T0302078

Collateral Frameworks

Central bank collateral frameworks are an often-overlooked feature of monetary policy that play a key role in the monetary and financial system. Readers will discover how central banks conduct and implement monetary policy beyond merely setting interest rates, and develop their understanding as to how collateral policies may affect financial markets, financial stability, and the real economy. This book studies the collateral framework in the euro area in detail and levers this analysis to provide an account of the euro crisis from the perspective of collateral policy. Readers gain access to a wealth of institutional and economic data and information with a level of density and accessibility unavailable elsewhere. This book, the first of its kind, is a valuable read for academic monetary and financial economists, those working in banking and policy-making financial institutions, and anyone who wishes to learn more about the role of central banks in society.

Kjell G. Nyborg is Chaired Professor of Finance at the University of Zurich, Senior Chair of the Swiss Finance Institute, Research Fellow of the Centre for Economic Policy Research, and Fellow of the Royal Society of Arts. He is also a former Director and the current Vice President and President-elect of the European Finance Association. Nyborg studied mathematics and economics at the University of Chicago before going on to do a PhD, with a specialization in finance, at the Graduate School of Business, Stanford University. He has previously taught at London Business School, UCLA, and the Norwegian School of Economics.

211

Collateral Frameworks

The Open Secret of Central Banks

KJELL G. NYBORG
University of Zurich
Swiss Finance Institute
and Centre for Economic Policy Research

CAMBRIDGE
UNIVERSITY PRESS

University Printing House, Cambridge CB2 8BS, United Kingdom

One Liberty Plaza, 20th Floor, New York, NY 10006, USA

477 Williamstown Road, Port Melbourne, VIC 3207, Australia

4843/24, 2nd Floor, Ansari Road, Daryaganj, Delhi - 110002, India

79 Anson Road, #06-04/06, Singapore 079906

Cambridge University Press is part of the University of Cambridge.

It furthers the University's mission by disseminating knowledge in the pursuit of education, learning and research at the highest international levels of excellence.

www.cambridge.org
Information on this title: www.cambridge.org/9781107155848
DOI: 10.1017/9781316659250

First published 2017

A catalogue record for this publication is available from the British Library

Library of Congress Cataloging in Publication data
Names: Nyborg, Kjell G., author.
Title: Collateral frameworks : the open secret of central banks /Kjell G. Nyborg.
Description: Cambridge, United Kingdom : Cambridge University Press, 2017.
Identifiers: LCCN 2016016319 | ISBN 9781316609545 (paperback)
Subjects: LCSH: Monetary policy. | Banks and banking, Central. |
   BISAC: BUSINESS & ECONOMICS/ Economics /Macroeconomics.
Classification: LCC HG230.3 .N93 2016 | DDC 339.5/3–dc23
LC record available at https://lccn.loc.gov/2016016319

ISBN   978-1-107-15584-8   Hardback
ISBN   978-1-316-60954-5   Paperback

Contents

List of Figures   page viii
List of Tables   ix
List of Exhibits   xi
List of Examples   xii
Preface   xiii
Acknowledgments   xv

1 Background and Motivation   1
   1.1 Money Matters in Financial Markets   3
   1.2 The Market for Liquidity   6
   1.3 The Financial Crisis and Unconventional Monetary
        Policy   7
   1.4 Central Bank Balance Sheets and the Increasing
        Importance of Collateral   11
   1.5 Collateral   14

2 Collateral Frameworks: Overview   18
   2.1 Potential Impact   19
   2.2 Collateral Eligibility and Usage   23
   2.3 Collateral Values, Haircuts, Ratings, and Guarantees   26
   2.4 Overview of Findings   29
   2.5 Rest of Book   32

3 Monetary Policy Implementation in the Euro Area
   over Time   35

4 Evidence on the Production and Usage of Collateral   52

5 Haircuts   59
   5.1 Documentation and Overview   59
   5.2 Detailed Haircut Rules and Main General Observations   63

5.3	Haircuts over Time	79
5.4	Extraordinary Haircuts	85
5.5	Evidence on Collateral Eligibility, Ratings, and Haircuts in Primary and Secondary Repo Markets	87
6	**Ratings and Guarantees**	**94**
6.1	Rating and Guarantee Rules over Time	96
6.2	Exemptions	112
6.3	Ratings and Haircuts: Two Examples	115
6.4	Fundamental Liquidity	118
6.5	Sovereign Ratings and the Impact of DBRS	119
6.6	Evidence on Guarantees	132
6.7	Government Guarantees: Italy	136
6.8	Government Guarantees: Germany	142
6.9	Government Guarantees and Irregular Haircuts: Greece	143
6.10	Corporate Guarantees and Access to Cheap Funding	146
7	**Market and Theoretical Prices**	**149**
7.1	Eligible Marketable Collateral	149
7.2	Pledged Collateral	162
7.3	Summary	166
8	**Collateral "Own Use"**	**168**
9	**Non-regulated Markets, Unsecured Bank Debt, and LTRO Uptake**	**171**
10	**Market Discipline**	**178**
10.1	Market Discipline Impairment	178
10.2	Biases and Systemic Arbitrage	183
10.3	Potential Costs	185
10.4	Introducing Market Forces	189
11	**Bailing Out the Euro**	**192**
11.1	Unconventional Monetary Policies: Broad Patterns and Key Issues	194

11.2 Full Allotment, Fragmentation, and Inefficient Bailouts   199

11.3 Buying Time and Sovereign Free-Riding   207

11.4 Bailing Out the Euro: Who Benefits? General Observations 212

11.5 Event Study: September 4, 2014   214

12 The Endgame of the Euro Crisis   224

12.1 Background   225

12.2 Eurosystem Purchases of Sovereign Bonds: Legal Issues   231

12.3 The Expanded Asset Purchase Program   233

12.4 Issues and Scenarios   236

12.5 The Importance of Buying Sovereign and Bank Bonds   242

13 Restoring Credibility   245

13.1 Organized Hypocrisy   248

13.2 Secure Sovereign Debt and Modify Haircuts   256

14 The Problem with Collateral   263

14.1 The Fundamental Problem   263

14.2 The Interbank Market   266

14.3 Full Reserve Banking   269

15 Concluding Remarks   274

Appendix: Haircut and Rating Rules Updates   281

A.1 Headline Changes   281

A.2 The Harmonized Rating Scale   282

A.3 Haircuts   284

A.4 Rating Rules   288

A.5 Greece and Cyprus   288

References   293

Index   313

Figures

1.1   EURO STOXX Index and Euribor–Eonia swap spread
(three months)   8

1.2   Central banks' balance sheets over time   12

2.1   Determination of collateral values in the collateral
framework   27

3.1   MRO and LTRO daily outstanding amounts and the
monetary base   47

4.1   Eligible assets and collateral used   57

6.1   Number of government-guaranteed issuers and
collateral   137

9.1   Number of eligible collateral by country and liquidity
category   174

11.1   Euribor–Eonia swap spread (three months) and usage
of standing facilities   200

11.2   Eurosystem liquidity injections vs aggregate liquidity
needs   201

12.1   Euro-area sovereign yield spreads over Germany
(ten years)   229

Tables

3.1   Main Eurosystem monetary policy instruments over time   36

3.2   Refinancing operations and monetary base   46

3.3   Consolidated Eurosystem balance sheet (asset side, in billion EUR)   50

4.1   Eligible marketable collateral across asset classes   53

4.2   Usage of collateral across asset classes   55

5.1   Haircuts and liquidity categories from March 8, 2004, to October 24, 2008   66

5.2   Haircuts and liquidity categories from October 25, 2008 (Temporary framework), and February 1, 2009 (General framework), to December 31, 2010   69

5.3   Haircuts and liquidity categories from January 1, 2011, to September 30, 2013   72

5.4   Haircuts and liquidity categories from October 1, 2013 (and November 1, 2013, for own-use covered bonds)   75

5.5   Greece and Cyprus: extraordinary haircuts   86

5.6   Distribution of collateral and comparison of haircuts in primary and secondary repo markets   89

6.1   Credit quality and ratings rules   98

6.2   Ratings for euro-area countries by year and rating agency   120

6.3   Yearly average DBRS ratings and rating differentials to other agencies   127

6.4   Extra collateral value from DBRS's pivotal ratings (or credit quality exemptions)   129

6.5   Distribution of collateral with guarantees   133

6.6   Extra collateral value to unrated Italian bank bonds from DBRS's pivotal rating and government guarantees   140

7.1	Incidence of market and theoretical prices for determining collateral values	154
9.1	Number of eligible collateral: impact of "non-regulated markets inclusion clause"	175
11.1	Event study of ECB announcements on September 4, 2014	217
12.1	Euro-area member state fiscal indicators	226
A.1	Harmonized rating scale	283
A.2	Haircuts and liquidity categories from May 1, 2015	285
A.3	Credit quality and ratings rules	289

Exhibits

6.1	Harmonized rating scale: long-term ratings per step	110
6.2	Issues with German government guarantees, August 15, 2013	142
6.3	Irregular haircuts of Greek government-guaranteed unsecured bank bonds, December 8, 2011	145
6.4	Long-term rating scales and scoring system	148
7.1	Pricing rule 2: incidence of theoretical and stale prices, January 13, 2015	160
7.2	Collateral usage by collateral value (billion EUR), 2014Q4	163
7.3	Collateral usage by count	165
9.1	LTRO by country (billion EUR)	176

Examples

6.1   Two Spanish government bonds, March 21, 2014   115
6.2   Two Italian government bonds, March 21, 2014   116

Preface

This book seeks to inform about a feature of monetary policy that is largely overlooked yet occupies a central role in the monetary and financial system, namely central bank collateral frameworks. They are much like G.K. Chesterton's famous "invisible" postman in that, like him, collateral frameworks are out in the open and utilized every single day of the year, but nevertheless go largely unnoticed.[1] Unlike the postman, however, collateral frameworks are obscured by opacity. Those that care can look up the nitty-gritty of how collateral frameworks work by studying the relevant official documentation, but it is not trivial reading. Furthermore, to understand how collateral frameworks actually function, it is not sufficient to merely read the official rules, it is also necessary to supplement these with empirical facts that shed light on how those rules are implemented and what their consequences are. This book does both. Its main objective is to bring the importance of collateral frameworks more out into the open.

I do this through an in-depth study of the collateral framework of the euro area. This is an especially interesting case because of the banking and sovereign debt problems in the euro area and the ongoing efforts of the European Central Bank (ECB) to, in Mario Draghi's words, preserve the euro. The Eurosystem's collateral framework provides a novel and useful frame of reference for looking at the unfolding crisis. The book shows that the collateral framework is integral to the unconventional monetary policies pursued by the ECB in its bid to stave off the crisis. The book also lays out the general pattern of the ECB's unconventional policies to preserve the euro and shows that these involve indirect bailouts of banks and sovereigns, with some countries benefiting more than others.

---

[1] Chesterton (1911).

As I thought I was nearing completion of this book in January 2015, several "euro events" occurred in rapid succession that I felt compelled to incorporate into my analysis because they reduced uncertainty with respect to future ECB actions to preserve the euro. This has led to a chapter on the endgame of the euro crisis to go along with a chapter on the euro's fundamental credibility problem and what to do about it. These chapters expand the scope of the book so that it can also be read as an analysis of the euro crisis that branches out from a detailed study of the Eurosystem's collateral framework.

The discussion of the euro crisis also serves to deepen the understanding of collateral frameworks provided by the book by illustrating, in part, their potential reach and, in part, how their design may ultimately be influenced by political forces. I believe this is especially relevant with respect to understanding the Byzantine structure of the Eurosystem's collateral framework.

The general picture that emerges from my research is that a collateral framework is a monetary policy tool that can be used, by design or inadvertently, to impinge on the role of markets. It can be used to nudge financial markets and the behavior of banks and sovereigns this way or that and, by implication, the real economy as well. A message of the book is that to gain a more complete understanding of the monetary and financial systems, it is essential to understand the structure, functionality, role, reach, and implications of collateral frameworks. The book shows that collateral frameworks are central to the operations and activities of central banks and the monetary and financial systems built up around their money. They can be used as part of a package of unconventional monetary policies to address crises or near-crises situations, but they can also cause market distortions and contribute to a misallocation of resources and to financial instability.

Acknowledgments

The work in this book represents a continuation of a line of research I have been carrying out over many years with several co-authors. Our joint research addresses issues in the market for liquidity, central banking, bank bailouts, and the role of money in financial markets. Studying collateral frameworks, the micro-foundation of the monetary and financial systems, is a natural progression from this. Thus, I would like to give a special thanks to these co-authors: Sudipto Bhattacharya, Ulrich Bindseil, Falko Fecht, Per Östberg, Ilya Strebulaev, and Jörg Rocholl.

The final draft of this book has benefited from the comments of four anonymous reviewers and the participants in a handful of seminars, including one at the ECB. In particular, I was invited by the ECB to give the keynote lecture in their September 2013 workshop on "Structural Changes in Money Markets: Implications for Monetary Policy Implementation" and used the opportunity to present some of my thoughts on their collateral framework. I argued that it should be viewed as an integral and important part of their monetary policy and pointed to some of the same issues that I discuss at more length in this book. I am thankful to the ECB for affording me this opportunity and for the useful feedback I received at that workshop. In addition, I would like to thank the ECB's legal department, outreach division, and collateral team for clarifying some issues relating to the Eurosystem's collateral framework.

I have also benefited from the comments of seminar participants at the Central Bank of Ireland in April 2014 and, closer to the finishing line of the book in the spring of 2015, at the University of Chicago, the University of Wisconsin, and the Swiss National Bank. The final touch-up in the fall of 2015 benefited from comments and clarifying remarks from Ulrich Bindseil and an anonymous reviewer and also from presentations at the Contract Theory and Banking workshop at the University of Zurich; the Yale Program on Financial Stability Annual Conference, August 2015; and Norges Bank, as well as from presentations on research relating to the book at the Deutsche Bundesbank/SAFE conference on Regulating Financial Markets, May 2015; the Federal Reserve Bank of San Francisco and Bank of Canada conference on "Recent Advances in Fixed Income Research and Implications for Monetary Policy," November 2015; and the Rady School of Management at the University of California, San Diego.

In writing this book, I have benefited greatly from the research assistance of my team: Lilia Mukhlynina, Cornelia Rösler, and Jiri Woschitz. Magnus Nybø also chipped in toward the end. I am grateful for their commitment to the project and for their many helpful comments on the manuscript itself. The responsibility for any errors is mine.

I Background and Motivation

It is commonly accepted that monetary policy affects the wider economy. There is also emerging evidence that there are monetary effects in financial markets. However, most work on these topics looks at broad-brush policy variables such as short-term interest rates or the quantity of money. There is a dearth of work on monetary economics or finance and banking that studies the micro-foundation of the monetary system and its impact on markets and the economy. The broad objective of this book is to contribute toward filling that gap. This is important in light of the ongoing challenges in the global economy, where central banks are engaged in quantitative easing and other forms of unconventional monetary policy in an effort to stabilize and support the economy, banks, and the financial markets. In the euro area, monetary policy is even in the vanguard in the fight to save the euro and European project itself.

Banking and finance are central to the broader economy because money flows through the banking sector and the financial system. A better understanding of how this works requires, in the first instance, a deeper and more detailed knowledge of monetary system architecture. Modern monetary systems are organized around central banks and their money, what bankers call liquidity. Central bank money is injected by central banks into the banking system against collateral on terms defined, not in a market, but by central banks through their collateral frameworks. In some jurisdictions, or currency areas, central bank independence means that collateral frameworks are not subject to formal supervision, review, or even much by way of discussion. Public focus is instead directed toward interest rates or monetary aggregates. This book therefore aims to bring to light the functioning, reach, and impact of collateral frameworks.

Different central banks have different collateral frameworks. There are common features, but details can vary a great deal. The focus in this book is on the framework of the Eurosystem, i.e., the collective structure of national central banks in the euro area spearheaded by the European Central Bank (ECB). The ECB plays a principal role because it is authorized to design and update the euro area's collateral framework. This is an especially interesting case to study because of the richness and complexity that arise from a single currency across multiple countries and the very wide range of collateral banks can use to obtain liquidity directly from the Eurosystem. The euro area also represents one of the largest economies in the world. Its well-publicized financial, economic, and political problems have significant impact on global markets and the world economy. Concerns about the euro itself are intermingled with and, arguably, at the core of these problems. Gaining a more sound understanding of the euro area's monetary system at the most fundamental level is therefore of great value.

In the main part of this book, I lay bare how the Eurosystem operates with respect to its collateral framework. This is done partly through a study of the details of the official rules that define the collateral framework. But equally importantly, to put flesh on the bare bones of these rules, the book provides a large number of empirical findings through a forensic-style analysis that help make the collateral framework more concrete and shed light on how monetary policy actually functions in the euro area.

As an example, the book documents that rating agencies and sovereign guarantees to bank-issued collateral play an important role in the implementation of the collateral framework and, by implication, Eurosystem monetary policy. This raises a host of questions, such as: Are some rating agencies more central than others? What is the distribution of sovereign guarantees across euro-area countries? Is there a link between ratings and guarantees? What is the estimated value of the guarantees? How much of this can be attributed to generous ratings? How do ratings and guarantees interact with other aspects of the collateral framework and (unconventional) monetary policy? This is only one example of the kind of issues that relate to collateral frameworks and that I study. The book provides an overall assessment of the Eurosystem's collateral framework, and, through that, general issues are raised.

Toward the end of the book, starting with Chapter 11, I use these findings and the insights they provide to comment on the ECB's usage of various unconventional monetary policies to preserve the euro. Combined, these policies essentially serve as indirect bailouts of banks and the weaker sovereigns. While many of the policies may be necessary to keep the eurozone together, they are not sufficient. The euro's fundamental problem lies outside the realm of monetary policy. Yet, I propose that it may be possible to address this fundamental problem, at least in part, through modifications to the collateral framework.

Finally, I use some of the insights gained from my study of collateral to comment on the organization of the interbank market for liquidity as well as on the idea of full reserve banking, a notion that has received increasing attention in recent years as a way to stabilize the financial system. Once one recognizes that full reserve banking places great demands on collateral, my comments on this topic are simply a corollary to my main investigation into collateral frameworks.

1.1 MONEY MATTERS IN FINANCIAL MARKETS

There is an enormous amount of work in economics on monetary policy transmission channels. This book complements and contributes to that literature, but does not emanate from it. Instead, it can be characterized as the product of the literatures on the market for liquidity, monetary effects in financial markets, collateral, and financial intermediation. With respect to the first of these, what is especially relevant for this book is the literature that studies open market operations and the interaction of banks and the central bank. I will touch on this in the next section. Collateral is discussed toward the end of this chapter, and the most relevant literature on financial intermediation is touched on in the next chapter. In this section, I briefly review the evidence on monetary effects in financial markets from a rather "selfish" perspective.

Work I have done with Per Östberg on the details of the interaction between the market for liquidity and the broader financial markets shows that money matters in financial markets in part because frictions in interbank markets spill over into the broader markets through what we call liquidity pull-back (Nyborg and Östberg 2014). There is also evidence that asset prices and measures of liquidity in financial markets are affected by monetary shocks (see, e.g., Fleming and Remolona 1997; Fair 2002; Flannery and Protopapadakis 2002; Bernanke and Kuttner 2005; Chordia, Sarkar, and Subrahmanyam 2005). Liquidity pull-back is a monetary phenomenon acted out in financial markets. It is based on the important role played by central bank money in modern banking and financial systems. Central bank money is the currency, or liquidity, banks need to satisfy reserve requirements, allow for depositor withdrawals, settle interbank transactions, etc. It is injected into the banking system through central bank operations and then reallocated among banks. For many transactions, there is no substitute for central bank money. Thus, for any bank, having sufficient central bank money at any point in time is a constraint that needs to be satisfied.

However, conditions in the interbank market may fluctuate. At times it may be "tight," in the sense that the price of liquidity is high and some banks may have exhausted interbank credit limits. If so, banks may seek alternative sources of central bank money. But, as observed by Friedman (1970): "One man can [increase] his nominal money balances only by persuading someone else to [decrease] his."[1]

---

[1] In Friedman (1970), the sentence reads: "One man can reduce his nominal money balances only by persuading someone else to increase his."

The same holds true for banks. Friedman's observation is echoed by Tobin (1980): "[T]he nominal supply of money is something to which the economy must adapt, not a variable that adapts itself to the economy – unless the policy authorities want it to." These restrictions can be overcome by borrowing from the central bank's lending facility (discount window), but this is expensive. A bank can also attempt to attract new, or retain old, deposits, but this is a slow process. Liquidity pull-back offers an alternative approach, namely to obtain liquidity through interacting with financial markets, by pulling liquidity back from them.

This can be done in several ways, most obviously by selling financial assets directly.[2] The mechanism within a bank through which this may happen is that the bank's internal liquidity management system feeds into trading desks' limits, reducing them. Alternatively, liquidity pull-back can be achieved by increasing margins to levered investors or haircuts in repos (repurchase agreements). In turn, this may lead to asset sales by the affected counterparties. Liquidity pull-back does not increase the quantity of central bank money in the system. However, the actions I have described can increase the selling (or acting) bank's liquidity balances, as long as the (ultimate) buyer banks with another bank.

Östberg and I emphasize that a feature of the theoretical idea we sketch in our paper is that financial assets serve as a storage facility for liquidity that a bank can tap into if it should face a shortfall. We draw out the implications of this idea with respect to the link between interbank tightness and volume, order flow, and returns in the broader financial markets. The empirical evidence is strongly supportive. A general conclusion of our work is that the way banks obtain central bank money affects financial markets. This supports the perspective in this book that collateral frameworks matter since they determine the terms at which banks can obtain liquidity directly from the central bank. The process of allocating central bank money

---

[2] See Kashyap and Stein (2000) for evidence on banks' holdings of securities.

in an economy starts with the interaction of the central bank vis-à-vis banks, and this interaction needs to obey the rules and constraints imposed by the central bank's collateral framework.

1.2 THE MARKET FOR LIQUIDITY

Before the crisis, money markets were viewed by many academics and policy makers alike as uninteresting with respect to the broader financial markets and the economy. This is not because they were thought of as not serving an important function, but because they were regarded as functioning extremely well. They were considered to be highly competitive and liquid – in a word, "boring" – with no significant impact on the broader financial markets. Yet, the money-market literature shows that this view was never quite correct.

Hamilton's (1996) seminal study finds that the federal funds rate (US overnight rate) reacts to calendar effects relating to the reserve maintenance period. There is also evidence that the overnight rate reacts to the supply of reserves (Hamilton 1997; Carpenter and Demiralp 2006). Similar effects can be found in the euro area (e.g., Nautz and Offermanns 2007; Angelini 2008; Beirne 2012). Fecht, Nyborg, and Rocholl (2008) and Rösler (2015) also document calendar effects with respect to volume. These findings are indications of a less-than-perfect market for liquidity. Furthermore, using primary market data from ECB main refinancing operations (repo auctions) well before the crisis, Bindseil, Nyborg, and Strebulaev (2009) find evidence that the market for liquidity is informationally efficient but, at the same time, allocationally inefficient.

The existence of inefficiencies in the market for liquidity explains the positive support in the data for the liquidity pull-back idea. Indeed, that work was motivated by the empirical evidence that interbank markets are not efficient, even during times of normalcy. An earlier ECB working paper by Nyborg, Bindseil, and Strebulaev (2002) also finds evidence consistent with the idea that the collateral framework affects banks' willingness to pay for liquidity.

After the onset of the financial crisis in August 2007, the significance of the market for liquidity and collateral has become greatly magnified, as will be explained below.

1.3   THE FINANCIAL CRISIS AND UNCONVENTIONAL MONETARY POLICY

A central (and much-studied) aspect of the financial crisis is the emergence of severe frictions in the interbank market for liquidity. Interestingly, therefore, the liquidity pull-back effect as a day-to-day phenomenon became weaker, or harder to identify statistically. A potential explanation for this is that the financial crisis represented a massive liquidity pull-back event, where money-like securities (e.g., Treasury bills) were sought by investors and banks, and the day-to-day liquidity pull-back effect was dwarfed by the much larger pattern of the crisis (think fractals). Kindleberger (1978) and Allen and Gale (1994, 2007) have stressed that financial crises often involve the (forced) sale of assets in order to obtain liquidity to, for example, settle financial obligations. In addition, the large injections of liquidity by central banks in response to the crisis eventually made it less necessary for banks to engage in liquidity pull-back. Instead, they could post collateral to the central bank and receive liquidity directly that way.

While the market for liquidity did not stop functioning during the crisis, it functioned less well than before.[3] Dysfunction in the market for liquidity was a central feature of the crisis. The price of liquidity shot up (Figure 1.1) while volume shifted in from longer to shorter maturities and fell overall (Abbassi, Bräuning, Fecht, and Peydró 2014; Gabrieli and Georg 2014; Rösler 2015). The turmoil in the interbank market for liquidity was accompanied by a massive loss of value in asset prices. This is also illustrated in Figure 1.1, using equities as an example. While Figure 1.1 uses euro-area data, graphs

---

[3] See, e.g., Cassola, Holthausen, and Lo Duca (2010) for the euro area and Afonso, Kovner, and Schoar (2011) for the United States.

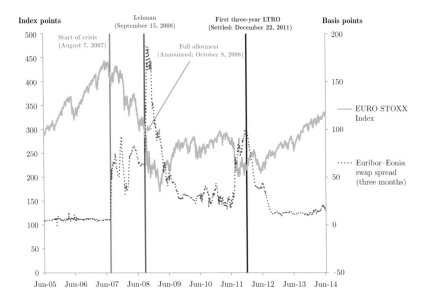

FIGURE 1.1   EURO STOXX Index and Euribor–Eonia swap spread (three months)

Time period: June 20, 2005, to June 30, 2014.
The spread is the difference between Euribor and the Eonia swap and is in basis points. Euribor: Euro Interbank Offered Rate. Eonia: Euro Overnight Index Average. *Data sources*: www.stoxx.com/indices/index_information.html?symbol =SXXE and www.emmi-benchmarks.eu/.

using corresponding data from other markets (e.g., the United States) would exhibit the same patterns.

Figure 1.1 shows the spread between the three-month Euribor and three-month Eonia swap rates (Euribor–Eonia swap spread), with values on the right axis, and a broad euro-area stock market index (EURO STOXX), with values on the left axis. As explained by Nyborg and Östberg (2014), while the Euribor–Eonia swap spread may reflect credit risk, it represents more directly the price of liquidity (here, over three months).[4] A high spread is tantamount to the interbank market for liquidity not working well. The sharp increase in the

---

[4] The alternative to borrowing a given quantity of liquidity at Euribor over three months, for example, is to attempt to borrow the same quantity overnight and hedge with the Eonia swap (an overnight index swap). But under this alternative strategy, the borrowing bank faces the risk that it may not be able to borrow the

spread in August 2007 represents the beginning of the financial crisis. The spread is seen to peak just after the Lehman bankruptcy, which occurred on September 15, 2008. That the bankruptcy of a US institution should trigger a severe tightening in the market for liquidity in the euro area illustrates the interconnectedness of global markets. Since then, the spread has come down substantially, though not to pre-crisis levels.

The pattern for the stock market is analogous. As the interbank market for liquidity saw severe tightening, the stock market almost collapsed, losing around 50 percent of its value from August 2007 to the bottom in March 2009. Since then the stock market has reversed, gaining back much of the lost ground. Stock markets around the world reacted similarly.

In response to the meltdown that ensued after Lehman Brothers' bankruptcy, the ECB made significant changes to its monetary operations. On October 8, 2008, the ECB announced that it would switch from auctioning a limited quantity of liquidity in its operations to running fixed rate tenders at the policy rate with full allotment. It would do this for both the main and longer-term refinancing operations (MROs and LTROs, respectively). This represents one of the most significant actions taken by the ECB in response to the crisis. Under full allotment, central bank money is not rationed in the refinancing operations. Instead, banks receive everything they ask for. The only restriction is that they have to pledge sufficient collateral to cover these amounts. In October 2008, LTRO money was available with three-month maturities. In response to further problems, the ECB lengthened the maturity in the LTROs to three years in two operations, held in December 2011 and February 2012.

The availability of unlimited amounts of three-year money was not enough to calm the markets. The threat to the euro was real enough to move Mario Draghi, President of the European Central Bank, to make his famous declaration in July 2012: "Within our

desired amount every day. The price of having the liquidity for sure over the three months is the Euribor–Eonia swap spread.

mandate, the ECB is ready to do whatever it takes to preserve the euro."[5]

On September 6, 2012, this was followed up by the launch of the Outright Monetary Transactions (OMT) program.[6] The OMT allows for unlimited purchases of sovereign bonds of countries under a European Financial Stability Facility/European Stability Mechanism program, but has yet to be used.[7] Even so, it is often viewed as representing the "whatever it takes" in Draghi's famous statement quoted above. For example, a 2013 *Financial Times* article reports that:[8]

> The size of the programme is unlimited, lending credence to Mr Draghi's remarks that he would do "whatever it takes" to save the euro... As of February 2013 no country had yet applied for help under OMT, but the very fact of its existence had greatly calmed financial markets.

But the problems in the eurozone did not go away after the introduction of the OMT, as evidenced, for example, by the continued use of the full allotment policy in open market operations and ongoing considerations of further unconventional measures.[9] The mere promise of unlimited purchases of troubled sovereigns' paper (the OMT) was not enough. Real action was required. Thus, on

---

[5] See "Verbatim of the remarks made by Mario Draghi: Speech by Mario Draghi at the Global Investment Conference in London 26 July 2012," www.ecb.europa.eu /press/key/date/2012/html/sp120726.en.html.

[6] See the ECB press release, September 6, 2012, on "Technical features of Outright Monetary Transactions," www.ecb.europa.eu/press/pr/date/2012/html/pr120906 _1.en.html.

[7] I have verified with the ECB (in November 2015) that no purchases have been made under the OMT. The Eurosystem's recent purchases of sovereign bonds are carried out under another program – the expanded asset purchase program. For details, see below.

[8] "Definition of outright monetary transactions OMT," *Financial Times*, ft.com/ lexicon, http://lexicon.ft.com/Term?term=outright-monetary-transactions-OMT.

[9] See, e.g., Chapter 11 in this book or "Monetary policy communication in turbulent times: Speech by Mario Draghi, President of the ECB, at the Conference De Neder- landsche Bank 200 years: Central banking in the next two decades, Amsterdam, 24 April 2014," www.ecb.europa.eu/press/key/date/2014/html/sp140424.en.html.

September 4, 2014, the ECB announced asset-backed security (ABS) and covered bond purchase programs that, at the time, were said to possibly add as much as EUR 1 trillion to the balance sheet of the Eurosystem. The exact quantity was subject to much speculation, but reconfirmed in December 2014 and then again in January 2015, when Draghi finally announced that the Eurosystem would go the extra mile and start buying sovereign bonds, though not under the OMT but as a part of the broader asset purchase program announced in September 2014 (see Chapters 11 and 12).

1.4 CENTRAL BANK BALANCE SHEETS AND THE INCREASING IMPORTANCE OF COLLATERAL

The accommodative monetary policies of central banks in response to the financial crisis have substantially increased their balance sheets. This is illustrated in Figure 1.2.

Figure 1.2a shows the growth in the consolidated balance sheet of the Eurosystem and, by way of comparison, six other central banks: the Federal Reserve System, Bank of Japan, People's Bank of China, Bank of Canada, Bank of England, and Norges Bank (Norway),[10] over the period 2000 to 2014. The data are for the end of each calendar year, except 2014, when the sizes of the balance sheets are taken at the end of June. For each central bank, each year is benchmarked against its 2004 balance sheet, which represents 100 percent. The variation in balance sheet growth across these countries is quite large. For example, over the 2004 to June 2014 period, it ranges from less than 100 percent for the central banks of Japan, Canada, and Norway to approximately 800 percent for the Bank of England (which, because of this very large increase, gets its own axis in the plot). The Eurosystem is in the middle, with an increase of 135 percent.

Figure 1.2b shows the size of the balance sheets as a percentage of the respective countries' (or currency area's) GDP, from 2000

---

[10] For the Norges Bank figures, the contribution of the "petroleum fund" to the balance sheet is excluded.

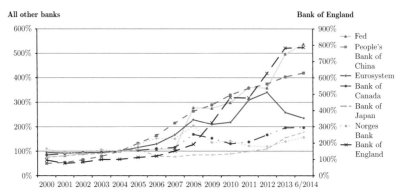

(a) Growth of central banks' balance sheets over time

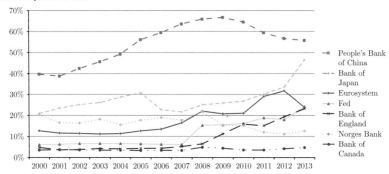

(b) Central banks' balance sheets as a percentage of GDP

FIGURE 1.2 Central banks' balance sheets over time

Figure 1.2a graphs the size of the Eurosystem's consolidated balance sheet over time as well as those of selected central banks. Numbers are normalized, with 2004 representing 100 percent for each central bank. Figure 1.2b graphs the balance sheet sizes as a percentage of GDP in the respective countries. For the Eurosystem, the aggregate GDP across euro-area countries on a year-by-year basis is used. Datapoints are year-end from 2000 to 2013 and, in (a), June 2014. *Data sources*: Balance sheet statistics are from the respective central banks' webpages, except for the People's Bank of China where they are taken from the National Bureau of Statistics of China for 2007–2013 and from Bloomberg and Trading Economics (www.tradingeconomics.com/) for other years. Figures for the Bank of England are taken from its consolidated balance sheet, available from 2005, and, prior to that, by adding the total assets from its Banking and Issue Department accounts. GDP data are from the respective central banks' web-pages (Norway, Japan, United States), Eurostat (Eurosystem), Office for National Statistics (United Kingdom), Statistics Canada, and the National Bureau of Statistics of China.

to 2013. The Eurosystem's balance sheet has increased from approximately 13 percent of euro-area GDP in 2000 to around 24 percent in 2013. This is approximately the same percentage in 2013 as for the Federal Reserve and the Bank of England, but less than the central banks of Japan (47 percent) and China (56 percent). A balance sheet to GDP ratio of more than 20 percent is unprecedented before the crisis over the period sampled here for these countries, with the exception of the Bank of Japan and the People's Bank of China. This illustrates the rising importance of central banks and, by implication, the assets they hold.

Central bankers are concerned that the growth in central bank balance sheets over the crisis is associated with these getting weaker as a result of ever worse collateral being taken on. For example, Thomas Jordan (2012), President of the Swiss National Bank, is on record as saying that

> as a result of the measures implemented during the crisis, central banks took much more risk onto their balance sheets, which could potentially lead to substantial losses ... there is no doubt that central banks have to play a role in an economic crisis at the market level as well as at the level of individual systemically important banks. In order to act appropriately, they need room to maneuver, which implies a sound central bank balance sheet with sufficient equity.

These sentiments are echoed by Klaas Knot (2013), Governor of the Dutch Central Bank:

> The unprecedented expansion of central banks' balance sheets since the start of the crisis is certainly revealing. It shows that central banks' balance sheets are becoming more and more exposed to economic risk and political pressure. Eventually, this may result in a substantial amount of negative capital in a central bank's balance sheet. This is undesirable, because it could undermine a central bank's credibility and independence ... An additional concern for

central banks is that unconventional monetary policy increasingly comes with some sense of "public unease" about the role central banks play...The fact that criticism of central banks is creeping more and more into the mainstream debate – whether or not this is justified – implies that the public is looking increasingly critically at central banks. While this may not put central banks' independence or room for maneuver immediately at risk, it does signify that central banks may need to step up their efforts on transparency and accountability.

The increased risk, associated with the expansion in central bank balance sheets as a result of the financial crisis, that these two prominent central bankers are speaking of, and that they are justly concerned about, is a consequence of the functioning of the collateral frameworks that central banks themselves have designed and the unconventional monetary policies they have pursued. The aforementioned quotes are, therefore, testament to the importance of collateral frameworks and that something is not quite right about them. The central bankers seem to imply that their collateral frameworks could be a source of risk that could create problems down the road.

1.5   COLLATERAL

The previous discussion points to the centrality of collateral with respect to monetary policy and the market for liquidity. Because conditions in the market for liquidity spill over to the broader financial markets, both collateral and collateral frameworks matter for financial markets. Furthermore, collateral is now more important than ever, in part, because of the growth in central bank balance sheets. There is also a push to increase the reliance on collateral in interbank and financial market transactions. Some policy makers and commentators view this as beneficial for financial stability.[11] But it could also

---

[11] This view is, for example, expressed in World Bank (2012, p. 153). See also Chapter 14.

contribute to tension between the usage of collateral in transactions with the central bank versus other counterparties.

During the financial crisis, the ECB broadened the Eurosystem collateral framework considerably, allowing a broader range of securities of the same credit quality and allowing securities of lower ratings.[12] A strand of the literature addresses the question as to what role the balance sheet of a central bank plays (Hawkins 2003; Bindseil, Manzanares, and Weller 2004; Caruana 2011; Miles and Schanz 2014) and also asks whether a central bank can default or impinge its credibility by weakening its balance sheet (Stella 1997; Ernhagen, Vesterlund, and Viotti 2002; Buiter 2008). The recent revisiting of these questions is a result of a concern in some quarters that central banks could be at risk, at least from being able to implement effective policies. By allowing riskier securities as collateral, the ECB has increased its risk, in both financial and political terms, as emphasized by Klaas Knot.

Collateral also plays a direct role in the secondary market for liquidity, notably in repos, and much research is devoted to this topic. As predicted by Duffie (1996), the evidence shows that collateral that trades special in the repo market also trades at a premium in the cash market (Jordan and Jordan 1997; Buraschi and Menini 2002). Not surprisingly, the risk of the underlying collateral adversely affects the repo rate (Bartolini, Hilton, Sundaresan, and Tonetti 2011).

Researchers have also asked the question as to whether the collateralization of transactions in the market for liquidity affects financial stability. Intuitively, collateral can be expected to have a stabilizing effect (Ewerhart and Tapking 2008; Heider and Hoerova 2009). However, theoretically, collateral can also turn out to be destabilizing (Kiyotaki and Moore 1997; Brunnermeier and Pedersen 2009) when it is combined with credit limits and shocks to asset values. Gorton and Metrick (2012) argue that the financial crisis in the United States was characterized by a run on bilateral

---

[12] This is investigated in detail in subsequent chapters.

repos with securitized assets as collateral. A run in this case means an extreme increase in haircuts. Their main argument is that the underlying securities became more risky and therefore more information sensitive (Gorton and Metrick 2010). Krishnamurthy, Nagel, and Orlov (2014) disagree with this view, arguing instead that the evidence is more consistent with a credit crunch than with a run. However, these authors study different segments of the repo market. Whatever the case, the evidence shows that repo markets were not unaffected by the crisis and may well have played an integral part in it.

The evidence also shows that an increase in market risk is associated with a shift toward safer collateral (Mancini, Ranaldo, and Wrampelmeyer 2014). Thus, default risk appears to be a consideration in the repo market. Furthermore, a shift toward higher-quality collateral in secondary market repos may leave lower-quality collateral to be used in repos with the central bank. Safety concerns and regulatory innovations such as the Liquidity Coverage Ratio (BCBS 2013) are likely to further increase banks' demand for high-quality assets. Thus, the efficient use and potential reuse of collateral emerge as important considerations (Singh and Stella 2012; CGFS 2013; Singh 2013).

Collateral also plays an important role in real transactions (Bernanke and Gertler 1989, 1990; Calomiris and Hubbard 1990; Kiyotaki and Moore 1997). This literature establishes a link between collateralized borrowing and asset prices and investments. Notably, the net worth of collateral impacts the investment capability of a firm. This is analogous to a repo transaction, where the form of collateral is not an asset or real estate, but a security.

While there is a substantial literature on collateral, as sketched above, little of this research looks directly at the design and consequences of a central bank's collateral framework, as I do in this book. Nyborg and Strebulaev (2001) show theoretically that allocational inefficiencies in the market for liquidity may depend on the size of the set of eligible collateral but do not consider collateral heterogeneity, which is a crucial issue handled by collateral frameworks in practice. In another theoretical contribution, Chapman, Chiu, and Molico (2011) show that haircuts in central bank collateral frameworks can influence investment decisions; when haircuts on illiquid assets are "too low," an overinvestment in these may take place, leaving the central bank at risk and reducing welfare. Related to this, Buiter and Sibert (2005) and Ashcraft, Gârleanu, and Pedersen (2010) argue that there may be an inverse relation between haircuts in repos with the central bank and the secondary market prices of the underlying collateral. The latter paper provides empirical evidence to back up this theoretical claim.

While central bank working groups have issued reports on collateral frameworks (e.g., Cheun, von Köppen-Mertes, and Weller 2009; Markets Committee (BIS) 2013), these are overviews that do not provide much by way of detail or go into depth with respect to the consequences of collateral framework design or their role in unconventional monetary policies. A theme that will emerge in subsequent chapters is that collateral frameworks may have distortive effects on financial markets and the broader economy.

2 Collateral Frameworks: Overview

Central bank collateral frameworks are fundamental institutional features of the monetary and financial system that have gone largely unstudied by researchers, perhaps because they are simply taken for granted and seem of little consequence in times of "normalcy." They are also often complex and opaque, requiring the studying of numerous legal documents to be accurately understood. Their basic function is to define the set of eligible collateral financial institutions can use in operations with central banks to obtain central bank money (liquidity). They also determine the quantity of liquidity that a central bank will supply for each eligible collateral, by, for example, setting haircuts in repos with eligible counterparties ("banks"). This places collateral frameworks at the core of the monetary system and the financial system that extends (from) it.

This chapter provides an overview of the role played by collateral frameworks and how they function in practice, with an emphasis on potential biases and distortions that may arise from their design. These issues are then investigated in subsequent chapters through a forensic-style analysis of the Eurosystem's collateral framework. The current chapter also previews the key findings of that investigation. A central characteristic of the Eurosystem's collateral framework is its broad eligibility criteria. The findings in this book are especially relevant with respect to understanding potential issues that arise in collateral frameworks sharing this characteristic. My general point is that collateral frameworks have potentially far-reaching effects on financial markets and the real economy. They are at the core of the monetary system and, as observed by Bagehot, "[m]oney is economical power."[1]

---

[1] Bagehot (1873).

An important strand of the monetary economics literature focuses on the distinction between what economists call "inside and outside money" (Gurley and Shaw 1960). The former can be defined as "an asset representing, or backed by, any form of private credit that circulates as a medium of exchange," with the latter being "money that is either of a fiat nature (unbacked) or backed by some asset that is not in zero net supply within the private sector of the economy" (Lagos 2006). According to Blanchard and Fischer (1989, chapter 4), "currency and bank reserves, high-powered money or the money base constitute outside money." Recent contributions by Kiyotaki and Moore (2003) and Holmström and Tirole (2011) show that outside money, or liquidity, can improve welfare in an economy where moral hazard reduces the effectiveness of inside money. In these models, heavy reliance on outside money is a sign of large frictions in financial markets. Based on the presumption that financial development will improve over time and reduce moral hazard, Kiyotaki and Moore (2003) conclude that: "Perhaps the model's sharpest prediction is that eventually outside money will cease to be used, driven out by liquid private paper that earns higher returns." Even if the underlying premise were true, Kiyotaki and Moore recognize that the conclusion may be controversial, because "after all, assets such as bonds [that serve as inside money] are promises to pay in outside money." In other words, inside money and, more generally, the financial system are anchored to outside money. In practice in modern economies, this means central bank money. It therefore becomes important to understand how central bank money is issued.

This takes us back to collateral frameworks and the quote from Bagehot above. If central bank money is economic power and is issued against collateral, it stands to reason that it is important to understand the nature of the collateral and the terms of the exchange.

2.1 POTENTIAL IMPACT

There are several dimensions to the potential impact of collateral frameworks. A security that is in the set of eligible collateral can be refinanced through, or bought by, the central bank. This may affect its repo rate, liquidity, and price in the secondary market. The haircuts applied by the central bank to different collateral may be set so that the impact of eligibility differs across asset classes and individual securities, possibly by design or even inadvertently.

For instance, in order to make banks' balance sheets more liquid, the central bank can favor especially illiquid collateral by giving these relatively low haircuts. While this may help channel liquidity "where it is needed," a side effect is that it may cause distortions in money and asset markets by reducing the role of market discipline. In addition, an impairment in the efficiency of the market for liquidity can spill over into the broader financial markets, as shown by Nyborg and Östberg (2014), and, from there, to the real economy.

Collateral frameworks that favor illiquid collateral may also stimulate the endogenous production of it. In turn, this may lead to a misallocation of funds in the real economy toward assets that are fundamentally less liquid in a real sense, that is, assets that have very long-dated returns in terms of goods and services.[2]

To follow the logic, it is important to understand that central banks control central bank money, that is, nominal balances. If there is a low level of current goods and services, there is little a central bank can do about it in the short run. When we speak of collateral being illiquid, we typically mean this in a nominal sense; selling it may involve accepting a discount in the price, and the more so the more one wishes to sell. While a policy of favoring illiquid collateral may serve a useful purpose in some situations, it can also give rise to problems if this collateral is also illiquid in a real sense, as seems plausible. Favoring illiquid collateral in the collateral framework may

---

[2] This relates to Chapman, Chiu, and Molico's (2011) result that low haircuts on illiquid assets may tilt portfolios in that direction and also to the arguments of Buiter and Sibert (2005) and Ashcraft, Gârleanu, and Pedersen (2010) that haircuts affect prices. In turn, these can be seen as special versions of Amihud and Mendelson's (1986) general point that portfolios may be optimally tilted away from illiquid assets by agents that have more immediate liquidity needs. However, these papers do not discuss nominal versus real liquidity.

then lead to an overproduction of illiquid real assets. Tilting the economy toward an overproduction of illiquid real assets is not only inefficient, but may exacerbate business cycles. A policy of favoring illiquid collateral in a depressed economy may make it harder for the economy to recover.

Housing, perhaps especially second homes, is an example of illiquid real assets. The real returns are long-dated and the usage relatively inflexible. Countries such as Spain and Ireland are still grappling with the aftermath of a prolonged construction boom. In the case of Spain, much of this was touristic housing, including second-home villas and apartments that stand empty much of the time. In subsequent chapters, I will address whether the collateral framework in the Eurosystem favors illiquid collateral.

The banking literature has raised the issue that banks may be underincentivized to channel funds to assets that are liquid in a real sense because of a free-rider problem among them. In particular, as emphasized by Bhattacharya and Gale (1987), the provisioning of liquidity is a public good. Thus, if liquid investments have lower returns than less liquid ones, banks have an incentive to free-ride on other banks. When each bank relies on other banks to promote liquid, low-return investments, the end result is an underprovisioning of "real liquidity" in the system as a whole.[3] To this I would add that a central bank that attempts to offset the problem of an underprovisioning of real liquidity by providing nominal balances on favorable terms to illiquid real assets does not solve the free-rider problem but

---

[3] The distinction between "liquid" and "illiquid" assets in Bhattacharya and Gale (1987) is based on the timing of returns in terms of goods or services. "Liquid" assets are ones with a relatively low duration. In other words, "liquidity" in their analysis refers to assets that are liquid in a real sense. For the most part, the theoretical banking literature has not considered the real-world distinction between nominal and real assets. Most of the literature is written in terms of real assets, ignoring money and the vital function of banks in the money creation process. Some exceptions are Champ, Smith, and Williamson (1996), Allen and Gale (1998), Diamond and Rajan (2006), Skeie (2008), and Allen, Carletti, and Gale (2014). Allen, and Gale's (2007) Clarendon Lectures on financial crises include insightful discussions on the important distinction between real and nominal debt contracts.

exacerbates it. Thus, a collateral framework that favors illiquid collateral may ultimately promote a misallocation of funds in the real economy because it affects individual banks' incentives seen in isolation, as discussed above, and also enhances the free-rider problem among banks with respect to the private provisioning of liquidity.

My general point here is that the incentives created by a central bank's collateral framework may affect the production of different eligible collateral and underlying real assets. As an extreme example, if central bank money is available only against igloos, or igloo-backed securities, igloos will be built. If the collateral framework favors housing, the risk of a bubble in property prices could be enhanced.

Collateral frameworks can also impinge on market discipline and banks' incentives to monitor creditors by accepting collateral that does not trade at all. They can support the influence of politics on banks and the financial system by extending favorable terms to collateral with local, regional, or central government guarantees. Haircut rules and guarantee policies can interact to increase market segmentation. Collateral frameworks can facilitate indirect bailouts, propping up poorly performing banks that should optimally be resolved instead.

What a central bank accepts in exchange for central bank money also affects its own balance sheet. Perceived weaknesses in a central bank's balance sheet can ultimately affect agents' trust in it, its money, and even the political body or bodies that created the central bank and support it. Witness the "end the Fed" and "back to gold" movements in the United States and the numerous calls to break up the euro.[4] The threat to the euro has been real enough to lead the ECB to engage in a prolonged battle to save it. Many commentators

[4] See, e.g., Paul (2009) and a Bloomberg National Poll in 2010 in which 16 percent of the respondents said the Federal Reserve should be abolished (www.bloomberg.com/news/2010-12-09/more-than-half-of-americans-want-fed-re ined-in-or-abolished.html), or "House Republicans resume efforts to reduce Fed's power," by Binyamin Appelbaum, *New York Times*, July 10, 2014 (www.nytimes.com/2014/07/11/business/house-republicans-restart-their-war-on -the-fed.html?).

have expressed the view that a break-up of the euro will also mean a break-up of the European Union.

To put the Eurosystem's collateral framework in context, the next chapter provides an overview of the monetary policy developments in the euro area from the introduction of the euro in January 1999 to January 2015. This is also essential to gain an appreciation of the role of the collateral framework in "saving the euro." Thus, I review the unconventional policies introduced to deal with the crisis. Of particular importance are the full allotment policy and the extension of the maturity of repos in longer-term refinancing operations (LTROs) to one and three years. Combined, these two policies provided banks with almost unlimited one- and three-year funding directly from the central bank, constrained only by banks' eligible collateral holdings. These and other policies facilitated the expansion of the Eurosystem's consolidated balance sheet from EUR 1 trillion at the end of 2006 to EUR 2.3 trillion at the end of 2013. The additional collateral pledged to the Eurosystem as a result of this expansion is freely chosen by banks, subject to the constraint that the collateral is eligible. Hence, the crisis has enhanced the importance of the collateral framework.

The large ABS and covered bond purchase programs announced on September 4, 2014, also emphasize the importance of the collateral framework. This initiative heralded the outright buying of sovereign bonds, which was eventually announced in January 2015. The Euroystem's buying of sovereign bonds is a highly contentious policy. The OMT, for example, has been the subject of a legal challenge that went all the way to the European Court of Justice. The fight to preserve the euro and the role of the collateral framework in this is discussed at length toward the end of the book.

2.2 COLLATERAL ELIGIBILITY AND USAGE

In most currency areas, banks can use a wide set of eligible collateral with potentially different liquidity and risk characteristics (ECB 2013; Markets Committee (BIS) 2013). The set of eligible collateral in the euro area is especially large. At times, more than 40,000 ISINs have been on the public list of eligible "marketable" collateral, with the number over time being around 30,000 to 40,000 ISINs.[5] This list is updated daily and posted on the ECB's webpage. The set of eligible collateral ranges from sovereign bonds to unsecured bank bonds and ABSs, with a large span of ratings within all asset classes. At the end of 2013, these had a value of around EUR 14 trillion. In addition, banks can pledge non-marketable assets such as credit claims. Guarantees by governments, corporations, and other entities can be, and are, used to provide eligibility to otherwise non-eligible collateral. "Marketable" collateral without such guarantees or external ratings can be made privately eligible through the use of approved in-house ratings. The same collateral is eligible across all operations, main and long-term refinancing operations and the marginal lending facility (discount window) alike. The Eurosystem therefore offers an ideal setting for gaining insight into collateral frameworks with broad eligibility criteria, in addition to being important in its own right.[6]

I begin the analysis of the collateral framework in Chapter 4 by presenting evidence, drawn from official statistics on collateral eligibility and usage, that the Eurosystem's collateral framework promotes collateral that we would ex ante think of as worse, for example, in terms of being less liquid or having a higher probability of default. Over time, ABSs, uncovered bank bonds, and other "lower-quality" marketable assets have become an increasingly larger proportion of eligible collateral. The increased production of such "low-end" collateral is a logical response to another trend, namely that these collateral classes have become increasingly attractive to use in repos with the Eurosystem, as revealed by the large increase in their usage. From

---

[5] ISIN is International Securities Identification Number.

[6] The Federal Reserve System also has wide eligibility criteria but restricts the securities it accepts at its open market operations to Treasury, agency, and agency mortgage-backed securities (see the Board of Governors of the Federal Reserve System webpage www.federalreserve.gov/monetarypolicy/bst_ratesetting.htm or Markets Committee (BIS) 2013).

2004 to 2013, the proportion of these low-end asset classes and non-marketable assets used in repos with the ECB has grown from around 35 percent to close to 60 percent by value.[7]

That banks use a relatively high proportion of lower-quality collateral in Eurosystem liquidity-injecting operations might be seen as the natural result of the efficient use of collateral by banks. Nyborg, Bindseil, and Strebulaev (2002) argue that there is heterogeneity in the opportunity costs among the collateral that is eligible to be used in Eurosystem repos which is not eliminated by haircuts. This may arise, for example, as a result of Eurosystem haircuts not reflecting market conditions. Consistent with this view, I document in Chapter 5 that years pass between each time Eurosystem haircuts are updated. That banks use relatively worse collateral in ECB operations suggests that lower-quality collateral have relatively low haircuts.

Lower-quality collateral may also have lower opportunity costs because of their limited use outside of Eurosystem operations. In addition to the approximately EUR 14 trillion (end of 2013) of eligible collateral that is marketable, banks can also use non-marketable collateral, with unknown aggregate value. In comparison, at the end of 2013, the refinancing operations soaked up collateral with a collateral value of less than EUR 1 trillion. Thus, there is a large excess quantity of eligible collateral, some of which is locked out of other markets. For example, the popular Eurex GC Pooling ECB Basket contracts include only around 7,000 to 8,000 ISINs of the roughly 35,000 ISINs that can be used in Eurosystem repos.[8]

In addition, as argued by Ewerhart and Tapking (2008), banks may have a preference for using higher-quality collateral in bilateral

---

[7] An ECB working paper by Bindseil and Papadia (2006) notes a similar trend in the 1999–2005 period as does an IMF working paper by Chailloux, Gray, and McCaughrin (2008) for the 2004–2007 period. The latter paper also shows a similar phenomenon occurring in the United States with the onset of the financial crisis in the third quarter of 2007.

[8] See www.eurexrepo.com/repo-en/products/gcpooling/. Eurex Clearing AG acts as a central counterparty (CCP) in these contracts.

repos as this may save on expected default costs. The logic revolves around two-way default risk. While larger haircuts have the advantage of protecting cash providers against defaults by cash takers (collateral providers), they have the drawback of leading to larger losses to collateral providers in the event that cash providers fail to return the underlying collateral at maturity. This gives rise to a preference for using higher-quality collateral in bilateral repos, since such collateral requires lower haircuts to protect the cash provider from cash-taker credit risk (assuming default costs are positively related to losses in default). In short, higher-quality collateral reduces the total costs of two-way credit risk. The flip side of this is a preference for using lower-quality collateral in repos with the central bank. Doing so is possible, of course, only in a system where the central bank does not require the highest quality collateral, as is the case in the euro area.

2.3 COLLATERAL VALUES, HAIRCUTS, RATINGS, AND GUARANTEES

Banks' preference for particular types of collateral in repos with the central banks is affected by the terms offered by the central bank. In the euro area, the repo rate is independent of the counterparty and the collateral that is being used. However, haircuts vary across eligible collateral. They therefore play a key role in the collateral framework.

Haircuts are applied, in principle, to the market value of eligible collateral to yield a collateral's *collateral value*. The collateral value is the amount that an eligible institution (which I refer to as a bank, for short) can borrow from the central bank with the specified collateral. For a specific eligible collateral i at time t, the collateral value, $V_{i,t}^c$, is given by

$$V_{i,t}^c = (1 - h_{i,t})V_{i,t}^m, \tag{2.1}$$

where $h_{i,t}$ is the haircut and $V_{i,t}^m$ is, in principle, the market price of the collateral. I say "in principle" because not all eligible collateral have market prices. Where a market price does not exist or is not sufficiently reliable, the central bank applies the haircut to a theoretical, or model, price instead. Thus, we can think of V^m equally as a model or market price.

Questions that naturally arise from these observations and that will be addressed in later chapters include the following: What are haircuts for different eligible collateral and how are they determined? What determines whether a market or a theoretical price is used? What does a market price actually mean? For example, how recent must it be to count or what kind of volume must it be good for? How are theoretical prices determined?[9] What fraction of all eligible collateral has a theoretical "market" price for the purpose of calculating collateral values?

Figure 2.1 unpacks Equation (2.1) to highlight the elements that determine collateral values in the Eurosystem's collateral framework. Markets affect collateral values directly when a market price of

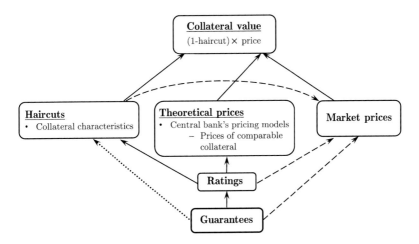

FIGURE 2.1 Determination of collateral values in the collateral framework

Solid lines and boxes indicate features and elements of the collateral framework. Dashed lines point to variables that may influence market prices and, thereby, collateral values indirectly. The dotted line indicates that guarantees can influence haircuts directly. Ratings may affect theoretical prices directly in the central bank's pricing models or indirectly through the choice of comparables.

[9] Unfortunately, the question as to how theoretical prices are actually calculated is not explored in depth in this book, due to a lack of information.

the underlying collateral exists, but non-market factors are also very important.

First, haircuts are not determined in a market, but directly by the ECB. As seen in Equation (2.1), haircuts have a direct effect on collateral values. They potentially also have an indirect effect because a collateral's haircut in Eurosystem operations may impact on its market value. I provide an empirical example in Chapter 6 that supports this view.

Second, ratings affect every aspect of the collateral value calculation. Haircuts are directly affected by them (details in Chapters 5 and 6). Market prices also tend to respond to ratings. They are also likely to be an input to the model used to calculate theoretical prices, when that is necessary (but the theoretical models used by the Eurosystem are not publicly available). This gives rating agencies substantial influence. Unfortunately, there is evidence that competition for business among rating agencies often leads to a "race to the bottom," that is, the rating agency most likely to give the highest rating wins the business (see, e.g., White 2010, for an overview). But ratings may also be derived from internal models (approved by individual countries' national central banks).

Third, ratings may be affected by guarantees provided to specific collateral or issuers by sovereigns and other players. This opens the door for politics to influence collateral values, since government guarantees may involve politics in some form or another. Guarantees can also influence haircuts directly. Chapter 6 provides further details on the role of ratings and guarantees.

In addition to these points, the influence of markets in determining collateral values is reduced by the fact that the ECB accepts a large number of securities that are trading on non-regulated markets as well as non-marketable collateral, for which market prices by definition do not exist. In short, markets play a potentially limited role when it comes to determining collateral values.

2.4 OVERVIEW OF FINDINGS

One of the contributions of this book is to distill official European Union/ECB documentation on the Eurosystem's collateral framework to make clear how haircuts are set and how this has evolved over time. The haircut rules are detailed over several tables, representing different time periods, that can be used as a reference by other researchers. The role of ratings and guarantees in determining eligibility and haircuts is also examined in detail. The rules give rise to a set of natural questions that are examined through various pieces of data.

For example, I look into the distribution of eligible collateral and their ratings across different asset classes, the relation between primary market and secondary market haircuts, the impact of haircuts on secondary market yields, cross-collateral haircut inconsistencies, the role of rating agencies, the usage and timing of government guarantees, and the incidence of eligible "marketable" collateral without market prices. These data are sometimes taken from individual, representative days. My objective is to get a sense of what the key issues with the collateral framework might be, leaving room for further research to look into these issues in more detail. The broad-theme conclusions that emerge are that the collateral framework of the Eurosystem is biased toward low-quality collateral, does not actively use markets but instead impinges on market discipline, and, in conjunction with the full allotment policy, has been used to facilitate indirect bailouts over the course of the crisis.

Some of the more specific findings are as follows. First, Eurosystem haircuts depend on collateral characteristics relating to liquidity and risk, but not on market conditions at particular points in time. Revisions to them are rare.

Second, around 76 percent, by count, of all assets on the public list of eligible collateral have prices that are theoretically determined, rather than taken from the market. Another 4 percent have stale market prices (more than one day old). By value, the percentage of collateral on the public list with theoretical or stale prices is approximately 20 percent. These numbers are estimated using the official collateral framework pricing rules and Bloomberg as a data source. The fraction of collateral with theoretical prices is higher for lower-quality collateral. Combining these findings with data on the usage of collateral, I estimate that approximately 44 percent, by value, of the collateral that is actually pledged, or used, by banks in repos with the Eurosystem have collateral values based on theoretical prices. Adding in stale market prices, this increases to 46 percent.

These two sets of findings can help explain why preferences for using particular asset classes arise and how this can persist and even strengthen over time.

Third, haircuts in the secondary repo market are often taken directly from the Eurosystem's collateral framework. In particular, I examine Eurex's important GC Pooling contracts. These repos are based on a subset of the eligible collateral in Eurosystem operations. According to Eurex officials, they set the haircuts in these contracts based on those of the Eurosystem, but may increase them for particular collateral that is perceived to be especially risky. I find that Eurex uses the same haircuts as the ECB in more than 90 percent of cases.

Fourth, by way of background, as of October 2008, eligible collateral is put into two rating categories: (i) A– or higher (using Standard & Poor's scale) and (ii) BBB+ to BBB–, with haircuts in the lower category being higher. I present evidence, however, that the vast majority (around 85 percent by count, 90 percent by value) of eligible collateral is rated A– or higher, thus receiving the lower haircuts.

Fifth, by way of background, until the onset of the financial crisis, the accepted external rating agencies were Standard & Poor's (S&P), Fitch, and Moody's.[10] In 2009, Dominion Bond Rating Services (DBRS) was added to that list. Only the highest rating counts in the

[10] The ECB refers to these as external credit assessment institutions, or ECAIs. I will use the simpler terminology of (accepted) rating agencies.

Eurosystem's collateral framework.[11] I document that DBRS has been pivotal in providing an A– rating for Italy, Ireland, and Spain, and a BBB– rating for Portugal. I estimate that the lower haircuts on government bonds from these countries as a result of the pivotal ratings by DBRS are worth around EUR 200 to 300 billion in increased collateral value. This is especially notable as it is under the full allotment policy, meaning that the full increase in collateral value is available as funding from the Eurosystem. This underscores the important role of DBRS in the Eurosystem's indirect bailout of the weaker sovereigns.

Sixth, exemptions to the standard minimum ratings requirements were granted to Greece, Cyprus, Ireland, and Portugal as the financial crisis progressed. Ireland and Portugal eventually exited from the bailout programs under which the exemptions were granted. Portugal's emergence from exemption in August 2014 was made possible by the ECB lowering the minimum acceptable rating from DBRS from BBB to BBBL in advance of that date.

Seventh, government guarantees are widely used, with the majority of credit institutions with such guarantees being Italian. The country with the largest number of government-guaranteed issues, however, is Germany (from a small number of issuers). The heavy provision of government guarantees to Italian credit institutions began in the run-up to the second three-year LTRO, held under the full allotment policy, in February 2012. The total value of the guaranteed collateral (from the Italian government to Italian credit institutions) amounts to more than EUR 80 billion and the marginal effect is to increase their total collateral value by around EUR 30 billion. Approximately 50 percent of this is due to the A– rating given to Italy by DBRS.

Eighth, as an exception, a handful of bank bonds guaranteed by Greece received haircuts commensurate with an A– rating over a two- to three-month period straddling 2011 and 2012, despite neither the issuers, Greece, nor the bonds themselves being rated that highly.

---

[11] There are some exceptions to this general rule relating to ABSs and covered bonds at different points in time. See Chapter 6.

It is unclear what part of the collateral framework justified this or whether it was simply a mistake. Whatever the underlying reason was, the banks and the holders of the paper in question should have benefited from these irregular haircuts.

Ninth, in the run-up to the second three-year LTRO, the ECB weakened collateral eligibility criteria by admitting 10,516 securities trading on non-regulated markets to the public list of eligible collateral. This increased the number of French and Italian eligible collateral by 198.5 and 70.8 percent, respectively. Practically all of this newly admitted collateral were unsecured bank bonds. Spanish, Italian, and French banks had by far the largest uptake in the three-year LTROs, in that order.

Tenth, the announcement on September 4, 2014, that the ECB would purchase ABSs and covered bonds, with an aggregate size that was believed at the time to be around EUR 1 trillion, was accompanied by abnormally large stock returns in the euro area. But these were not spread equally across countries. The largest stock returns were seen in the same countries that have benefited from high ratings from DBRS – Portugal, Italy, Ireland, and Spain – as well as Greece. These countries' bank stocks reacted especially positively. The event study findings are consistent with the purchase program being a part of an indirect bailout especially coming to the aid of the financially weaker sovereigns and their banks.

2.5 REST OF BOOK

The rest of the book is organized as follows. Chapter 3 reviews monetary policy implementation in the euro area, with a focus on the role of collateral, different types of operations, and the many changes that took place after the Lehman bankruptcy in the fall of 2008. Chapter 4 presents statistics on the composition, over time, of eligible collateral into different asset classes. It also presents statistics on the usage of collateral across asset classes.

Chapters 5 to 10 contain the heart of the book, an in-depth study of the Eurosystem's collateral framework. The first three of these chapters discuss the main elements that determine collateral values. Chapter 5 explains how haircuts are set and traces this out over the March 2004 to January 2015 period. Data on the distribution of ratings across eligible collateral and a comparison of eligibility and haircuts in ECB operations and Eurex's GC Pooling contracts are also provided. Chapter 6 contains a description of the ratings and guarantee rules as they pertain to eligibility and haircuts. Several pieces of evidence on ratings and guarantees and cross-collateral inconsistencies are provided. Chapter 7 describes the rules for how prices are determined, including what triggers the use of a theoretical price in the calculation of collateral values. It also furnishes estimates of the reliance on theoretical prices. In Chapter 8, I move on to "own-use" collateral, that is, eligible collateral used by an entity that has close links with the institution that issued the collateral. Chapter 9 provides evidence on the admittance of unsecured bank bonds trading on non-regulated markets to the list of eligible collateral. Finally, Chapter 10 distills the findings of the previous chapters and discusses the limited role of market discipline afforded by the Eurosystem's collateral framework. It also provides some ideas as to how market forces may be introduced back into the collateral framework.

The next three chapters are devoted to the euro crisis. Chapter 11 discusses the role of the ECB's unconventional monetary policy in saving the euro through providing an indirect bailing out of banks and sovereigns. This chapter also provides the evidence on the stock market's reaction to the announcement of the ABS and covered bond purchase programs on September 4, 2014. Chapter 12 discusses what I call "the endgame of the euro crisis." This includes a discussion of the role of the European Court of Justice in the ECB's decision to go ahead with sovereign bond purchases and an analysis of where things may be headed. Chapter 13 takes the analysis outside the realm of collateral frameworks and unconventional monetary policies to the euro's fundamental problem of a lack of credibility. I propose that this can be mitigated by securing sovereign debt and linking Eurosystem collateral framework haircuts to fiscal and other measures.

Before concluding in Chapter 15, the book considers, in Chapter 14, some proposals to stabilize financial markets that have been tabled by others in response to the financial crisis. These proposals, which relate to the organization of interbank markets and larger reserve requirements (specifically, full reserve banking), place large demands on collateral. The findings in earlier chapters suggest that there is a limited quantity of what we may think of as high-quality collateral. This is a problem for these proposals. I offer some alternative solutions for improving the interbank market and also argue that unsecured markets can play an important role with respect to the third pillar of the Basel regulatory framework, market discipline. A general observation from the findings in this book is that market forces are conspicuously weak at the core of the monetary system.

3 Monetary Policy Implementation in the Euro Area over Time

The collateral framework is a part of the monetary policy framework. Through its monetary policy operations, a central bank provides central bank money against eligible collateral, as determined by the collateral framework. To put the role of the Eurosystem's collateral framework in context, this chapter sketches out the main features of the ECB's monetary policy framework and updates to these over time.[1] It also provides data on the magnitudes of the ECB's operations over time and therefore the value of collateral that needs to be pledged by banks, in the case of repos, or purchased. This is then compared to the monetary base and the Eurosystem's consolidated balance sheet, which helps to illustrate the centrality of the collateral framework.

Table 3.1 lists the main instruments of monetary policy implementation in the euro area and significant modifications to these from January 1999 to January 2015. The ECB's basic approach is to use reverse operations that inject liquidity into the banking sector through repos, or collateralized loans. Banks' counterparties in these transactions are their respective national central banks (NCBs). Some NCBs operate with systems where the pledged collateral is earmarked for a particular operation, but most use a pooling system in which the total collateral value of each bank's collateral inventory

---

[1] For a more in-depth overview, see ECB (2011). For up-to-date details, see the "Monetary Policy" tab on www.ecb.europa.eu. Briefer summaries can also be found in Bindseil and Nyborg (2008) and the literature on repo auctions using ECB data, e.g., Bindseil, Nyborg, and Strebulaev (2009) and Cassola, Hortaçsu, and Kastl (2013). An excellent textbook covering monetary policy in the Eurosystem is Bindseil (2014). Bofinger (2001) provides an insightful and more traditional treatment of monetary policy without much by way of discussion of collateral.

Table 3.1 *Main Eurosystem monetary policy instruments over time*

	Main refinancing operation (MRO)	Longer-term refinancing operation (LTRO)	Maintenance period	Marginal lending facility	Deposit facility	Outright purchase programs
Jan-99	**Fixed rate tender** (weekly) Limited allotment (liquidity neutral) 2 weeks, overlapping maturities	**Variable rate tender** (monthly) As of March 24, 1999: Discriminatory auctions Limited allotment (fixed) 3 months, overlapping maturities	24th of month to 23rd of the following month	As of April 1999 policy rate + 100bp	As of April 1999 policy rate – 100bp	
Jun-00	**Variable rate tender** Discriminatory auctions					
Nov-01	Policy rate subject to change only every other General Council meeting (previously every GC meeting)					
Mar-04	1 week maturity		Varies from 21 to 43 days Starts at settlement date of first MRO after every second Governing Council meeting			

Date		policy rate +	policy rate −	
Aug-07	Sometimes more than one per month			
Oct-08	**Fixed rate tender** Full allotment	**Fixed rate tender**[1] Full allotment Maturity varies: 1, 3, and 6 months	policy rate + 50bp	policy rate − 50bp	
Jan-09			policy rate + 100bp	policy rate − 100bp	
May-09			policy rate + 75bp	policy rate − 75bp	
Jun-09		First 1-year LTRO,[2] June 24 (EUR 442 billion)			
Jul-09					First Covered Bond Purchase Programme (CBPP1, EUR 60 billion) starts. End: June 30, 2010
May-10					Securities Markets Programme (SMP) starts. Last purchase in February 2012. Official End: September 2012

Table 3.1 (cont.)

	Main refinancing operation (MRO)	Longer-term refinancing operation (LTRO)	Maintenance period	Marginal lending facility	Deposit facility	Outright purchase programs
Nov-11						CBPP2 (EUR 40 billion), End: October 31, 2012
Dec-11		3-year LTRO, December 21 (EUR 489 billion)				
Jan-12			Reserve req. ratio lowered from 2 to 1 percent, January 18			
Feb-12		3-year LTRO, February 29 (EUR 530 billion)				
Jul-12					Deposit rate set equal to zero	
Sep-12						Outright Monetary Transactions (OMT) program. No ex ante limits w.r.t. the quantity purchased.

Feb-13	ECB allows early repayment of the 3-year LTROs at banks' convenience.		
May-13 **Nov-13**		policy rate + 50bp	policy rate − 50bp[3]
Jun-14	ECB announces future usage of Targeted LTROs (TLTROs). The first two will be in September and December 2014.	policy rate + 25bp	policy rate − 25bp[3] Deposit rate negative
Jul-14	Further technical details of TLTROs announced: eight TLTROs to be allotted. Interest rate equal to the current policy rate plus 10 bps. Legal Act published on July 29.	Governing Council monetary policy meeting moves to 6-week cycle in January 2015. Length of maint. period will also change to six weeks.	

Table 3.1 *(cont.)*

	Main refinancing operation (MRO)	Longer-term refinancing operation (LTRO)	Maintenance period	Marginal lending facility	Deposit facility	Outright purchase programs
Sep-14	Policy rate set to historical low of 5bp	First TLTRO allotted on September 18, volume of EUR 82.6 billion				ECB announces on September 4 the implementation of an ABS purchase program (ABSPP) and a new covered bond program (CBPP3). Starting October (CBPP3) and November 2014 (ABSPP) with durations of at least two years.
Dec-14		Second TLTRO allotted on December 11, volume of EUR 129.8 billion				

| Jan-15 | Interest on remaining six TLTROs equal to the current policy rate (no spread). | Expansion on January 22 of asset purchase program to include bonds issued by euro-area governments and agencies and European institutions. Initially EUR 60 billion per month until September 2016, but open-ended. |

Source: www.ecb.europa.eu/press/html/index.en.html

Notes: [1] The fixed rate, full allotment LTROs were initially held at the policy rate, as for the MROs. Starting with the one-year LTRO on December 16, 2009, the ECB gradually started charging the weighted average of the policy rates over the tenor of an LTRO. This was initially done for LTROs with tenors of more than three months. From October 27, 2010, the averaging scheme was used for three-month LTROs as well (see www.ecb.europa.eu/press/pr/date/2010/html/pr100902_1.en.html). One three-month variable rate tender LTRO was held on April 28, 2010. [2] The one-year LTRO on June 24, 2009 was the first of four such LTROs. The other three had a combined size of EUR 229 billion. [3] In these cases, the change to the difference between the deposit rate and the policy rate is caused by changes to the policy rate. The deposit rate is maintained at zero.

account with its NCB is used to cover all its loans across all operations. For example, a bank that has outstanding repos, or loans, of 1 billion needs to have eligible collateral with an official collateral value of at least 1 billion in its collateral pool, or account. Subject to the eligibility and value constraints, banks have complete discretion over what collateral they pledge in Eurosystem operations.

Each new reverse operation offers banks the opportunity to refinance, or roll over, maturing repos (or loans). They are therefore referred to as refinancing operations.

Table 3.1 delineates the evolution of the two most important types of refinancing operations, namely the main refinancing operations (MROs) and the longer-term refinancing operations (LTROs).[2] The MROs were initially run as fixed rate tenders with a limited allotment. Under this procedure, the ECB lends central bank money to participating financial institutions (banks, for short) at its policy rate.[3] Banks submit quantity (only) bids and receive a prorated share of the alloted amount. In June 2000, the ECB switched to variable rate tenders using the discriminatory auction format (Nyborg, Bindseil, and Strebulaev 2002), for reasons discussed by Ayuso and Repullo (2001), Breitung and Nautz (2001), and Nyborg and Strebulaev (2001). Theoretical models of fixed and variable rate refinancing operations are provided by Nyborg and Strebulaev (2001) and (2004), respectively. With the introduction of the discriminatory auctions, the policy rate became the minimum bid rate in the MROs. Initially,

---

[2] The ECB also holds some foreign currency reverse operations as well as liquidity absorbing operations. The latter have been used, for example, to "sterilize" purchases from the Securities Markets Programme (see below). These operations, which are abbreviated OT by the ECB, are not listed in Table 3.1.

[3] One can think of the ECB's policy rate as its target rate (Bindseil and Nyborg 2008). The benchmark allotment is "the amount that allows counterparties to smoothly fulfill their reserve requirements until the settlement of the next MRO ...[It] is the allotment normally required to establish balanced conditions in the short-term money market, given the ECB's complete liquidity forecast. Balanced liquidity conditions should normally result in an overnight rate close to the minimum bid rate" (ECB 2004, p. 16). The introduction of the full allotment policy (see below) has resulted in the overnight rate moving closer to the deposit rate rather than the minimum bid rate as before.

the main refinancing operations had maturities of two weeks, but this was changed to one week in March 2004. The discriminatory format was also used in the LTROs. Before the crisis, the LTROs had maturities of approximately three months.

The financial crisis ushered in several changes, especially after Lehman Brothers' default in September 2008. On October 8, 2008, the ECB announced that it would switch to a fixed rate tender at the policy rate with full allotment, for both the MROs and the LTROs.[4] This represents one of the most significant actions taken by the ECB in response to the crisis. Under this mechanism, central bank money is not rationed in the refinancing operations. Instead, banks receive what they ask for. The only restriction is that they have to pledge sufficient collateral to cover these amounts.

A second major change was extending the maturity of some LTROs, initially to six months (first time in April 2008) and later to one and three years. Given the full allotment policy, this means that banks can receive unlimited one- and three-year funding directly from the ECB, subject to having sufficient collateral. The impact was massive. The first one-year LTRO was held in June 2009 and had a volume of approximately EUR 442 billion.[5] Two three-year LTROs were held, one in December 2011 and one in February 2012, through which the ECB lent more than EUR 1 trillion in aggregate to banks. This is almost as much as the consolidated Eurosystem balance sheet in 2006 (EUR 1.142 trillion; see Table 3.3), the last full pre-crisis year.

A third change was the initiation of outright purchases of securities for monetary policy purposes, starting on a limited scale (EUR 60 billion) with covered bonds in July 2009. Outright purchasing was subsequently expanded with the introduction of the Securities Markets Programme (SMP) in May 2010. The Outright

---

[4] Starting in December 2009, LTROs were gradually settled at the weighted average of the policy rates in force over their respective tenors. One three-month LTRO was held under the variable rate tender format in April 2010. See Table 3.1 for details.

[5] Specifically, June 24, 2009. Three other one-year LTROs were held, on September 30, 2009, December 16, 2009, and October 26, 2011, with sizes of EUR 75.2, 96.9, and 56.9 billion, respectively.

Monetary Transactions (OMT) program then replaced the SMP on September 6, 2012.[6] The OMT allows for unlimited purchases of sovereign bonds of countries under a European Financial Stability Facility/European Stability Mechanism, but has yet to be employed.

According to ECB press releases, purchases under the SMP and OMT would be sterilized.[7] That is, the money created by the purchases would be absorbed through other operations. The way this was done, under the SMP, was through one-week deposits, which were available at weekly competitive tenders. Since participation in these tenders was voluntary, there was no guarantee that the asset purchases would be fully sterilized. Maybe more importantly, the ECB ran full allotment MROs and LTROs at the same time as the SMP and its associated sterilizing operations. Thus, the money taken out of the market in the sterilizing operations could return into the market in the refinancing operations. Collateral availability was not a concern in this case because the deposits created by the sterilizing operations could be used with zero haircut in the refinancing operations (Chapter 5). One might therefore take the assertion that SMP purchases were sterilized with a grain of salt.

Even though the OMT has never been used, as mentioned earlier, it is often viewed as representing the "whatever it takes" in Draghi's famous statement to save the euro.

However, the fourth change I want to emphasize here shows that the mere promise of unlimited purchases was not enough.[8] On September 4, 2014, the ECB announced an asset-backed security (ABS) and covered bond purchase program where collateral actually would be purchased. This event is studied in detail in Chapter 11.

[6] See ECB press release, September 6, 2012, "Technical features of Outright Monetary Transactions," www.ecb.europa.eu/press/pr/date/2012/html/pr120906_1.en.html.
[7] See www.ecb.europa.eu/press/pr/date/2010/html/pr100510.en.html (SMP) and www.ecb.europa.eu/press/pr/date/2012/html/pr120906_1.en.html (OMT).
[8] The legality of the OMT has also been challenged in court. See, e.g., "Euro week ahead: OMT hearings, data slate highlight key tests," by Martin Baccardax, *MNI Deutsche Börse Group*, October 10, 2014, https://mninews.marketnews.com/print/1050693. This is discussed further in Chapters 11 and 12.

On January 22, 2015, the ECB finally announced that it would start buying sovereign bonds with a total value, combined with the other two asset purchase programs, of more than EUR 1 trillion. This will be covered in further detail in Chapter 12.

A fifth notable change was decreasing the reserve requirements from 2 to 1 percent of short-term liabilities (in January 2012). Thus, the ECB modified its monetary policy to be super-accommodative while at the same time lowering its reserve requirements. The "headline" effects of this are shown in Table 3.2, Figure 3.1, and Table 3.3 and discussed below.

Table 3.2 compares the daily outstanding amounts of central bank money injected via MROs and LTROs to each other and to the monetary base. It covers the time period January 1999 to December 2014, dividing this into five subperiods, reflecting major changes to the monetary policy instruments, as reported in Table 3.1. There are five main observations, which are also graphically shown in Figure 3.1.[9]

First, the monetary base and the daily outstanding amounts injected into the banking system from the MROs and LTROs have grown over time, even pre-crisis, suggesting an accommodative monetary policy.

Second, the quantity of central bank money injected via the MROs and the LTROs jumped substantially with the introduction of full allotment fixed rate tenders. Pre full allotment, from September 2007 to September 2008, the quantity from these operations was EUR 461.8 billion in terms of the average daily outstanding amount. Post full allotment, from October 2008 to November 2011, this had increased to EUR 633.1 billion.

---

[9] Table 3.2 and Figure 3.1 account for the fact that in the three-year LTRO that settled on December 22, 2011, banks had the option to transfer in loans from the one-year LTRO that settled on October 27, 2011. EUR 45,721.45 million out of EUR 56,934.45 million were shifted. So only EUR 11,213 million fell due in the one-year LTRO on November 1, 2012. Reference: press release on December 8, 2011 (www.ecb.europa.eu/press/pr/date/2011/html/pr111208_1.en.html). This effect is also taken into account in Figure 11.2.

Table 3.2 *Refinancing operations and monetary base*

Panel A

	Obs.	Mean	St. Dev.	Min	Max	Mean	St. Dev.	Min	Max
		MRO (billion EUR)				LTRO (billion EUR)			
Jan 99 – Mar 04	1,339	160.2	34.4	75.0	253.0	52.7	8.2	45.0	75.0
Apr 04 – Aug 07	878	285.9	27.4	205.5	338.0	105.2	26.4	75.0	190.0
Sep 07 – Sep 08	276	183.6	40.9	128.5	368.6	278.2	22.3	190.0	420.0
Oct 08 – Nov 11	815	156.3	72.9	46.2	339.5	476.7	140.4	298.2	728.6
Dec 11 – Dec 14	805	109.0	36.4	17.5	291.6	757.7	244.0	371.6	1,110.3

Panel B

	Obs.	Mean	St. Dev.	Min	Max	Mean	St. Dev.	Min	Max
		MRO+LTRO (billion EUR)				Monetary Base (billion EUR)			
Jan 99 – Mar 04	1,339	212.8	32.7	75.0	298.0	471.1	34.3	415.6	561.4
Apr 04 – Aug 07	878	391.1	46.1	280.5	465.5	696.3	76.8	561.0	832.1
Sep 07 – Sep 08	276	461.8	38.6	397.0	637.1	865.1	23.8	832.3	901.2
Oct 08 – Nov 11	815	633.1	123.7	407.4	896.5	1,120.9	80.3	921.0	1,307.5
Dec 11 – Dec 14	805	866.7	235.9	503.5	1,285.2	1,402.0	223.5	1,162.8	1,774.6

Panel C

	Obs.	Mean	St. Dev.	Min	Max	Mean	St. Dev.	Min	Max
		MRO+LTRO, as percent of Monetary Base				MRO+LTRO, as percent of Balance Sheet			
Jan 99 – Mar 04	1,339	45.2	4.1	34.7	56.8	27.0	3.3	10.9	36.7
Apr 04 – Aug 07	878	56.2	2.4	48.1	61.9	38.3	1.6	32.8	42.1
Sep 07 – Sep 08	276	53.4	4.7	45.6	75.7	33.8	2.8	27.3	49.5
Oct 08 – Nov 11	815	56.5	10.7	38.5	89.7	32.8	6.8	21.6	46.9
Dec 11 – Dec 14	805	60.9	8.6	40.5	72.9	33.6	4.6	19.8	42.7

The table presents statistics on the daily outstanding amount of central bank money injected via MROs and LTROs and the monetary base. The sample period (January 1999 to December 2014) is subdivided into five subperiods, each representing major changes to monetary policy implementation as shown in Table 3.1. Statistics on MROs and LTROs have been calculated from the data available on www.ecb.europa.eu/mopo/implement/omo/html/top_history.en.html. Statistics on the monetary base and on the ECB balance sheet have been collected from the Statistical Data Warehouse of the ECB (http://sdw.ecb.europa.eu/home.do). The balance sheet is provided on a weekly basis and the monetary base on a monthly basis. Monetary base and balance sheet numbers are converted to daily data from the original data in the obvious way (i.e., values are carried forward for one month (week) until the monetary base or balance sheet numbers are updated).

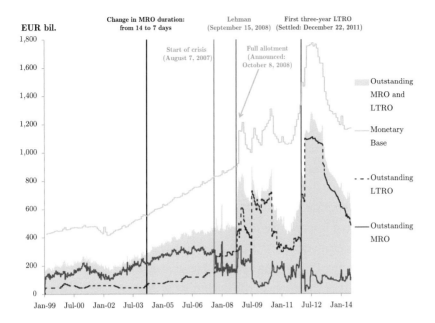

FIGURE 3.1 MRO and LTRO daily outstanding amounts and the monetary base

Time period: January 1, 1999, to June 30, 2014.
The sampling frequency of the outstanding MRO and LTRO amounts is daily, while that of the monetary base is monthly.
Data sources: www.ecb.europa.eu/mopo/implement/omo/html/top_history
.en.html and www.ecb.europa.eu/stats/monetary/res/html/index.en.
html.

Third, a further jump occurred with the introduction of the three-year LTROs. In the December 2011 to December 2014 period, the average daily outstanding amount from the MROs and LTROs was EUR 866.7 billion. Over these last two time periods, the monetary base averaged to EUR 1,120.9 and 1,402 billion, respectively, up from EUR 865.1 billion over the September 2007 to September 2008 period.

Fourth, over time, the central bank money injected via the MROs and LTROs has come to comprise the majority of the monetary base. In all but the first subperiod in Table 3.2, the average fraction is well above 50 percent. In the subperiod October 2008 to

November 2011, right before the introduction of three-year LTROs, the average fraction was 56.5 percent, rising to 60.9 percent over the December 2011 to December 2014 period. At the peak, the MROs and LTROs comprised 89.7 percent of the monetary base. This was at the end of June 2009, right after the implementation of the first one-year LTRO, which had a size of EUR 442 billion.[10] More generally, these figures show that the MROs and LTROs account for a relatively larger fraction of the monetary base in the three-year LTRO era than previously.

Fifth, the financial crisis brought about a change with respect to the relative importance of the MROs and LTROs. Until the start of the crisis, substantially more liquidity was injected through the MROs than the LTROs. As seen in Figure 3.1, this reversed shortly after the start of the crisis in the beginning of August 2007. The exact date of the reversal is September 19, 2007, when extant MRO loans from the previous week of EUR 269 billion fell due and were replaced with new one-week loans totaling only EUR 155 billion. The ECB had already injected EUR 165 billion through LTROs since early August, and this was sufficient to make the LTROs larger than the MROs on September 19. The increased usage of the LTRO relative to the MRO initially reflects a policy decision to provide more long-term money. But after the introduction of the full allotment policy in October 2008, it also represents a preference for longer-term money by the banks.

The three-year LTROs can be viewed as having supplied funding to the banks, rather than just mere "liquidity." That it should have been necessary to inject EUR 1.5 trillion of one- and three-year funding is highly suggestive of other sources of funding drying up, as the monetary system "delevered." It is difficult to interpret such large injections of medium-term funds as anything but an indirect bailout of large swathes of the banking system.[11] It also aided the sovereigns. By alleviating the pressure on the banking system, it reduced the

---

[10] Specifically, over the June 25 to June 30, 2009, period.
[11] See Chapter 11 for further discussion.

need for sovereigns to step in. In addition, the funds received by the banks could be used to fund the purchase of sovereign debt, either by themselves or levered investors. While the full allotment policy in principle allowed for nearly unlimited funding to banks, they, their creditors, and the sovereigns were faced with uncertainty with respect to how long the full allotment policy would be in place. By extending the maturity to three years, this uncertainty was reduced. This may help explain the heavy uptake of the three-year LTROs. The three-year maturity bought time for banks and sovereigns to work through their problems and avoid default. However, this may not have worked as well as one may have hoped (Chapter 11).

The increase in the MROs and LTROs did not only increase the monetary base but also the ECB's balance sheet. Because the money is injected against collateral, the properties of that collateral affect the properties of the asset side of the ECB's balance sheet, for example in terms of risk. The ECB's balance sheet is also affected by outright purchase programs.

Table 3.3 takes a more in-depth look at the asset size of the Eurosystem's consolidated balance sheet from 1999 to 2013. My focus here is on those items that relate to the collateral framework, namely items 5 (monetary policy operations) and 7 (securities of euro-area residents in euros, i.e., purchases of euro-denominated collateral). Note that item 5 consists primarily of MROs and LTROs, but it also includes fine-tuning and structural operations, the marginal lending facility, and credits relating to margin calls.[12]

Focusing on the 2004 to 2013 period, Table 3.3 reports that item 5 increased from EUR 345.1 billion in 2004 to a peak of EUR 1,122.3 billion in 2012, a 225 percent increase. Repayments to the three-year LTROs brought this item down to EUR 717.1 billion at the end of 2013. As a percentage of the total balance sheet, the monetary policy

---

[12] For example, on December 25, 2009, the breakdown of item 5 was as follows: MROs, 59,221; LTROs, 669,296; fine-tuning operations, 0; structural operations, 0; marginal lending facility, 40; credits related to margin calls, 27. Source: www.ecb.int/press/pr/wfs/2009/html/fs091229.en.html.

Table 3.3 *Consolidated Eurosystem balance sheet (asset side, in billion EUR)*

Assets	1999	2000	2001	2002	2003	2004	2005	2006	2007	2008	2009	2010	2011	2012	2013
1 Gold and gold receivables	116.5	117.1	126.8	130.9	130.2	125.7	148.1	174.0	184.5	219.8	238.1	334.4	419.8	479.1	343.9
2 Claims on non-euro-area residents denominated in foreign currency	254.9	258.7	264.6	248.6	189.5	153.8	152.0	147.0	137.6	152.8	191.9	220.2	236.8	258.0	245.7
3 Claims on euro-area residents denominated in foreign currency	14.4	15.8	25.2	19.9	18.0	17.0	24.0	22.9	35.7	221.4	31.7	26.0	95.4	33.7	23.0
4 Claims on non-euro-area residents denominated in euro	4.8	3.7	5.7	4.0	6.0	6.8	9.3	11.6	13.6	8.9	15.7	19.1	26.0	19.1	19.5
5 Lending to euro-area credit inst. (monetary pol. op.) denominated in euro	250.1	268.6	203.6	236.6	276.0	345.1	404.0	441.5	617.1	829.6	728.6	513.1	879.1	1,122.3	717.1
6 Other claims on euro-area credit institutions denominated in euro	–	0.6	0.5	0.1	0.7	3.8	3.5	10.8	23.8	54.8	25.8	42.0	95.0	208.3	75.0
7 Securities of euro-area residents denominated in euro	23.5	26.0	28.0	33.1	54.1	70.2	94.4	78.0	97.2	120.8	329.5	459.6	610.6	585.2	586.1
8 General government debt denominated in euro	59.2	57.7	68.7	66.3	42.9	41.3	40.3	39.9	37.1	37.5	36.2	35.0	33.9	30.0	28.3
9 Other assets	79.8	87.0	91.5	93.1	117.8	120.4	144.1	216.7	326.3	375.9	254.9	276.9	336.6	275.4	246.8
Total assets	803.2	835.1	814.7	832.6	835.2	884.2	1,019.7	1,142.3	1,473.0	2,021.5	1,852.5	1,926.2	2,733.2	3,011.2	2,285.4

Data sources: For each year, the last consolidated weekly financial statement of the Eurosystem. For example, for 2013, see www.ecb.europa. eu/press/pr/wfs/2013/html/index.en.html.

operations (item 5) fluctuate from a low of 26.6 percent in 2010 to a high of 41.9 percent in 2007.

Item 7 is outright holdings of collateral. This was small prior to the fall of 2008, constituting less than 7 percent of the Eurosystem's consolidated balance sheet in 2006 and 2007, the last full year prior to the financial crisis and the first year of the crisis, respectively. After the onset of the crisis, this eventually grew to a peak of EUR 610.6 billion in 2011 and to EUR 586.1 billion in 2013. These numbers constitute 22.3 and 25.6 percent of the total balance sheet, respectively, of EUR 2,733 and 2,285 billion.[13]

Combined, items 5 and 7 stood at around the 47 percent level from 2004 to 2008, jumping up to a high-water mark of 57.1 percent in 2009. The percentage fell to 50.5 percent in 2010 before climbing back up to the 57 percent mark in 2013. These numbers show that the importance of the collateral framework has grown as a result of the crisis. That around a third of the Eurosystem's assets is comprised of repos or loans to the European banking sector against collateral that banks choose themselves makes it particularly interesting to ask what kind of collateral banks actually choose to use when obtaining liquidity (or funding) from the ECB.

[13] Interestingly, the ECB was accumulating large quantities of collateral prior to introducing the first outright purchase program in July 2009. This can be seen by comparing item 7 in 2008 and 2009; the increase is larger than the covered bond purchase program introduced in 2009. What happened is that from the last week of 2008 to the first week of 2009, the ECB reclassified approximately EUR 147 billion from item 9 (other assets) to item 7 (see ECB press release, January 7, 2009, "Consolidated financial statement of the Eurosystem as at 31 December 2008").

4 Evidence on the Production and Usage of Collateral

Eligible collateral comes from many different asset classes, ranging from government bonds to asset-backed securities. Non-marketable assets can also be eligible. This chapter reports on the nominal amounts of eligible collateral across different marketable asset classes from 2004 to 2013. It also reports on banks' actual usage of collateral across these asset classes and non-marketable assets. By comparing the usage data with the eligible collateral value data, it is possible to get a sense of the extent to which there are biases in the collateral framework. If all eligible collateral have the same opportunity costs, we would expect to see no distinct preference for using collateral from particular asset classes. Thus, in this chapter, I compare the fraction of eligible collateral that is used across asset classes.

Table 4.1 provides the nominal value of eligible marketable collateral from 2004 to 2013. The data are compiled by the ECB and available on its webpage (see the caption of Table 4.1). The ECB provides the data broken down into seven asset classes. These are, from top to bottom in the table, central government securities, regional government securities, supranational and agency securities ("other marketable assets"), covered bank bonds, corporate bonds, uncovered bank bonds, and asset-backed securities.[1] As will be shown in Chapter 5, collateral haircuts in the Eurosystem are increasing in these asset classes in the order just cited. Thus, we can think of these asset classes as having decreasing "quality" in terms of risk and liquidity, as reflected by haircuts.

---

[1] The category that is labeled "other marketable assets" on the ECB's webpage and in Table 4.1 represents, according to emails from the ECB, predominantly securities issued by supranational institutions and agencies. The category labeled "corporate bonds" also includes equities (until May 2005).

Table 4.1 *Eligible marketable collateral across asset classes*

Years	2004	2005	2006	2007	2008	2009	2010	2011	2012	2013
Central government securities	3,980	4,145	4,260	4,409	4,641	5,215	5,793	6,036	6,054	6,404
percent of total	*52*	*50*	*49*	*47*	*42*	*41*	*42*	*47*	*44*	*45*
Regional government securities	215	239	263	288	302	328	384	407	438	424
percent of total	*3*	*3*	*3*	*3*	*3*	*3*	*3*	*3*	*3*	*3*
Other marketable assets[1]	292	310	312	340	558	496	618	683	939	1,155
percent of total	*4*	*4*	*4*	*4*	*5*	*4*	*5*	*5*	*7*	*8*
Covered bank bonds	1,256	1,215	1,191	1,166	1,248	1,392	1,391	1,537	1,662	1,576
percent of total	*16*	*15*	*14*	*12*	*11*	*11*	*10*	*12*	*12*	*11*
Corporate bonds[2]	680	745	828	825	944	1,279	1,482	1,224	1,289	1,496
percent of total	*9*	*9*	*9*	*9*	*9*	*10*	*11*	*10*	*9*	*11*
Uncovered bank bonds	905	1,172	1,372	1,648	2,192	2,828	2,716	1,882	2,408	2,329
percent of total	*12*	*14*	*16*	*18*	*20*	*22*	*20*	*15*	*18*	*16*
Asset-backed securities	318	392	510	712	1,057	1,290	1,294	981	928	799
percent of total	*4*	*5*	*6*	*8*	*10*	*10*	*9*	*8*	*7*	*6*
Total	7,646	8,217	8,736	9,387	10,941	12,828	13,677	12,751	13,719	14,183

Nominal amounts in billion EUR (averages of end-of-month values for each year) and percentages of eligible amounts per year.

Data source: ECB webpage; collateral data from February 14, 2014; www.ecb.europa.eu/paym/coll/html/index.en.html; downloaded on March 20, 2014.

Notes: [1] "Other marketable assets" are, according to emails from the ECB, predominantly supranational and agency debt. [2] According to an email from the ECB, the corporate bonds category also contains equities (until May 2005).

Table 4.1 shows that, in aggregate, the nominal value of eligible marketable collateral has nearly doubled from 2004 to 2013, going from EUR 7,646 to 14,183 billion. These are relatively large numbers in comparison with the size of the ECB's operations and balance sheet as well as the monetary base, as discussed above. For example, the nominal value of eligible marketable collateral in 2013 is approximately 19.8 times the amount lent through the ECB's operations (item 5 on the balance sheet) and 10.9 times the combined size of item 5 and item 7 (outright collateral holdings). Government securities account for roughly half of the eligible collateral, by nominal value, going from 52 percent in 2004 to 45 percent in 2013. Their lowest share is 41 percent in 2009. In 2013, the next largest asset classes are uncovered bank bonds (16 percent), covered bank bonds (11 percent), and corporate bonds (11 percent). In 2004, covered bank bonds accounted for 16 percent of the eligible assets by value, while uncovered bonds accounted for 12 percent. Asset-backed securities have increased from 4 to 6 percent of eligible collateral from 2004 to 2013.

Table 4.2 reports on the use of eligible collateral, covering both marketable and non-marketable assets. By "use of collateral" is meant what banks have pledged for the purpose of borrowing from the Eurosystem. Table 4.2 shows that total usage has grown from EUR 817 billion in 2004 to EUR 2,348 billion in 2013, of which EUR 593 billion are non-marketable assets. These total usage numbers are larger than total borrowing from the ECB's operations (as reported in Chapter 3), reflecting that banks put more collateral in their pools than they need to. The numbers in Tables 3.3 and 4.2 show that, in 2013, banks pledged 2,348/717, or 3.27, times more collateral than was necessary given their aggregate liquidity uptake. This suggests a negligible opportunity cost for much of the eligible collateral and for the majority of the pledged collateral. Banks are free to withdraw the excess collateral at any time.

Table 4.2 shows that the fraction of eligible marketable securities that are used by banks varies considerably across asset classes.

Table 4.2 *Usage of collateral across asset classes*

Years	2004	2005	2006	2007	2008	2009	2010	2011	2012	2013
Central government securities	252	234	206	177	158	225	262	255	359	331
percent of eligible central gov. securities	*6*	*6*	*5*	*4*	*3*	*4*	*5*	*4*	*6*	*5*
Regional government securities	58	65	61	53	62	71	71	82	99	92
percent of eligible regional gov. securities	*27*	*27*	*23*	*19*	*21*	*21*	*19*	*20*	*23*	*22*
Other marketable assets[1]	19	22	20	16	16	21	33	58	82	123
percent of eligible other marketable assets	*6*	*7*	*6*	*5*	*3*	*4*	*5*	*8*	*9*	*11*
Covered bank bonds	213	190	173	163	174	273	265	288	454	438
percent of eligible covered bank bonds	*17*	*16*	*14*	*14*	*14*	*20*	*19*	*19*	*27*	*28*
Corporate bonds[2]	27	44	60	77	96	115	102	96	91	116
percent of eligible corporate bonds	*4*	*6*	*7*	*9*	*10*	*9*	*7*	*8*	*7*	*8*
Uncovered bank bonds	169	227	294	371	440	562	430	269	354	309
percent of eligible uncov. bank bonds	*19*	*19*	*21*	*22*	*20*	*20*	*16*	*14*	*15*	*13*
Asset-backed securities	45	84	109	182	444	474	490	358	385	345
percent of eligible asset-backed securities	*14*	*21*	*21*	*26*	*42*	*37*	*38*	*36*	*41*	*43*
Non-marketable[3]	34	35	36	109	190	295	359	419	633	593
Credit Claims[3]										439
Fixed-term and cash deposits[3]										154
Total	817	900	959	1,148	1,579	2,035	2,010	1,824	2,457	2,348

Billion EUR, after valuation and haircuts. Averages of end-of-month values for each year.
Each "main row" represents the total collateral value of the indicated collateral type. The "subrows" (in italics) are these collateral values expressed as a percentage of the corresponding total nominal values in Table 4.1.
Data source: ECB webpage; collateral data from February 14, 2014, www.ecb.europa.eu/paym/coll/html/index.en.html; downloaded on March 20, 2014.
Notes: [1] "Other marketable assets" are, according to an email from the ECB, predominantly supranational and agency debt. [2] According to an email from the ECB, the corporate bonds category also contains equities (until May 2005). [3] The split of non-marketables into credit claims and fixed-term and cash deposits is available only since Q1 of 2013.

For example, in 2013, only 5 percent of central government securities (by value) were used. In contrast, the usage fraction was 22 percent for regional government securities, 28 percent for covered bank bonds, and 43 percent for asset-backed securities. These different usage fractions suggest that there are systematic differences across asset classes with respect to how "desirable" banks view it to use one or the other type of collateral. It suggests that there are biases in the collateral framework and, as seen in the table, these biases generally favor the usage of lower-quality collateral.

Figure 4.1 provides another way to see the bias toward lower-quality collateral. It contains two graphs, one for nominal values of eligible marketable collateral (4.1a) and one for usage of marketable and non-marketable assets (4.1b). The different asset classes are color-coordinated, to lump them into three broad categories. First, the higher-quality collateral is indicated by blue colors. This is comprised of central and regional government securities as well as supranational and agency debt.[2] Second, the medium-quality collateral, comprised of covered bank bonds and corporate bonds, is indicated by red colors. Third, the lower-quality collateral is indicated by green colors and is composed of uncovered bank bonds and asset-backed securities. When looking at usage, the "green" category of lower-quality collateral is augmented by non-marketable assets.

Comparing Figures 4.1a and 4.1b provides a striking illustration of the preference for lower-quality collateral exhibited by banks and how this has increased over time. While low-quality collateral has ranged from around 16 to 32 percent of the nominal value of eligible marketable collateral, the low-quality collateral group constitutes from around 30 to 68 percent of usage. The usage fraction of the low-quality group always exceeds its fraction by nominal value by at least 14 percentage points and typically much more. For example, in 2013

---

[2] What I refer to as supranational and agency debt here is the category labeled "other marketable assets" in Tables 4.1 and 4.2, for reasons explained in Footnote 1 and in the tables themselves. Note also that given the sovereign debt crisis in the euro area, it can clearly be argued that not all government debt is of particularly high quality. Here, this is not taken into account.

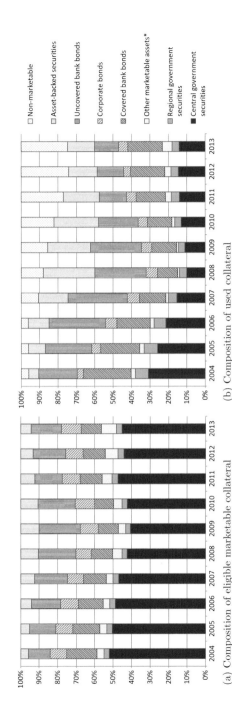

Legend:
- □ Non-marketable
- □ Asset-backed securities
- ▤ Uncovered bank bonds
- ▨ Corporate bonds
- ▩ Covered bank bonds
- □ Other marketable assets*
- ▥ Regional government securities
- ■ Central government securities

(a) Composition of eligible marketable collateral

(b) Composition of used collateral

FIGURE 4.1 Eligible assets and collateral used

Figure 4.1a shows the composition of eligible marketable assets across collateral classes based on nominal values. Figure 4.1b shows the composition of used collateral, including non-marketable assets, based on collateral values. Both sets of figures are based on averages of end-of-month values within each year.

Data source: ECB webpage; collateral data from February 14, 2014; www.ecb.europa.eu/paym/coll/html/index.en.html; downloaded on March 20, 2014. *"Other marketable assets" are, according to emails from the ECB, predominantly supranational and agency debt.

it constitutes approximately 22 percent by nominal value and 53 percent by usage. Figure 4.1 shows that the preference for low-quality collateral has increased over time, but it has slightly abated since the peak in 2008 when lower-quality collateral constituted 68 percent of total usage. Of course, since then, the quality of many government bonds has deteriorated substantially. Taking this into account would change the complexion of Figure 4.1 and, most likely, show a continued increase in the reliance on lower-quality collateral.

Figure 4.1a shows that the preference for lower-quality collateral has also come with an increase in its production. The lower-quality group of collateral (green color) has grown, in terms of nominal value, from 16 percent of eligible marketable collateral in 2004 to 22 percent in 2013. While this is not as dramatic as the increase in usage over the same time period, from 30 to 53 percent, it illustrates that lower-quality collateral is not only being used, but also produced at a higher rate.

Overall the evidence points to (i) a preference among banks for using lower-quality collateral in repos with the Eurosystem; (ii) an increase in the relative usage of lower-quality collateral over time; and (iii) an increase in the production of lower-quality collateral over time. These findings suggest that collateral values of lower-quality collateral are relatively high, for example because the haircuts of such collateral are relatively small.

5 Haircuts

This chapter documents in detail the haircut policy of the Eurosystem and how it has evolved over time. A detailed description of haircuts necessarily also provides further information on the large range of collateral that banks can use to obtain credit from the Eurosystem and how eligibility rules have been relaxed over the course of the financial crisis. The chapter ends by presenting evidence on the Eurosystem's haircuts across different types of collateral versus those applied in two widely used and comparable central counterparty (CCP) contracts.

5.1 DOCUMENTATION AND OVERVIEW

The ECB provides a list of documents that describe the collateral framework, including the rules for collateral eligibility and haircuts, on a dedicated webpage.[1] These documents are also published in the *Official Journal of the European Union* and represent legally binding acts or decisions.[2] In addition to the publication date itself, each of these documents shows the date when the act, or decision, was legally adopted. These "adopted on," or formal approval, dates should not be confused with press-release dates; the ECB sometimes communicates decisions by the Governing Council through press releases before they become legal acts, if at all. When describing the haircut rules in this chapter, and the ratings rules in the next, I have relied on the contents of the legal documentation provided by the ECB on its webpage and published in the *Official Journal*.[3]

---

[1] See www.ecb.europa.eu/paym/coll/html/index.en.html.
[2] Until February 2003, the name of the journal was the *Official Journal of the European Communities*.
[3] The ECB could, in theory, modify the collateral framework without publishing this in the *Official Journal*. However, since the collateral framework relates to the

The earliest dated collateral framework document posted on the ECB's webpage is the *Guideline of the European Central Bank of 31 August 2000 on monetary policy instruments and procedures of the Eurosystem* (ECB 2000/7). The preamble to this document establishes that it is produced under the "Treaty establishing the European Community":

> The achievement of a single monetary policy entails the need to define the instruments to be used by the national central banks of Member States that have adopted the euro... The ECB is vested with the authority to establish the necessary Guidelines for the implementation of the single monetary policy and the NCBs [National Central Banks] have an obligation to act in accordance with such Guidelines... ECB Guidelines form an integral part of Community law.
>
> ECB (2000/7, p. 1)

Thus, the Guidelines on monetary policy instruments and procedures are legal documents that lay out, among other things, the Eurosystem's collateral framework, including the requirements for collateral to be eligible to be used in Eurosystem operations and how haircuts are set on eligible collateral.

As seen from the evidence in Chapter 4, collateral eligibility rules are fairly relaxed, allowing for marketable collateral ranging from government securities to uncovered (unsecured) bank bonds and asset-backed securities (ABSs), as well as some non-marketable assets. The basic collateral eligibility rules, as laid out in the official documentation, are that the collateral should be a non-subordinated debt instrument denominated in euros, issued in the European Economic Area (EEA), or, under certain conditions, in the euro area,

interaction of the Eurosystem with third parties, namely banks, it makes sense that it is made public through publication in the *Official Journal*. See Council of the European Union (2012b) [Consolidated versions of the Treaty on European Union and the Treaty of the Functioning of the European Union], articles 297 and 132(2), and ECB (1999, pp. 53–59).

by an entity domiciled in the EEA or one of the G-10 countries.[4] However, until May 2005, equities could also be used (see Table 5.1, Panel B), and from October 25, 2008, to December 31, 2010, the non-subordination requirement was dropped if an adequate guarantee was provided (see Table 5.2). Subordinated bonds may also have been accepted as "Tier 2 assets" until December 31, 2006 (see below). As a general rule, to be eligible, collateral needs to have sufficiently high credit standards, roughly meaning that the collateral's rating must be "sufficiently high." The credit standards (rating rules), including the role of guarantees from third parties, have varied over time and are studied in detail in the next chapter.

My focus in this chapter is on the rules for haircuts and how these have evolved. Because haircuts are a function of collateral characteristics, some issues regarding eligibility are discussed as well. Further issues relating to collateral eligibility are covered in Chapters 8 and 9, where I discuss the rules governing own-use collateral and the eligibility of securities trading on non-regulated markets, respectively.

The initial Guidelines are updated and amended in subsequent Guidelines and other documentation that is published on the ECB's webpage (see Footnote 1). These updates are categorized as either amending the "General" or "Temporary" frameworks. Measures that are initially introduced as temporary are sometimes eventually adopted into the General framework, as evidenced by subsequent General framework updates. The "Temporary" label was first used in the wake of the Lehman default, with the first Temporary framework document being formally adopted on October 23, 2008, and recorded in the *Official Journal* two days later.[5]

---

[4] See ECB (2000/7), ECB (2005/2), ECB (2006/12), ECB (2011/14), and the other collateral framework references listed in the back of the book for details. See also Eberl and Weber (2014). The G-10 include the following non-EEA countries, Canada, Japan, Switzerland, and the United States. See, e.g., www.imf.org/external/np/exr/facts/groups.htm#G10.

[5] The relevant *Official Journal* publication is listed in the references as ECB (2008/11).

The time period reported on in this chapter is March 8, 2004, to January 31, 2015. The start date is chosen because it marks the introduction of collateral *liquidity categories* as a factor, and organizational tool, by which to set haircuts for Tier 1 (later, marketable) assets (ECB 2003/16). The liquidity categories represent a classification of eligible collateral into groups depending on the type of security and type of issuer (e.g., central government bonds versus ABSs). This is described in detail below.

A second significant modification to the system for classifying collateral occurred at the beginning of 2007. Up to that point, the ECB operated with a two-tier framework for eligible collateral. Tier 1 consisted of marketable debt instruments fulfilling uniform eurozone-wide eligibility criteria specified by the ECB. Tier 2 consisted of additional assets, marketable and non-marketable, for which eligibility criteria were set by the national central banks, but subject to the minimum eligibility criteria established by the ECB. This two-tier system was replaced by a single tier (or "single list") on January 1, 2007 (ECB 2005/2 and 2006/12). Thus, from 2007 on, eligible collateral can be divided into marketable and non-marketable assets rather than Tier 1 and Tier 2 assets.[6] The liquidity categories established in March 2004 for Tier 1 assets were initially also applied to the new grouping of "marketable assets." Like Tier 2 assets before them, non-marketable assets essentially form a separate (and lower) liquidity category. Prior to the introduction of liquidity categories, haircuts for Tier 1 assets were determined only by their residual maturity and coupon (ECB 2000/7, pp. 37–38; ECB 2002/2, pp. 38–39).

In Chapter 2, I suggested that haircuts in central bank operations will be felt in financial markets and, ultimately, the real

---

[6] Ostensibly, the single list means that the same collateral can be used vis-à-vis all NCBs. However, with respect to non-marketable assets this can clearly not be an entirely correct description *de facto*, since a bank that has its charter in one country obtains Eurosystem credit from the NCB of that country. So, for example, Spanish bank loans (non-marketable assets) can be used in repos with the Banco de España, but not with the Deutsche Bundesbank unless the loans are transferred to a German bank. Chapter 6 describes other ways the full set of eligible collateral may end up varying across NCBs under the single list regime.

economy. This does not conflict with the perspective that haircuts, as well as a requirement of sufficiently high credit standards of eligible collateral, may be motivated by risk management concerns. Haircuts are a way for the central bank to control credit risk exposure to counterparties in its operations. The legal documentation also reveals that risk management concerns are important with respect to the collateral policy of the ECB.[7] While my objective in this book is not to assess the Eurosystem's collateral framework from a traditional risk management perspective, it is clear that having the haircut rules and credit standards laid out in some detail, as I do in this and the next chapters, is helpful also with respect to carrying out a risk management exercise. Still, it is not clear that the risk management methods that would be appropriate for a regular bank, for example, are also appropriate for a central bank. This is so because the haircuts set by a central bank's collateral framework may influence, for example, the production and design of collateral by banks, as discussed in Chapter 2. A message of this book is that central bank collateral frameworks should not be seen as mere risk management tools; they are an important element of monetary policy, having potentially far-reaching impact on financial markets and the wider economy.

5.2 DETAILED HAIRCUT RULES AND MAIN GENERAL OBSERVATIONS

This section provides the ECB's rules for setting haircuts for eligible collateral in Eurosystem operations over the almost eleven-year period from March 8, 2004, to January 31, 2015. The discussion below emphasizes the following six general points:

Observation 1 (ECB haircut policy: General features)

1. Haircuts are rarely revised over time. Thus, they do not depend on market conditions at particular points in time.

---

[7] See ECB (2000/7), ECB (2006/12), and the other collateral framework references listed in the back.

2. Haircuts increase in asset class illiquidity, as measured by the liquidity category.
3. Haircuts increase in risk, as captured by the duration.
4. As of October 25, 2008, haircuts increase in risk, as captured by the rating. There are two rating categories.
5. Within asset classes (liquidity categories), controlling for duration and the two rating categories, there is little differentiation in haircuts between different eligible collateral.
6. Haircuts do not depend on the counterparty.[8]

Details of the rules are provided in Tables 5.1 to 5.4. The information in these tables is taken from ECB General and Temporary framework documentation, as outlined above and referenced in the table captions. Panel A in each table provides haircuts by liquidity category over time for Tier 1 and, as of January 1, 2007, marketable assets. Panels B, C, and D (as applicable) deal with Tier 2 and non-marketable assets. My discussion focuses on the "A" panels, as these represent the most important collateral (by usage, as seen in Chapter 4).

The rules are presented in four tables because over the eleven-year period that is being studied, changes to the haircut rules for Tier 1 (later, marketable) assets were made only three times. This is the basis for Observation 1.1 above, namely that haircuts are rarely revised. This will become clearer as I go through the tables.

I start by scanning the tables to capture the general points emphasized in Observation 1. Further details dealing with changes over time are discussed in the next section.

Note first that, as shown in Table 5.1, Panel A, over the time period March 8, 2004, to October 24, 2008 (inclusive), there were four liquidity categories (plus inverse floaters) for Tier 1/marketable securities, namely, central government and central bank debt (category I); local and regional government debt, jumbo covered bonds

---

[8] There is one exception to this, namely the additional haircuts introduced as of November 1, 2013, for "own-use" collateral. Further details are below and a more in-depth discussion of what exactly "own use" means is in Chapter 8.

(pfandbrief), agency and supranational debt instruments (category II); traditional pfandbrief, credit institution and corporate debt (category III); and asset-backed securities (category IV). As seen, for the same residual maturity and coupon policy (zero, fixed, or floating), haircuts are increasing in the liquidity category, with the exception of inverse floaters for which haircuts are the same across liquidity categories. For example, for a residual maturity of between one and three years and any fixed coupon, the haircuts are 1.5 percent (category I), 2.5 percent (category II), 3.0 percent (category III), and 3.5 percent (category IV). This effect of the liquidity category on haircuts is also a key feature of Tables 5.2 to 5.4 and leads to Observation 1.2.

While the liquidity categories are intended to reflect different liquidity levels, they might also reflect different risk levels. For example, the least liquid category (IV), ABSs, arguably consists of riskier securities than the most liquid group (I), central government bonds and central bank debt instruments. For example, as noted by Calomiris (2009b), ratings across asset classes are not comparable with respect to default probabilities.[9] Of course, later developments in the euro area proved that, in many cases, risk and illiquidity could be substantial for central government bonds as well.

Haircuts are also seen to be increasing in the residual maturity of the collateral, and for paper with more than three years to run, zero-coupon securities have higher haircuts than corresponding fixed-coupon paper. These residual maturity and coupon effects constitute a rough-and-ready control for duration, or the sensitivity of the value of the collateral to changes in interest rates. In other words, haircuts increase in risk, as measured by duration. The same pattern can be observed in Tables 5.2 to 5.4. This leads to Observation 1.3.

From the introduction of the "single list" of eligible collateral in January 1, 2007, until October 24, 2008 (Table 5.1), the minimum rating for eligible collateral is A− (using Standard & Poor's rating

---

[9] Calomiris reports that according to Moody's, in 2005 five-year default probabilities were ten times larger for Baa rated CDOs than for Baa rated corporate bonds, the numbers being 20 and 2 percent, respectively.

Table 5.1 *Haircuts and liquidity categories from March 8, 2004, to October 24, 2008*
(Dates in table heading refer to tier one and marketable assets)

Panel A: Haircuts applied to tier one assets (March 8, 2004, to December 31, 2006) or marketable securities (January 1, 2007, to October 24, 2008)

	Liquidity categories[1]							
	Category I Central government debt instruments, Debt instruments issued by central banks[3]		**Category II** Local and regional government debt instruments, Jumbo Pfandbrief-style debt instruments,[4] Agency debt instruments,[5] Supranational debt instruments		**Category III** Traditional Pfandbrief-style debt instruments, Credit institution debt instruments, Debt instruments issued by corporate and other issuers[5]		**Category IV** Asset-backed securities[2]	
Residual maturity (years)	Fixed coupon	Zero coupon	Fixed coupon	Zero coupon	Fixed coupon	Zero coupon	Fixed coupon	Zero coupon
0–1	0.5	0.5	1.0	1.0	1.5	1.5	2.0	2.0
1–3	1.5	1.5	2.5	2.5	3.0	3.0	3.5	3.5
3–5	2.5	3.0	3.5	4.0	4.5	5.0	5.5	6.0
5–7	3.0	3.5	4.5	5.0	5.5	6.0	6.5	7.0
7–10	4.0	4.5	5.5	6.5	6.5	8.0	8.0	10.0
>10	5.5	8.5	7.5	12.0	9.0	15.0	12.0	18.0

Tier one floating rate debt instruments:
Haircut is the same as for the zero-to-one-year maturity bucket of fixed coupon instruments in the liquidity category to which the instrument is assigned.

Tier one inverse floating rate debt instruments:
Haircuts are the same for all liquidity classes, but differ with respect to residual maturity as follows (residual maturity, haircut):
0–1, 2.0; 1–3, 7.0; 3–5, 10.0; 5–7, 12.0; 7–10, 17.0; >10, 25.0.

Panel B: Haircuts applied to eligible tier two assets from March 8, 2004, to December 31, 2006

Equities: A haircut of 22 percent is applied to all eligible equities (equities are phased out with ECB 2005/2, which is applied from May 30, 2005).

Tier two marketable debt instruments with limited liquidity and fixed or zero coupons:

Majority of tier two assets falls into this category. They generally have a small secondary market, prices may not be quoted daily, and normal size trades can generate price impacts. Haircuts as a function of residual maturity, by coupon (residual maturity, haircut):

fixed coupon: 0–1, 2.0; 1–3, 3.5; 3–5, 5.5; 5–7, 6.5; 7–10, 8.0; >10, 12.0.   zero coupon: 0–1, 2.0; 1–3, 3.5; 3–5, 6.0; 5–7, 7.0; 7–10, 10.0; >10, 18.0.

Credit institution debt instruments which do not comply strictly with the criteria set out in Article 22(4) of the UCITS Directive (Directive 85/611/EEC, as amended): Add 10 percent to the tier two haircut.

Tier two floating rate debt instruments: Same rules apply as for tier one assets (unless otherwise determined by the ECB).

Tier two inverse floating rate debt instruments: Haircuts applied are identical to those applied to tier one inverse floating rate instruments.

Tier two debt instruments with restricted liquidity and special features:

Assets which require extra time to be liquidated in the market despite enjoying some aspects of marketability. In general, non-marketable assets with special features that introduce some marketability (e.g., market auction procedures and a daily price valuation). Haircuts as a function of residual maturity, by coupon (residual maturity, haircut):

fixed coupon: 0–1, 4.0; 1–3, 8.0; 3–5, 15.0; 5–7, 17.0; 7–10, 22.0; >10, 24.0.   zero coupon: 0–1, 4.0; 1–3, 8.0; 3–5, 16.0; 5–7, 18.0; 7–10, 23.0; >10, 25.0.

Panel C: Haircuts applied to eligible tier two non-marketable debt instruments from March 8, 2004, to December 31, 2006[§]

Trade bills: 4 percent for instruments with a residual maturity of up to six months.

Bank loans (later on called credit claims, which is the legal term): 12 percent (22 percent) for loans with a residual maturity of up to six months (between six months and two years).

Mortgage-backed promissory notes: 22 percent.

Panel D: Haircuts applied to eligible non-marketable assets from January 1, 2007, to October 24, 2008[§]

Credit claims (bank loans) with fixed interest payments:

Haircuts applied to fixed interest credit claims differ according to the residual maturity and the valuation methodology applied by the NCB. Haircuts as a function of residual maturity (residual maturity, haircut) if the valuation is based on

(1) a theoretical price assigned by the NCB: 0–1, 7.0; 1–3,   9.0; 3–5, 11.0; 5–7, 12.0; 7–10, 13.0; >10, 17.0.

(2) the outstanding amount assigned by the NCB: 0–1, 9.0; 1–3, 15.0; 3–5, 20.0; 5–7, 24.0; 7–10, 29.0; >10, 41.0.

Table 5.1 *(cont.)*

Panel D – continued

Credit claims with variable interest payments:

The haircut applied to variable interest credit claims is 7 percent, irrespective of the valuation methodology applied by the NCB.

Retail mortgage-backed debt instruments:

Non-marketable retail mortgage-backed debt instruments are subject to a valuation haircut of 20 percent.

Until December 31, 2006, the ECB operated with a two-tier system for eligible assets. Tier one consists of marketable debt instruments fulfilling uniform euro-area-wide eligibility criteria specified by the ECB. Tier two consists of additional assets, marketable and non-marketable, for which eligibility criteria are established by the national central banks, subject to minimum eligibility criteria established by the ECB. Tier two assets need explicit approval by the ECB. With Guidelines ECB (2005/2) and ECB (2006/12), the ECB replaced the two-tier system with a single list, in force from January 1, 2007. Panel A reports haircuts for tier one assets (March 8, 2004, to December 31, 2006) or marketable securities (January 1, 2007, to October 24, 2008) by liquidity category, residual maturity, and coupon (zero, fixed, or floating). This panel is copied from ECB (2003/16). It is not changed in the General or Temporary framework documentation before October 25, 2008 (see Table 5.2). Panel B shows haircuts for tier two assets from March 8, 2004, to December 31, 2006 (ECB 2003/16), if not otherwise indicated. It disappears with the introduction of the single list as of January 1, 2007. Panel C shows haircuts for tier two non-marketable assets from March 8, 2004, to December 31, 2006 (ECB 2003/16). Panel D replaces Panel C as of January 1, 2007 (ECB 2006/12).

§Panel C: Non-marketables are part of tier two until December 31, 2006 (ECB 2003/16). Panel D replaces Panel C as of January 1, 2007: the names of the non-marketable subclasses and haircuts change with the introduction of the single list (ECB 2006/12).

Notes: (As reported in ECB 2003/16, Table 6, updates in square brackets and italic type) [1] In general, the issuer classification determines the liquidity category. However, Jumbo Pfandbrief-style debt instruments [*Jumbo covered bank bonds*] are included in category II, in contrast to other debt instruments issued by credit institutions which are included in category III. [2] Also, asset-backed securities fall into liquidity category IV regardless of the issuer classification. [3] Debt certificates issued by the ECB and debt instruments issued by the national central banks prior to the adoption of the euro in their respective Member State are included in liquidity category I. [4] Only instruments with an issuing volume of at least EUR 500 million [*1 billion*], for which at least two [*three*] market makers provide regular bid and ask quotes, fall into the asset class of Jumbo Pfandbrief-style instruments [*Jumbo covered bank bonds*]. [5] Only securities [*marketable assets*] issued by issuers that have been classified as agencies by the ECB are included in liquidity category II. Securities [*Marketable assets*] issued by other agencies are included in liquidity category III.

Table 5.2 *Haircuts and liquidity categories from October 25, 2008 (Temporary framework), and February 1, 2009 (General framework), to December 31, 2010 (Dates in table heading refer to marketable assets)*

Panel A: Haircuts applied to eligible marketable assets

		Liquidity categories for marketable assets[1]								
		Category I Central government debt instruments, Debt instruments issued by central banks[2]		Category II Local and regional government debt instruments, Jumbo covered bank bonds,[3] Agency debt instruments,[4] Supranational debt instruments		Category III Traditional covered bank bonds, Debt instruments issued by corporate and other issuers[4]		Category IV* Credit institution debt instruments (unsecured)*		Category V* Asset-backed securities[5]*
Credit quality[†]	Residual maturity (years)	Fixed coupon	Zero coupon	Fixed coupon	Zero coupon	Fixed coupon	Zero coupon	Fixed coupon	Zero coupon	
AAA to A−[†]	0–1	0.5	0.5	1.0	1.0	1.5	1.5	6.5*	6.5*	12*
	1–3	1.5	1.5	2.5	2.5	3.0	3.0	8.0*	8.0*	
	3–5	2.5	3.0	3.5	4.0	4.5	5.0	9.5*	10.0*	
	5–7	3.0	3.5	4.5	5.0	5.5	6.0	10.5*	11.0*	
	7–10	4.0	4.5	5.5	6.5	6.5	8.0	11.5*	13.0*	
	>10	5.5	8.5	7.5	12.0	9.0	15.0	14.0*	20.0*	
BBB+ to BBB−[†]	Add 5 percent to AAA to A− according to residual maturity, coupon structure, and liquidity category. Note that ABSs with a rating below A− are not eligible.[†]									

Table 5.2 (cont.)

Panel A – continued

Floating rate debt instruments:

Haircut applied to marketable debt instruments *included in categories I to IV** is that applied to zero-to-one-year maturity buckets of fixed coupon instruments in liquidity and credit quality category[†] to which the instrument is assigned.

Inverse floating rate debt instruments:

Haircuts applied to inverse floating rate debt instruments *included in categories I to IV** are the same but differ with respect to maturity bucket and credit quality categories.[†] Haircuts as a function of residual maturity (residual maturity, haircut) *for AAA to A– rated instruments*[†] are:
0–1, 2.0; 1–3, 7.0; 3–5, 10.0; 5–7, 12.0; 7–10, 17.0; >10, 25.0. For BBB+ to BBB– add 5 percent.[†]

Marketable assets denominated in foreign currency (yen, pounds sterling, and US dollars): *Add 8 percent to the haircut*[†] [applies from November 14, 2008 [ECB 2008/11]].

Debt instruments issued by credit institutions and traded on non-regulated markets: *Add 5 percent to the haircut.*[†]

Subordinated debt instruments with guarantees: *Shall be eligible if a financially sound guarantor provides an unconditional and irrevocable guarantee. Add 10 percent to the haircut of such assets plus an additional 5 percent valuation markdown if theoretically valued.*[†]

Panel B: Haircuts applied to eligible non-marketable assets*

Credit claims (bank loans) with fixed interest payments:

Haircuts applied to fixed interest credit claims differ according to the residual maturity, *the credit quality category*[†] *and the valuation methodology applied by the NCB.* Haircuts as a function of residual maturity (residual maturity, haircut) *for ratings of AAA to A–*[†] *if the valuation is based on*

(1) a theoretical price assigned by the NCB: 0–1, 7.0; 1–3, 9.0; 3–5, 11.0; 5–7, 12.0; 7–10, 13.0; >10, 17.0. For BBB+ to BBB– add 5 percent.[†]
(2) the outstanding amount assigned by the NCB: 0–1, 9.0; 1–3, 15.0; 3–5, 20.0; 5–7, 24.0; 7–10, 29.0; >10, 41.0. For BBB+ to BBB– add 5 percent.[†]

Credit claims with variable interest payments:

For ratings of AAA to A– the haircut applied to variable interest credit claims is 7 percent, irrespective of the valuation methodology applied by the NCB. *For BBB+ to BBB– add 5 percent.*[†]

Retail mortgage-backed debt instruments:

For ratings of AAA to A– non-marketable retail mortgage-backed debt instruments are subject to a valuation haircut of 20 percent.

Fixed-term deposits (with Eurosystem): *No haircut.*[†]

The table shows both General and Temporary framework updates from October 23, 2008. General framework updates apply from February 1, 2009 (ECB 2008/13), and are indicated in (red) italic type and starred, ∗. Temporary framework updates are indicated in (blue) slanted type with a dagger, †. They are introduced in ECB (2008/11), applied from October 25 to November 30, 2008, and subsequently extended first by ECB (2008/18, from November 21, 2008) from December 1, 2008, to December 31, 2009, and second by ECB (2009/24, from December 10, 2009) from January 1, 2010, to December 31, 2010. For an explanation of the credit quality (ratings) categories and rules, see Table 6.1, Panel C.

Notes: (As reported in ECB 2008/13, Tables 6 and 7) [1] In general, the issuer classification determines the liquidity category. However, all asset-backed securities are included in category V^*, regardless of the classification of the issuer, and jumbo covered bank bonds are included in category II, *while traditional covered bank bonds and other debt instruments issued by credit institutions are included in categories III and IV*. [2] Debt certificates issued by the ECB and debt instruments issued by the *NCBs*∗ prior to the adoption of the euro in their respective Member State are included in liquidity category I. [3] Only instruments with an issuing volume of at least EUR 1 billion, for which at least three market-makers provide regular bid and ask quotes, fall into the asset class of jumbo covered bank bonds. [4] Only marketable assets issued by issuers that have been classified as agencies by the ECB are included in liquidity category II. Marketable assets issued by other agencies are included in liquidity category III. [5] *Individual debt instruments included in category V that are theoretically valued according to Section 6.5 [of the General framework] are subject to an additional valuation haircut. This haircut is directly applied at the level of theoretical valuation of the individual debt instrument in the form of a valuation markdown of 5 percent.*∗

Table 5.3 *Haircuts and liquidity categories from January 1, 2011, to September 30, 2013 (Dates in table heading refer to marketable assets)*

Panel A: Levels of valuation haircuts applied to eligible marketable assets

Credit quality	Residual maturity (years)	Category I — Central government debt instruments, Debt instruments issued by central banks[2]		Category II[6] — Local and regional government debt instruments, Jumbo covered bank bonds,[3] Agency debt instruments,[4] Supranational debt instruments		Category III[6] — Traditional covered bank bonds, *Debt instruments issued by non-financial corporations and other issuers,*[4]* *Other covered bank bonds*[5]*		Category IV[6] — Credit institution debt instruments (unsecured), *Debt instruments issued by financial corporations other than credit institutions (unsecured)**		Category V[6] — Asset-backed securities[a] — Backed by commercial mortgages / all others	
		Fixed coupon	Zero coupon	Fixed coupon	Zero coupon	Fixed coupon	Zero coupon	Fixed coupon	Zero coupon	commercial mortgages	all others
Steps 1 and 2 (AAA to A−)[7]	0–1	0.5	0.5	1.0	1.0	1.5	1.5	6.5	6.5		
	1–3	1.5	1.5	2.5	2.5	3.0	3.0	8.5*	9.0*		
	3–5	2.5	3.0	3.5	4.0	5.0*	5.5*	11.0*	11.5*		
	5–7	3.0	3.5	4.5	5.0	6.5*	7.5*	12.5*	13.5*	16.0*	16.0*
	7–10	4.0	4.5	5.5	6.5	8.5*	9.5*	14.0*	15.5*		
	>10	5.5	8.5	7.5	12.0	11.0*	16.5*	17.0*	22.5*		
Step 3 (BBB+ to BBB−)[7]	0–1	5.5	5.5	6.0	6.0	8.0*	8.0*	15.0*	15.0*		*Applies from June 29, 2012*[b]
	1–3	6.5	6.5	10.5*	11.5*	18.0*	19.5*	27.5*	29.5*		
	3–5	7.5	8.0	15.5*	17.0*	25.5*	28.0*	36.5*	39.5*	32.0†	26.0†
	5–7	8.0	8.5	18.0*	20.5*	28.0*	31.5*	38.5*	43.0*		
	7–10	9.0	9.5	19.5*	22.5*	29.0*	33.5*	39.0*	44.5*		
	>10	10.5	13.5	20.0*	29.0*	29.5*	38.0*	39.5*	46.0*		

Liquidity categories for marketable assets[1]

Floating rate debt instruments:

Haircut applied to marketable debt instruments included in categories I to IV is that applied to zero-to-one-year maturity buckets of fixed coupon instruments in liquidity and credit quality category to which the instrument is assigned.

Inverse floating rate debt instruments: Eligibility revoked in ECB (2012/25) with effect from January 3, 2013.[‡]

Haircuts applied to inverse floating rate debt instruments included in categories I to IV are the same but differ with respect to maturity bucket and credit quality categories. Haircuts as a function of residual maturity (residual maturity, haircut):

AAA to A−: 0–1, *7.5**; 1–3, *11.5**; 3–5, *16.0**; 5–7, *19.5**; 7–10, *22.5**; >10, *28.0**. BBB+ to BBB−: 0–1, *21.0**; 1–3, *46.5**; 3–5, *63.5**; 5–7, *68.0**; 7–10, *69.0**; >10, *69.5**.

Marketable assets denominated in foreign currency (yen, pounds sterling, and US dollars): *There is an additional haircut which is applied in the form of a valuation markdown before applying the regular haircut. Valuation markdowns are as follows: Pounds sterling and US dollars: 16 percent; Yen: 26 percent*[†] *|applies from November 9, 2012 [ECB 2012/23; ECB 2012/34; ECB 2013/4]|.*

Uncovered debt instruments issued by credit institutions and traded on ECB approved non-regulated markets:[*] Not eligible from January 1, 2011, to December 31, 2011. *Eligible from January 1, 2012, onward (ECB 2011/14) with same haircuts as for comparable collateral trading on regulated markets.*[*§]

Panel B: Haircuts applied to eligible non-marketable assets

Credit claims (bank loans) with fixed interest payments:

Haircuts applied to fixed interest credit claims differ according to the residual maturity, the credit quality category and the valuation methodology applied by the NCB. Haircuts as a function of residual maturity (residual maturity, haircut), if the valuation is based on

(1) a theoretical price assigned by the NCB:

AAA to A−: 0–1, *8.0**; 1–3, *11.5**; 3–5, *15.0**; 5–7, *17.0**; 7–10, *18.5**; >10, *20.5**. BBB+ to BBB−: 0–1, *15.5**; 1–3, *28.0**; 3–5, *37.0**; 5–7, *39.0**; 7–10, *39.5**; >10, *40.5**.

(2) the outstanding amount assigned by the NCB:

AAA to A−: 0–1, *10.0**; 1–3, *17.5**; 3–5, *24.0**; 5–7, *29.0**; 7–10, *34.5**; >10, *44.5**. BBB+ to BBB−: 0–1, *17.5**; 1–3, *34.0**; 3–5, *46.0**; 5–7, *51.0**; 7–10, *55.5**; >10, *64.5**.

Table 5.3 (cont.)

Panel B – continued

Credit claims with variable interest payments:

The haircut is that applied to fixed interest credit claims in the zero-to-one-year maturity bucket corresponding to the same credit quality and the same valuation methodology.*

Retail mortgage-backed debt instruments:

Non-marketable retail mortgage-backed debt instruments are subject to a valuation haircut of 24 percent*. *The rating must be A– at least** [ECB 2010/13].

Fixed-term deposits (with Eurosystem): No haircut.

[taken over to General framework by ECB (2010/30, from December 13, 2011), applied from January 1, 2011].

The information in this table is published in ECB (2010/13, from September 16, 2010), if not otherwise indicated. Updates to the General framework are in [red] italic type and starred, *, with the exception of updates that absorb previous Temporary framework measures into the General framework (what they are can be seen by comparing the current table with Table 5.2). Temporary framework updates are indicated in (blue) slanted type with a dagger, †. *ᵃ Except ABSs backed by residential mortgages or loans to SMEs issued before June 20, 2012, that do not fulfill certain standard eligibility criteria, but have a credit quality of at least BBB–. These have a haircut of 32 percent (see ECB 2012/11).† ᵇ ABSs in this credit quality category are ineligible before this date. For details see ECB (2011/25), ECB (2012/11), ECB (2012/18), and ECB (2013/4).† For an explanation of the credit quality (ratings) categories and rules, see Table 6.1, Panel D.*

‡ However, inverse floaters still appeared in the public list of eligible collateral until April 17, 2013.

§ The importance of this clause is that it reintroduces eligibility for uncovered bank debt trading on ECB-approved non-regulated markets, after a one-year absence (see Table 5.2). Note that covered bank bonds trading on these approved non-regulated markets never had a blanket exclusion.

Notes: (As reported in ECB 2010/13, Tables 6 and 7) [1] In general, the issuer classification determines the liquidity category. However, all asset-backed securities are included in category V, regardless of the classification of the issuer, and jumbo covered bank bonds are included in category II, while traditional covered bank bonds, *other covered bank bonds**, and other debt instruments issued by credit institutions are included in categories III and IV. [2] Debt certificates issued by the ECB and debt instruments issued by the NCBs prior to the adoption of the euro in their respective Member State are included in liquidity category I. [3] Only instruments with an issuing volume of at least EUR 1 billion, for which at least three market-makers provide regular bid and ask quotes, fall into the asset class of jumbo covered bank bonds. [4] Only marketable assets issued by issuers that have been classified as agencies by the ECB are included in liquidity category II. Marketable assets issued by other agencies are included in liquidity category III or IV, depending on the issuer and asset type. [5] *Non-UCITS-compliant covered bonds, including both structured covered bonds and multi-issuer covered bonds are included in liquidity category III.** [6] *Individual asset-backed securities, covered bank bonds (jumbo covered bank bonds, traditional covered bank bonds and other covered bank bonds) and uncovered bank bonds* that are theoretically valued in accordance with Section 6.5 [of the General framework] are subject to an additional valuation haircut. This haircut is directly applied at the level of theoretical valuation of the individual debt instrument in the form of a valuation markdown of 5 percent.* [7] *Ratings as specified in the Eurosystem's harmonized rating scale, published on the ECB's website (www.ecb.europa.eu).**

Table 5.4 Haircuts and liquidity categories from October 1, 2013 (and November 1, 2013, for own-use covered bonds) (In force as of January 31, 2015. Dates in heading refer to marketable assets. See the Appendix to this book for further updates.)

Panel A: Levels of valuation haircuts applied to eligible marketable assets

Credit quality	Residual maturity (years)	Category I — Central government debt instruments, Debt instruments issued by NCBs[2]		Category II[6] — Local and regional government debt instruments, Jumbo covered bank bonds,[3] Agency debt instruments,[4] Supranational debt instruments		Category III[6] — Traditional covered bank bonds, Debt instruments issued by non-financial corporations and other issuers,[4] Other covered bank bonds[5]		Category IV[6] — Credit institution debt instruments (unsecured), Debt instruments issued by financial corporations other than credit institutions (unsecured)		Category V[6] — Asset-backed securities[a]
		Fixed coupon	Zero coupon	Fixed coupon	Zero coupon	Fixed coupon	Zero coupon	Fixed coupon	Zero coupon	
Steps 1 and 2 (AAA to A−)[7]	0–1	0.5	0.5	1.0	1.0	1.0^*_d	1.0^*_d	6.5	6.5	
	1–3	1.0^*_d	2.0^*	1.5^*_d	2.5	2.0^*_d	3.0	8.5	9.0	
	3–5	1.5^*_d	2.5^*_d	2.5^*_d	3.5^*_d	3.0^*_d	4.5^*_d	11.0	11.5	10.0^*_d
	5–7	2.0^*_d	3.0^*_d	3.5^*_d	4.5^*_d	4.5^*_d	6.0^*_d	12.5	13.5	
	7–10	3.0^*_d	4.0^*_d	4.5^*_d	6.5	6.0^*_d	8.0^*_d	14.0	15.5	
	>10	5.0^*_d	7.0^*_d	8.0^*	10.5^*_d	9.0^*_d	13.0^*_d	17.0	22.5	
Step 3 (BBB+ to BBB−)[7]	0–1	6.0^*	6.0^*	7.0^*	7.0^*	8.0^*	8.0	13.0^*_d	13.0^*_d	
	1–3	7.0^*	8.0^*	10.0^*_d	14.5^*	15.0^*_d	16.5^*_d	24.5^*_d	26.5^*_d	
	3–5	9.0^*	10.0^*	15.5	20.5^*	22.5^*_d	25.0^*_d	32.5^*_d	36.5^*_d	$22.0^†$
	5–7	10.0^*	11.5^*	16.0^*_d	22.0^*	26.0^*_d	30.0^*_d	36.0^*_d	40.0^*_d	
	7–10	11.5^*	13.0^*	18.5^*_d	27.5^*	27.0^*_d	32.5^*_d	37.0^*_d	42.5^*_d	
	>10	13.0^*	16.0^*	22.5^*	33.0^*	27.5^*_d	35.0^*_d	37.5^*_d	44.0^*_d	

Table 5.4 (cont.)

Panel A – continued

Floating rate debt instruments:

Haircut applied to marketable debt instruments included in categories I to IV is that applied to zero-to-one-year maturity buckets of fixed coupon instruments in liquidity and credit quality category to which the instrument is assigned.

Marketable assets denominated in foreign currency (yen, pounds sterling, and US dollars): There is an additional haircut which is applied in the form of a valuation markdown before applying the regular haircut. Valuation markdowns are as follows: Pounds sterling and US dollars: 16 percent; Yen: 26 percent.

Debt instruments issued by credit institutions and traded on non-regulated markets: Same haircuts as for other marketable assets.

Panel B: Haircuts applied to eligible non-marketable assets

Credit claims (bank loans) with fixed interest payments:

Haircuts applied to fixed interest credit claims differ according to the residual maturity, the credit quality category, and the valuation methodology applied by the NCB. Haircuts as a function of residual maturity (residual maturity, haircut), if the valuation is based on

(1) a theoretical price assigned by the NCB:

AAA to A-: 0–1, 10.0^*; 1–3, 12.0^*; 3–5, 14.0_d^*; 5–7, 17.0, 7–10, 22.0^*; >10, 30.0^*. BBB+ to BBB-: 0–1, 17.0^*; 1–3, 29.0^*; 3–5, 37.0, 5–7, 39.0; 7–10, 40.0^*; >10, 42.0^*.

(2) the outstanding amount assigned by the NCB:

AAA to A-: 0–1, 12.0^*; 1–3, 16.0_d^*; 3–5, 21.0_d^*; 5–7, 27.0_d^*; 7–10, 35.0^*; >10, 45.0^*. BBB+ to BBB-: 0–1, 19.0^*; 1–3, 34.0; 3–5, 46.0, 5–7, 52.0^*; 7–10, 58.0^*; >10, 65.0^*.

Credit claims with variable interest payments:

The haircut is that applied to fixed interest credit claims in the zero-to-one-year maturity bucket corresponding to the same credit quality and the same valuation methodology.

Retail mortgage-backed debt instruments:

Non-marketable retail mortgage-backed debt instruments are subject to a valuation haircut of *39.5 percent* *. The rating must be A− at least (ECB 2011/14).

Fixed-term deposits (with Eurosystem): No haircut.

Updates to the General framework, published in ECB (2013/35, from September 26, 2013), are either in (red) italic type and starred, *, if haircuts increase compared to Table 5.3 or in (green) italic type, starred with a subscript *d* if haircuts decrease. These apply from October 1, 2013, except for updates with respect to own-use covered bonds, which apply from November 1, 2013 (ECB 2013/35, Article 8(4)). Temporary framework updates (ECB 2013/36) apply from October 1, 2013, and are indicated in (blue) slanted type with a dagger, †. This relates to haircuts of ABSs with a second-best rating below A− that do not fulfill additional (temporarily applied) requirements. *aExcept ABSs backed by residential mortgages or loans to SMEs issued before June 20, 2012, that do not fulfill certain standard eligibility criteria, but have a credit quality of at least BBB−. These have a haircut of 22 percent (see ECB 2013/36).*† For an explanation of the credit quality (ratings) categories and rules, see Table 6.1, Panel E.

Notes: (As reported in ECB 2013/35, ANNEX I, and ECB 2011/14, Table 6)[1] In general, the issuer classification determines the liquidity category. However, all asset-backed securities are included in category V, regardless of the classification of the issuer, and jumbo covered bank bonds, are included in category II, while traditional covered bank bonds, other covered bank bonds and other debt instruments issued by credit institutions are included in category III and IV. [2] Debt certificates issued by the ECB and debt instruments issued by the NCBs prior to the adoption of the euro in their respective Member State are included in liquidity category I. [3] Only instruments with an issuing volume of at least EUR 1 billion, for which at least three market-makers provide regular bid and ask quotes, fall into the asset class of jumbo covered bank bonds. [4] Only marketable assets issued by issuers that have been classified as agencies by the ECB are included in liquidity category II. Marketable assets issued by other agencies are included in liquidity category III or IV, depending on the issuer and asset type. [5] Non-UCITS-compliant covered bank bonds, including both structured covered bank bonds and multi-issuer covered bank bonds, are included in liquidity category III. [6] Individual asset-backed securities, covered bank bonds (jumbo covered bank bonds, traditional covered bank bonds, and other covered bank bonds), and uncovered bank bonds that are theoretically valued in accordance with Section 6.5 *of Annex I to Guideline ECB/2011/14** are subject to an additional valuation haircut. This haircut is directly applied at the level of the theoretical valuation of the individual debt instrument in the form of a valuation markdown of 5 percent. *Furthermore, an additional valuation markdown is applied to own-use covered bonds. This valuation markdown is 8 percent for own-use covered bonds in Credit Quality Steps 1 and 2, and 12 percent for own-use covered bonds in Credit Quality Step 3** ["For these purposes, 'own-use covered bonds' means covered bank bonds issued by either a counterparty or entities closely linked to it, and used in a percentage greater than 75 percent of the outstanding notional amount by that counterparty and/or its closely linked entities" (ECB 2013/35, p. 9)]. [7] Ratings are as specified in the Eurosystem's harmonized rating scale, published on the ECB's website at www.ecb.europa.eu.

scale), but the exact rating does not affect haircuts. From October 25, 2008, eligible collateral is put into two categories, those rated A– or higher and those rated BBB+ to BBB–. I will refer to these categories as rating category 1 and 2, respectively.[10] Collateral rated below BBB– is not eligible and I will sometimes refer to this as rating category 3. One can think of collateral rated below BBB– as having a haircut of 100 percent. As seen in Tables 5.2 to 5.4, collateral in rating category 2 have higher haircuts than those in category 1, given residual maturity, liquidity category, and coupon type. For example, over the October 25, 2008, to December 31, 2010, period, going from rating category 1 to 2 adds 5 percent to the haircut. This leads to Observation 1.4.

Given the liquidity category, residual maturity, rating, and type of coupon, there is no variation in haircuts across securities. For example, measures of volatility or standard measures of liquidity are not included. There is no consideration to idiosyncratic features of a security or particular market conditions relevant to it at particular points in time. This holds for Tables 5.1 to 5.4 and forms the basis of Observation 1.5.

Unlike what is common in bilateral repos, counterparty risk is not taken into account when setting haircuts. This property of the haircut rules has remained in place throughout the time period that I am studying here, with one exception, and forms the basis of Observation 1.6 above. The exception relates to so-called own-use collateral, for which additional haircuts were introduced in the collateral framework update adopted on September 26, 2013 (see Table 5.4), and valid from November 1, 2013. Own use refers to collateral that is issued by an entity with which the bank using it has close links (see

[10] The ECB operates with what it calls "credit quality steps" (see, e.g., ECB 2010/13). My rating category 1 combines the ECB's Credit Quality Steps 1 and 2 because collateral in these two steps receive the same haircuts (as seen in Tables 5.3 and 5.4 and discussed in further detail in Chapter 6 and the Appendix to this book). My rating category 2 corresponds to the ECB's Step 3. Throughout this book, I use Standard & Poor's scale when referring to ratings, unless otherwise specified. So, for example, a rating of AAA (A–) also represents Aaa (A3) using Moody's scale.

Chapter 8 for the definition of close links and further discussion of the own use of collateral).

5.3 HAIRCUTS OVER TIME

This section comments further on Tables 5.1 to 5.4, focusing more on the details in those tables and tracing out the changes over time. The discussion is organized around each of the four subperiods represented by the four haircut tables.

March 8, 2004, to October 24, 2008. Table 5.1
The lowest haircut for Tier 1 (later, marketable) assets is 0.5 percent. This is for liquidity category I assets with residual maturity of less than one year. The highest haircut is 25 percent and is for inverse floaters with more than ten years to run. Ignoring the inverse floaters, the highest haircut is for zero-coupon asset-backed securities (liquidity category IV) with residual maturity of more than ten years, for which the haircut is 18 percent. Thus, there is substantial variation in haircuts across securities as a function of residual maturity, coupon type, and liquidity category, with less liquid and more risky securities having larger haircuts. There is no variation, however, in these differences in the more than four-year period covered by Table 5.1.

Panel B summarizes the haircuts applied to Tier 2 assets as of March 8, 2004. For the most part, these stayed in force until the introduction of the single list on January 1, 2007. The exceptions relate to collateral eligibility. For example, equities were struck from the list of eligible collateral as of May 30, 2005 (ECB 2005/2). Panels C and D summarize haircuts for non-marketable assets. Haircuts for Tier 2 and non-marketable collateral are by and large somewhat higher than for Tier 1 (later, marketable) assets, but few of them exceed the haircut of 25 percent for Tier 1 inverse floaters. The highest haircut is 41 percent and is for credit claims without even a theoretical price. The haircut in this case is applied to the nominal value. The most interesting feature of the collateral framework reported on in Panels B to D might well be the great variety of eligible collateral, for example equities, trade bills, bank loans, and "marketable" assets with restricted liquidity features.

October 25, 2008, to December 31, 2010. Table 5.2

These updates are published in two *Official Journal* documents, both formally adopted on October 23, 2008. One of these is the first Temporary framework document (ECB 2008/11); the other updates the General framework (ECB 2008/13). As reported in Table 5.2, only the new Temporary framework is actually effective from October 25, 2008. General framework updates are effective from February 1, 2009. Table 5.2 includes all these updates, indicating General framework updates in (red) italic type and starred. Temporary framework updates are in (blue) slanted type and with a dagger (†). In addition to the changes indicated in Table 5.2, the ECB also introduced the full allotment policy in October 2008. The impetus for all these changes was the turmoil in the financial markets after the Lehman default in September 2008.

On the face of it, one of the biggest updates in Table 5.2 is the introduction of two rating categories. Among marketable collateral, the old minimum threshold of A– stayed in place for ABSs only. Even some non-marketable assets now get by with a BBB– rating. Chapter 6 provides further information as to how the ratings are set and how minimum rating requirements have evolved.

Additional notable changes to haircuts (and eligibility) are as follows:

1. The number of liquidity categories increases from four to five. Unsecured (uncovered) credit institution debt instruments are moved from category III to the new category IV, and asset-backed securities are moved from the old category IV to the new category V. This is part of the General framework.
2. Unsecured bank debt trading on ECB-approved non-regulated markets is included in the public list of eligible collateral (liquidity category IV). An additional haircut of 5 percent applies to such collateral. This is studied separately in Chapter 9 (Temporary framework).

3. Subordinated debt can be eligible provided it has adequate guarantees. An additional haircut of 10 percent applies. A valuation markdown of 5 percent also applies if a theoretical, rather than a market, price is used.

4. Haircuts are increased for unsecured credit institution debt instruments (General framework).

5. There is a single haircut of 12 percent on asset-backed securities (with a rating of A− or higher), regardless of the maturity. A valuation markdown of 5 percent also applies if a theoretical, rather than a market, price is used.

6. Foreign-denominated marketable securities may be eligible collateral (Temporary framework).

7. Fixed-term deposits with the Eurosystem are included in the set of eligible non-marketable collateral, without a haircut (Temporary framework).

Several of these features involve an expansion of the set of eligible collateral. Specific examples are the inclusion of unsecured bank bonds trading on non-regulated markets and foreign-denominated collateral.

The most visible, or talked about, change, however, may well be the lowering of minimum rating requirements, from A− to BBB−. Still, it is not clear how many marketable securities actually were affected by this particular change. The raw data on this, though ostensibly public, have not been made available by the ECB. But more recent raw data on marketable eligible collateral are publicly available, and, in Section 5.5, I present evidence that the vast majority of eligible marketable collateral on the public list of eligible collateral are rated A− or higher. If this were also the case in October 2008, one may question the relaxation of the rating requirement. This is an interesting question, especially given the excess of eligible collateral as documented in Chapter 4. A plausible hypothesis is that the lowering of the minimum ratings threshold was especially important for non-marketable collateral in countries with weak sovereigns and banking sectors.

The lowest haircut is 0 percent for fixed-term deposits with the Eurosystem. This apart, the lowest haircut is still 0.5 percent (liquidity category I, rating category 1, residual maturity less than one year) and the highest haircut for "regular" euro-denominated marketable securities is 30 percent for inverse floaters in rating category 2 and with more than ten years to run. Ignoring inverse floaters, the highest haircut among "regular" euro-denominated marketable assets is 25 percent for zero-coupon securities in liquidity category IV (unsecured bank bonds in rating category 2) and with more than ten years to maturity. As listed above, additional haircuts apply if the collateral is trading on non-regulated markets or is subordinated. While haircuts are increased for some instruments (going from Table 5.1 to Table 5.2), they remain unchanged for marketable assets with a rating of A− or higher and in liquidity categories I–III.

The additional haircut for ABSs that are theoretically valued is essentially an adjustment to the model price. Footnote 5 in Table 5.2 states that "[t]his haircut is directly applied at the level of theoretical valuation" (ECB 2008/13). Of course, whether the haircut is applied before or after the "regular" haircut is immaterial. But the footnote is suggestive of the ECB viewing the need for a theoretical price as a sign of higher risk. Such risk could be model risk, the risk that the model overstates the "true" value of the security, or that the need to use a theoretical price implies that the security is less liquid and more risky than its liquidity category and residual maturity would suggest. It is unclear why this is not already addressed in the model used to determine theoretical prices.

January 1, 2011, to September 30, 2013. Table 5.3
These updates mostly relate to the General framework and, as before, are indicated in (red) italics and starred.[11] Notable updates include absorbing the two-tiered credit rating system from the Temporary framework into the General framework. This is mostly a change in form rather than substance, but it may also reduce uncertainty for financial institutions with respect to collateral eligibility since the General framework is viewed as more permanent (even though it

---

[11] Temporary framework features that are taken over by the General framework are not flagged, but what they are can be seen by comparing Table 5.3 to Table 5.2.

is also subject to change). This would be especially important with respect to the three-year LTROs introduced later in 2011 and 2012. In addition, haircuts increase for marketable securities in liquidity categories II–V, especially for lower-rated securities, and for inverse floaters. Haircuts for non-marketable securities also increase. Finally, as of June 29, 2012, ABSs with ratings down to BBB– may qualify as eligible collateral at a haircut of 32 percent if the underlying loans are commercial mortgages, or 26 percent for ABSs backed by other types of loans.

The lowest haircut is still for fixed-term deposits with the Eurosystem (0 percent). Apart from this, the lowest haircut is 0.5 percent (liquidity category I, rating category 1, residual maturity less than one year) and the highest haircut for marketable securities is 69.5 percent for inverse floaters in rating category 2 and more than ten years to run. Ignoring inverse floaters, the highest haircut for marketable assets is 46 percent (liquidity category IV, rating category 2, residual maturity more than ten years). These are for euro-denominated collateral. Foreign-denominated eligible collateral attract higher haircuts.

The additional haircut of 5 percent for marketable securities whose value is determined by a model is extended from ABSs only to covered bonds and unsecured bank bonds (Table 5.3, Footnote 6). This presumably reflects that the usage of marketable securities without an adequate market price has become a larger concern for the ECB. This can be understood with reference to the finding in Chapter 4 that banks have a preference for using lower-quality collateral and the increased usage of such collateral over time, something which would be a concern for the ECB, especially under the full allotment policy.

A notable feature in Table 5.3 is the off-again, on-again clause regarding unsecured debt instruments issued by credit institutions and trading on non-regulated markets. Before October 2008, such instruments were not eligible collateral. Their eligibility expired on December 31, 2010, but was reintroduced one year later, as of January 1, 2012, but this time as a part of the General framework and with the same haircut as comparable marketable collateral. This is notable, in part because it was just in time for the second of the two three-year LTROs. Chapter 9 discusses this further.

October 1, 2013, to January 31, 2015. Table 5.4[12]

As shown in Table 5.4, the fourth and final update to haircuts in the March 8, 2004, to January 2015 time period was adopted on September 26, 2013, with effect from October 1, 2013, except for own-use covered bonds for which the updates take effect November 1, 2013. As of this date, the *liquidity categories* are officially referred to as *haircut categories*, as indicated in Table 5.4 This may reflect an understanding that these categories do not only reflect liquidity but also risk, thus the use of a more neutral label. However, I will continue to use the terminology *liquidity category*.

The update in Table 5.4 represents the first time over the time period that is studied that the ECB decreased haircuts for some marketable (earlier, Tier 1) assets. Such decreases are indicated in (green) italic type in the table with a *d* subscript (a star superscript continues to denote updates to the General framework). Overall, for marketable collateral in liquidity categories I, II, and III with a rating of A− or better, haircuts have never been lower over the almost eleven-year period studied here.

The additional haircut of 8 percent (12 percent) for own-use covered bonds in rating category 1 (2) represents the first time the haircut rules take into account the counterparty that submits the collateral (and is the only exception to Observation 1.6). Own use essentially refers to securities issued by an entity with which the counterparty has close links, which roughly means that the counterparty has a 20 percent or larger stake in the issuer. Chapter 8 provides further details and discussion on own-use collateral.

Finally, note that with respect to Observation 1.1, the average time between each new haircut table over the period March 8, 2004,

---

[12] Some of the updates in Table 5.4 do not apply before November 1, 2013. See Table 5.4 for details. The end date, January 31, 2015, is simply the last date covered by this book. This is not the last date the haircuts in Table 5.4 were in force. See the Appendix to this book for subsequent developments.

to October 1, 2013, is 1,164.7 days, equivalent to 38.3 months or 3.2 years. But this underestimates the average time between haircut updates across securities, conditional on asset class, residual maturity, and coupon type. For example, Tables 5.1 to 5.4 reveal that for securities (i) in liquidity categories I or II rated A− or better and with any period of maturity or (ii) liquidity category III rated A− or better and residual maturity less than three years, haircuts remained the same throughout the 3,493-day, March 8, 2004, to September 30, 2013, period.

Thus, apart from infrequent updates to the haircut tables, the only events that bring about a haircut change for an individual security are (i) the yearly reduction in residual maturity (for securities with maturities less than eleven years) and (ii) a possible ratings change should the security's rating fall below A− or below BBB−. The only direct input from the market itself to a security's collateral value in Eurosystem operations is therefore the market price, if any, of the collateral.

5.4 EXTRAORDINARY HAIRCUTS

In addition to the rules summarized in Tables 5.1 to 5.4, there are two extraordinary sets of haircut rules that apply to debt instruments issued or guaranteed by Greece or Cyprus. These countries did not meet regular minimum rating requirements for many of the years covered by this book and have been under restructuring/bailout programs, so-called Economic Adjustment Programmes (EAPs). These programs are jointly organized by the IMF, European Commission, and the ECB, commonly referred to as the "Troika." As part of their respective EAPs, Greece and Cyprus received exemptions from standard collateral eligibility rules, eventually with non-standard haircuts.[13] The extraordinary haircut rules for Greece and Cyprus entered into force on December 21, 2012 (updated December 15, 2014), and May 9, 2013, respectively, and are reported in Table 5.5. They were still in force as of January 31, 2015.[14] Haircuts for Greek

---

[13] Section 6.2 contains further details and references regarding these exemptions.
[14] See the Appendix to this book for subsequent developments.

Table 5.5 *Greece and Cyprus: extraordinary haircuts*

Panel A: Hellenic Republic, applied as of

Maturity bucket	December 21, 2012		December 15, 2014	
	Fixed coupons and floaters	Zero coupon	Fixed coupons and floaters	Zero coupon
Government bonds				
0–1	15.0	15.0	6.5	6.5
1–3	33.0	35.5	11.0	12.0
3–5	45.0	48.5	16.5	18.0
5–7	54.0	58.5	23.0	26.0
7–10	56.0	62.0	34.0	39.5
> 10	57.0	· 71.0	40.0	52.5
Government-guaranteed bank and non-financial corporate bonds				
0–1	23.0	23.0	13.5	14.0
1–3	42.5	45.0	19.0	20.0
3–5	55.5	59.0	24.5	26.5
5–7	64.5	69.5	31.5	35.0
7–10	67.0	72.5	43.5	49.5
> 10	67.5	81.0	50.0	62.0

Panel B: Republic of Cyprus, applied as of May 9, 2013

Maturity bucket	Fixed coupons and floaters	Zero coupon
Government bonds		
0–1	14.5	14.5
1–3	27.5	29.5
3–5	37.5	40.0
5–7	41.0	45.0
7–10	47.5	52.5
> 10	57.0	71.0
Government-guaranteed bank and non-financial corporate bonds		
0–1	23.0	23.0
1–3	37.0	39.0
3–5	47.5	50.5
5–7	51.5	55.5
7–10	58.0	63.0
> 10	68.0	81.5

This table shows the extraordinary haircut schedules temporarily applying to marketable debt instruments issued or fully guaranteed by the Hellenic Republic (ECB 2012/32; ECB 2013/4; ECB 2013/5; ECB 2014/12; ECB 2014/46) and the Republic of Cyprus (ECB 2013/13; ECB 2013/21; ECB 2013/22). Panel A shows the extraordinary haircuts for the Hellenic Republic announced on December 19, 2012, and entered into force on December 21, 2012. On November 19, 2014, the ECB announced updates that apply from December 15, 2014, and are still in use as of January 31, 2015. Panel B shows the extraordinary haircuts for the Republic of Cyprus announced on May 2, 2013, entered into force May 9, 2013, and still in use as of January 31, 2015. For a detailed description on temporary eligibility criteria exemptions for both the Hellenic Republic and the Republic of Cyprus also see ECB (2010/3), ECB (2012/2), ECB (2012/3), ECB (2012/14), ECB (2014/31), and ECB (2014/32). See the Appendix to this book for further updates.

government bonds (paper guaranteed by Greece) were initially in the range from 15 percent (23 percent) for maturities of less than one year to 71 percent (81 percent) for zero-coupon bonds with maturity of more than ten years. As shown in Table 5.5, they were reduced in the update on December 15, 2014. For Cyprus, the corresponding numbers are 14.5 percent (23 percent) and 71 percent (81.5 percent).

5.5   EVIDENCE ON COLLATERAL ELIGIBILITY, RATINGS, AND HAIRCUTS IN PRIMARY AND SECONDARY REPO MARKETS

This section compares collateral eligibility and haircuts in the primary and secondary repo markets. By the primary market I mean the ECB's refinancing operations and the marginal lending facility, the haircuts in which are as described above in Tables 5.1 to 5.4. The secondary market is represented by two widely used general collateral central counterparty (CCP) repo contracts that are based on subsets of the Eurosystem's eligible collateral list. I provide statistics on the distribution of eligible collateral across liquidity categories and ratings, in both the primary and secondary market, and then compare haircuts on an ISIN-by-ISIN basis. I do this using data from a representative date. It might be interesting to expand on this by looking at the evolution of the patterns I document over time.

The secondary market I use is Eurex's GC Pooling market. In particular, I use the GC Pooling ECB Basket and the GC Pooling ECB Extended Basket.[15] Since their inception in 2005, contracts on these general collateral baskets have grown to become a mainstay of the repo market in Europe (Mancini, Ranaldo, and Wrampelmeyer 2014; Rösler 2015), with a growth in daily volume of less than EUR 20 billion in 2006 to around EUR 150 billion in 2013.[16] Eurex provides anonymous electronic trading in these contracts, with itself as a central counterparty. It also provides a real-time collateral management

---

[15] See www.eurexrepo.com/repo-en/products/gcpooling/ for details and a list of the eligible ISINs in these baskets and the haircuts Eurex applies to these.

[16] See www.eurexrepo.com/repo-en/market-data/statistics/.

system, with the actual collateral received by the cash provider being determined by Eurex within this system.[17]

Repos carried out on both the GC Pooling ECB and ECB Extended baskets allow for the reuse of received collateral within the GC Pooling market and the Eurex Clearing Margining process. The ECB Basket also enables reuse within Eurosystem/Bundesbank operations. This is not possible with the Extended Basket. The ECB Basket has stricter ratings requirements, at least A−, and contains fewer ISINs, around 7,000 to 7,500, than the Extended Basket, which allows for a rating down to BBB− and has around 20,000 to 25,000 ISINs (the exact numbers vary over time).

To get a sense of the distributions of primary and secondary market eligible collateral and the haircuts applied to them, I collected the lists of eligible collateral from the Eurosystem and the two GC Pooling baskets on August 14, 2013. The findings are reported in Table 5.6.

Panel A shows the distribution of eligible marketable collateral in Eurosystem operations across liquidity and ratings categories. More than 80 percent of the eligible collateral fall under liquidity categories III and IV; the number of ISINs in these two categories are 6,965 and 24,587, respectively, out of a total number of ISINs of 38,051. The rating categories are backed out from the haircuts using the rules in Table 5.3. This is possible because the daily Eurosystem collateral eligibility lists contain information on the collateral's liquidity category, maturity, and coupon type. Approximately 85 percent of eligible collateral have an A− or higher rating, the number being 32,493. The number in the BBB+ to BBB− range is 5,264.

The high fraction of eligible collateral rated A− or higher is at first glance surprising, especially compared to ratings of corporations. For example, in 2013 Fitch had approximately the same number of

[17] To be precise, the trading infrastructure is provided by Eurex Repo GmbH and the central counterparty is Eurex Clearing AG. Both of these are subsidiaries of Eurex Frankfurt AG, which is owned by Deutsche Börse AG (deutsche-boerse.com/dbg/dispatch/en/kir/dbg_nav/investor_relations/10_The_Company/20_Organizational_Structure).

Table 5.6 *Distribution of collateral and comparison of haircuts in primary and secondary repo markets*

	Liquidity Category					Total
	I	II	III	IV	V	
Panel A: Number of ECB eligible marketable collateral						
Number, AAA to A–	1,701	3,053	5,881	20,967	891	32,493
Number, BBB+ to BBB–	153	378	1,060	3,562	111	5,264
Irish government securities	33	–	–	–	–	33
Irish government guarantees	–	0	2	14	0	16
Portuguese government securities	37	–	–	–	–	37
Portuguese government guarantees	–	0	16	20	0	36
Greek government securities	87	–	–	–	–	87
Greek government guarantees	–	0	6	22	0	28
Cypriot government securities	55	–	–	–	–	55
Cypriot government guarantees	–	0	0	2	0	2
Total	**2,066**	**3,431**	**6,965**	**24,587**	**1,002**	**38,051**
Panel B: GC Pooling ECB Basket (all rated A– or higher)						
Same haircut	975	2,270	3,224	267	0	6,736
Higher haircut	34	224	201	41	0	500
Lower haircut	0	0	0	0	0	0
Total	**1,009**	**2,494**	**3,425**	**308**	**0**	**7,236**
Panel C: GC Pooling ECB Extended Basket, AAA to A–						
Same haircut	1,308	2,489	3,947	10,222	0	17,966
Higher haircut	54	268	291	1,139	0	1,752
Lower haircut	0	0	0	3	0	3
Total	**1,362**	**2,757**	**4,238**	**11,364**	**0**	**19,721**
Panel D: GC Pooling ECB Extended Basket, BBB+ to BBB–						
Same haircut	84	5	383	696	0	1,168
Higher haircut	1	1	13	38	0	53
Lower haircut	0	0	0	0	0	0
Total	**85**	**6**	**396**	**734**	**0**	**1,221**

This table provides information on the distribution of eligible collateral across liquidity and rating categories in Eurosystem operations (Panel A) as well as in two secondary market repo contracts traded on Eurex Repo, namely the GC Pooling ECB Basket contract (Panel B) and the GC Pooling ECB Extended Basket contract (Panels C and D). The ECB list on August 14, 2013 (published on August 13, 2013) can be found on www.ecb.europa.eu/paym/coll/assets/html/index.en.html and the two Eurex Repo files that apply on August 14, 2013, on www.eurexrepo.com/repo-en/products/gcpooling/. Panel A includes all eligible marketable collateral in the public list, including all securities that are exempt from the standard minimum rating requirements. The exempted securities are made up of government and government-guaranteed securities from Ireland, Portugal, Greece, and Cyprus. There is no collateral in the GC Pooling ECB Basket that is rated below A–. There is no collateral in the GC Pooling ECB Extended Basket rated below BBB–. Panels B, C, and D compare haircuts in the GC Pooling baskets to the haircuts set by the ECB (Table 5.3). The row labeled "same" (higher, lower) gives the number of collateral where the Eurex contract uses the same (higher, lower) haircut for eligible collateral as the Eurosystem.

European corporations in the BBB+ to BBB− range as in the A− or higher range (Fitch 2014).[18] However, ratings tend to be quite high for banks. Hau, Langfield, and Marques-Ibanez (2013) report that 74 percent of banks in the United States and EU15 have an average rating (from Standard & Poor's (S&P), Moody's, and Fitch) of A− or higher. This relates to the argument put forth by many commentators that there is, or have been, ratings inflation in the United States, whereby, for example, the rating agencies themselves are alleged to have helped issuers get higher ratings (see, e.g., Calomiris 2009a; White 2010; Griffin, Nickerson, and Tang 2013; and the references therein). The literature suggests that ratings may be inflated both because of ratings shopping, on the part of issuers, and ratings catering by the rating agencies. Several advantages to higher ratings are discussed in the literature, such as leading to lower capital requirements and facilitating a broader investor base.

The Eurosystem's collateral framework offers an additional source of gain to higher ratings, namely an increase in collateral value in central bank repos as a result of lower haircuts. As described above, these are essentially reduced from 100 percent in the case of collateral that goes from a rating of below BBB− to the BBB+ to BBB− range, and they are further reduced for collateral obtaining a rating of A− or higher. The large haircut differential between the Eurosystem's rating categories provides a potential gain to the issuer even if the market would see through a "massaged" (or "catered") rating with respect to pricing the collateral. Further evidence on ratings and their impact is provided in Chapter 6.

Panel B provides the distribution of collateral in the GC Pooling ECB Basket across liquidity categories, as on August 14, 2013. In total, there are 7,236 ISINs. This represents 19.0 percent of all Eurosystem-eligible collateral and 22.3 percent of those rated A− or higher. Recall that only collateral rated A− is eligible for inclusion in the GC Pooling ECB Basket. The liquidity groups with the highest

---

[18] According to Fitch (2014), 34 percent of European corporations had a BBB+ to BBB− rating year-end 2013, and 30 percent had a rating of A− or higher.

representations are II and III, with 2,494 and 3,425 ISINs, respectively. For each liquidity category, I define the "acceptance rate" as the fraction of ECB eligible collateral rated A− or higher that is included in the GC Pooling ECB Basket. Liquidity category II has the highest acceptance rate (81.7 percent), with liquidity categories IV and V having the lowest (1.5 and 0 percent, respectively). Liquidity categories I and III have almost identical acceptance rates of 59.3 and 58.2 percent, respectively. Thus, ignoring government bonds (liquidity category I), the less liquid and risky a security is, the less likely it is to be accepted into the GC Pooling ECB Basket.

With respect to government bonds and the GC Pooling ECB Basket, only government bonds issued by the following countries are in the ECB Basket collateral list for August 14, 2013: AT, BE, CA, CZ, DE, DK, FI, FR, LU, NL, PL, SE, SK.[19] So, for example, countries such as Spain and Italy are excluded even though both countries have A− ratings (due to their rating from DBRS, see Chapter 6). However, on August 14, 2013, bonds from Spain and Italy and most other countries that are excluded from the ECB Basket are included in the GC Pooling ECB Extended Basket. These countries have identifiers: BG, ES, HR, IE, IS, IT, LT, LV, MT, RO, and SL. On the selected date, government paper from the following countries are totally excluded from the GC Pooling market: CY, GR, and PT. The list of countries with bonds in the two baskets varies over time. For example, on February 16, 2015, IT-denominated ISINs were even excluded from the Extended Basket contract.

A restrictive policy with respect to eligible collateral makes sense from a risk management perspective for Eurex. As a central counterparty, it is ultimately liable in case of default by one of the

---

[19] I have used standard country identifiers (e.g., used for ISINs) to abbreviate countries. This does not mean, however, that the government bonds of, for example, PL (Poland) are issued with a PL ISIN. To continue with this example, with respect to the GC Pooling eligible collateral list for August 14, 2013, all Polish government bonds in the list are Eurobonds with a CLBL "country of location" identifier and with ISINs that start with XS. The list was downloaded from www.eurexrepo.com/repo-en/products/gcpooling/.

two other counterparties. That Eurex excludes a large number of A– and higher-rated paper from the GC Pooling ECB Basket suggests that there is substantial variation in the liquidity and risk of instruments with the same rating, at least as assessed by Eurex. This relates to Calomiris' (2009b) observation (see Footnote 9) that the same letter rating has different implications with respect to default probabilities for different types of securities. Eurex's excluding ABSs from both of its baskets suggests that it, and the market it caters to, does not view ABS ratings as comparable to those of other asset classes.

Panel B also compares the haircuts used by Eurex in the ECB Basket to those set by the ECB for Eurosystem operations. For 6,736, or 93 percent, of the ISINs, these are the same. For the ECB Extended Basket, Panels C (AAA to A–) and D (BBB+ to BBB–) show that the fraction of ISINs that have the same haircut as in Eurosystem operations is only marginally lower. That more than 90 percent of the haircuts applied to collateral in Eurex's two GC Pooling contracts are the same as those applied by the ECB in its operations is consistent with what has been communicated by Eurex, namely that in their GC Pooling contracts their policy is to rely on the haircuts set by the ECB in its collateral framework, though they may add a supplementary margin at their discretion if their risk assessment differs.

This shows that haircuts in the Eurosystem collateral framework have direct impact on the secondary repo market. Monetary policy goes beyond just steering overnight rates. It also affects the collateral values of securities in the secondary market. Furthermore, any biases that may creep into the collateral framework of the central bank, for example from infrequently revised haircuts, will carry over to the secondary markets. It is rather remarkable that for many repo contracts in the euro area, haircuts are set by a Eurosystem committee rather than in the markets.

Eurex has excluded government bonds from Spain and Italy from its GC Pooling ECB Basket over a long time period. This is noteworthy because a basic criterion to be in this basket is a rating of A– or higher, something that both Spain and Italy had on the sampled date, August 14, 2013, in Table 5.6. They still fulfilled this criterion in June 2014 and were still excluded from the ECB Basket. Instead, Eurex pooled Spanish and Italian bonds with instruments rated in the BBB+ to BBB− range by including them in the ECB Extended Basket only. As mentioned above, in February 2015, Italian paper was even excluded from the Extended Basket. The implication is that Eurex does not view the A− ratings of Italy and Spain as entirely reliable. The next chapter provides further information on the ratings of different countries and the rating and guarantee rules used by the Eurosystem. This will shed light on why some market participants may take the ratings of Italy and Spain with a pinch of salt.

6 Ratings and Guarantees

As seen in the previous chapter, ratings are a central feature of the collateral framework, both with respect to eligibility and haircuts. Furthermore, despite the problematic times experienced over the last few years in Europe, a surprisingly large fraction of Eurosystem eligible collateral have a rating of A− or higher. Understanding the rating rules and their implications is therefore important. This chapter starts by summarizing these rules and how they have evolved over time. This is followed by discussions of exemptions and of evidence that relates to the important role of rating agencies and government guarantees.

I want to emphasize seven points up front. First, since January 2007, rating agencies have come to play a well-defined legal role in the rating process within the Eurosystem's collateral framework.

Second, since that time, the basic rule is that only the highest rating from one of the official rating agencies matters. These were initially Fitch, Standard & Poor's (S&P), and Moody's. Dominion Bond Rating Services (DBRS) was added to the list in February 2009. Similar collateral can have different haircuts and therefore different collateral values, as a function of which rating agencies they are rated by. I present specific examples that illustrate such cross-collateral inconsistencies. Using one of these examples, I also present cursory evidence that higher ratings lead not only to lower haircuts and higher collateral values but also to higher market prices (lower yields), *ceteris paribus*. This is further evidence that the collateral framework has direct impact on secondary markets.

Third, I compare and contrast the ratings given by the four accepted agencies to all euro-area countries over time. The evidence shows that as a result of the inclusion of DBRS into the collateral framework (with its first set of sovereign ratings given in 2010), Italy and Spain have received A– ratings (on the S&P scale) they otherwise would not have had. This has reduced the haircuts, and thus increased the collateral value, of Italian and Spanish government securities within the Eurosystem's collateral framework. The extra collateral value from DBRS's pivotal ratings of these two countries is substantial. I estimate that in August 2013, it was worth around EUR 115 billion, growing to around EUR 165 and 180 billion by July 2014 and January 2015, respectively. These estimates do not account for the impact the higher ratings may have had on market values or the gain in collateral value to government-guaranteed bank bonds from a higher government rating.

Fourth, exemptions for sovereigns from the minimum rating thresholds are part and parcel of the ECB's collateral policy. All countries whose best rating has dipped below the minimum standard laid down in the collateral framework have received exemptions. These are Portugal, Greece, and Cyprus. Portugal is a particularly interesting example because its emergence out of exempt status on August 20, 2014, was possible only because the ECB relaxed its ratings rules in advance of Portugal emerging from the bailout program under which it had received exempt status. In particular, the ECB lowered the minimum rating from DBRS that would establish collateral eligibility, from BBB to BBBL. Without the BBBL rating from DBRS, Portuguese sovereign securities would not have met the minimum rating threshold.

The increase in the collateral value of Portuguese government bonds from DBRS's pivotal rating is worth around EUR 100 billion, relative to these securities being ineligible as collateral. Thus, in January 2015, the total increase in collateral value from DBRS's pivotal ratings to euro-area sovereigns is around EUR 280 billion.

Fifth, the effective rating of collateral within the Eurosystem's collateral framework can be boosted by guarantees from governments and other entities, including corporations. This can affect haircuts and thus collateral and market values. I present evidence that the majority of guarantees are provided by local, regional, and central governments. The country with the largest number of credit institutions with government guarantees is Italy. For example, out of the 329 credit institutions with government-guaranteed collateral in the public list of eligible collateral published on August 14, 2013, 257 were Italian. This large provision of government guarantees in Italy started in the run-up to the second three-year LTRO in February 2012, a time when guarantees were declining in the rest of the euro area. I estimate that these guarantees to Italian credit institutions were worth approximately EUR 30 billion in extra funding from the Eurosystem.

Approximately half of the estimated extra collateral value arising from Italian government guarantees is due to Italy's A− rating from DBRS. This EUR 15 billion is an example of the indirect effect of high ratings which flows via guarantees. It is also likely to be an underestimate because it does not take into account the additional value generated by the higher market price the guarantees are likely to result in, especially as a result of the A− rating.

Sixth, while ratings by external rating agencies play a central role in the framework, they are not required for a specific collateral to be eligible. Acceptable ratings can also be supplied by in-house models. Such "ad hoc" or "privately" eligible collateral is not included in the public list of eligible collateral.[1]

Seventh, corporations with banking subsidiaries that have the right to participate in Eurosystem operations can use these as vehicles to cheap funding directly from the Eurosystem. This can be facilitated through the usage of guarantees from the corporation to the banking subsidiary.

6.1 RATING AND GUARANTEE RULES OVER TIME

The official rating rules of the Eurosystem's collateral framework are described in the same set of legal documents, published in the

---

[1] See ECB (2006/12, p. 44, 2011/14, p. 40, and 2014/60, p. 48).

Official Journal, used to study haircuts in Chapter 5. This section summarizes these rules and how they have evolved over the period January 1, 2001, to January 31, 2015. It is instructive to start with 2001 because the rules established at that point were in force in March 2004, which is the start date for the haircut rules reported on in the previous chapter.

To be eligible to be used in Eurosystem operations in exchange for central bank money, collateral has to meet with *high credit standards*. This central concept with respect to the ratings rules is referred to, defined, and modified throughout the official documentation. So high credit standards is a fluid concept. It is whatever it is defined to be by the ECB at a particular point in time.

My main focus is on the rules that establish high credit standards for marketable (and tier one) collateral. These are summarized in Table 6.1, which also provides references to the relevant documentation. As also explained in Table 6.1, the rules are similar for non-marketable assets.

Table 6.1 is organized into five panels, designed to cover the same time periods as the haircut tables, that is, Tables 5.1 to 5.4. The first two panels cover the Table 5.1 period, with the remaining three panels covering the same periods as Tables 5.2 to 5.4, respectively. This makes it easy to check the rating rules that were in effect for each haircut table. It also reflects that major updates to the rating and haircut rules tend to occur at the same time. Each panel provides the baseline rule for high credit standards that is in force at the start of the time period covered by the panel. This is followed by significant updates to the basic rule. As time progresses, the majority of these updates relate to asset-backed securities, for which the rules started to diverge from other marketable securities when the minimum rating standards for the latter were relaxed in October 2008. The rating standards for asset-backed securities are eventually relaxed as well. I discuss each panel in turn.

Table 6.1 *Credit quality and ratings rules*

Credit Quality Rules	Applies to:
*Panel A: January 1, 2001, to December 31, 2006 (covers first half of **Haircut Table 5.1** period)*	All Tier 1 assets.[1]
Baseline Rule [ECB 2000/7, p. 32, G]	
1. "They must meet *high credit standards* [author's italics]. In the assessment of the credit standard of debt instruments, the ECB takes into account, *inter alia*, available ratings by market agencies, as well as certain institutional criteria which would ensure particularly high protection of the holders . . ."	
2. Debt instruments issued by credit institutions that are not UCITS-compliant covered bonds " . . . are accepted in tier one only if each issue as such is awarded a rating [by a rating agency] which indicates, in the view of the Eurosystem, that the debt instrument meets high credit standards" [ECB 2000/7, p. 32, G]. [UCITS-compliant covered bonds are credit institution debt instruments that comply with Article 22(4) of the UCITS Directive [Directive 85/611/EEC, Article 22(4), p. 7, amended by Directive 88/220/EEC, Article 1, pp. 1–2].]	
Comment: What "high credit standards" exactly mean is not specified in the documentation.	
Updates	
1. Applies from July 7, 2002 [ECB 2002/2, p. 32, G]: "[T]hey must meet high credit standards. In the assessment of the credit standard of debt instruments, the ECB takes into account, *inter alia*, available ratings by market agencies, *guarantees . . . provided by financially sound guarantors* [author's italics], . . . as well as certain institutional criteria which would ensure particularly high protection of the instrument holders . . ." The guarantees and the guarantors must meet certain criteria, as specified in ECB [2002/2, p. 32, G].	
2. Subsequent updates expand on what constitutes acceptable guarantees [ECB 2003/16, p. 33, G; ECB 2005/2, p. 34, G].	
3. Applies from May 30, 2005 [ECB 2005/2, pp. 34 and 37, G]:	
(i) UCITS-compliant covered bonds "are eligible in tier one." [These are credit institution debt instruments that comply with Article 22(4) of the UCITS Directive [Directive 85/611/EEC, Article 22(4), p. 7, amended by Directive 88/220/EEC, Article 1, pp. 1–2, Directive 2001/107/EC, and Directive 2001/108/EC].]	
(ii) Debt instruments issued by credit institutions that are not UCITS-compliant covered bonds (see 3.(i) for exact references) "may be accepted in tier one only if they are listed or quoted on a regulated market as defined in Directive 2004/39/EC."	

*Panel B: January 1, 2007, to October 24, 2008 (covers second half of **Haircut Table 5.1** period)*

Baseline Rule [ECB 2006/12, pp. 42–44, G]

Introduces the Eurosystem Credit Assessment Framework (ECAF), which clarifies what "high credit standards" mean:

(i) at least one long-term rating of A– or better from Fitch or Standard & Poor's, or A3 from Moody's, for either the issue or, in the absence of an issue rating, the issuer.

(ii) "In the absence of an [A– (or higher) long-term rating (on the S&P scale]] of the issuer, high credit standards can be established on the basis of guarantees provided by financially sound guarantors" [ECB 2006/12, p. 43, G]. Financial soundness is defined in terms of an A– long-term rating (on the S&P scale) by one of the approved rating agencies (see (i) above].

(iii) UCITS-compliant covered bonds are exempted from the above rules. (These are credit institution debt instruments that comply with Article 22(4) of the UCITS Directive [Directive 85/611/EEC, Article 22(4), p. 7, as last amended by Directive 2005/1/EC].)

If neither the issue, issuer or the guarantor is rated then:

(i) if the issuer or guarantor is a local or regional government or a public sector entity, the relevant supervisory authorities can give the collateral a rating of at most a rating of the relevant central government. Thus, the determination of "high credit quality" is at the discretion of the relevant supervisory authorities, provided the central government rating meets the minimum rating requirement (which here is A– long-term rating on the S&P scale).

(ii) if the issuer or guarantor is a non-financial corporation then "high credit standards" are determined by in-house, NCB, or third-party rating models. See ECB [2006/12, pp. 42–44, G] for further details.

Update

Applies from November 19, 2007 [ECB 2007/10, p. 38, G]:

Modifies baseline rule item (iii): UCITS-compliant covered bonds are exempt only if issued before January 1, 2008.

*Panel C: October 25, 2008, to December 31, 2010 (covers **Haircut Table 5.2** period)*

Baseline Rules [ECB 2008/11, p. 18, T; ECB 2008/13, p. 36, G]

Same as for Panel B except "high (or 'minimum') credit standards" are now "... a 'BBB–' equivalent credit assessment ... [except for] asset-backed securities ..., for which the requirement for high credit standards shall remain unchanged [at 'A–']" (ECB 2008/11, p. 18, T].

All marketable assets.[1]

The rules for non-marketable assets are roughly the same, but issue ratings may not exist. In the case of credit claims, third-party ratings of the debtor or guarantor may supersede ratings from the accepted rating agencies (see ECB 2006/12, pp. 44–46).[2]

All marketable assets[1] except for asset-backed securities.

Table 6.1 *(cont.)*

Credit Quality Rules	Applies to:
*Panel C – continued (covers **Haircut Table 5.2** period)*	
<u>Comment</u>: There is some lack of clarity with respect to precisely what "a 'BBB-' equivalent credit assessment" means. But taken in context, it appears to refer to the "equivalent" of a long-term rating of BBB– (on the S&P scale).	
As of February 1, 2009 [ECB 2008/13, p. 36, G]: Dominion Bond Rating Service (DBRS) appears with Fitch, Standard & Poor's, and Moody's in the set of acceptable rating agencies for the first time in the *Official Journal* collateral framework documentation.	All marketable assets.[1]
Updates 1. Applies from March 1, 2009, [ECB 2009/1, p. 60, G]: For ABSs issued on March 1, 2009, or later, high credit standards mean a long-term rating (on the S&P scale) of: (i) AAA at the time of issue, and (ii) A–, or better after issuance over the life of the issue. (Note that ABSs do not have issuer ratings.)	Asset-backed securities.
2. ECB (2010/1, pp. 22–23, G]: Second-highest rating rule a. Applies from March 1, 2010: For ABSs issued on March 1, 2010, or later, high credit standards mean at least two long-term ratings *for the issue* of (on the S&P scale) (i) AAA at the time of issue, and (ii) A–, or better after issuance. b. Applies from March 1, 2011: Modification to Update 2.a.(ii): All ABSs, regardless of the issuance date, need at least two long-term ratings for the issue of A–, or better after issuance. Note: It is recognized that ABSs issued before March 1, 2010, may not have more than one rating at issuance. In this case, the effective "issuance date" for the second rating is the first rating date by the rating agency giving that second rating. These ABSs must also comply with the rating rules in force when they were issued (as the second highest rule represents a tightening of the rating rules).	Asset-backed securities.

*Panel C – continued (covers **Haircut Table 5.2** period)*

<u>Comment</u>: This update does not clarify whether the terminology "for the issue" rules out high credit standards being established by guarantees in the absence of an issue rating (note that ABSs do not have issuer ratings). See Panel E, 2.(b) for a clarifying update on this point.

3. Applies from October 10, 2010 (ECB 2010/13, p. 35, G):
At issuance, the AAA requirement (see Update 2.a.(i)) can be met with short-term ratings of 'F1+' by Fitch, 'A–1+' by Standard & Poor's, or 'R-1H' by DBRS. Thus, until this clause is canceled (see Update 1, Panel E), these short-term ratings are equivalent to a AAA rating (on the S&P scale).

Asset-backed securities.

*Panel D: January 1, 2011, to September 30, 2013 (covers **Haircut Table 5.3** period)*

ECB 2010/13, p. 51, G
Introduces the terminology "harmonised rating scale" into the official documentation. Defines credit quality in terms of Steps 1, 2, and 3 (the terminology "credit quality steps" is introduced in ECB 2006/12). The long-term ratings that go with these steps are as follows:

Step 1 (LT): S&P and Fitch, AAA to AA–; Moody's, Aaa to Aa3; DBRS, AAA to AAL
Step 2 (LT): S&P and Fitch, A+ to A–; Moody's, A1 to A3; DBRS, AH to AL
Step 3 (LT): S&P and Fitch, BBB+ to BBB–; Moody's, Baa1 to Baa3; DBRS, BBBH to BBB

Each step may also include short-term ratings (that may vary over time). However, historically, as described below, high credit standards are not defined by the (full) credit quality steps, but in terms of them. For example, until May 2015, rating thresholds were defined largely by long-term ratings, with short-term ratings being accepted only in a few exceptions, as indicated in this table.

Baseline Rule (ECB 2010/13, p. 51, G)
1. Same as for Panels B and C. Clarification: The high credit standard (or credit quality) threshold of BBB– means "a minimum long-term rating of 'BBB–' by Fitch or Standard & Poor's, of 'Baa3' by Moody's, or of 'BBB' by DBRS"; in other words, Step 3 (LT).

All marketable assets[1] except for asset-backed securities.

2. For ABSs the rules in updates 1 to 3 from Panel C apply.

Asset-backed securities.

Table 6.1 (cont.)

Credit Quality Rules	Applies to:
Panel D – continued (*covers* **Haircut Table 5.3** *period*) Updates 1. Applies from December 19, 2011 [ECB 2011/25, pp. 65–66, T]: High credit standards for ABSs mean two long-term ratings in Step 2, or better, at issuance and thereafter (see Update 3, Panel C). ABSs with a second highest rating below (on the S&P scale) AAA/A–1+ (long-term/short-term) at issuance have stricter eligibility criteria (e.g., with respect to the underlying assets and the incidence of non-performing loans). 2. Applies from June 29, 2012 [ECB 2012/11, pp. 17–18, T]: High credit standards for ABSs mean two long-term ratings in Step 3, or better, at issuance and thereafter (see Update 3, Panel C). ABSs with a second highest rating below (on the S&P scale) AAA/A–1+ (long-term/short-term) at issuance or below A– (on the S&P scale) after issuance have stricter eligibility criteria (e.g., with respect to the underlying assets and the incidence of non-performing loans).	Asset-backed securities. Asset-backed securities.
Panel E: *October 1, 2013, to January 31, 2015* (*covers* **Haircut Table 5.4** *period*) (See the Appendix to this book for further updates.) Baseline Rule [ECB 2013/35, pp. 8–9, G] 1. The new baseline rule with respect to determining high credit standards modifies the priority of external rating agency ratings (see Panel B). The basic principle is that the order of priority is: issue, programme/issuance series, issuer or guarantor ratings. Details are as follows: (a) "At least one credit assessment from an accepted [rating agency] for either the issue or, in the absence of an issue rating from the same [rating agency], the programme/issuance series under which the asset is issued, must comply with the Eurosystem's credit quality threshold [of a long-term rating in Step 3, or better]" (ECB 2013/35, p. 8, G). (b) "If multiple … credit assessments are available … the first-best rule … is applied" (ECB 2013/35, p. 8, G). (c) Clarification: "If the first-best credit assessment for the issue or, if applicable, for the programme/issuance series does not comply with the Eurosystem's credit quality threshold, the asset is not eligible, even if a[n acceptable] guarantee … exists" (ECB 2013/35, p. 8, G).	All marketable assets[1] except for asset-backed securities.

*Panel E – continued (covers **Haircut Table 5.4** period)*

(d) "In the absence of [a] ... credit assessment for the issue or, if applicable, the programme/issuance series, the best available [rating agency] credit assessment for the issuer or the guarantor (if the guarantee is acceptable ...) must comply with the Eurosystem's credit quality threshold [of a long-term rating in Step 3, or better]" (ECB 2013/35, p. 8, G).

(e) For issuer ratings, short-term ratings can be used for assets with original maturity of less than (and including) 390 days.

Comment: The acceptable short-term issuer ratings are not specified, but logic suggests they are the ones ascribed to Step 3 in the harmonized rating scale (to substitute for a long-term rating in Step 3).

2. For ABSs, the rules in Panel D apply, with the following modifications:

(a) Weakening of the rule in Update 2, Panel D: ABSs with a second highest rating below a long-term rating in Step 2 at issuance or thereafter (see Update 3, Panel C) have stricter eligibility criteria (e.g., with respect to the underlying assets and the incidence of non-performing loans).

(b) Clarification: For ABSs a guarantee cannot be used to establish high credit standards if an ABS has no issue rating.

Asset-backed securities.

Updates
1. Applies from April 1, 2014 [ECB 2014/10, p. 37, G; see also ECB 2014/12, p. 43, T]:
(i) Cancellation of Update 3 in Panel C: Short-term ratings cannot substitute for long-term AAA (on the S&P scale) ratings.
(ii) Weakening of high credit standards: Step 3 (LT) is changed for DBRS to be BBBH to BBBL (from BBBH to BBB before).

Asset-backed securities.
All marketable assets.

2. Applies from December 15, 2014 [ECB 2014/38, pp. 21–23, G]:
Modification to the baseline rule: For collateral from public issuers, only the issuer or guarantor ratings matter.

Marketable assets issued by central governments, regional or local governments, agencies (except agency-issued covered bonds), and supranational institutions.

This table provides eligibility criteria with respect to credit quality standards for Tier 1 assets (January 1, 2001, to December 31, 2006) and marketable assets (from January 1, 2007, onward). The table lays out the baseline rule over five time periods, as specified above, and subsequent updates, until January 2015. General framework documents are denoted by a "G," Temporary framework documents by a "T." Notes: [1]By "all Tier 1 assets" and "all marketable assets" the table refers to all these assets except debt certificates issued by (i) the ECB, or (ii) the national central banks prior to the adoption of the euro in their respective Member State. Securities in (i) and (ii) are eligible without rating considerations. [2] This comment regarding non-marketable assets also applies to subsequent panels in this table (see e.g., ECB 2011/14, pp. 41–43).

January 1, 2001, to December 31, 2006. Table 6.1, Panel A (Covers first half of Haircut Table 5.1 period)

The importance of high credit standards for eligible collateral is established by the following passage, which one can also think of as establishing a baseline rule (for Tier 1 collateral):

> [Eligible collateral] must meet high credit standards. In the assessment of the credit standard of debt instruments, the ECB takes into account, *inter alia*, available ratings by market agencies, as well as certain institutional criteria which would ensure particularly high protection of the holders. [A footnote adds:] Debt instruments issued by credit institutions which [are not UCITS-compliant covered bonds] are accepted in tier one only if each issue as such is awarded a rating (by a rating agency) which indicates, in the view of the Eurosystem, that the debt instrument meets high credit standards.
>
> ECB (2000/7, p. 32)[2]

Interestingly, the official documentation does not define in unambiguous terms what "high credit standards" exactly mean. This does not exclude the possibility that the Eurosystem did not have internal guidelines that offered more precision. It might well be that the two-tier structure of eligible collateral, with substantial influence from the NCBs, may have made it difficult to make more precise official and legal definitions of high credit standards than what is offered in the baseline rule above. The lack of precision in the minimum rating requirement indicates that there is a degree of discretion given to NCBs in determining the set of eligible collateral. From the added footnote, it appears that UCITS-compliant covered bonds do not need a rating at all.

---

[2] UCITS-compliant covered bonds are debt instruments issued by credit institutions that "comply strictly with the criteria set out in Article 22(4) of the UCITS Directive [Directive 88/220/EEC amending Directive 85/611/EEC]." This is from ECB (2000/7), p. 32, footnote 38. UCITS is an acronym for Undertakings for Collective Investment in Transferable Securities.

An important update to the baseline rule, applicable from July 7, 2002, inserts a clause about the possibility of achieving the high credit standards requirement through guarantees by "financially sound guarantors" (ECB 2002/2, p. 32). Again, the wording is somewhat vague. Subsequent updates expand on what constitutes acceptable guarantees (e.g., ECB 2003/16, ECB 2005/2). These specific updates are not listed in Table 6.1. Guarantees in later periods more relevant for this book are covered in more detail below.

January 1, 2007, to October 24, 2008. Table 6.1, Panel B (Covers second half of Haircut Table 5.1 period)
The introduction of the single list (of eligible collateral, see Chapter 5) also saw the introduction of the Eurosystem Credit Assessment Framework, ECAF (ECB 2006/12). This framework, which is part of the collateral framework, introduces a more precise definition of what high credit standards actually mean and also updates the rules with respect to acceptable guarantees. Under ECAF, whether collateral has a high credit standard is determined by the rating assigned to it. The minimum acceptable level is a long-term rating of A− (on the S&P scale).[3]

Within the collateral framework, there are several ways the A− rating can be established. The ratings of the issue, issuer, and if the collateral has a guarantee, that of the guarantor, may all come into play. The baseline procedure is as follows.

First one looks at the issue's long-term rating by the acceptable rating agencies. Over the period covered here, these were S&P, Fitch, and Moody's. If the issue is rated by more than one of these agencies, the highest is picked. Thus, to meet with high credit standards, it is sufficient that the highest external long-term issue rating from one of the accepted rating agencies is A− or above.

If the issue does not have a long-term rating from one of the approved agencies, one looks at the external rating of the issuer and,

---

[3] Recall that, unless otherwise specified, ratings throughout this book are given on the S&P scale.

if applicable, the rating of the guarantor. The highest of these is then picked to determine the rating of the issue.[4] A high credit standard is thus met if (i) the issue has at least one external long-term rating of A− or better, or (ii) if there is no issue rating, the issuer or the guarantor, if any, has an external long-term rating of at least A− or higher.

While guarantees can be used to override issuer ratings, there is some ambiguity in the official text with respect to whether they can also be used to override issue ratings (see ECB 2006/12, p. 43). However, according to email correspondence from the ECB to my research team, the correct interpretation of the Guidelines is that "guarantor ratings could not have overridden issue ratings." Nevertheless, I present two examples in Section 6.9 where issue ratings appear to be overridden. At any rate, the ambiguity was cleared up in 2013, when the official text explicitly says that guarantor ratings cannot override issue ratings.[5]

For some collateral, it may be the case that neither the issue, issuer, nor guarantor has an external rating (from one of the approved agencies). In this case, one looks closer at the issuer or the guarantor. If one of these is a local or regional government, or a public sector entity, the relevant supervisory authority has the power to determine the rating of the issue. But it cannot exceed the external rating of the central government. Thus, for high credit standards to be met at a date in the subperiod studied here, the central government would need at least one external rating of A− or higher. If the issuer or guarantor is a non-financial corporation, the rating is determined by in-house, NCB, or third-party rating models that have been approved by the relevant supervisory authority. In other words, if no rating exists, banks can use their own models to determine whether the collateral meets with the required high credit standards. Thus, the more precise rules for the minimum rating requirement introduced with

---

[4] Certain conditions with respect to the guarantee must also be met, see ECB (2006/12) and the other references in Table 6.1 for details.
[5] See Table 6.1, Panel E, Baseline rule 1(c).

the single list still provide potentially large discretion to the NCBs and national supervisory authorities. This also means that the public list of eligible securities is incomplete because it does not include the securities that are eligible under these "private eligibility" rules.

Finally, an update from November 2007 says that UCITS-compliant covered bonds are exempt from the normal ratings rules only if issued before January 1, 2008.

October 25, 2008, to December 31, 2010. Table 6.1, Panel C (Covers Haircut Table 5.2 period)

The basic procedure for determining the rating of collateral for the purpose of the Eurosystem's collateral framework is the same as in Panel B. However, as a part of the Temporary framework in force from October 25, 2008, the minimum rating requirement is reduced from A– to "a 'BBB–' equivalent credit assessment."[6] The official document is not entirely clear as to precisely what a "BBB– equivalent credit assessment" means. But taken in context, it appears to refer to the equivalent of a long-term rating of BBB– (on the S&P scale).

This relaxation in rating standards is applied to all collateral except for asset-backed securities.[7] These still need a rating of A– or higher.

The rules for asset-backed securities are subsequently updated in various steps. From March 1, 2009, onward, high credit standards for ABSs require these to have a AAA long-term rating at issuance (but only A– thereafter). A year later, the ECB introduced the second-highest rating rule for ABSs, whereby it is the second highest rating that counts, rather than the highest as for other marketable assets. Thus, from March 1, 2010, ABSs are required to have at least two

---

[6] ECB (2008/11, p. 18).

[7] The ratings rules in Table 6.1 also apply to the covered bond and ABS purchase programs listed in Table 3.1, with minor exceptions. In the first covered bond purchase program, starting in July 2009, the issue's first-best rating by an approved rating agency had to be at least AA. The other programs were more consistent with the rules in Table 6.1. For details, see ECB (2009/16), ECB (2011/17), ECB (2014/40), and ECB (2014/45) for the three covered bond and the ABS purchase programs, respectively.

AAA long-term ratings at issuance and at least two A− ratings thereafter. From October 10, 2010, short-term ratings can substitute for long-term ratings to establish the AAA requirement at issuance.

A subtle but highly significant update to the rating rules in this period is the inclusion of Dominion Bond Rating Services (DBRS) in the set of acceptable rating agencies from February 1, 2009. This can be seen as an implicit weakening of collateral standards, since only the highest rating matters with respect to determining high credit standards.[8] The likelihood of getting one A− (or higher) rating is expected to be larger with four rating agencies to draw from than with three.[9] Furthermore, as will be documented later in this chapter, DBRS has proved to have a material impact on collateral values because its ratings are often higher than those of the other agencies, especially when it makes a difference.

From the documents that are available on the ECB's webpage or otherwise in the public domain, there is some uncertainty with respect to the exact date when DBRS was included among the official rating agencies within the Eurosystem's collateral framework. For example, according to ECB (2007):

> On 19 October 2007 the Governing Council decided to accept the rating agency Dominion Bond Rating Service (DBRS) as a new external credit assessment institution (ECAI) source for the purposes of the Eurosystem credit assessment framework ... The go-live [date] of DBRS eligibility will immediately follow the finalization of the necessary adaptations in the relevant IT infrastructure. The go-live date will be pre-announced on the ECB's website, most likely by the beginning of 2008.

Press releases from DBRS repeat this information, yet the promised press release from the ECB regarding the go-live date is not available

---

[8] Except for ABSs after March 1, 2010, as just noted in the paragraph above.

[9] For example, if the ratings were distributed around some mean with independent errors. Also, there is evidence that rating agencies compete by catering to issuers by giving them inflated ratings (Griffin, Nickerson, and Tang 2013). We might expect the catering inflation effect to be increasing in the number of competitors (thinking in terms of Cournot oligopoly).

anywhere. After extensive email correspondence and phone conversations with the ECB's legal department as well as with DBRS's press office, the ECB eventually informed my research team via email:

> Following your inquiry of 6 May 2015, [we] would like to inform you that in February 2009, the Eurosystem list of accepted ECAIs was expanded by a fourth agency: Dominion Bond Rating Service (DBRS). DBRS itself states in its press release of 20.12.2007 that it has been accepted as an ECAI since 1 January 2008. However, legally, DBRS appeared as an accepted ECAI for the first time in the text of Guideline ECB/2008/13, of 23 October 2008, which came into force on 1 February 2009. Hence, it is as of 1 February 2009 that DBRS has been accepted, legally and practically, as an ECAI by the Eurosystem.

In addition to establishing the exact date when DBRS was included among the approved rating agencies, this also illustrates the importance of the ECB Guidelines published in the *Official Journal*.

January 1, 2011, to September 30, 2013. Table 6.1, Panel D (Covers Haircut Table 5.3 period)
The baseline procedure for determining collateral ratings for the purpose of the collateral framework continues to follow the procedure laid out in Panel B. The lower rating standards introduced in Panel C are adopted into the General framework in a Guideline that also introduces the terminology "harmonised rating scale" (ECB 2010/13). This scale defines credit quality, or standards, in terms of three steps. These are already referred to in Table 5.3 and are defined primarily in terms of long-term ratings from the four accepted rating agencies, as shown in Exhibit 6.1.[10]

---

[10] The notion of "credit quality steps" is initially introduced in ECB (2006/12). Step 3 is introduced into the General framework as of January 1, 2011 (ECB 2010/13). Further details are in Table 6.1 and the Appendix to this book.

Exhibit 6.1 Harmonized rating scale: long-term ratings per step.

	S&P and Fitch	Moody's	DBRS
Step 1	AAA to AA−	Aaa to Aa3	AAA to AAL
Step 2	A+ to A−	A1 to A3	AH to AL
Step 3	BBB+ to BBB−	Baa1 to Baa3	BBBH to BBB

Each step may also include short-term ratings. These are of less practical importance than the long-term ratings and may vary over time. As revealed by the documentation in the *Official Journal*, the baseline rule for high credit standards after January 1, 2011, is, at a minimum, one long-term rating in Step 3 or better (for marketable assets except ABSs).

A point to note here is that the lowest acceptable rating from DBRS (BBB) is one notch higher than the lowest acceptable ratings of the three other rating agencies. This is suggestive of ratings by DBRS being viewed as not quite equal to the ratings of the other agencies. This seemingly innocuous detail turns out to play an interesting role with respect to how the ECB dealt with the credit standards of Portuguese government securities when Portugal was emerging from its exempt status in August 2014 (see Sections 6.2 and 6.5).

For ABSs, the second-highest rule continues to apply. They also continue to face stricter requirements than other marketable assets in terms of the letter rating required for high credit standards. However, the rules for ABSs established in Panel C are gradually weakened over time. In December 2011, the minimum rating requirement at issuance is reduced to at least two long-term ratings of A− or better (from one AAA and one A− before). This is eventually reduced to two long-term ratings in Step 3 or better, but with sufficiently high short-term ratings being able to substitute for this requirement.[11]

---

[11] As described in Table 6.1, Panel C, Update 3.

October 1, 2013, to January 31, 2015.[12] *Table 6.1, Panel E (Covers Haircut Table 5.4 period)*

Panel E sees significant modifications to the basic procedure used to establish high credit standards, if not the minimum ratings threshold itself, which remains at Step 3. It is still long-term ratings that matter, with a couple of exceptions discussed below.

As of October 1, 2013, the rating of the programme/issuance series is introduced as one of the items to consider when determining the rating of collateral in the Eurosystem's collateral framework. In particular, "[a]t least one credit assessment from an accepted [rating agency] for either the issue or, in the absence of an issue rating from the same [rating agency], the programme/issuance series under which the asset is issued, must comply with the Eurosystem's credit quality threshold [of a long-term rating in Step 3, or better]" (ECB 2013/35, p. 8).

As before, issuer and guarantor ratings can also be considered. Furthermore, it is now unambiguously clear that guarantees cannot be used to override issue (or programme/issuance series) ratings.[13] If these are below the Step 3 level, guarantees cannot be used to lift the collateral up to eligible status. Issuer or guarantor ratings are only considered if issue or programme/series ratings from one of the four accepted rating agencies do not exist. Short-term ratings for the issuer can be used instead of long-term ratings if the original maturity of the collateral is 390 days or less. Guarantees can still override issuer ratings.

From December 15, 2014, only issuer or guarantor ratings matter for collateral issued by central governments, regional or local governments, agencies (except agency-issued covered bonds), and

---

[12] January 31, 2015, simply represents the end date of this study. The validity of the rating rules in Table 6.1, Panel E stretches beyond this date. In particular, ECB (2014/60) introduces new rules that apply from May 1, 2015. These appear to blur the distinction between long- and short-term ratings.

[13] See Table 6.1, Panel E, Baseline rule 1(c). There is some lack of clarity in the official documentation whether this no-override of issue ratings clause was already in place. It is therefore listed in Table 6.1 as a clarification.

supranational institutions. This final clause eliminates situations where similar bonds issued by the same sovereign have different ratings and therefore different haircuts.

Finally, as of April 1, 2014, the lower limit of the Step 3 range for DBRS is reduced from BBB by the ECB to BBBL. The significance of this change relates to Portuguese exemptions.

6.2 EXEMPTIONS

In relation to the sovereign debt crisis in the euro area, Ireland, Portugal, Greece, and Cyprus received exemptions from the normal rating rules. In particular, each of these countries received suspensions of the minimum requirement for credit quality thresholds for marketable debt instruments issued or guaranteed by their governments. These exemptions are all in the Temporary framework and are tied to Economic Adjustment Programmes (EAPs) organized by the Troika.[14] Financial bailout support came from a variety of sources, including the EU and the IMF. EU funding was largely channeled through the European Financial Stabilisation Mechanism (EFSM), the European Financial Stability Facility (EFSF), and the European Stability Mechanism (ESM).[15]

Ireland and Portugal were under EAPs from December 2010 to December 2013 and from May 2011 to May 2014, respectively.[16]

---

[14] The initial relevant Temporary framework documents are ECB (2010/3) for Greece, ECB (2011/4) for Ireland, ECB (2011/10) for Portugal, and ECB (2013/13) for Cyprus. These were subsequently updated as events unfolded.

[15] See the webpages of the European Commission and the IMF for further details. European Commission: http://ec.europa.eu/economy_finance/assistance_eu_ms /index_en.htm; IMF: www.imf.org/external/np/exr/facts/europe.htm.

[16] The details of the adjustment programs have changed over time. For Ireland, see European Commission (February 2011, Box 4, p. 18) for a timeline of events in 2010, and European Commission (June 2014) for a post-program analysis and more details on Ireland's exit of the program. For Portugal, see European Commission (June 2011, Box 4, p. 15) for a timeline of events in 2011, and European Commission (April 2014) for a post-program analysis and more details on Portugal's exit of the program. A more complete list of documents and further links related to the EAPs for Ireland and Portugal can be found on the webpage of the European Commission under http://ec.europa.eu/economy_finance/assistance_eu_ms/index_en.htm and on the IMF webpage under www.imf.org/external/np/exr/facts/europe.htm.

They had exempt status from April 1, 2011, to April 1, 2014 (Ireland), and July 7, 2011, to August 20, 2014 (Portugal). Greece and Cyprus were still under EAPs as of January 2015.[17]

The case of Portugal is especially interesting because it would not have been possible for it to emerge from its exempt status without a change to the official rating rules. In particular, since January 2012, when S&P and DBRS downgraded Portugal from BBB− to BB and BBB to BBBL, respectively, all agencies have rated Portugal below Step 3.[18] Its highest rating since then has been a steady BBBL from DBRS. This is "almost" Step 3, since it corresponds to a BBB− by S&P on a simple notch count basis. Reducing the Step 3 lower limit for DBRS by one notch, from BBB to BBBL, was all that was needed to allow Portugal to obtain non-exempt status. As luck would have it, this is exactly what the ECB did on March 12, 2014, effective from April 1, 2014 (ECB 2014/10 and 2014/12). Thus, Portugal's emergence from exempt status was made possible by an active collateral policy decision by the ECB. This is one example as to how collateral policy can be used to support, or, perhaps more correctly in this case, indirectly prolong a bailout to a relatively weak sovereign.

---

[17] Greece was essentially under two EAPs. The first one was meant to last from May 2010 to June 2013, while the second one is meant to cover the periods 2012 to 2014 (EFSF) and March 2012 to March 2016 (IMF) (see European Commission, May 2010, Box 3, pp. 8–9, for more details on the timeline of events in 2010, and European Commission, March 2012, p. 4, for a short summary on who disburses how much over which time period). A more complete list of documents and further links related to the two EAPs for Greece can be found on the webpages of the European Commission under http://ec.europa.eu/economy_finance/assistance _eu_ms/greek_loan_facility/index_en.htm and the IMF under www.imf.org/ external/np/exr/facts/europe.htm. For Cyprus, the EAP covers the period 2013 to 2016 (European Commission, May 2013, p. 7). See European Commission (May 2013, Box 5, pp. 37–39) for the exact details on the timeline of events in 2013. A more complete list of documents and further links related to the EAP for Cyprus can be found on the webpage of the European Commission under http://ec.europa.eu/economy_finance/assistance_eu_ms/cyprus/index_en.htm or the IMF under www.imf.org/external/np/exr/facts/europe.htm.
[18] At least until January 2015, which is the last time this was checked for the purpose of this book.

Exemptions were temporarily suspended at various points in time for Greece and Cyprus when these countries took action that in the view of the Troika threatened collateral values. Greece was initially granted exempt status on May 6, 2010 (ECB 2010/3). But when it "decided to launch a debt exchange offer in the context of private sector involvement to holders of marketable debt instruments issued by the Greek Government" (ECB 2012/2), Greece was temporarily suspended from its exempt status over the period February 28 to March 7, 2012. As explained in ECB (2012/2), the reason for the suspension was that "[t]he adequacy as collateral for Eurosystem operations of the marketable debt instruments issued by the Greek Government, or issued by entities established in Greece and fully guaranteed by the Greek Government, has been further negatively affected by such decision of [Greece]" (ECB 2012/2).[19] Greece also lost its exempt status over the period July 25 to December 20, 2012 (ECB 2012/14 and 2012/32). When this was reintroduced on December 21, 2012, it was accompanied by an extraordinary haircut schedule, specifying larger than normal haircuts (see Table 5.5 and the discussion in Chapter 5).

With respect to Cyprus, on June 27, 2013, the Cypriot authorities announced they would launch a voluntary debt exchange of Cypriot sovereign bonds (European Commission, June 2013). As a result, Cyprus temporarily lost its exempt status (ECB 2013/21) on June 28, 2013. The reason was the same as in the Greek case, namely that "[t]he adequacy as collateral for Eurosystem operations of the marketable debt instruments issued or fully guaranteed by the Republic of Cyprus has been further negatively affected by the decision to launch a debt management exercise" (ECB 2013/21). From July 5, 2013, onward, Cyprus regained its exempt status (ECB 2013/22) on the same terms as before. Exemptions from standard eligibility criteria, albeit with conditions attached, are thus a regular feature of the Eurosystem's collateral framework.

---

[19] See also ECB (2012/3).

6.3 RATINGS AND HAIRCUTS: TWO EXAMPLES

This section provides two examples that illustrate how the rating rules work and the implications for haircuts. The two examples also illustrate cross-collateral inconsistencies. The second example is used to examine the impact of haircuts on yields. Both examples are based on the public list of eligible collateral published on March 21, 2014. But the examples are not particular to this date. They describe situations that persisted over long time periods.

Example 6.1 Two Spanish government bonds, March 21, 2014.

ISIN	Maturity	Issue rating	Country rating	Haircut	Applied rating category
ES0000011975	January 31, 2023	None	A− (DBRS)	4%	AAA to A−
ES0000011926	January 31, 2018	BBB (Fitch)	A− (DBRS)	10%	BBB+ to BBB−

Ratings are from Bloomberg and translated into the S&P scale.

The rather bizarre situation here is that the longer-dated Spanish bond, ISIN ES0000011975, has a lower haircut. This has to do with the ratings rules.

The longer-dated bond is not rated by any of the approved agencies. Spain's ratings by Fitch, S&P, and Moody's were all in the BBB+ to BBB− range. However, DBRS gave Spain a rating of AL (or A(low)), equivalent to A− on the S&P scale. Since only the highest rating matters, the longer-dated bond gets an A− "Eurosystem rating" and, commensurate with its residual maturity, a haircut of 4 percent.

In contrast, the shorter-dated bond, ISIN ES0000011926, is rated BBB by Fitch. This is its only external rating and, according to the rating rules, takes precedence over the issuer rating. The bond therefore gets a haircut of 10 percent, commensurate with this rating and the bond's residual maturity.

If Fitch had also rated the longer-dated bond, it would presumably have given this a BBB rating as well, since this was also Fitch's rating of Spain. The same goes for Moody's and S&P, which rated Spain Baa2 (BBB) and BBB−, respectively. Since the longer-dated bond was not rated by any of these agencies and DBRS rated Spain A−, holders of the longer-dated and more risky bond got 6 percent more financing from the Eurosystem than holders of the shorter-dated bond.

Note that while the haircuts in this example are consistent with the rating rules described in Table 6.1 and the haircut rules in Table 5.4, the haircuts I have reported are not inferred from these tables. They are taken directly from the ECB's public list of eligible collateral published on March 21, 2014.

The sovereign bond cross-collateral inconsistency illustrated in Example 6.1 is no longer possible because of the new rule in December 2014 that issue ratings do not count, with respect to determining haircuts, for sovereign bonds (Table 6.1, Panel E, Update 2). This also applies to the example below. However, cross-collateral inconsistencies can still arise for other collateral that is similar but, for some reason or another, rated by different agencies.

The second example is ideal for examining the potential effects of haircuts on yields. It involves two inflation-linked Italian government bonds with identical maturity dates (September 15, 2014). One of these, IT0003625909, carries a 2.15 percent inflation-linked coupon with semi-annual payments and the other, IT0003631212, is a zero-coupon bond (strip). The last coupon prior to maturity on IT0003625909 was on March 15, 2014. After this date, both bonds are in essence bullet bonds, though a small fraction of the total payment at maturity from IT0003625909 is due to the final coupon of 1.075 percent. The other details of the two bonds are as follows:

Example 6.2 Two Italian government bonds, March 21, 2014.

ISIN	Maturity	Issue rating	Country rating	Haircut	Applied rating category
IT0003625909	September 15, 2014	A− (DBRS)	A− (DBRS)	0.5%	AAA to A−
IT0003631212	September 15, 2014	BBB+ (Fitch)	A− (DBRS)	6%	BBB+ to BBB−

Ratings are from Bloomberg and translated into the S&P scale.

Although the bonds are in essence identical, there is a large difference in their haircuts, as determined by the Eurosystem's collateral framework. Again, this has to do with the rating agencies.
IT0003625909 is rated A− by DBRS and BBB+ by Fitch. The rules
say that the highest rating applies and thus the bond gets a haircut
of 0.5 percent. IT0003631212 is only rated by Fitch, and, consistent with the rating of the other bond and Fitch's rating of Italy,
Fitch rates IT0003631212 at BBB+. It therefore gets a haircut of
6 percent. Again, these haircuts are as reported in the ECB's official eligible collateral list. They are also consistent with the rating
and haircut rules described in the tables above. The point is that
these rules can lead to essentially arbitrary inconsistencies in haircuts across securities. IT0003625909 can be almost fully refinanced
from the ECB, while only 94 percent of IT0003631212 can be
refinanced.

We might expect that haircuts affect market prices because a
smaller haircut means that a larger fraction of an investment can
be funded, in this case directly from the Eurosystem. The case of
the two Italian bonds considered here offers a near-perfect setting
to examine this hypothesis since they are essentially identical, once
the coupon on March 15, 2014, has been paid. This is especially so
because the haircuts are determined exogenously within the collateral framework. Thus, we would expect the yield of IT0003631212,
which has the higher haircut, to be larger than that of IT0003625909.
To investigate this, the yields of these two bonds over the time
period March 18, 2014, to May 27, 2014, were downloaded from
Bloomberg. Over this time period, there were forty-eight days with
price (and yield) data for both bonds. Taking real yields (under simple compounding) of the two securities from Bloomberg, I get an
average difference (IT0003631212 − IT0003625909) in these of 75.4
basis points (bp), with a standard error of 6.8 bp. This is a large
difference, especially benchmarked against other rates over that
period. For example, three-month and six-month Euribor were in
the range 30.9 to 34.7 bp and 40.0 to 44.4 bp, respectively, over

the same time period.[20] This supports the hypothesis that haircuts affect market yields and, in particular, that yields increase in haircuts.[21]

An alternative hypothesis is that the higher-rated bond is priced higher, not because it has a lower haircut, but because the higher rating makes it more attractive to investors, independent of the effect the rating has on the haircut. This is hard to justify since there is no apparent difference in risk between the two bonds and since all agencies' ratings of Italy are common knowledge.

6.4 FUNDAMENTAL LIQUIDITY

That Eurosystem haircuts affect yields is by itself important. It not only implies that the collateral framework can affect market prices but also speaks directly to what it means for an asset to be "more liquid." We can think of a relatively low haircut as meaning that the security has relatively high *fundamental liquidity*, since a lower haircut means that it can be converted to a higher quantity of central bank money (liquidity) in a direct repo with the central bank. The point illustrated by the second example above is then that a higher fundamental liquidity translates into a higher price, equivalently lower yield. Financial economists typically think of the liquidity of a security as being captured by the "ease" with which it can be converted into "cash." The hypothesis I propose here is that a higher fundamental level of liquidity (lower haircut or favored in some other way in transactions with the central bank) translates not only into a higher market price but also into a higher measured level of liquidity, and lower liquidity risk, in the market. Examining this in more generality would be a very interesting exercise.

---

[20] Eonia swap rates were even lower, ranging from 11.4 to 19.7 bp and 8.5 to 19.2 bp for the three- and six-month maturities, respectively. Euribor and Eonia swap rates are taken from www.euribor.org.

[21] Note that the coupon bond, IT0003625909, trades on an exchange, whereas IT0003631212 does not. This might make it relatively more liquid, resulting in a relatively lower yield. However, it is difficult to see how this could account for as much as 75 bp.

6.5 SOVEREIGN RATINGS AND THE IMPACT OF DBRS

This section compares the ratings of sovereigns by the four official rating agencies. DBRS was seen to be instrumental in the two examples in the previous section. In this section, I document the pivotal role DBRS frequently plays with respect to sovereign ratings. The evidence is in Table 6.2. This gives the year-end long-term rating for each eurozone member state by each of the four accepted rating agencies over the time period 2004 to 2014, as well as at the end of June 2014.[22] All ratings are given numerical values as follows: A− (Fitch and S&P) is 0, and every notch above (below) it increases (decreases) the value by one. For Moody's and DBRS, the equivalents of A− are A3 and AL, respectively. A− is chosen as the benchmark zero value since a rating of A− or higher puts the country into the upper Eurosystem rating category that results in the lowest haircuts, as seen in Tables 5.1 to 5.4 and discussed in the examples in Section 6.3. The highest score is thus a 6, representing AAA on the S&P scale. Further details of the scoring system, along with the rating scales of the four agencies, can be found in the Appendix to this chapter.

The impact of each rating agency can be seen by looking at the frequency of pivotal ratings. By this I mean a rating that changes the rating category of the sovereign, given the other ratings. From the haircut tables (Tables 5.1 to 5.4), there are three rating categories: scores of 0 (A−) or higher, scores from −1 (BBB+) to −3 (BBB−), and scores below −3. Thus, a pivotal rating (for a country-year) is the case where (i) one rating is 0 or higher and the other ratings are below 0, or (ii) the case where one rating is in the range −1 to −3 and the others are below −3. The first scenario is especially important because a sovereign rating of A− or higher means that a sovereign can provide guarantees that result in the lowest possible haircuts, given the residual maturity and coupon of the collateral in question.

---

[22] The ratings history has been taken from Bloomberg and cross-referenced by documentation from each rating agency's webpage. DBRS gave its first euro-area sovereign ratings in 2010.

Table 6.2 *Ratings for euro-area countries by year and rating agency*

	2004	2005	2006	2007	2008	2009	2010	2011	2012	2013	6/2014	12/2014	Pivotal A−	Pivotal BBB−
Austria (AT)														
S&P	6	6	6	6	6	6	6	6	5	5	5	5		
Fitch	6	6	6	6	6	6	6	6	6	6	6	6		
Moody's	6	6	6	6	6	6	6	6	6	6	6	6		
DBRS	–	–	–	–	–	–	–	6	6	6	6	6		
Belgium (BE)														
S&P	5	5	5	5	5	5	5	4	4	4	4	4		
Fitch	4	4	5	5	5	5	5	5	4	4	4	4		
Moody's	5	5	5	5	5	5	5	3	3	3	3	3		
DBRS	–	–	–	–	–	–	–	5	5	5	5	5		
Finland (FI)														
S&P	6	6	6	6	6	6	6	6	6	6	6	5		
Fitch	6	6	6	6	6	6	6	6	6	6	6	6		
Moody's	6	6	6	6	6	6	6	6	6	6	6	6		
DBRS	–	–	–	–	–	–	–	–	6	6	6	6		
France (FR)														
S&P	6	6	6	6	6	6	6	6	5	4	4	4		
Fitch	6	6	6	6	6	6	6	6	6	5	5	4		
Moody's	6	6	6	6	6	6	6	6	5	5	5	5		
DBRS	–	–	–	–	–	–	–	6	6	6	6	6		
Germany (DE)														
S&P	6	6	6	6	6	6	6	6	6	6	6	6		
Fitch	6	6	6	6	6	6	6	6	6	6	6	6		
Moody's	6	6	6	6	6	6	6	6	6	6	6	6		
DBRS	–	–	–	–	–	–	–	6	6	6	6	6		

Ireland (IE)											
S&P	6	6	6	6	4	1	-1	-1	-1	0	1
Fitch	6	6	6	6	3	-1	-1	-1	-1	-1	0
Moody's	6	6	6	6	5	-1	-4	-4	-4	-1	-1
DBRS	–	–	–	–	–	2	0*	0*	0*	0	0 DBRS 4/2011–5/2014[1]
Italy (IT)											
S&P	3	2	2	2	2	2	1	-1	-2	-2	-3
Fitch	4	3	3	3	3	3	2	0	-1	-1	-1
Moody's	4	4	4	4	4	4	1	-2	-2	-2	-2
DBRS	–	–	–	–	–	–	2	1	0*	0*	0* DBRS 3/2013–12/2014
Luxembourg (LU)											
S&P	6	6	6	6	6	6	6	6	6	6	6
Fitch	6	6	6	6	6	6	6	6	6	6	6
Moody's	6	6	6	6	6	6	6	6	6	6	6
DBRS	–	–	–	–	–	–	–	–	–	–	–
Netherlands (NL)											
S&P	6	6	6	6	6	6	6	6	5	5	5
Fitch	6	6	6	6	6	6	6	6	5	5	6
Moody's	6	6	6	6	6	6	6	6	6	6	6
DBRS	–	–	–	–	–	–	–	6	6	6	6

Table 6.2 *(cont.)*

	2004	2005	2006	2007	2008	2009	2010	2011	2012	2013	6/2014	12/2014	Pivotal A−	Pivotal BBB−
Portugal (PT)														
S&P	4	3	3	3	3	2	0	−3	−5	−5	−5	−5		
Fitch	4	4	4	4	4	4	2	−4	–	–	–	–		
Moody's	4	4	4	4	4	4	2	−5	−6	−6	−5	−4		
DBRS	–	–	–	–	–	–	0	−2	−3	−3	−3†	−3†	DBRS 4/2014–12/2014[1]	
Spain (ES)														
S&P	6	6	6	6	6	5	4	3	−3	−3	−2	−2		
Fitch	6	6	6	6	6	6	5	3	−2	−2	−1	−1		
Moody's	6	6	6	6	6	6	5	2	−3	−3	−2	−2		
DBRS	–	–	–	–	–	–	4	3	0*	0*	0*	0*	DBRS 6/2012–12/2014	
Greece (GR)														
S&P	1	1	1	1	1	−1	−4	−13	−9	−9	−9	−8		
Fitch	1	1	1	1	1	−1	−3†	−11	−11	−9	−8	−8		Fitch 6/2010–12/2010[1]
Moody's	2	2	2	2	2	1*	−4	−13	−14	−12	−12	−10	Moody's 12/2009–5/2010	
DBRS	–	–	–	–	–	–	–	–	–	−10	−10	−8		
Slovenia (SI)														
S&P	4	4	4	4	4	4	4	3	1	0*	0*	0*	S&P 5/2013–12/2014	

Fitch	4	4	4	4	4	4	4	3	0	−1	−1	−1
Moody's	3	3	4	4	4	4	4	2	−2	−4	−4	−4
DBRS	–	–	–	–	–	–	–	–	–	–	–	–
Cyprus (CY)												
S&P	1	1	1	1	2	2	1	−2	−10	−9	−8	−7
Fitch	4	4	3	3	3	3	3	−2	−6	−11	−9	−9
Moody's	1	1	2	3	3	3	3	−3	−9	−12	−12	−9
DBRS	–	–	–	–	–	–	–	–	–	−11	−9	−9
Malta (MT)												
S&P	2	1	1	1	1	1	1	1	0	−1	−1	−1
Fitch	3	3	2	2	2	2	2	2	2	1	1	1
Moody's	0	0	1	2	2	2	2	1	0	0	0	0
DBRS	–	–	–	–	–	–	–	–	–	–	–	–
Slovakia (SK)												
S&P	0	1	1	2	2	2	2	2	1	1	1	1
Fitch	2	2	2	2	2	2	2	2	2	2	2	2
Moody's	0	1	2	2	2	2	2	2	1	1	1	1
DBRS	–	–	–	–	–	–	–	–	–	–	–	–
Estonia (EE)												
S&P	1	1	1	1	1	0	0	3	3	3	3	3
Fitch	2	2	2	2	1	0	1	2	2	2	2	2
Moody's	2	2	2	2	2	2	2	2	2	2	2	2
DBRS	–	–	–	–	–	–	–	–	–	–	–	–

Table 6.2 (cont.)

	2004	2005	2006	2007	2008	2009	2010	2011	2012	2013	6/2014	12/2014	Pivotal A−	Pivotal BBB−
Latvia (LV)														
S&P	0	0	0	−1	−3	−5	−4	−4	−2	−1	0	0		
Fitch	1	1	1	0	−2	−3	−3	−2	−1	−1	0	0		
Moody's	–	–	1	1	0*	−3	−3	−3	−3	−2	−1	−1	Moody's 10/2008–12/2008	
DBRS	–	–	–	–	–	–	–	–	–	–	–	–		

Table 6.2 reports the year-end ratings of all eurozone countries from 2004 to 2014. All ratings from officially accepted rating agencies are reported. These are Standard and Poor's (S&P), Moody's, Fitch, and Dominion Bond Rating Services (DBRS). DBRS became an accepted rating agency on February 1, 2009. The table reports numerical values for the actual ratings according to the following scheme: A− (Fitch and S&P) gets a score of 0, and every notch above (below) it increases (decreases) the value by one. For Moody's and DBRS, the equivalents of A− are A3 and AL (or A(low)), respectively. Thus, a rating from S&P or Fitch of BBB−, for example, results in a numerical value of −3. For each rating agency, the highest score is 6 (equivalent to AAA on the S&P scale). A− is chosen as the benchmark zero value since a rating of A− or higher puts the country into rating category 1 (A− or higher, or Step 1 or 2) and thus results in lower haircuts, as seen in Tables 5.1 to 5.4. The two far right columns report on end-of-month pivotal ratings. A rating agency is pivotal for a given country on a given date if the country's rating would fall into a lower rating category without the rating of the agency in question. A rating that is pivotal to put a country in rating category 1, alternatively 2, is referred to as Pivotal A−, alternatively BBB−. Recall that the ECB uses the highest rating to assign the rating category. Pivotal A−, alternatively BBB−, ratings are indicated by boldface red and an asterisk, *, alternatively, boldface blue and a dagger, †. Data on ratings are from Bloomberg and cross checked by information on each rating agency's webpage: S&P: www.standardandpoors.com/ Fitch: www.fitchratings.com/ Moody's: www.moodys.com/ DBRS: www.dbrs.com/.

Note: [1] Some of the pivotal ratings for Ireland, Portugal, and Greece occurred when these countries had exempt status. Haircuts in these cases were commensurate with the ratings. See the text for discussion.

There is one exception to the general rule described in the paragraph above for determining pivotal ratings. As discussed in Section 6.1, the minimum threshold for DBRS in terms of "rating notches" was higher than for the other agencies until April 1, 2014. In particular, before that time, the lowest acceptable rating from DBRS was BBB, equivalent to −2 in my ratings-score system. It became BBBL, or −3, from that date onward. Thus, until April 1, 2014, a "lower" pivotal rating for DBRS is −2, with −4 or smaller from the other agencies. But this scenario has hardly ever occurred.[23]

Table 6.2 shows that DBRS has been pivotal in providing central governments with an A− rating for three countries, Italy (2013–2014), Spain (2012–2014), and Ireland (2011–5/2014), for a combined total of approximately eight country-years. DBRS is also pivotal in providing Portugal with a BBB− to BBB+ rating in 2014.[24]

No rating agency besides DBRS is pivotal in cases where all four rating agencies provide a rating. However, Moody's is pivotal in placing Greece in rating category 1 (with an A2 rating) in 2009 and Latvia in 2008, before the entry of DBRS. S&P is pivotal in giving Slovenia an A− rating in 2013 and 2014 (not rated by DBRS). Fitch is pivotal in placing Greece in rating category 2 (with a rating of BBB−) in 2010, if we ignore Greece's exempt status at that time. So, while there are instances where all agencies are pivotal, DBRS has by far the highest frequency of being pivotal.

Caution should arguably be exercised with respect to labeling an agency as being pivotal for a country that is exempt from the standard rating rules. This relates to Ireland, Portugal, and Greece, as indicated in Table 6.2. For example, DBRS is labeled as being pivotal for Portugal on June 2014, because of its rating score of −3. However,

---

[23] It never occurred at the end of any month over the period sampled in Table 6.2. It occurred once, however, over a two-week period in January 2012, until DBRS downgraded Portugal from BBB (−2) to BBBL (−3) on the 30th of that month. I have not found other examples.

[24] Year-end 2014 is the last entry in Table 6.2. However, DBRS's pivotal role with respect to the ratings for Spain, Italy, and Portugal extended to the end of January 2015, which is the last time I checked for the purpose of this book. S&P upgraded Ireland to A− on June 6, 2014, making DBRS no longer pivotal as of that date.

Portugal was exempt at that time (until August 20, 2014). Ireland had exempt status for the duration of the period for which DBRS is listed in the table as giving Ireland a pivotal A— rating (score of 0). Greece was exempt during the period in 2010 when Fitch is indicated as being pivotal with a BBB— (score, 3) rating. I have therefore taken a closer look at the haircuts received by these countries' bonds while exempt. The evidence is that they received haircuts commensurate with the indicated pivotal ratings, with a few individual exceptions.[25] Thus, the pivotal ratings indicated for Ireland, Portugal, and Greece in Table 6.2 are appropriate.

With respect to exemptions and ratings, Portugal is an especially interesting case, as noted in Section 6.2. During most of its time as exempt, Portugal's highest rating was a BBBL from DBRS. While this was not in rating category 2 (Step 3) before April 2014, Portuguese sovereign paper nevertheless received haircuts commensurate with this rating category. This suggests that DBRS's BBBL rating of Portugal helped secure the standard rating category 2 haircuts for Portuguese sovereign bonds, even before the ECB reduced its minimum acceptable rating from DBRS to BBBL in April 2014. In this sense, DBRS could even be said to have been pivotal for Portugal from January 2012 onward, although it is not labeled as such in Table 6.2.

Table 6.3 compares the average scores of the rating agencies at year-end 2011 to 2014 and June 2014, across countries rated by all four agencies.[26] Panel A presents the average yearly scores of DBRS. At mid-year and year-end 2014, the average DBRS rating of 1.45 and 1.64, respectively, is approximately two notches below that at the end of 2011 (3.56). Panel B compares the average DBRS ratings to those of the other agencies. DBRS ratings are statistically significantly higher than those of Moody's at every year-end and June 2014, those of Fitch on three of the five sample dates, and those of S&P on all dates

---

[25] Some Irish bonds had haircuts commensurate with a BBB rating rather than DBRS's A—, perhaps due to lower issue ratings by other agencies.

[26] The year 2010 is not included because DBRS rated only three countries that year (see Table 6.2).

Table 6.3 *Yearly average DBRS ratings and rating differentials to other agencies*

	2011	2012	2013	6/2014	12/2014
Number of countries	9	9	11	11	11
Panel A: Average rating across countries (A– = 0)					
DBRS	3.56	4.00	1.27	1.45	1.64
Panel B: Average rating differentials across countries (DBRS – alternative agency)					
S&P	0.44^b	1.00^b	0.73	0.64^c	0.73
	(0.18)	(0.33)	(0.43)	(0.34)	(0.43)
Fitch	0.33	0.56^c	0.45^c	0.27	0.45^c
	(0.24)	(0.24)	(0.25)	(0.27)	(0.21)
Moody's	1.22^c	1.44^b	1.36^a	1.18^a	0.91^b
	(0.49)	(0.53)	(0.41)	(0.33)	(0.28)
Panel C: Number of pivotal ratings					
DBRS	1	1	3	2^1	2
All others	0	0	0	0	0

Panel A of this table reports the average rating of DBRS for a given year across countries for which all four rating agencies provided ratings in that year (see Table 6.2). Using the same set of countries, Panel B provides the averages and standard errors of the differential between the ratings of DBRS and the three other agencies (DBRS – alternative agency). Ratings are standardized according to the scheme in Table 6.2 whereby A– (Fitch and S&P) gets a score of 0, and every notch above (below) it increases (decreases) the value by one. For Moody's and DBRS, the equivalents of A– are A3 and AL (or A(low)), respectively. Panel C summarizes pivotal ratings for a given year across countries for which all four rating agencies provided ratings in that year. Statistical significance at the 1, 5, and 10 percent level is indicated by *a*, *b*, and *c* respectively.

Note: [1] S&P upgraded Ireland on June 6, 2014.

except year-end 2013 and 2014. Interestingly, despite DBRS ratings only being statistically different on average from Fitch and S&P on three of the five dates, neither of the other two rating agencies have pivotal ratings for the countries and time period sampled in Table 6.3.

Moreover, DBRS is pivotal in one to three cases in those three years where either Fitch's or S&P's mean ratings are not statistically different from that of DBRS. Thus, the true impact of DBRS is not seen from the mean ratings but from the number of times it provides pivotal ratings. Panel B of Table 6.3 shows that over period 2011–2014, DBRS was pivotal at year-end in seven cases (country-years) for the countries rated by all four agencies.[27]

Table 6.4 estimates the extra collateral value of DBRS's pivotal ratings, or from exemptions, to Italy, Spain, Ireland, and Portugal on four dates. These are August 15, 2013 (Panel A); July 17, 2014 (Panel B); August 29, 2014 (Panel C); and January 13, 2015 (Panel D). Ireland appears in Panel A only, since DBRS lost its pivotal status for Ireland in June 2014. Portugal was exempt on the first two dates, as indicated in the table. The estimation is implemented using the public lists of eligible collateral published on the ECB's website the evening before the four sample dates. These files provide the ISINs for government securities from these countries that are eligible on the sample dates as well as the haircuts that are applied. These ISINs

---

[27] This does not include DBRS's pivotal rating of Portugal on December 2014, since Portugal was not rated by Fitch. In addition, DBRS had two pivotal ratings in June 2014. That DBRS can make a difference to ratings (especially on the upside) is also found by Kisgen and Strahan (2010) in the context of the inclusion in 2003 of DBRS in bond investment regulation in the United States. The important role of DBRS in determining ratings of sovereigns in the euro area (under ECAF) is also noted in the popular press and by market participants. For example, *FTAlphaville* quotes a JP Morgan report (from May 2012) as saying that:

> [F]or Italy to fall below the A− threshold the following downgrades would need to occur: Moody's (1 notch), Fitch (1), and DBRS (3). For Spain to fall below the A− threshold: Moody's (1), Fitch (2) and DBRS (3). I.e. DBRS keeps Italy and Spain rated A+, two notches higher than the other agencies, according to the ECB's rules. Overall, one could argue that rating changes by DBRS are the most important for sovereign bonds held as collateral at the ECB, given current levels.

(See "The fourth rater," by Joseph Cotterill, May 23, 2012, http://ftalphaville.ft .com//2012/05/23/1012871/). I have verified this statement by looking up the historical ratings in Bloomberg. Furthermore, DBRS became pivotal for Spain in June 2012, when both Fitch and Moody's downgraded Spain by three notches to BBB and BBB−, respectively. S&P kept it at BBB+ and DBRS kept it at A+. DBRS became pivotal for Italy in March 2012.

Table 6.4 *Extra collateral value from DBRS's pivotal ratings (or credit quality exemptions)*

	DBRS rating	Second highest rating	Amount outstanding (million EUR)	Haircut actual (qw)	Haircut (qw) without		Estimated extra collateral value (million EUR)		Total # of securities	Amount outstanding		
					DBRS	Exemption	DBRS	Exemption		available	missing	zero
Panel A: Estimated extra collateral value on August 15, 2013												
Italy	A−	BBB+	1,634,434	2.69	7.69	–	81,689	–	394	146	101	147
Spain	A−	BBB	690,829	2.69	7.63	–	34,127	–	158	53	4	101
Ireland	A−	BBB+	116,887	2.46	7.46	7.46	5,844	0	33	33		
Portugal	BBB−	BB	118,356	7.65	7.65	100.00	0	109,298	37	37		
Total			2,560,507	2.91	7.66		121,660	109,298	622	269	105	248
Panel B: Estimated extra collateral value on July 17, 2014												
Italy	A−	BBB+	1,773,751	2.57	9.12	–	116,181	–	475	154		321
Spain	A−	BBB+	756,994	2.66	9.13	–	48,909	–	196	57	6	133
Portugal	BBB−	BB	113,454	9.01	9.01	100.00	0	103,237	35	35		
Total			2,644,198	2.87	9.11		165,090	103,237	706	246	6	454
Panel C: Estimated extra collateral value on August 29, 2014												
Italy	A−	BBB+	1,745,553	2.54	9.11	–	114,735	–	483	151	1	331
Spain	A−	BBB+	741,209	2.59	9.12	–	48,423	–	192	56		136
Portugal	BBB−	BB+	110,813	9.08	100.00	–	100,752	–	35	35		
Total			2,597,574	2.83	12.99		263,910	0	710	242	1	467

Table 6.4 (cont.)

Panel D: Estimated extra collateral value on January 13, 2015

DBRS rating	Second highest rating	Amount outstanding (million EUR)	Haircut actual (qw)	Haircut (qw) without		Estimated extra collateral value (million EUR)		Total # of securities	Amount outstanding		
				DBRS	Exemption	DBRS	Exemption		available	missing	zero
Italy	A–	BBB+	1,765,114	2.09	9.09	–	123,664	–	485	153		332
Spain	A–	BBB+	791,518	2.07	9.11	–	55,723	–	223	71		152
Portugal	BBB–	BB+	109,818	9.24	100.00	–	99,671	–	34	34		
Total			2,666,450	2.38	12.84	0	279,057	0	742	258	0	484

The numbers in Panel A are produced by feeding into Bloomberg all ISINs of government bonds from Ireland, Italy, Spain, and Portugal on the public list of Eurosystem eligible collateral for August 14, see www.ecb.europa.eu/paym/coll/assets/html/list.en.html). The amount outstanding for each ISIN is retrieved using the Bloomberg variable AMOUNT_OUTSTANDING_HISTORY. The column "Haircut actual (qw)" is the quantity-weighted haircut across ISINs, using the outstanding amounts as weights and the haircuts taken from the public list. "Haircut (qw) without DBRS" does the same, but recalculates haircuts using the rating rules in Table 6.1 and haircut rules in Table 5.3 with DBRS rating excluded. "Haircut (qw) without Exemption" shows the haircut without exemption status. Only Ireland and Portugal got exemptions. The "Estimated extra collateral value DBRS" is the difference in actual haircuts and haircuts without DBRS ratings multiplied by the outstanding amount if there is no exemption or the exemption is not needed. The "Estimated extra collateral value Exemption" is the same using the "Haircut (qw) without Exemption" if the exemption is needed. The number of ISINs for which the outstanding amount for August 15 is missing or zero is also reported. Panel B repeats the same exercise for July 17, 2014 (published on July 16). This does not include Ireland, since Ireland had no exemption status and DBRS was no longer pivotal for Ireland on that date. Also, Panel B uses the Bloomberg variable AMT_OUTSTANDING, since the amount outstanding data was taken end of day on July 16, 2014. Panels C and D repeat the exercise for August 29, 2014 (published on August 28), and January 13, 2015 (published on January 12), with the Bloomberg variables AMOUNT_OUTSTANDING_HISTORY and AMT_OUTSTANDING, respectively. The column "Second highest rating" refers to the highest rating from Fitch, Moody's, and S&P. Ratings are translated into S&P equivalents. Panels B, C, and D use Table 5.4 to infer haircuts without DBRS ratings.

are then fed into Bloomberg to get the outstanding amounts (if available) on the sample dates. From this information, and using Tables 5.3 and 5.4, it is possible to calculate the quantity-weighted (by outstanding amount) haircuts that is actually applied by the Eurosystem and that which would have been applied if DBRS had rated the relevant countries one notch lower. The extra collateral value is then the difference in quantity-weighted haircuts multiplied by the total outstanding amount, by country. On the two dates on which Portugal is exempt, the extra collateral value is attributed in the table to the exemption itself rather than to DBRS.

Table 6.4 reports that the extra collateral value from DBRS's pivotal ratings on August 15, 2013, and July 17, 2014, are estimated to be EUR 122 and 165 billion, respectively. Italian government bonds account for EUR 81.7 and 116.2 billion, respectively, of the extra collateral value on these two dates.[28]

The contribution of Ireland is a relatively small EUR 5.8 billion on August 15, 2013. This is attributed to DBRS in the table rather than to the exemption because Irish government bonds received haircuts commensurate with the pivotal A− rating provided by DBRS. Thus, the exemption did not play much of a direct role for Ireland.

If we assume that Portuguese bonds would have received a haircut of 100 percent if Portugal did not have exempt status, as they should according to the collateral framework, the extra collateral value from its exemption is in excess of EUR 100 billion on both August 15, 2013, and July 17, 2014. On the latter date, without the exemption, DBRS would actually have provided Portugal with a pivotal BBB− rating. So without the exemption, the collateral value of Portuguese government bonds would have been the same, *ceteris paribus*, as with the exemption. Of course, in this case, the

---

[28] Several securities have missing or zero values in the outstanding amount columns in Table 6.4. So the DBRS-induced extra collateral value estimates may be too low. On the other hand, many of the ISINs with outstanding amounts of zero in Bloomberg are strips. If these had positive amounts outstanding, there could be a double-counting problem instead.

extra collateral value would be attributable to DBRS instead of to the exemption.

As seen in Panels C and D, on August 29, 2014, and January 13, 2015, the extra collateral value from the pivotal ratings of DBRS to Italy, Spain, and Portugal were worth approximately EUR 264 and 279 billion, respectively. This is all unambiguously attributable to DBRS because Portugal was not exempt after August 20, 2014. These estimates do not take into account the additional indirect effect arising from higher market values as a result of lower haircuts.

In conclusion, the relatively generous and pivotal ratings offered to Italy, Spain, and Portugal by DBRS have substantially boosted the collateral values of these countries' securities. That one rating agency can have such a large impact is the result of the rating within the Eurosystem's collateral framework being determined by the highest external rating rather than, for example, an average. As it turns out, the agency with the highest rating is typically DBRS when it really makes a difference.

6.6 EVIDENCE ON GUARANTEES

Table 6.5 provides evidence on the incidence of guarantees by different types of guarantors. The data come from the public list of eligible collateral on August 15, 2013 (published the previous day). On this date, the list consists of 38,081 different ISINs.

Panel A reports on the number of eligible collateral on the public list that have a guarantee, broken down by liquidity category and type of guarantor. Table 6.5 also provides all potential types of guarantors, even if there is no paper guaranteed by that type. For example, the table reveals that although central banks, supranationals, and agencies are potential guarantors, there is no collateral that is guaranteed by such institutions.

In total, 4,276 securities have guarantees. As shown in Panel B, Table 6.5, this represents 11.23 percent of all eligible marketable securities (on the public list). The largest number of guaranteed securities are found in liquidity category IV, namely 3,241, representing

Table 6.5 *Distribution of collateral with guarantees*

Guarantor	Liquidity Category					Total
	I	II	III	IV	V	
Panel A: Number of issues with guarantees						
Central Bank	0	0	0	0	0	0
Central Government	0	352	135	884	0	1,371
Corporate and other issuers	0	0	15	525	0	540
Credit institutions (excl. agencies)	0	9	20	833	0	862
Regional/ Local Government	0	312	58	881	0	1,251
Supranational Issuer	0	0	0	0	0	0
Agency – non credit inst.	0	0	0	0	0	0
Agency – credit inst.	0	0	0	0	0	0
Financial corp. (excl. credit inst.)	0	35	98	118	1	252
Total	**0**	**708**	**326**	**3,241**	**1**	**4,276**
Panel B: Percentage of issues with guarantees						
Central Bank	0	0	0	0	0	0
Central Government	0	10.27	1.93	3.59	0	3.60
Corporate and other issuers	0	0	0.21	2.13	0	1.42
Credit institutions (excl. agencies)	0	0.26	0.29	3.38	0	2.26
Regional/ Local Government	0	9.10	0.83	3.58	0	3.29
Supranational Issuer	0	0	0	0	0	0
Agency – non credit inst.	0	0	0	0	0	0
Agency – credit inst.	0	0	0	0	0	0
Financial corp. (excl. credit inst.)	0	1.02	1.40	0.48	0.10	0.66
Total	**0**	**20.66**	**4.67**	**13.17**	**0.10**	**11.23**
Panel C: Number of issues with governmental (central, regional, local) guarantees						
Central Bank	0	0	0	0	0	0
Central Government	0	0	0	0	0	0
Corporate and other issuers	0	0	190	0	0	190
Credit institutions (excl. agencies)	0	0	1	1,736	0	1,737
Regional/ Local Government	0	15	0	0	0	15
Supranational Issuer	0	0	0	0	0	0
Agency – non credit inst.	0	132	0	0	0	132
Agency – credit inst.	0	517	0	0	0	517
Financial corp. (excl. credit inst.)	0	0	2	29	0	31
Total	**0**	**664**	**193**	**1,765**	**0**	**2,622**

Table 6.5 (cont.)

Panel D: Number of issues with governmental (central, regional, local) guarantees across countries

Country	Corporate and other issuers	Credit institutions (excl. agencies)	Regional & local government	Agency – non credit inst.	Agency – credit inst.	Financial corp. (excl. credit inst.)	Total
Austria	24	230	2	0	0	0	256
Belgium	51	0	3	0	0	0	54
Cyprus	0	2	0	0	0	0	2
Czech Republic	1	22	0	0	0	0	23
Germany	0	684	9	80	456	0	1,229
Denmark	0	0	0	0	0	3	3
Spain	30	86	0	4	61	0	181
Finland	0	14	0	0	0	1	15
France[1]	41	311	1	0	0	4	357
Great Britain	0	2	0	0	0	14	16
Greece	6	22	0	0	0	0	28
Ireland	2	13	0	0	0	1	16
Iceland	15	0	0	0	0	0	15
Italy	0	325	0	0	0	0	325
Luxembourg[2]	0	0	0	48	0	1	49
Netherlands	0	7	0	0	0	1	8
Portugal	16	14	0	0	0	6	36
Sweden	0	1	0	0	0	0	1
Slovenia	2	4	0	0	0	0	6
Slovakia	2	0	0	0	0	0	2
Total	**190**	**1,737**	**15**	**132**	**517**	**31**	**2,622**

Panel E: Number of issuers with governmental (central, regional, local) guarantees across countries

Country	Corporate and other issuers	Credit institutions (excl. agencies)	Regional & local government	Agency – non credit inst.	Agency – credit inst.	Financial corp. (excl. credit inst.)	Total
Austria	6	14	1	0	0	0	21
Belgium	2	0	2	0	0	0	4
Cyprus	0	1	0	0	0	0	1
Czech Republic	1	1	0	0	0	0	2

Germany	0	13	3	2	4	0	22
Denmark	0	0	0	0	0	2	2
Spain	4	14	0	1	1	0	20
Finland	0	1	1	0	0	1	2
France	2	3	0	0	0	1	7
Great Britain	0	1	0	0	0	4	5
Greece	3	5	0	0	0	0	8
Ireland	1	4	0	0	0	1	6
Iceland	1	0	0	0	0	0	1
Italy	0	257	0	0	0	0	257
Luxembourg	0	0	0	2	0	1	3
Netherlands	0	5	0	0	0	1	6
Portugal	10	7	0	0	0	4	21
Sweden	0	1	0	0	0	0	1
Slovenia	1	2	0	0	0	0	3
Slovakia	1	0	0	0	0	0	1
Total	**32**	**329**	**7**	**5**	**5**	**15**	**393**

This table presents the distribution of collateral with guarantees in five different ways. Panel A (B) shows the number (percentage) of issues with guarantees across liquidity categories and type of guarantor. Panel C shows the number of issues with governmental guarantees (central, regional, local) across liquidity categories and type of issuer. Panel D shows the number of issues with governmental guarantees (central, regional, local) across countries (of the guaranteeing government) and type of issuer. Panel E shows the number of issuers with governmental guarantees (central, regional, local) across countries (of the guaranteeing government) and type of issuer. There are no other guarantor types than the ones listed in this table. The data is taken from the public list of eligible collateral for August 15, 2013 (published on August 14, 2013) on www.ecb.europa.eu/paym/coll/assets/html/index.en.html. Liquidity categories are as in Table 5.3.

Notes: [1] Nine securities in column "Credit institutions (excl. agencies)" are issued by Dexia France and guaranteed by Belgium. [2] The forty-eight securities issued with guarantees in the "agency" column are issued by the EFSF or ESM (issuer residence=Luxembourg) and are guaranteed by the German government.

13.17 percent of the eligible securities in this category. However, liquidity category II has the highest frequency of guaranteed paper, namely 20.66 percent. Guarantees are thus significant.

Panel A also provides the number of securities guaranteed by different guarantors. For example, 1,371 securities have central government guarantees and 1,251 have regional or local government guarantees. Combined this amounts to 61.3 percent of all guarantees.

Panel C reports on how these governmental guarantees are distributed across issuers and liquidity categories. In all, 1,765 government guarantees are provided to collateral in liquidity category IV, and 1,737 guarantees are provided to credit institutions (excluding agencies). In total, 329 credit institutions have issued eligible collateral with government guarantees. Of these 257 are from Italy (Panel E). This represents 96.6 percent of the 266 Italian credit institutions with eligible marketable collateral. There are 1,897 Italian credit institution securities in total on the eligibility list, and 387, or 20.4 percent, of these have guarantees. The heavy provision of government guarantees to credit institutions in Italy suggests a severe weakness in the Italian banking sector. It may also reflect a relatively large willingness of Italy to provide guarantees to unsecured paper issued by its banks. Either of these reasons carries its own obvious concerns. According to the *New York Times International*, August 30–31, 2014, p. 4, "a new crisis in Italy could reignite fears that the eurozone will come apart."

6.7 GOVERNMENT GUARANTEES: ITALY

The heavy provision of guarantees by the Italian government to Italian credit institutions seen above makes it interesting to take a closer look at Italy. Figure 6.1 traces out the number of Italian and non-Italian credit institutions with government-guaranteed eligible collateral (on the public list). The vertical dotted lines mark the dates for the two three-year LTROs that, as discussed in Chapter 3, provided a total of EUR 1.1 trillion in funding to banks. It can be seen that the finding in the previous section is not a one-off.

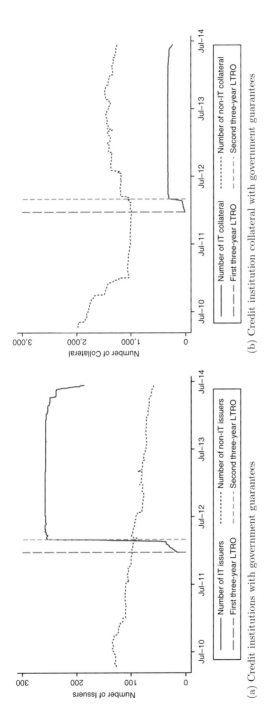

(a) Credit institutions with government guarantees

(b) Credit institution collateral with government guarantees

FIGURE 6.1 Number of government-guaranteed issuers and collateral

Time period: April 8, 2010, to June 11, 2014.

These figures graph the number of issuers with government (central, regional, local) guaranteed collateral as well as the number of such collateral over time on the Eurosystem's public list of eligible collateral. Figures 6.1a and 6.1b contain the graphs for credit institutions only, while Figures 6.1c and 6.1d cover all issuers and collateral. Separate graphs are provided for Italian (IT) and non-Italian (non-IT) issuers and issues. The vertical lines represent the two three-year LTROs, held on December 21, 2011, and February 29, 2012, respectively.

Data source: www.ecb.europa.eu/paym/coll/assets/html/list.en.html.

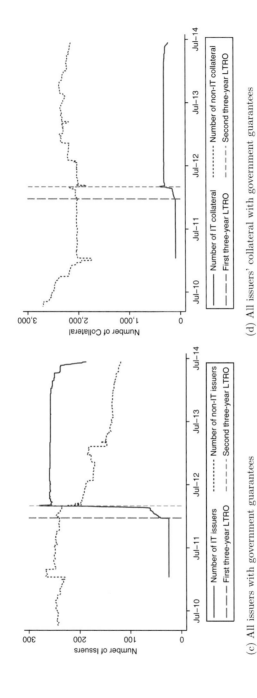

(c) All issuers with government guarantees

(d) All issuers' collateral with government guarantees

FIGURE 6.1 (cont.)

Figure 6.1 illustrates four points. First, the number of Italian credit institutions with government guarantees increased rapidly from close to zero to more than 250 over a few days prior to the second three-year LTRO. Second, the number of Italian credit institutions with government guarantees remained stable until spring/early summer of 2014, when it fell to just below 200. This is still a large number. Third, the number of non-Italian credit institutions with government-guaranteed eligible collateral has decreased steadily from before the first three-year LTRO to the spring of 2014. Fourth, since the second three-year LTRO, there have been substantially more Italian credit institutions with government guarantees than non-Italian ones. This speaks to a severe worsening of the credit worthiness of the banking sector in Italy over the period covered here. It suggests that the three-year LTROs, and the indirect bailout these represented, were especially important for the Italian banking sector.

To get a sense of the size and impact of these guarantees, data on the individual securities and issuers were collected from Bloomberg for August 15, 2013, and May 28, 2014. With respect to the former date, of the 325 Italian securities with central government guarantees, 294 could be found on Bloomberg. For each of these securities, Bloomberg was used to find the rating of the issue and the long-term issuer rating. I then used the procedure described in Table 6.1 and discussed above in order to determine the rating that would have applied without the guarantee.

Table 6.6, Panels A and B, report the results for August 15, 2013, and May 28, 2014, respectively. My discussion below focuses on Panel A. The findings in Panel B are similar. Without the guarantees, the distribution of collateral across the different rating categories is as follows. Rating category 1 (A− or higher), none; rating category 2 (BBB+ to BBB−), 42; rating category 3 (below BBB−), 14; no rating, 238. The absence of a rating means that there is neither an external rating for the issue nor for the issuer. Thirty-one ISINs could not be found in Bloomberg.

Table 6.6 *Extra collateral value to unrated Italian bank bonds from DBRS's pivotal rating and government guarantees*

Panel A: August 15, 2013

Issuer rating	N	Amount outstanding	Haircut actual (qw)	Haircut without guarantee (qw)	Estimated extra collateral value
A– and better	0				
BBB+ to BBB–	42	64,280,000,000	8.75	27.24	11,888,600,032
Below BBB–	14	8,050,000,000	8.94	100.00	7,330,249,984
Not rated	238	12,031,650,000	8.91	100.00	10,959,307,178
N.a. in Bloomberg	31				
Total	**325**	**84,361,650,000**	**8.79**	**44.56**	**30,178,157,194**

Panel B: May 28, 2014

Issuer rating	N	Amount outstanding	Haircut actual (qw)	Haircut without guarantee (qw)	Estimated extra collateral value
A– and better	0				
BBB+ to BBB–	25	25,630,000,000	6.77	14.49	1,979,500,000
Below BBB–	14	7,550,000,000	7.30	100.00	6,998,750,016
Not rated	210	10,970,150,000	6.95	100.00	10,208,270,186
N.a. in Bloomberg	30				
Total	**279**	**44,150,150,000**	**6.91**	**50.36**	**19,186,520,202**

Unrated bonds receive the rating of the issuer, but this is superseded by that of the guarantor, if any, should it be higher than that of the issuer (see Table 6.1 for details). Guarantees can therefore serve to reduce haircuts and boost collateral values. This table provides an estimate of the extra collateral value to unrated Italian bank bonds that have government guarantees on the dates specified below. Because of DBRS's pivotal A– (A[low]) rating of Italy, these bonds receive rating category 1 haircuts, which in all cases is better than what the issuer rating would give. Panel A uses the public list of eligible collateral on August 15, 2013 (published on August 14), and Panel B that for May 28, 2014 (published on May 27). Issuer long-term ratings are from Bloomberg, as are amounts outstanding. Each panel reports on: (i) the (external) ratings of all bonds without considering guarantees (in accordance with Table 6.1 this is based on issuer ratings); (ii) amounts outstanding; (iii) quantity-weighted actual haircuts (from the public list); (iv) quantity-weighted haircuts when ignoring the guarantees (haircuts are inferred using Tables 5.3 and 5.4); (v) the estimated extra collateral value due to the guarantees (using amounts outstanding as estimates of market values).

For each rating category, Table 6.6 also reports on the aggregate amount outstanding (by face value), the quantity-weighted average haircut, and the quantity-weighted average haircut that would have applied if these securities did not have government guarantees (inferred using Table 5.3), and the extra collateral value due to the guarantee. The total amount outstanding is EUR 84.4 billion and the quantity-weighted average haircut is 8.79 percent. Without the guarantee, the quantity-weighted average haircut would increase to 44.56 percent. The extra collateral value due to the government guarantees is thus EUR 30.2 billion.[29] This is a conservative estimate, since 10 percent of the credit institution securities with guarantees could not be found in Bloomberg. It is also a sizeable sum. It is equivalent to approximately 5 percent of the pre-crisis monetary base, or around 7 percent of the pre-crisis MRO and LTRO outstanding amounts.

Next, I ask how much of the extra EUR 30 billion is due to Italy having received an A− rating from DBRS. Without this, Italy's rating would be in the BBB+ to BBB− range, with haircuts on guaranteed collateral being commensurately higher. With this lower rating, only the collateral with issue/issuer ratings below BBB− (or unrated) would benefit from the guarantee. As seen in Table 6.6, the total amount outstanding of this collateral is approximately EUR 20.1 billion. The extra collateral value from a guarantee would therefore be this EUR 20.1 billion less the haircut that a BBB+ to BBB− rating would provide, which we can approximate by 27 percent, giving EUR 14.6 billion.[30] Thus, the A− rating from DBRS is worth approximately EUR 15.6 billion (30.2 minus 14.6). In other words, approximately 50 percent of the extra collateral value from the guarantee is due to the A− rating from DBRS.

---

[29] I have used the outstanding amount by face value rather than the market value of the securities. So this is only an approximation. However, the few securities for which prices could actually be found had prices above face value (because of falling interest rates), suggesting that the EUR 30 billion (increase in collateral value) estimate is biased down. For May 28, 2014 (Table 6.6, Panel B), I estimate the extra collateral value to be around EUR 19 billion.

[30] The 27 percent figure is taken from the quantity-weighted average haircut the paper with BBB+ to BBB− ratings (in Table 6.6) would have without the guarantee.

6.8 GOVERNMENT GUARANTEES: GERMANY

While Italy has the largest number of credit institutions with governmental guarantees, Germany has the largest number of issues with government guarantees. Table 6.5, Panel D, shows the breakdown across different kinds of issuers, according to the official issuer classification used in the public list of eligible collateral on August 15, 2013. There are 1,229 issues in total. Most of these are from credit institutions, of which the public list identifies thirteen (as seen in Table 6.5, Panel E). These credit institutions are, with only two exceptions, Landesbanken/Girozentralen or state development banks (Förderbanken). Of the twenty-two German issuers with government guarantees, there are nine Landesbanken/Girozentralen, five state development banks and agencies, two state-owned financial corporations, two "bad bank" agencies, two credit institutions, and one agricultural development agency.[31]

The total amount outstanding (of issues with government guarantees) is huge: EUR 513.2 billion.[32] The breakdown across the different kinds of institutions is in Exhibit 6.2.

Exhibit 6.2 Issues with German government guarantees, August 15, 2013.

	Landesbanken/ Girozentralen	State development banks and agencies	Other credit institutions
Billion EUR	121.440	283.838	2.009
	Other state-owned financials	Bad bank agencies	Other
Billion EUR	8.428	78.182	19.299

---

[31] By state-owned, I mean either German Länder, the federal government, or a combination.

[32] Outstanding amounts are downloaded from Bloomberg, as described in the caption to Table 6.4. Three have zero outstanding amount in Bloomberg and eleven issues could not be found.

With respect to these numbers, the Landesbanken have tradi-
tionally had state guarantees. However, in July 2001, the European
Commission and the German government decided that these would
be phased out by July 2005 for new issues maturing no later than
December 2015. Of the EUR 121.4 billion in guaranteed collateral
issued by Landesbanken/Girozentralen, EUR 114.5 billion relate to
such transition period securities. The single largest issuer with guarantees is Kreditanstalt für Wiederaufbau, a development agency that
originated under the Marshall Plan, with a guaranteed outstanding
amount of EUR 184.7 billion. The second largest, by outstanding
amount, is FMS Wertmanagement (EUR 76.2 billion), a "bad bank"
that was set up under the SoFFin on July 8, 2010, and is owned by
the federal government.[33] "Normal" credit institutions only account
for EUR 2.0 billion of the guarantees. Thus, while German guarantees are very large, the vast majority of these are given to state or
near-state institutions.

6.9 GOVERNMENT GUARANTEES AND IRREGULAR HAIRCUTS: GREECE

Greece is also an interesting case to look at because of its high visi-
bility with respect to the euro crisis. As seen in Chapter 5 (Table 5.5),
it is one of only two countries that have been in such bad financial
shape that they have received their own haircut schedules, the other
country being Cyprus. Even Portugal, despite having ratings below
the official minimum threshold during its time of exemption, has
not had the haircuts on its paper increased beyond those of rating
category 2. The extraordinary haircuts on Greek government bonds
are substantially larger. Marketable debt instruments guaranteed by
the Greek government have also been subject to extraordinary haircuts. As seen in Table 5.5, these are roughly 8 to 11 percentage

---

[33] The SoFFin (Sonderfonds Finanzmarktstabilisierung – Special Financial Market Stabilization Funds) was created during the financial crisis to provide funding and
liquidity to troubled financial institutions in Germany through recapitalizations
and the purchasing of assets. It stopped offering new services from 2011 onward.

points larger than for those of Greek government paper with similar maturities.

As discussed in Section 6.2, before the introduction of the extraordinary haircuts on December 21, 2012, Greece had been, on and off, under exempt status since May 2010. However, its highest rating did not fall below the minimum official BBB– threshold before January 2011, when it was downgraded to BB+ by Fitch. As seen in Table 6.2, Greek ratings subsequently deteriorated rapidly. By the end of 2011, its best rating was a CCC by Fitch. When the extraordinary haircuts were introduced, its best rating was a B– by S&P, six notches below BBB–. Nevertheless, before this time when Greece had exempt status, haircuts on its paper were commensurate with those of a BBB+ to BBB– rating.

During the Greek exempt-but-not-extraordinary-haircut period, one would expect that debt instruments guaranteed by the Greek government would also receive haircuts commensurate with a BBB+ to BBB– rating. To examine this, I have looked at the haircuts of such paper, as revealed by the public list of eligible collateral. I find that, for the most part, eligible collateral guaranteed by the Greek government have the expected BBB haircuts. However, there are exceptions. Throughout the period, there are occasions when the haircuts on a handful of unsecured bank bonds are commensurate with a AAA to A– rating. Exhibit 6.3 presents several such examples, gleaned from information on the public list of eligible collateral on December 8, 2011 (and using ratings as found in Bloomberg).

The case of the last example in Exhibit 6.3, XS0703365451 issued by Piraeus Bank, is especially interesting because the bond has an issue rating of B. As seen in Table 6.1 and discussed in Section 6.1, government guarantees are not supposed to be able to override issue ratings. Nevertheless, here is an example where this essentially has happened.[34] And this is not all. The rating applied to the bond,

---

[34] Another example is XS0570763218 issued by ATE Bank, which was on the public list of eligible collateral over the period May 26 to June 3, 2011, with a

Exhibit 6.3 Irregular haircuts of Greek government-guaranteed unsecured bank bonds, December 8, 2011.

ISIN	Issuer	Maturity	Issue rating (max)	Issuer rating (max)	Haircut	Inferred rating
XS0704183127	Alpha Bank	February 7, 2012	–	B–	6.5	AAA to A–
XS0702937060	Eurobank	February 7, 2012	–	B–	6.5	AAA to A–
XS0706144051	Eurobank	February 13, 2012	–	B–	6.5	AAA to A–
XS0703356542	Piraeus Bank	February 6, 2012	–	B–	6.5	AAA to A–
XS0703365451	Piraeus Bank	February 7, 2012	B	B–	6.5	AAA to A–

All ISINs are in liquidity category IV and are guaranteed by the Greek government, whose largest rating at the time was CCC (from Fitch). Issue and issuer ratings are from Bloomberg. Inferred ratings: backed out from Table 5.3 using Eurosystem haircuts (from the public list of eligible collateral). Eurobank is short for EFG Eurobank Ergasias.

for the purpose of setting its haircut, exceeds what the guarantee should imply. This feature is shared with the other examples in the exhibit.

In all cases, the haircut-inferred rating is A– (or higher), rather than the BBB– (to BBB+) one would expect. I base this expectation on the haircut policy used by the ECB for other exempt countries (as discussed above) and based on the fact that Greek sovereign paper had haircuts commensurate with a BBB– rating, before the extraordinary haircuts were introduced. The examples are exceptions. Most

haircut-inferred rating of A– (to AAA). At the same time, the security's largest issue rating was BBB– by Fitch (according to information on Bloomberg). The security was also guaranteed by the Hellenic Republic, whose best rating at the time was a B+, also from Fitch. Moody's downgraded Greece from B1 (equivalent to B+) to Caa1 on June 1, while S&P had Greece at B. It is a puzzle as to how a guarantee by an entity rated below investment grade could give the security its lowest possible haircut.

Greek government-guaranteed marketable collateral received haircuts consistent with BBB— ratings rather than the A— rating seen in the examples. However, these irregular haircuts are not a one-off for December 8, 2011. Each and every one of the ISINs in my example received rating category 1 haircuts over the period November 17, 2011, to February 4, 2012. Some of them on other dates too.

It is not clear why these cases of irregular haircuts exist. I have not found a rule that justifies them, but perhaps it is lurking somewhere in the very fine print of the collateral framework, perhaps as a part of a bailout program. Or perhaps they are simply mistakes. After all, keeping track of 30,000 to 40,000 ISINs is not trivial. Whatever the case, these irregular haircuts would have benefited Greek banks and the holders of their paper.

Over the periods in 2012 when Greece lost its exempt status, one would expect Greek banks to have received extraordinary amounts of emergency liquidity assistance (ELA) to help keep them afloat. Consistent with this, in 2012, the Bank of Greece provided EUR 191.5 billion in ELA, up from EUR 84.8 billion in 2011 and much higher than the EUR 58.3 billion of ELA in 2013.[35] From the examples I have provided in this section, it appears that assistance of a different kind was also forthcoming when Greece's exempt status was "on."

6.10 CORPORATE GUARANTEES AND ACCESS TO CHEAP FUNDING

Another interesting feature of Table 6.5 is that corporations guarantee 540 securities. Such corporate guarantees are for the most part extended to the financial arms of corporations, for example, VW and Peugeot guarantee notes issued by their banking subsidiaries. Since it is possible to use a limited amount of own-issued securities (see Chapter 8), the implication is that some corporations can fund loans

---

[35] See the annual reports of the Bank of Greece, available on www.bankofgreece.gr /Pages/en/Publications/GovReport.aspx?Filter_By=8.

to customers, for example, directly from the Eurosystem. More generally, under the full allotment policy, the only limit to how much funding corporations with eligible banking subsidiaries can obtain is provided by the Eurosystem's assessment of the value of the collateral the banking subsidiaries can pledge. In effect, the central bank is competing with commercial banks and other funding markets. The Eurosystem's terms are also exceptionally good. The policy rate when the two three-year LTROs were held was 1.0 percent. As stated in a *Financial Times* article from 2012:[36]

> Stefan Rolf, head of asset backed securitisation at Volkswagen Financial Services, said that the competitive pricing on the [three-year] LTRO meant it made economic sense to put it into the mix as one of a number of ways of funding VW.
>
> Suki Mann, head of credit strategy at Société Générale in London, said carmakers and other industrial groups that have banking arms clearly believe that they may be able [to] take part in the second phase of the [three-year] LTRO, potentially using consumer loans as collateral.
>
> "This is an alternative source of funding and a very cheap one at that," he said.

Access to cheap funding directly from the Eurosystem may create a competitive advantage for those corporations that have this possibility. Important empirical questions include the following: How much funding is obtained this way and what is the effect on firms' weighted average costs of capital? The anecdotal evidence suggests that the sums involved are significant. For example, according to the same FT article, "Peugeot-Citroen, Europe's second-largest carmaker by sales, has also said that its Banque PSA lending arm is in talks with the ECB about borrowing money and would potentially offer about [euro] 1bn as collateral." More generally, it is not clear that central banks should be extending credit to non-bank firms.

---

[36] "VW and Peugeot eye ECB loans offer," by Mary Watkins and John Reed, *Financial Times*, February 16, 2012.

APPENDIX: RATING SCALES

The exhibit below provides the rating scales of the four accepted rating agencies and translates these into the scoring system used in this book. The matching across scales for Moody's, S&P, and Fitch is as provided by the BIS.[37] DBRS is added on a simple notch-by-notch basis.

Exhibit 6.4 Long-term rating scales and scoring system.

Moody's	Standard & Poor's and Fitch	DBRS	Score
Aaa	AAA	AAA	6
Aa1	AA+	AAH	5
Aa2	AA	AA	4
Aa3	AA−	AAL	3
A1	A+	AH	2
A2	A	A	1
A3	A−	AL	0
Baa1	BBB+	BBBH	−1
Baa2	BBB	BBB	−2
Baa3	BBB−	BBBL	−3
Ba1	BB+	BBH	−4
Ba2	BB	BB	−5
Ba3	BB−	BBL	−6
B1	B+	BH	−7
B2	B	B	−8
B3	B−	BL	−9
Caa1	CCC+	CCCH	−10
Caa2	CCC	CCC	−11
Caa3	CCC−	CCCL	−12
Ca	CC	CC	−13
C	C	C	−14
–	D	D	−15

Data sources: Moody's, Standard & Poor's, Fitch, and DBRS webpages. DBRS may also subdivide the CC and C rating categories.

---

[37] See www.bis.org/bcbs/qis/qisrating.htm.

7 Market and Theoretical Prices

As shown in Equation (2.1), the collateral value of a security in Eurosystem operations is its market, or in some cases, model, price less its haircut. The rules that determine whether a market or theoretical (model) price is used are laid down in the official documentation of the Eurosystem's collateral framework. As one would expect, there are separate pricing rules for marketable and non-marketable collateral. This chapter describes changes to these rules over time, with a focus on marketable collateral. Non-marketable collateral is discussed toward the end. The chapter also provides evidence on the incidence of theoretical prices, initially in terms of the public list of eligible marketable collateral. This is followed by an estimate of the incidence of theoretical prices among pledged collateral.

7.1 ELIGIBLE MARKETABLE COLLATERAL

From January 1, 2007, to January 2, 2013, the pricing rule for marketable collateral was:

Pricing rule 1
The value of a marketable asset is calculated on the basis of the most representative price on the business day preceding the valuation date. If more than one price is quoted, the lowest of these prices (normally the bid price) is used. In the absence of a representative price for a particular asset on the business day preceding the valuation date, the last trading price is used. If the reference price obtained is older than five days, or has not moved for at least five days, the Eurosystem defines a theoretical price.

ECB (2006/12)

This passage reveals that both stale and theoretical prices are built into the collateral framework. Theoretical prices are used if market prices do not exist or are too stale, that is, more than five days old over the 2007–2012 time period. The pricing rule before 2007 was similar, but without the five-day staleness limit (ECB 2000/7 and 2005/2). The combination of haircuts that are rarely revised (Chapter 5) and stale or theoretical prices has the potential to create biases, along the lines of those documented in Chapter 4.[1]

As of January 3, 2013, the pricing rule for marketable collateral was modified to:

Pricing rule 2
The value of a marketable asset is calculated on the basis of the most representative price on the business day preceding the valuation date. In the absence of a representative price for a particular asset on the business day preceding the valuation date, the Eurosystem defines a theoretical price.

ECB (2012/25)

This rule was still in force at the end of January 2015. It differs in two respects from the previous one. First, it is more vague with respect to how the "representative" price is chosen. While market prices are not referred to in the wording of the new rule, it seems fair to assume that it is implicit in the word "representative." But no algorithm is provided for the choice of a market price, unlike under the old rule. Second, the factors that determine whether a market price is used are different. Whereas the old rule would go back five days to find a market price, the new rule requires a market price on the day preceding the valuation day, i.e., the day the list of eligible collateral is published. Furthermore, whereas the old rule assigned a theoretical price

---

[1] Theoretical prices are also part of the Fed's collateral framework. A webpage of the Board of Governors of the Federal Reserve System (www.federalreserve.gov /monetarypolicy/bst_ratesetting.htm) under the heading *Collateral Eligibility, Valuation, and Haircuts by Program* reports that "For assets that cannot be marked to market, a haircut is applied to an internally modeled fair market value estimate."

if the market price had not moved for five days, the new rule makes no mention of such a requirement.

There is no official statistic that tells us how many securities have their prices determined by a model rather than the market. I have therefore first conducted a "random check" using the eligible collateral list published January 12, 2015, and valid for January 13. The 33,679 ISINs on the list were fed into Bloomberg on the evening of January 12, 2015, after the close of market. Importantly, Bloomberg includes a variable that describes whether the price of a given ISIN on its system is derived from a model (theoretically). While it is possible that the Eurosystem collects prices from a variety of platforms, Bloomberg is an industry standard that is used by other central banks to determine collateral values in their operations. The pricing information on the Bloomberg system, including the usage of theoretical prices, should thus give at least a good approximation of the information that is available to the Eurosystem.

Of the 33,679 ISINs on the public list, 7,045 could not be found in Bloomberg on January 12, 2015. The vast majority of these trade on non-regulated markets. Of the remaining securities, 17,149 have model prices in Bloomberg and would therefore have a theoretical price within the collateral framework (unless a market price can be found elsewhere). This represents 64.4 percent of the "found" securities. Combined, the "not found" and "model price" categories account for 71.8 percent of all securities. Another 1.5 percent are in Bloomberg without a pricing source. These missing-pricing-source ISINs are a subset of the ISINs with missing prices. Thus, a first estimate of the usage of theoretical prices in determining Eurosystem collateral values is 73.3 percent. If we add in the ISINs that are labeled as having market prices in Bloomberg, but where these are actually missing, the estimate of the incidence of theoretical prices increases to a whopping 76.6 percent. It bears emphasis that the majority of this is accounted for by theoretical prices in Bloomberg itself.

To take a longer horizon look at the incidence of theoretical prices, I have also fed into Bloomberg the ISINs on the daily public lists of eligible collateral that apply over the period December 12, 2014, to June 16, 2015 (with a break from December 20, 2014, to January 4, 2015). As a daily average, 72.8 percent of these ISINs are in Bloomberg with a model as the pricing source, no pricing source (and therefore having missing prices), or cannot be found. There is hardly any fluctuation in the percentage from day to day. The standard deviation is 0.5 percent. If we only count those ISINs that can be found, the average percentage of ISINs with model prices is 63.4 percent, with a standard deviation of 0.7 percent. Adding in the securities with no pricing source, the average increases to 65.2 percent. These averages are very similar to the corresponding figures for January 13, 2015. Thus, that date can be said to be representative.

Next, I carry out a more detailed exercise to examine the incidence of theoretical prices across liquidity categories, both by count (as above) and by value. I am also interested in studying the incidence of stale prices. Doing the latter requires a history of prices and pricing sources of eligible collateral. A snag with respect to the data is that the pricing source is only available on the download date. Since there are small changes in the public list of eligible collateral from day to day, it is not possible to download historical pricing sources for all ISINs. That would require time travel. So I have downloaded prices and pricing sources for all ISINs on the public list for each of the six trading days prior to January 13, 2015. The number of days is chosen with a view to Pricing rule 1, which applies a theoretical price if market prices are more than five days old or have not moved for five days. Only 568 ISINs are lost because of this snag. In addition, 6,570 securities cannot be found in Bloomberg. Thus, I have complete six-day pricing and pricing source histories for 26,541 of the 33,679 ISINs that were on the public list of eligible collateral on January 13, 2015.

For those ISINs that have a market price, the *price staleness* is the number of days prior to the day of interest (January 13, 2015) that the price was actually new. This can be defined more precisely using the following notation. Let t be the day of interest. For a given security, let p_{t-i} be the "price" i trading days before t, $i = 1, \ldots, 6$. For each i, this is either missing, calculated from a model, or an actual market price.[2]

Definition 1 (Price staleness) Let t be the day of interest and suppose that p_{t-1} is a market price.

1. If there are no market prices for $i = 2, \ldots, 6$, *staleness* is 1.
2. Else, let i^* be the smallest $i \leq 5$ for which p_{t-i} is a market price and $p_{t-i} \neq p_{t-j}$, where $j \leq 6$ is the smallest number larger than i for which p_{t-j} is a market price. If such i^* exists, *staleness* is equal to i^*.
3. Else, the price is *too stale.*

Securities for which staleness exceeds five days ("too stale") would require a theoretical price under the old Pricing rule 1. Under Pricing rule 2, however, they are given a stale market price instead. It is not clear if one is better than the other.

A "fresh" market price is where staleness equals one. A staleness of zero is not possible because the freshest price used by either pricing rule is one day old.

Table 7.1 reports, by liquidity category, on the usage of theoretical prices and the distribution of staleness across issues that have market prices. Panel A does this by count, while Panel B does it by outstanding nominal amounts. The first two sections of the panels cover securities in rating categories 1 and 2, and the third covers collateral that are exempted from the normal rating rules. For rating category 1, Panel A shows that only 6,623 out of 28,606 securities can be found in Bloomberg with a market price. Of these, 5,442 have fresh prices (staleness of one day). So, 1,181, or 17.8 percent, of the market prices are stale (staleness larger than one day). Not counting the 397 securities that are not in all six public lists that have been used, these numbers mean that only 19.3 percent of all securities have fresh market prices. For securities in rating category 2, the percentages are similar. In aggregate, of the 33,111 eligible collateral ISINs

---

[2] A market price here could be a quote, a transactions price, or an average of quotes or transactions prices. This is indicated in the Bloomberg system.

Table 7.1 *Incidence of market and theoretical prices for determining collateral values*

Panel A: Number of collateral with market and theoretical prices (January 13, 2015)

ECB rating class and staleness	Liquidity category					Total	Non-regulated markets
	I	II	III	IV	V		
AAA to A-							
Market price	1,080	1,299	1,215	2,762	267	6,623	885
Staleness 1	1,023	1,179	1,013	1,985	242	5,442	555
2	29	79	60	206	4	378	80
3	12	16	22	147	5	202	80
4	5	2	4	60	3	74	35
5	2	2		35	1	40	19
Too stale	9	21	116	329	12	487	116
Theoretical price	1,024	1,831	4,176	13,940	615	21,586	7,067
Model or missing price	1,008	1,580	3,752	9,502	592	16,434	2,879
Security not in Bloomberg	16	251	424	4,438	23	5,152	4,188
Security not in all public lists	8	36	31	322		397	351
Total	2,112	3,166	5,422	17,024	882	28,606	8,303
Non-regulated markets	167	514	756	6,859	7	8,303	8,303
BBB+ to BBB-							
Market price	38	82	377	668	11	1,176	206
Staleness 1	27	81	361	488	11	968	165
2	2		9	22		33	10
3	2			6		8	4
4	1			6		7	2
5				3		3	1

Too stale	6	1	7	143		157	24
Theoretical price	6	221	573	2,756	20	3,576	1,364
Model or missing price	6	177	266	1,689	20	2,158	537
Security not in Bloomberg		44	307	1,067		1,418	827
Security not in all public lists			64	101		165	142
Total	44	303	1,014	3,525	31	4,917	1,712
Non-regulated markets	*1*	*1*	*369*	*1,341*	*0*	*1,712*	*1,712*
Exempted							
Market price	33	0	2	0	0	35	0
Staleness 1	29		2			31	
2	4					4	
3						0	
4						0	
5						0	
Too stale						0	
Theoretical price	93	0	3	19	0	115	2
Model or missing price	93		3	19		115	2
Security not in Bloomberg				0		0	
Security not in all public lists	3		3	3		6	
Total	129	0	5	22	0	156	2
Non-regulated markets	*2*	*0*	*0*	*0*	*0*	*2*	*2*
Grand total	2,285	3,469	6,441	20,571	913	33,679	10,017
Non-regulated markets	*170*	*515*	*1,125*	*8,200*	*7*	*10,017*	*10,017*

Table 7.1 *(cont.)*

Panel B: Amount outstanding of collateral with market and theoretical prices (January 13, 2015)

ECB rating class and staleness	Liquidity category					Total	Non-regulated markets
	I	II	III	IV	V		
AAA to A-							
Market price	6,342,978	1,789,732	810,704	1,228,688	99,004	10,271,105	680,951
Staleness 1	6,102,377	1,706,290	777,158	1,137,969	86,409	9,810,202	583,134
2	171,075	64,073	19,931	45,500	1,380	301,958	53,269
3	53,039	9,035	2,801	15,375	3,912	84,161	24,291
4	5,819	1,250	1,490	6,238	3,978	18,774	3,447
5	2,500	110		1,752	4	4,367	2,925
Too stale	8,169	8,975	9,324	21,854	3,322	51,643	13,886
Theoretical price	95,030	196,408	463,080	632,404	527,015	1,913,937	205,361
Model or missing price	95,030	196,408	463,080	632,404	527,015	1,913,937	205,361
Security not in Bloomberg						0	0
Security not in all public lists	14,270	3,646	342	6,693		24,951	17,419
Total	6,452,278	1,989,785	1,274,126	1,867,785	626,018	12,209,993	903,732
Non-regulated markets	*499,325*	*89,615*	*60,007*	*245,358*	*9,426*	*903,732*	*903,732*
BBB+ to BBB-							
Market price	119,160	48,937	241,780	287,153	4,294	701,324	76,957

Staleness 1	111,349	48,933	232,274	274,715	4,294	671,565	73,588
2	1,800		7,428	6,176		15,404	3,141
3	4,344			121		4,465	36
4	1,552			1,319		2,871	5
5				88		88	3
Too stale	115	4	2,078	4,734		6,931	184
Theoretical price	2,481	16,420	43,307	102,902	8,061	173,169	30,576
Model or missing price	2,481	16,420	43,307	102,902	8,061	173,169	30,576
Security not in Bloomberg						0	0
Security not in all public lists			290	199		489	194
Total	121,641	65,356	285,377	390,254	12,355	874,983	107,727
Non-regulated markets	*1,062*	*20*	*16,296*	*90,350*	*0*	*107,727*	*107,727*
Exempted							
Market price	48,670	0	575	0	0	49,245	0
Staleness 1	43,959		575			44,534	0
2	4,711					4,711	0
3						0	0
4						0	0
5						0	0
Too stale						0	0
Theoretical price	35,417	0	584	36,872	0	72,874	317
Model or missing price	35,417		584	36,872		72,874	317
Security not in Bloomberg						0	0

Table 7.1 (cont.)

Panel B – continued

ECB rating class and staleness	Liquidity category						
	I	II	III	IV	V	Total	Non-regulated markets
Security not in all public lists	2,218			7,287		9,505	0
Total	86,305	0	1,159	44,159	0	131,623	317
Non-regulated markets	*317*	*0*	*0*	*0*	*0*	*317*	*317*
Grand Total	6,660,223	2,055,141	1,560,662	2,302,199	638,373	13,216,598	1,011,776
Non-regulated markets	*500,705*	*89,635*	*76,302*	*335,708*	*9,426*	*1,011,776*	*1,011,776*

The table uses the public list of eligible marketable collateral for January 13, 2015 (published on January 12, 2015, henceforth "the public list"). Each security (ISIN) is placed in one of three groups based on its rating backed out from the information in the public list and using the haircut rules in Table 5.4: "AAA to A–," "BBB+ to BBB–," and "Exempted." The latter consists of eligible collateral issued or guaranteed by the governments of Greece and Cyprus. Price and pricing histories were downloaded from Bloomberg from January 5 to January 12, 2015 (six business days), on a day-by-day basis (necessary for the pricing source) and the amount outstanding for each ISIN on January 13, 2015. Bloomberg provides information on whether the reported prices are market or model prices. If the pricing source on January 12, 2015, reveals that a security has a market price and this price exists, the security is classified as having a "Market price." Otherwise, the security is classified as having a "Theoretical price". This classification consists of securities with a model (vast majority) or missing price, or securities not found in Bloomberg. Market price staleness is determined according to Definition 1 in Chapter 7 and measured in trading days. Securities with a staleness exceeding five days are labeled "Too stale." Panel A (B) reports the number of issues (amount outstanding) across the categories described above by rating and liquidity category. The column labeled "Non-regulated markets" breaks out separate numbers for securities traded on non-regulated markets (see Chapter 9).

on January 13, 2015 (that are also in the January 5 to 12 lists), only 19.5 percent have market prices that are "fresh." 76.3 percent have their prices determined theoretically or are not found in Bloomberg (in which case we can assume they are so illiquid that a theoretical price is needed). In other words, based on this investigation, more than three fourths of eligible collateral would have to be assigned a theoretical price. On top of this, 4.2 percent of all securities have stale market prices. So 80.5 percent of all eligible marketable collateral are estimated to have theoretical or stale prices (under Pricing rule 2).

The corresponding Panel B numbers, which are based on amount outstanding, are less dramatic. Still 16.4 percent of the eligible collateral on the public list, by value, are theoretically valued. This amounts to approximately EUR 2.2 trillion of the EUR 13.2 trillion or so of total value. Thus, the value of the eligible collateral that is theoretically valued is more than adequate to cover all outstanding Eurosystem repos.[3] In addition, 3.8 percent of all securities have stale market prices. Thus, by nominal value, approximately 20 percent of all assets on the public list of eligible collateral have their collateral values determined by theoretical or stale prices.

Using the numbers in Table 7.1, it can be seen that the incidence of theoretical prices is increasing in the liquidity category. This is shown in Exhibit 7.1.[4] The incidence of theoretical or stale prices

---

[3] Because I have used outstanding nominal values and not made adjustments for haircuts, the EUR 2.2 and 13.2 trillion figures are overestimates. Still, after such adjustments, there should be more than enough to cover outstanding Eurosystem repos. At the end of 2014, these were only EUR 592,486 million (www.ecb.europa.eu/press/pr/wfs/2014/html/fs141230.en.html).

[4] The "by count" numbers are calculated from Table 7.1, Panel A as follows: For each liquidity category, I first add up the number of issues classified as having theoretical prices (or staleness of two or more) across the three rating categories, AAA to A−, BBB+ to BBB−, and Exempted. I then calculate the percentage this represents of the Grand Total number of securities within each liquidity category, but with "Security not in all public lists" collateral excluded. The "by value" numbers are calculated analogously, using the amount outstanding figures in Panel B. While download limits preclude me from carrying out this exercise on a large number of dates, I have also done it for December 19, 2015 (by count), with very similar results. Note that the "by value" figures are likely to be underestimates because many ISINs have an outstanding value of zero in the Bloomberg system (see Table 6.4 in Chapter 6,

Exhibit 7.1 Pricing rule 2: incidence of theoretical and stale prices, January 13, 2015.

Liquidity category	I	II	III	IV	V	Total
Theoretical prices						
By count	49.4%	59.8%	74.9%	83.0%	69.6%	76.3%
By value	2.0%	10.4%	32.5%	33.7%	83.8%	16.4%
Stale						
By count	3.2%	3.5%	3.4%	4.8%	2.7%	4.2%
By value	3.8%	4.1%	2.8%	4.5%	2.0%	3.8%
Combined						
By count	52.6%	63.3%	78.3%	87.7%	72.3%	80.5%
By value	5.8%	14.4%	35.3%	38.3%	85.8%	20.1%

Stale means price staleness of two days or more. Liquidity categories are as in Table 5.4.

among liquidity category I securities (government bonds) is 52.6 percent by count and 5.8 percent by value. These numbers increase to 78.3 and 35.3 percent, respectively, for liquidity category III securities and to 72.3 and 85.8 percent, respectively, for liquidity category V securities.[5]

I have also estimated the incidence of theoretical and stale prices for marketable collateral using the old Pricing rule 1. The numbers are extremely similar. The fractions of all collateral that would have theoretical prices are 77.4 percent by count and 16.5 percent by value. The respective fractions with stale prices are 3.2 percent and 3.6 percent. The reason why it does not make much of a difference which pricing rule is used relates to the large stability over time with

Footnote 28), and these tend to be in the system as having a model as their pricing source (around 60 percent on January 13, 2015). This is not adjusted for in the calculations.

[5] Liquidity categories III and V include traditional covered bonds and ABSs, respectively. See Table 5.4 for details. The numbers in the first two panels of Exhibit 7.1 do not add up exactly to those in the third panel because of rounding.

respect to whether a security is in Bloomberg and, if it is in, has a market or model price. Thus, whether the absence of a market price on the day is a trigger for giving a theoretical price (as in Pricing rule 2) or whether it is the absence of a new market price over the last five days (Pricing rule 1) is unimportant empirically.

That there is a heavy reliance on theoretical prices within the Eurosystem's collateral framework is arguably not surprising given the very large number of eligible collateral. It is hard to conceive of there being 30,000 to 40,000 actively traded debt securities. What may be more surprising is that as many as almost 20 percent of all securities, 6,441 ISINs in Table 7.1, on the public list of eligible collateral have fresh market prices on a daily basis. This may well be an overestimate. Of the ISINs I have classified as having market prices, 75 percent, by count, and 99 percent, by value, have the standard "BGN" pricing source. According to Bloomberg, "BGN is a real-time composite based on quotes from multiple contributors. Where executable quotes are available BGN provides an indication of the executable market. Where limited executable prices are available BGN provides an indicative level of where a bond is priced." Thus, many of these ISINs do not necessarily have proper, tradeable market prices, at least not as found in Bloomberg. My estimate of the incidence of market prices may, therefore, be biased upward. Conversely, my estimate of the incidence of theoretical prices may be too low.

One may also speculate that the relatively larger number of securities with market prices is influenced by small trades that are made for the purpose of establishing a price. Since the Eurosystem's pricing rule does not say anything about volume, it seems plausible that one can manipulate, or move, the market price and thus the collateral value of a thinly traded security.[6] Regardless of whether there is collateral price-manipulation, the large reliance on

---

[6] Recent examples of manipulation, or alleged manipulation, in financial markets include Libor, gold, and exchange rates. Regarding allegations of foreign exchange manipulation, see, e.g., "US offers immunity to forex traders," *Financial Times Europe*, Monday July 14, 2014, p. 1.

theoretical prices gives rise to the potential for biases. This is explicitly recognized in the collateral framework by assigning a valuation markdown of 5 percent to collateral of certain types where a theoretical price is used (see Tables 5.1 to 5.4). Paradoxically, this may, in turn, create an incentive for banks possessing thinly traded securities to manipulate prices in order to avoid the extra 5 percent markdown. I have not examined, however, whether this actually takes place.

7.2   PLEDGED COLLATERAL

The evidence above looks at the incidence of theoretical and stale prices among eligible marketable collateral. This section does the same for pledged, or used, collateral, using the same conservative classification as in Section 7.1. Because the incidence of theoretical prices is increasing in the liquidity category and because usage percentages tend to be larger among eligible collateral in the higher liquidity categories (Table 4.2), the incidence of theoretical and stale prices among marketable collateral that is actually used is likely to be larger than for all eligible marketable collateral. Furthermore, to gauge the overall incidence of theoretical and stale prices among all pledged collateral, it is also necessary to take into account non-marketable collateral.

By definition, non-marketable collateral necessarily have theoretical prices of some kind or another. The pricing rule in the official documentation is that one uses either what is referred to as a theoretical price or the nominal, or outstanding, amount (ECB 2006/12, 2011/14, and 2014/60). Higher haircuts may apply in the latter case. Taking the nominal amount can be viewed as using a primitive theoretical pricing model, where credit risk and discounting are ignored. I classify all non-marketable collateral as having a theoretical price.

To estimate the fraction of pledged collateral that have their collateral values based on theoretical or stale prices, I start with the "combined" frequencies in the last panel of Exhibit 7.1. These give the frequencies of theoretical or stale prices for the eligible marketable collateral on January 13, 2015, for each of the five liquidity categories. To get corresponding numbers for the collateral that was actually pledged, I employ usage statistics available on the ECB's website to calculate usage fractions, or weights, for each of the liquidity groups. That is, I estimate the percentages of the pledged marketable collateral that falls into each of the five liquidity categories. I then employ the usage statistics again to calculate the split between pledged marketable and non-marketable collateral. With these figures in hand, I can proceed to estimate the incidence of theoretical or stale prices among the pledged collateral. Specifically, I proceed as follows.

I start with the same kind of aggregate collateral usage statistics as analyzed in Table 4.2 and Figure 4.1. Since the data in Section 7.1 is from January 2015, I employ collateral usage figures for 2014Q4.[7] These numbers and the implied usage fractions (weights) by value are as tabulated in Exhibit 7.2.

Exhibit 7.2 Collateral usage by collateral value (billion EUR), 2014Q4.

Liquidity category	I	II	III	IV	V	Non-marketable
Value	372.6	382.8	240.9	180.9	309.2	362.1
Usage fraction by collateral value						
Marketable	25.1%	25.8%	16.2%	12.2%	20.8%	
Non-marketable						19.6%

[7] When this exercise was carried out, this was the closest available time period. See www.ecb.europa.eu/mopo/assets/charts/html/index.en.html. The ECB provides these numbers for the categories shown in Figure 4.1, which can be allocated to liquidity categories using Table 5.4. As observed in Chapter 4, Footnote 1, "other marketable assets" represents securities issued by supranational institutions and agencies. The ECB numbers do not distinguish between jumbo covered bonds (liquidity category II) or traditional pfandbrief (liquidity category III). I have therefore split the covered bond usage equally between these two liquidity categories. A different split would result in slightly different estimates for the usage incidence of theoretical and stale prices, but not more than about 2.5 percentage points either way.

To understand these figures, note that the usage fraction of 25.1 percent for liquidity category I is 372.6 as a percentage of the sum of collateral values across all five liquidity categories. The five liquidity categories comprise the set of marketable collateral. Thus, the tabulated usage fraction for each liquidity category, I to V, is its fraction of usage within the set of marketable collateral. The 19.6 percent usage fraction of non-marketable collateral is not taken into account in those figures.

By applying the usage fractions above to the theoretical and stale price frequencies tabulated in Exhibit 7.1 on a liquidity category by liquidity category basis, *the incidence of pledged marketable collateral that is theoretically valued or stale is estimated to be 33.4 percent, by value.*[8] For theoretical prices alone, the figure is 30.0 percent.

Taking into account that 19.6 percent of pledged collateral is non-marketable and, therefore, have collateral values based on theoretical prices, *the incidence of pledged collateral with theoretical or stale prices is estimated to be 46.4 percent, by value.*[9] For theoretical prices alone, the figure is 43.7 percent – so not much different. That close to half of the aggregate collateral value of the assets that are pledged in Eurosystem operations is based on theoretical valuations or stale prices is highly suggestive of a collateral framework where market forces are relatively unimportant.

It is also interesting to estimate the theoretical or stale price usage among pledged collateral on a "by count" basis. This is only possible for marketable collateral. However, the usage fractions in Exhibit 7.2 cannot be used because they are based on total collateral values within each liquidity group, rather than the number of ISINs. We know from Table 7.1, for example, that the less liquid categories (except V) are comprised of a large number of small issues. Thus, to estimate the "by count" usage of theoretical or stale prices, I combine

---

[8] Multiply the usage fractions in Exhibit 7.2 by the corresponding "by value" percentages in the "combined" panel in Exhibit 7.1 and take the sum.

[9] This is calculated as follows: $0.196 + (1 - 0.196) \times 0.334 = 0.464$.

the information in Table 7.1 with that in the first row of Exhibit 7.2, to estimate the relative number of ISINs pledged in each liquidity category.

Exhibit 7.3 lays out the estimation procedure. For each liquidity category, I first use the figures for the total outstanding amount and total number of distinct collateral (ISINs) in Table 7.1 to estimate the average amount outstanding per ISIN. I then take the total collateral value (taken from Exhibit 7.2) for each liquidity category and divide it by the estimated average amount per ISIN. This yields what I refer to as the "relative ISIN count" for each liquidity category. These numbers are not estimates of the number of ISINs with theoretical or stale prices, because it is unlikely that the entire outstanding amount of an individual ISIN is pledged. However, if the pledged fraction of the total outstanding amount is the same across each ISIN in the set of pledged collateral, the relative ISIN counts provide consistent measures of the relative number of ISINs within each liquidity category. I use the relative ISIN counts in this way, although the underlying assumption is unlikely to be perfectly met. My objective is only to get a sense of the frequency with which theoretical or stale prices are used with respect to calculating collateral values. Analogously to the usage fractions by collateral value in Exhibit 7.2, the usage fractions by count are then each liquidity category's relative ISIN count as a fraction of their sum.

Exhibit 7.3 Collateral usage by count.

Liquidity category	I	II	III	IV	V
From Table 7.1					
Amount outstanding (billion EUR)	6,660.2	2,055.1	1,560.7	2,302.2	638.4
Number of ISINs	2,285	3,469	6,441	20,571	913
Amount per ISIN (billion EUR)	2.915	0.592	0.242	0.112	0.699
Collateral pledged					
Value 2014Q4 (billion EUR)	372.6	382.8	240.9	180.9	309.2
Relative ISIN count	127.83	646.15	994.22	1,616.41	442.22
Usage fraction by count	3.34%	16.88%	25.98%	42.24%	11.56%

The exhibit shows that the usage fraction by count is increasing in the liquidity category, though falling back for liquidity category V (ABSs). Applying these usage fractions as weights to the combined theoretical or stale frequencies in Exhibit 7.1, yields the result that, *by count, approximately 78.2 percent of pledged marketable collateral have prices that are either theoretical or stale.*[10]

7.3 SUMMARY

This chapter has looked at the determination of market versus theoretical prices with respect to calculating Eurosystem collateral values. The incidence of theoretical prices and the incidence of stale prices are estimated by feeding the ISINs on the public list of eligible collateral into Bloomberg. Over a sample period covering more than half a year, the fraction of ISINs that are in Bloomberg with a model as a pricing source, no pricing source, or are not found is approximately 73 percent as a daily average. Unless there is a systematic bias in the Bloomberg data, this 73 percent represents a lower bound on the percentage of ISINs on the public list, by count, that have their collateral values determined by theoretical prices. This is so because not all ISINs with missing prices are in Bloomberg with the "no pricing source" label.

Taking price histories into account, the fractions of assets that have collateral values determined by theoretical or stale prices are estimated to be, approximately:

1. 80%, by count, and 20%, by value, for eligible marketable collateral;
2. 78%, by count, and 33%, by value, for pledged (used) marketable collateral;
3. and 46%, by value, for all pledged (used) collateral.

[10] The estimation does not take into account that haircuts vary systematically across liquidity categories. I have also run slightly more complicated estimation procedures where this is controlled for. If I assume that the average pledged collateral has a residual maturity of one to three years and has a fixed coupon, then, using the division of collateral between rating categories 1, 2, and "exempt," from Table 7.1 and haircuts from Table 5.4, the estimate of the incidence of theoretical or stale prices among pledged marketable collateral is 79 percent. This does not change if I assume a typical residual maturity of three to five years. Thus, the 78 percent estimate cited in the text is fairly robust.

The overall conclusion is therefore that theoretical and stale prices are significant features of the Eurosystem's collateral framework. Exhibit 7.1 shows that it is especially theoretical prices that are important. Section 7.2 estimates that the total fraction of pledged collateral with theoretical prices is approximately 44 percent, by value. That almost half of the pledged value in Eurosystem operations are based on theoretical prices, and more than 70 percent of eligible marketable assets have their collateral values determined theoretically, point to a surprisingly small role for market discipline in the money creation process.

8 Collateral "Own Use"

"Own use" of collateral is the case that a counterparty uses collateral (in a Eurosystem operation) issued by itself or an entity with which it has "close links." As defined in the official documentation, close links are said to exist between two parties, A and B, (i) if at least one of the parties owns or controls, directly or indirectly, 20 percent or more of the capital or voting rights of the other, or (ii) a third party owns or controls, directly or indirectly, the majority of the capital or voting rights of both A and B.[1] As of January 1, 2007, this is refined to include issuers, debtors, and guarantors (ECB 2006/12). In October 2008, the trigger level with respect to the third party in (ii) is changed from "majority of the capital" to "more than 20% of the capital of the counterparty [using the collateral in a Eurosystem operation] and more than 20% of the capital of the issuer/debtor/guarantor, either directly or indirectly, through one or more undertakings" (ECB 2008/13). Own-use collateral is sometimes also referred to as "retained collateral" in the official documentation.

With respect to eligibility, the baseline rule is that:

> Despite their inclusion in the tier one list, National Central Banks shall not accept as underlying assets debt instruments issued or guaranteed by the counterparty, or by any other entity with which the counterparty has close links.

> ECB (2000/7, p. 33).

While this would make own use of collateral impossible, there are and have always been exemptions to the baseline rule.

[1] This is based on Directive (2000/12/EC), ECB (2005/2, footnote 50), and ECB (2006/12). Only the first of these specifically refers to voting rights. The two more recent references specify own use in terms of ownership of capital.

The exemptions are initially laid out in ECB (2000/7). Specifically, footnote 45 of this document states that the prohibition against
own-use collateral does not apply to

1. "close links between the counterparty and the public authorities of EEA
   countries;" ECB (2003/16, footnote 52) adds the following parenthetic
   clause to this: "(including the case where the public authority is a guarantor of the issuer)"; ECB (2008/13) adds that the public authority acting as
   guarantor should have "the right to levy taxes" and
2. "debt instruments which comply strictly with the criteria set out in
   Article 22(4) of the UCITS Directive (Directive 88/220/EEC amending
   Directive 85/611/EEC)" or "cases in which debt instruments are protected
   by specific legal safeguards [that are] comparable."

The criteria in Article 22(4) referred to in point 2 above are essentially that the debt instrument is a covered bond.[2] This is made
explicit in subsequent collateral framework updates (first time in
ECB 2006/12). In other words, instruments that either have government guarantees or are covered bonds are exempted from the own-use
prohibition. Subsequent updates expand on the exemption by, for
example, including uncovered bonds, as long as these do not comprise more than 10 percent of a bank's collateral pool by value after
haircuts (ECB 2009/1). This percentage is later reduced to 5 percent
(ECB 2011/14). Exemptions are also given to "non-marketable retail
mortgage-backed debt instruments (RMBDs) which are not securities" (ECB 2008/13, p. 35) and "certain covered bonds not declared
UCITS-compliant...that fulfil all the criteria that apply to assset-
backed securities...and [some] additional criteria" (ECB 2010/13,
p. 32).[3]

Own use has the potential to weaken market discipline since
it means that if a bank cannot place an issue fully in the market,
it can turn around and refinance the unsold portion from the ECB,

---

[2] The UCITS Directive was updated in July 2009, with the old Article 22 replaced
by the new Article 52. Thus, the old Article 22(4) is replaced by the new Article
52(4). See Directive (2009/65/EC).
[3] See also ECB (2010/30 and 2011/14). ECB (2014/60) provides some updates.

after a haircut. Up until November 1, 2013, own-use collateral could be used without any penalty in the form of a larger haircut. Since then, however, a valuation markdown (penalty haircut) of 8 to 12 has been applied (Table 5.4, Footnote 6). This is a signal that own use of collateral is viewed as undesirable by the ECB. It is therefore odd that the rules for own-use collateral have been relaxed, as documented in this chapter. However, it does fit in with the general picture of there being a large number of weak credit institutions in the euro area, with the collateral framework being used to support them.

That collateral with government guarantees have been exempted from the prohibition on own use is especially important in light of the relatively large incidence of government guarantees in some countries, especially after the introduction of the three-year LTROs under the full allotment policy. It reinforces the view that the collateral framework, in conjunction with the full allotment policy and very long-maturity LTROs, opens a back door to bailouts. The ECB froze the usage (by nominal value) of own-use collateral with government guarantees on July 3, 2012, at the level at that time (ECB 2012/12). This was just four months after the second three-year LTRO. The view that there is a link between own-use collateral with government guarantees and the three-year LTROs is supported by the decision of the ECB in March 2013 that such collateral would no longer be eligible once the second of the two three-year LTROs matured – except in "exceptional cases" (ECB 2013/6).[4]

---

[4] The second three-year LTRO matured on February 26, 2015.

9   Non-regulated Markets, Unsecured Bank Debt, and LTRO Uptake

From the beginning, the Eurosystem's collateral framework granted eligibility status to marketable securities traded on either regulated or non-regulated markets (ECB 2000/7). Regulated markets include exchanges such as the "Frankfurter Wertpapierbörse (Regulierter Markt)" operated by Deutsche Börse AG and "Eurex Deutschland" operated by Eurex Frankfurt AG in Germany as well as "Euronext Paris" and "MATIF" operated by Euronext Paris in France, or the "Wholesale Italian and Foreign Government Bond Markets (MTS)" operated by Società per il Mercato dei Titoli di Stato – MTS S.p.A. in Italy. On October 4, 2014, for example, the list included eighty-eight regulated markets.[1]

Examples of non-regulated markets that are currently accepted by the ECB include the "STEP market" in the EU, the "French Medium-Term Notes (BMTN) market," and "the unofficial market (Freiverkehr) of a German exchange." On October 4, 2014, the list included twenty accepted non-regulated markets.[2]

While securities could potentially trade on different types of markets, the initial collateral framework described in ECB (2000/7) specifies that collateral issued by credit institutions is only eligible if it trades on a regulated market, except in the case of covered bonds.[3]

---

[1] See European Commission (2010b). The list of regulated markets is regularly updated on http://ec.europa.eu/internal_market/securities/isd/mifid/index _en.htm.

[2] See www.ecb.europa.eu/paym/coll/standards/marketable/html/index.en.html.

[3] Strictly speaking, the exception initially applied to debt instruments that complied with the criteria set out in Article 22(4) of the UCITS Directive 88/220/EEC (amending Directive 85/611/EEC). This is essentially the same as saying that the instrument is a covered bond. The UCITS Directive was updated in July 2009, with Article 22 being replaced by Article 52 in Directive (2009/65/EC). See Chapter 8, Footnote 2.

Thus, unsecured debt issued by credit institutions, or banks for short, trading on non-regulated markets was not eligible collateral, except in exceptional circumstances at the discretion of the Eurosystem.

This changed after the Lehman bankruptcy in the fall of 2008. In particular, as of October 25, 2008 (ECB 2008/11, Article 4):

> Debt instruments issued by credit institutions, which are traded on certain non-regulated markets, as specified by the ECB shall constitute eligible collateral for the purposes of Eurosystem monetary policy operations.

Hence unsecured bank bonds trading on non-regulated markets are subject to eligibility from October 25, 2008. As shown in Table 5.2, bank debt trading on non-regulated markets was initially subject to an additional haircut of 5 percent as compared with corresponding instruments trading on regulated markets. This reflects the increased risk and illiquidity of such collateral. Nevertheless, this extra haircut was later dropped (see Tables 5.3 and 5.4). I will refer to the inclusion of unsecured bank debt trading on non-regulated markets into the public list of eligible collateral as the "non-regulated markets inclusion clause."

The non-regulated markets inclusion clause was an emergency measure. It was part of a large swathe of unconventional monetary policy introduced as a result of the financial crisis. It was initially meant to last until November 30, 2008, but was prolonged twice until it finally expired on December 31, 2010.[4] It was reintroduced one year later, as of January 1, 2012, but this time into the General framework.[5] The timing of the reintroduction is notable because it was in time for the second of the two three-year LTROs (see Table 3.1). In other words, it was reintroduced at the time of the second spurt in unconventional monetary policy. Thus, the two-time inclusion of unsecured bank debt trading on non-regulated markets coincided with the two most significant measures taken by the ECB to deal

---

[4] See ECB (2008/18) and ECB (2009/24).
[5] See ECB (2011/14).

with the financial and sovereign debt crisis before 2014, namely the full allotment policy and the three-year LTROs.

The non-regulated markets inclusion clause had a huge impact on the set of eligible collateral. While I do not have access to the eligible collateral lists before April 8, 2010, the impact can nevertheless be seen by examining the set of eligible collateral since then. This is shown in Figure 9.1.

Figure 9.1a shows the time series of the number of eligible collateral on the public list, broken down by the country of residence of the issuer. The nine largest countries, by number of eligible collateral, are shown, with all other countries lumped together as one ("Others"). Figure 9.1b shows the same time series, but now broken down by liquidity category. Table 9.1 shows the precise numbers for the countries represented in Figure 9.1.

The impact of the exclusion of unsecured bank debt trading on non-regulated markets at the year-change 2010/2011 is seen as a large downward jump in the time series. In particular, the number of eligible collateral falls from 42,717 on December 31, 2010, to 28,198 on January 1, 2011, a decrease of 34.0 percent. The number of eligible collateral stays close to this low level for the duration of 2011. On January 1, 2012, it jumps up again to 39,642 from 29,126 on December 31, 2011, an increase of 36.1 percent. Figure 9.1b confirms that these changes are almost exclusively arising from liquidity category IV, i.e., unsecured bank debt. Indeed, liquidity category IV accounts for 79.3 percent of the aggregate decrease at the year-change 2010/2011 and 99.7 percent of the subsequent increase at the year-change 2011/2012 when unsecured bank bonds trading on non-regulated markets were once again considered for the public list of eligible collateral.[6]

Figure 9.1a reveals which countries were more affected by these changes. Overall, Germany and France can be seen to contribute more

---

[6] On December 31, 2010, other temporary measures, such as foreign currency debt instruments or subordinated instruments with guarantees being eligible in the collateral framework, expired as well (see Tables 5.2 and 5.3). This helps explain why unsecured bank bonds (liquidity category IV) comprise "only" 79.3 percent of the decrease at the year-change 2010/2011.

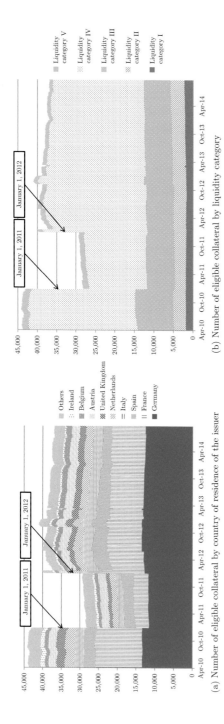

FIGURE 9.1 Number of eligible collateral by country and liquidity category

Time period: April 8, 2010, to September 15, 2014.

These figures show the number of securities in the public list of eligible collateral over time by the country of residence of the issuer (Figure 9.1a) and liquidity category (Figure 9.1b). The nine largest (by count) countries are shown individually. The sharp down and up turns at the year-changes 2010/2011 and 2011/2012, respectively, arise because of the withdrawal and reintroduction, respectively, of the "non-regulated markets inclusion clause." The effect of this clause is to include, in the public list of eligible collateral, credit institution unsecured debt instruments trading on ECB-approved non-regulated markets.

Data sources: Public lists of eligible collateral, published on the ECB webpage, www.ecb.europa.eu/paym/coll/assets/html/list.en.html.

Table 9.1 *Number of eligible collateral: impact of "non-regulated markets inclusion clause"*

Panel A: Number of securities by issuer residence

| | Year-end 2010 | | | | | Year-end 2011 | | | | |
| | Number of securities | | Change | | | Number of securities | | Change | | |
Issuer residence	Dec 31, 2010	Jan 1, 2011	Count	Percent	Percent of aggregate	Dec 31, 2011	Jan 1, 2012	Count	Percent	Percent of aggregate
Germany	13,329	11,596	−1,733	−13.0	11.9	11,692	12,713	1,021	8.7	9.7
France	11,598	3,384	−8,214	−70.8	56.6	3,743	11,174	7,431	198.5	70.7
Spain	2,985	2,952	−33	−1.1	0.2	3,579	3,607	28	0.8	0.3
Italy	2,535	1,656	−879	−34.7	6.1	1,626	2,778	1,152	70.8	11.0
Netherlands	2,411	1,493	−918	−38.1	6.3	1,450	1,777	327	22.6	3.1
United Kingdom	2,268	957	−1,311	−57.8	9.0	963	1,180	217	22.5	2.1
Austria	2,143	2,024	−119	−5.6	0.8	2,101	2,187	86	4.1	0.8
Belgium	933	662	−271	−29.0	1.9	812	943	131	16.1	1.2
Ireland	880	630	−250	−28.4	1.7	515	532	17	3.3	0.2
Others	3,635	2,844	−791	−21.8	5.4	2,645	2,751	106	4.0	1.0
Total	42,717	28,198	−14,519	−34.0	100.0	29,126	39,642	10,516	36.1	100.0

Panel B: Number of securities by liquidity category

| | Year-end 2010 | | | | | Year-end 2011 | | | | |
| | Number of securities | | Change | | | Number of securities | | Change | | |
Liquidity category	Dec 31, 2010	Jan 1, 2011	Count	Percent	Percent of aggregate	Dec 31, 2011	Jan 1, 2012	Count	Percent	Percent of aggregate
I	1,918	1,803	−115	−6.0	0.8	1,738	1,739	1	0.1	0.0
II	3,178	2,823	−355	−11.2	2.4	3,165	3,179	14	0.4	0.1
III	9,557	7,122	−2,435	−25.5	16.8	6,750	6,760	10	0.1	0.1
IV	26,387	14,869	−11,518	−43.7	79.3	16,147	26,634	10,487	64.9	99.7
V	1,677	1,581	−96	−5.7	0.7	1,326	1,330	4	0.3	0.0
Total	42,717	28,198	−14,519	−34.0	100.0	29,126	39,642	10,516	36.1	100.0

This table reports on the overnight changes in the number of securities in the public list of eligible collateral from December 31, 2010, to January 1, 2011, and from December 31, 2011, to January 1, 2012. For both year-changes, the table shows the number of eligible marketable assets on December 31 and January 1, and the changes in absolute terms (count), in relative terms within a group (percent), and as a percentage of the total change (percent of aggregate) by issuer residence (Panel A) and by liquidity category (Panel B). The 2010/2011 and 2011/2012 year-changes saw the "non-regulated markets inclusion clause" being repealed and reintroduced, respectively. *Data source:* Public lists of eligible collateral, published on the ECB webpage, www.ecb.europa.eu/paym/coll/assets/html/list.en.html.

than 50 percent of securities on the public list of eligible collateral. However, France is substantially more affected by the non-regulated markets inclusion clause. While 27.2 percent of all eligible collateral on the public list at the end of 2010 is French (the issuer has residence in France), 56.6 percent of the reduction in collateral is accounted for by France. Similarly, while only 12.9 percent of all eligible collateral on the public list at the end of 2011 is French, France accounts for 70.7 percent of the increase.

In terms of the impact across countries, Table 9.1 shows that at the year-change 2010/2011, the impact is the largest for France, with a reduction in the number of eligible collateral of 8,214, or 70.8 percent of all eligible French securities. More interestingly, perhaps, because of the relevance for the second three-year LTRO, at the year-change 2011/2012, France sees the biggest gain (198.5 percent), followed by Italy (70.8 percent), and then the Netherlands and the United Kingdom (22.6 and 22.5 percent, respectively).

Exhibit 9.1 reports on the aggregate level of Eurosystem credit to banks in eight countries, in September 2011 (three months before the first three-year LTRO), December 2011 (the month of the first three-year LTRO), and March 2012 (the month after the second three-year LTRO, which was held at the end of February 2012).

Exhibit 9.1 LTRO by country (billion EUR).

	March 2012	December 2011	September 2011
Spain	315.3	85.3	46.4
Italy	267.6	160.6	58.5
France	144.3	63.4	30.7
Ireland	79.0	76.3	77.3
Germany	73.2	47.1	18.4
Portugal	50.6	39.0	31.5
Belgium	39.8	18.0	7.4
Greece	36.8	60.9	72.7

Data source: National Central Banks (from Bloomberg).

The countries are ordered from the largest to the smallest in terms of LTRO uptake, measured in March 2012. This also roughly corresponds to the order of the largest increase in LTRO uptake from September 2011 to March 2012. In other words, the three-year LTROs had the biggest aggregate impact on Spanish banks, followed by Italian and French banks. While the numbers are not normalized for the size of the respective economies or banking sectors, it does indicate that the three-year LTROs were particularly important for these three countries. Italian and French banks were also those that benefited the most from the inclusion of unsecured bank debt trading on non-regulated markets in the public list of eligible collateral, in terms of having the largest increase in the number of eligible collateral at the year-change 2011/2012. This is consistent with the view that the non-regulated markets inclusion clause is part of an overall package to support, or indirectly bail out, banks. The evidence in this chapter also shows that many of these support, or bailout, measures had quite substantially heterogeneous impact across banks in different countries.

10 Market Discipline

Market forces and discipline are important notions in the context of collateral frameworks for several reasons. As illustrated by Equation (2.1) and Figure 2.1, collateral values are determined by applying haircuts to, in principle, market prices. Furthermore, market discipline is typically viewed as an important complement to financial regulation. It is one of the three pillars in both the Basel II and III bank regulation frameworks (BCBS 2011). The idea is that banks, like other enterprises, should be regulated not only through formal regulatory rules, but through the competitive forces of the market. More generally, market and competitive forces are central to the efficient allocation of capital and resources. We would expect this principle to be relevant also in the case of the market for liquidity and the money creation process.

An issue raised in this book, however, is that markets are utilized to a relatively small degree by the Eurosystem's collateral framework. Indeed, it appears that many features of the framework are designed to circumvent market discipline. Chapters 5 to 9 offer much by way of detail that speaks to this. The current chapter distills these findings and discusses some of the consequences of the relative lack of market discipline allowed for by the Eurosystem's collateral framework.

10.1 MARKET DISCIPLINE IMPAIRMENT

Several features of the Eurosystem's collateral framework impinge on market discipline. Some of the most noteworthy of these are listed below.

First, non-marketable assets are included in the set of eligible collateral. Thus, banks can obtain liquidity without having themselves or their assets assessed in the market. The evidence shows that the usage of non-marketable collateral has increased in the euro area over time, reaching approximately 10 percent in 2007 and more than 20 percent in 2011 where it has remained (Figure 4.1).

Second, a substantial fraction of marketable collateral on the public list of eligible collateral trades on non-regulated markets (more than 30 percent, Table 9.1). One might expect prices in such markets to be fairly unreliable as compared with regulated markets. This view is supported by the evidence in Table 7.1 that the incidence of theoretical prices is much higher for collateral trading on non-regulated markets than for other marketable collateral.

Third, there is vastly more eligible collateral than what is needed in aggregate (Chapter 4). Furthermore, the fact that banks pledge substantially more collateral than is necessary suggests that much of the eligible collateral has no opportunity cost. The ratio of the value of pledged collateral to aggregate liquidity uptake in 2013 is more than three to one. It is unclear that this is optimal. It contributes to reducing market discipline and the incentive for the private provision of liquidity.

Fourth, a large portion of the eligible collateral is so illiquid that it has no market price (Chapter 7). Around 76 percent, by count, of the 30,000 to 40,000 ISINs on the public list of eligible collateral have their prices determined theoretically. This is based on feeding all ISINs on the public list of eligible collateral into Bloomberg. This platform is perhaps the most important source of market data in the financial industry. The large incidence of eligible collateral without market prices in Bloomberg is strong support for the thesis that market forces and discipline are not central pillars of the Eurosystem's collateral framework.

Fifth, stale prices are also a feature of the Eurosystem's collateral framework. Over some subperiods, the collateral framework explicitly allows market prices to be up to five days old before a price is estimated theoretically (Chapter 7). Over other subperiods, the market prices that are used to estimate Eurosystem collateral values simply turn out to be stale (two or more days old). I estimate that prices are stale for close to 20 percent of the collateral with market prices. Thus, approximately 80 percent of all ISINs on the public list have theoretical or stale prices. By value, about a fifth of eligible marketable assets have collateral values that are based on theoretical or stale price. For the marketable collateral that is actually pledged, this fraction increases to about one third. When we include non-marketable collateral, the fraction, by value, of pledged collateral with theoretical or stale prices is almost one half. This illustrates the ease with which banks can side-step the influence of markets when acting within the "constraints" of the Eurosystem's collateral framework.

Sixth, with respect to determining market prices of eligible collateral, there is no official rule that addresses depth, that is, the volume observed prices are good for. This opens up the possibility of manipulating the prices of thinly traded eligible collateral. This can also affect theoretical prices, since these must necessarily be based on prices of comparable securities. While the collateral framework thus provides incentives for price manipulation, this book does not examine whether it actually takes place. The lack of market depth is especially a concern for illiquid collateral that, by definition, have low volumes.

Seventh, in Eurosystem operations, a bank is allowed to use collateral issued by an entity with which it has close links. The rules with respect to such "own use" have become increasingly lenient over the course of the crisis (Chapter 8). Evidence based on detailed bank-level data from Germany shows that own-use collateral has increased over time, especially among large banks (Fecht, Nyborg, Rocholl, and Woschitz 2016).

Eighth, Eurosystem haircuts are set by the ECB rather than determined in the market (Chapter 5). Indeed, influence appears to flow in the reverse direction, with the fixed haircuts set by the ECB being adopted by some segments of the market (Section 5.5). Furthermore, the second example in Section 6.3 suggests that Eurosystem haircuts influence market prices of eligible collateral, with larger haircuts reducing prices, *ceteris paribus*.

Ninth, revisions to Eurosystem haircuts are rare (Tables 5.1 to 5.4). The average time between new overall haircut rules is more than three years, but some classes of collateral have not had their haircuts changed over the entire March 2004 to January 2015 period of study of this book.

Tenth, the only market-based, or near-market-based, information that affects haircuts is ratings by external rating agencies (since October 2008). However, there is no aggregation of ratings by different agencies. Instead, except for ABSs, only the highest rating matters ("highest rating rule"), which invites ratings shopping and catering.[1]

There are four accepted rating agencies, S&P, Fitch, Moody's, and DBRS. The inclusion of DBRS to this list has contributed to higher ratings. A purely statistical effect is that the distribution of the highest rating shifts to the right as one adds agencies (unless rating agencies become more conservative as one adds competitors to their business). In addition, as evidenced from sovereign ratings, DBRS also gives higher ratings than the other agencies. It has been pivotal in giving Italy, Spain, and Ireland A− ratings and Portugal a BBB− rating over several years. No other agency has been pivotal for a country rated by DBRS (Table 6.2).

Eleventh, there are only two ratings categories for the purpose of setting haircuts for eligible collateral, above A− and BBB+ to BBB−. The ineffectiveness of ratings as a tool by which to differentiate haircuts can be seen from the finding that the vast majority of marketable eligible collateral on the public list are rated A− or higher, the percentage being approximately 85 percent by count (Tables 5.5 and 6.6) and 90 percent by value

---

[1] For ABSs, the most recent rule is that the second highest rating is what matters (Table 6.1).

(Table 7.1). This is surprising, but may be the result of the highest-rating rule.

Twelfth, collateral with ratings below BBB− are in principle not eligible, but exemptions from this rule for sovereign bonds with lower ratings are standard (Section 6.2).

Thirteenth, while a rating from an approved external rating agency, either for the issue, the issuer, or the guarantor, is necessary to be on the public list, collateral can also be made eligible privately through the use of an NCB or approved in-house or third-party rating. The collateral framework recognizes that banks have an incentive to shop around for the most favorable model or tweak their own model, by not allowing banks to use more than one model per year (ECB 2006/12). This is implicit recognition that private ratings models pose a potential problem. Given the abundance of eligible collateral on the public list, it is an open question as to why privately eligible collateral is allowed.

Fourteenth, guarantees can be used to boost ratings. This reduces the role of markets and potentially enhances the role of politics. Government guarantees increased greatly in advance of the second three-year LTRO in February 2012, especially in Italy (Figure 6.1). The run up to this LTRO also saw the inclusion of more than 10,000 securities trading on non-regulated markets into the set of eligible collateral.

The full allotment policy introduced in October 2008 enhances these potential sources of market discipline impairment. This is so because, under this policy, banks can obtain all the liquidity and funding they wish directly from the central bank. Banks are only constrained by the value of their collateral within the Eurosystem, as determined by Equation (2.1). Indeed, as seen in Figure 3.1, the quantity of central bank money has increased substantially after the introduction of the full allotment policy, thus placing more demands on collateral and magnifying the distortions that arise from the impairment of market forces.

10.2   BIASES AND SYSTEMIC ARBITRAGE

The evidence in Chapter 4 suggests that the collateral framework in the euro area is biased toward what we can think of as lower-quality collateral. There appears to be a preference, or bias, toward the usage of more illiquid and risky collateral that has increased over time (Table 4.2 and Figure 4.1). The production of lower-quality collateral has increased as well.

These findings are consistent with the anecdotal evidence that there is a pecking order for the use of collateral as follows:

- Lowest-quality collateral used with central bank.
- Intermediate-quality collateral used in CCP repos.
- Highest-quality collateral used in bilateral repos.

This pecking order must reflect the efficient use of collateral by banks. That the lowest quality collateral is used in repos with the Eurosystem may, in part, result from CCPs not accepting the very worst collateral and, in part, that two-sided credit risk in bilateral repos tends to favor higher-quality collateral, as discussed in Chapter 2. But it is also likely a reflection of collateral values in Eurosystem repos being relatively high for low-quality collateral, since banks have an incentive to use collateral in repos with the central bank that is valued relatively highly within the collateral framework as compared to in the markets.

We can say that the collateral framework provides the banks with an opportunity for engaging in *collateral arbitrage* vis-à-vis the central bank. Banks can use the worst quality collateral in repos with the Eurosystem to obtain central bank money and then turn around and reallocate that liquidity amongst themselves, saving on the best quality collateral in the process. This can also be thought of as a form of *systemic arbitrage* by the banks in aggregate, since they are essentially arbitraging the monetary system.

Equation (2.1) shows that relatively high collateral values of low-quality collateral can result from relatively small haircuts or relatively large prices. Haircuts are under the control of the central bank. For the most illiquid collateral, prices are also ultimately controlled by the central bank since such collateral has its price determined theoretically. Hence, the more illiquid the collateral, the bigger is the role of the central bank in setting the collateral value. Given the preference for using illiquid collateral in repos with the Eurosystem, this suggests that the Eurosystem is especially generous when it comes to illiquid collateral.

Such central bank generosity may well be the result of a deliberate intent to "channel liquidity where it is needed." The preference can get stronger over time, as the evidence suggests is the case, if the gap in liquidity between more liquid and less liquid collateral increases. This is so because haircuts are stale (Tables 5.1 to 5.4) and, more generally, because haircuts and collateral values do not respond much to market forces, as documented above. These features of the collateral framework also mean that the bias can increase over time through banks (endogenously) creating illiquid collateral to take advantage of the good terms on such collateral on offer in Eurosystem repos. This is especially a concern under the full allotment policy. It is also important to note that a direct corollary of a central bank policy to directly "channel liquidity where it is needed" is that interbank trade, and thereby market discipline, is undermined.

Some specific features that impair market discipline and that may contribute to the bias toward illiquid collateral are as follows. First, years pass between haircut updates. Second, theoretical models to determine prices may not adequately reflect the illiquidity of the collateral to be priced. The very fact that a particular collateral is so illiquid that it needs to be priced theoretically suggests that it could only be realized for cash in the market by giving a discount to similar, traded collateral. That the ECB adds a valuation markdowns to some collateral assigned a theoretical price, first time in October 2008 (Table 5.2), suggests that the models used to determine theoretical prices do not reflect this point. Static haircuts and non-market prices may contribute to biases building up in the collateral framework over time.

Third, the incentives to engage in ratings shopping and catering are larger for collateral that is of lower quality. Haircuts are reduced for collateral whose rating moves up to A−, but not beyond that. Furthermore, it is presumably easier to tweak a rating of more illiquid collateral since it is likely to be more opaque, with less market-based information regarding its value and volatility available. That ratings are (most likely) inputs to the models used for theoretical pricing provides added incentive to tweak ratings for lower-quality collateral.

Fourth, haircuts and theoretical prices can also be increased by guarantees. The evidence shows that guarantees are predominantly given to unsecured collateral where the default probability would otherwise be high, i.e., to relatively illiquid and risky collateral (Table 6.5).

Fifth, own-use collateral is likely to be more important for lower-quality collateral, since higher-quality collateral could more easily be placed in the market. The evidence is that the incidence of own-use collateral has grown over time (Fecht, Nyborg, Rocholl, and Woschitz 2016). This is consistent with the increased leniency over time of the own-use rules.

More generally, a collateral framework that is not responsive to market forces is almost destined to favor one type of collateral or another. The different features of the Eurosystem's collateral framework that impinge on market discipline may contribute in different ways to the observed bias toward illiquid collateral. However, there is much to suggest that this bias is by design.

10.3 POTENTIAL COSTS

The undermining of market discipline in the market for liquidity means that market signals are obscured, thus making supervisors' and regulators' jobs harder. The bias toward lower-quality collateral that the Eurosystem's collateral framework appears to promote has several additional implications. These issues are of increasing importance as the volume of central bank repos grows under the full allotment policy.

For example, as discussed in Chapter 2, favoring illiquid collateral in central bank repos may stimulate the production of such collateral and distort investments in the real economy away from assets that are liquid in a real sense. A contributing factor to such distortions is the free-rider problem inherent in the private provision of liquidity (Bhattacharya and Gale 1987). A collateral framework that is biased in favor of illiquid financial assets can exacerbate this free-rider problem, especially if these assets are also illiquid in a real sense, as seems plausible. In other words, favoring illiquid financial assets through the collateral framework can lead to suboptimal investment decisions and intertemporal consumption patterns. In more plain language, it can contribute to an amplification of business cycles.

In addition, promoting illiquid collateral through the collateral framework can also make the banking, and financial, system more vulnerable to liquidity shocks. Several authors have suggested that the breakdown in the interbank market during the financial crisis was related to increased levels of information asymmetry among banks with respect to the quality of their balance sheets (see, e.g., Heider, Hoerova, and Holthausen 2009). A collateral framework that is biased toward more illiquid collateral can make such a systemic crisis more likely.

The promotion of lower-quality collateral also weakens the balance sheet of the central bank. This can make the central bank less able to respond to problems in the banking system and, in extreme scenarios, undermine its credibility. One typically thinks of the soundness of the central bank as being important for the well functioning of the financial system. For example, Stella (1997, p. 33) concludes that a weak and deteriorating central bank balance sheet is likely to lead to price instability or financial repression. Stella (2005) also emphasizes the importance of the strength of the balance sheet to maintain central bank independence and thus support the credibility of its policies (see also Sims 2004; Jeanne and Svensson 2007). In the theory developed by Kiyotaki and Moore (2003), for example, the effectiveness of outside money is fragile in the sense it relies on the acceptance of agents in the economy. Such acceptance may be less likely to be achieved for outside money that is issued against a weak central bank balance sheet. In the euro area, it is hard to predict the outcome of the turmoil that is likely to ensue should the ECB need recapitalization.

As noted in Chapter 1, central bankers such as Thomas Jordan and Klaas Knot, among others, have also expressed concern about increasingly weak central bank balance sheets over the course of the crisis. Klaas Knot goes as far as saying that weak balance sheets can "undermine a central bank's credibility" and that "central banks may need to step up their efforts on transparency and accountability" (Knot 2013). Given this view, it is notable that the Eurosystem's collateral framework promotes risky and illiquid collateral.

A weak central bank can also affect economic activity negatively because economic agents start to lose faith in the central bank's money and the financial system it supports. As suggested by Nyborg (2011), we can think of the assets of a central bank as representing the "gold" that backs up the money. Reductions in the value or liquidity of those assets, such as the debasement of gold coins, can result in reduced faith in the central bank's money. In turn, this can lead to a lower willingness to trade and invest. This perspective may be relevant with respect to the recent crisis, with the price of gold skyrocketing while the economy went into deep recession.

A final important feature of the collateral framework in the euro area that has the potential to create distortions is that haircuts are independent of the counterparty. Individual banks' credit risk is not taken into account. Such a policy may well be justified as "levelling the playing field" by providing access to liquidity at similar terms (but against heterogeneous collateral). It could also be justified on logistical grounds, given that there are 30,000 to 40,000 eligible ISINs and thousands of banks. However, a counterparty-independent haircut policy also creates the potential for distortions because it provides incentives for a bank to submit collateral whose default probability is highly correlated with a default of the bank itself (Fecht, Nyborg, Rocholl, and Woschitz 2016).

The incentive created by the collateral framework to use highly correlated collateral may have contributed to the increasing level of segmentation across countries in the euro area. A report by the ECB states that "[i]n mid-2012 the share of cross-border use of collateral within the euro area stood at around 20% compared with around 50% in 2006" (ECB 2012). Probabilities of sovereign defaults increased significantly over the crisis, as evidenced by the sovereign debt crisis (and the accompanying increase in yield spreads between Germany and other sovereigns), and the solvency of a bank in a particular country is more closely linked to the solvency of that country than that of another country. The increasing use of guarantees from governments to credit institutions in the same country tightens this bond. Government guarantees thereby also contribute to segmentation.

Market fragmentation may also have intensified as a result of the ECB (2012/4) decision that:

> NCBs shall not be obliged to accept as collateral for Eurosystem credit operations eligible bank bonds guaranteed by a Member State under a European Union/International Monetary Fund programme, or by a Member State whose credit assessment does not comply with the Eurosystem's benchmark for establishing its minimum requirement for high credit standards for issuer and guarantors.

This would have affected banks in Cyprus, Greece, Ireland, and Portugal at various points in time (Chapter 6). The decision was adopted approximately three weeks after the second three-year LTRO. It may reflect a concern by central banks of other euro-area countries that they might be on the hook if severe problems should arise in these four troubled countries.

Fragmented markets are unattractive as they are a hindrance to the free flow of capital. That fragmentation may also represent increased bank default probabilities is an additional cause for concern. Worries about market fragmentation were an important driver behind the push for a European banking union. As observed by Benoît Cœuré, member of the executive board of the ECB, in the context of the establishment of the European Banking Union: "The negative feedback loop between banks and sovereigns as well as signs of market fragmentation made European leaders take an extraordinary decision last summer, namely to establish the European Banking Union" (Cœuré 2013).

To summarize, there are numerous features of the Eurosystem's collateral framework that impair market discipline. The more market forces are neutralized, the more likely it is that the committees that decide on haircuts and "market prices" get it wrong, leading in the first instance to financial market distortions as well as influencing bank behavior.

The evidence suggests that the collateral framework is biased toward lower-quality collateral. This affects the balance sheet of the Eurosystem. It also affects banks because the collateral framework provides a set of incentive constraints with respect to the behavior of banks and bankers. In turn, this must necessarily affect the real economy, since the money creation process is intimately linked to the channeling of funds to the real economy. Because these biases were present pre-crisis, it may well be that they have been a contributing factor to the prolonged problems in the euro area. An important question that is raised by the discussion in this chapter is to what extent it is desirable to design and use collateral frameworks to favor certain assets or institutions or encourage particular behavior.

10.4 INTRODUCING MARKET FORCES

There are several ways market forces could be introduced into the collateral framework. But how best to do it is complicated by our relatively limited understanding of the full extent of the implications of collateral policy. Still, an obvious element of a collateral policy that seeks to engage market forces more actively is to make use of the haircuts that banks would face in the market. To actually collect these, however, is not trivial in practice. Furthermore, as argued elsewhere in this book, the haircuts set by the central bank are likely to influence market haircuts (and prices). A more feasible approach, therefore, is to try to elicit information on "neutral" market haircuts for different counterparties through open market operation design. As a simple example, suppose there is only one type of collateral and that the central bank runs fixed rate tenders with fixed quantities of liquidity provided in each tender. In the standard design, banks submit quantity bids and receive a pro rata share of the liquidity supplied by the central bank. This design was used by the ECB in the first two years of its existence (Table 3.1). What the central bank can do instead is to ask banks to submit quantity–haircut pairs and then discriminate in favor of banks submitting the highest haircuts.

Running discriminatory tenders, or auctions, is nothing new to the ECB. As seen in Table 3.1, it employed discriminatory repo auctions from June 2001 to October 2008. In these auctions, banks submitted quantity–rate pairs. The liquidity went to those submitting the highest repo rates. These operations were first studied empirically by Nyborg, Bindseil, and Strebulaev (2002). My idea here can be seen as an offshoot of this approach. The novelty lies in discriminating along the haircut dimension. Of course, nothing stops the central bank from running operations that discriminate on both the repo rate and haircut dimensions. A dual approach may well be the way that gets market discipline most effectively into the collateral framework.

Discriminating in favor of the highest haircuts still leaves significant design details open. An important question is whether the central bank should hold banks to the haircuts they bid or use some other rule, for example, applying a uniform haircut to all repos (remember that I am considering, for now, a simple scenario where there is only one type of collateral). This is a well-researched question in the multiple unit auctions literature. What is new here is that the haircut, rather than the price or interest rate, is being considered as the discriminating variable. In Treasury auctions, the uniform rule has been shown empirically to offer many advantages (Nyborg and Sundaresan 1996; Keloharju, Nyborg, and Rydqvist 2005). This may well carry over to haircut-discriminating repo auctions. A uniform haircut rule may also lead to a more efficient interbank market for liquidity, along the lines of Nyborg and Strebulaev's (2004) model of repo auctions.

One of the biggest challenges with respect to using haircuts more actively in open market operations involves dealing with heterogeneity in collateral and counterparty risk. Proponents of an inactive haircut policy applied to a wide range of eligible collateral, such as what has always been pursued by the ECB, may also argue that because of such heterogeneity it is not practical or even desirable to use haircuts more actively. Central bank liquidity should flow "where it is needed." I would argue, however, that an important reason to use haircuts more actively is precisely heterogeneity with respect to collateral and counterparty risk. To handle collateral heterogeneity, it may be necessary to set limits to different types of collateral, or perhaps run a multi-round process, where one starts with the highest quality collateral and then runs down the ladder as necessary.

While central banks can use collateral policy to tilt the playing field to support banks with illiquid collateral, it is not clear that this is concordant with having a healthy, well-integrated banking sector and a healthy economy. Banks that need assistance should arguably be helped through extraordinary, targeted means, not by distorting the playing field for all banks. If market forces and discipline are taken out of collateral policy, this is likely to lead to financial and economic distortions that can build up over time and contribute to crises and recessions. This is especially critical within a currency union of heterogeneous countries such as the euro area.

11 Bailing Out the Euro

Within our mandate, the ECB is ready to do whatever it takes to
preserve the euro. And believe me, it will be enough.

– Mario Draghi, President of the ECB, Speech at the Global Investment Conference
in London July 26, 2012[1]

This declaration speaks volumes as to the threat the euro was, and
continues to be, under. The first signs of the problems to come
emerged in August 2007 with the advent of the broad financial crisis.
In the eurozone, this later morphed into a sovereign debt crisis and its
corollary, a crisis of the euro itself, that is still not fully resolved. In
this chapter, I examine some of the key measures taken by the ECB
to deal with the banking and sovereign debt crisis in the euro area
and the ongoing work to preserve the euro. The potency of some of
these measures derives from the richness of the underlying collateral
framework.

That the euro would eventually encounter difficulties was not
a surprise to many economists. The potential problems with having
a common currency for a dispersed set of countries such as those in
the euro area have been articulated numerous times by several commentators, including one of the most influential macroeconomists of
our times, the late Milton Friedman, who viewed the introduction of
the euro as a mistake. In August 2002, he reiterated this point by saying that "I will be surprised if you do not have very serious problems
arising in the next five years or so among the 12 countries in the euro
regime."[2] As we now know, Friedman's prediction came true.

---

[1] www.ecb.europa.eu/press/key/date/2012/html/sp120726.en.html.

[2] " 'Milton Friedman assesses the monetarist legacy and the recent performance
of central banks:' Milton Friedman interviewed by Robert Pringle," August 2002,
Central Banking. Available on www.centralbanking.com.

The unconventional monetary policies introduced by the ECB in response to the crisis are outlined in Table 3.1 and reviewed in Chapter 3. The main focus in the current chapter is on the full allotment policy (October 2008) and on the asset purchase programs announced in the ECB press conference on September 4, 2014. The former facilitated a growth in the ECB's balance sheet by around EUR 1 trillion, and there were indications from Draghi on September 4, 2014, that the new asset purchase programs being introduced would have similar impact.[3]

The projected EUR 1 trillion expansion was eventually confirmed in a press conference on January 22, 2015, where it was also announced that purchases of bonds of euro-area sovereigns, agencies, and institutions would be included in that total figure. This important event represents the beginning of the endgame of the ECB's efforts to preserve the euro and is discussed separately in Chapter 12.

I argue in Section 11.2 that the full allotment policy can be viewed as an indirect bailout mechanism of banks and sovereigns. While it is hard to maintain that emergency measures were not necessary in the turmoil that ensued after the Lehman bankruptcy, it is noteworthy that the full allotment policy is still in force more than six years later, in 2015. This is especially so because, as I will argue below, viewed as a bailout mechanism, the full allotment policy is inefficient.

After discussing further issues that relate to the full allotment policy and, more generally, the fight to preserve the euro in Section 11.3, I go on to examine who has benefited the most from the ECB's unconventional policies in Sections 11.4 and 11.5. This is partly done by reviewing some of the evidence put together in previous chapters. But I also introduce new evidence; in particular, I carry out an event study around the September 4, 2014, policy announcement to learn about its perceived benefits and the distribution of

[3] See ECB press conference with Mario Draghi, September 4, 2014, www.ecb.europa.eu/press/pressconf/2014/html/is140904.en.html.

those benefits across countries, as inferred from the stock market's reaction to it.

Before getting to these issues, in the next section I draw on Table 3.1 to put the full allotment policy and the September 4, 2014, policy announcement in context. I show that there is a systematic pattern to the ECB's unconventional monetary policies that repeats over time, only with slightly different modalities. The next section demonstrates the significance of the full allotment policy and the September 4, 2014, press conference by placing them within this repeating pattern.

11.1   UNCONVENTIONAL MONETARY POLICIES: BROAD PATTERNS AND KEY ISSUES

In addition to modifying its collateral framework, the ECB has made use of three sets of policies to deal with the crisis. The first involves increasing the quantity of central bank money injected through refinancing operations. This is achieved primarily through the full allotment policy and LTROs with one-, three-, and four-year maturities. The second policy involves purchasing assets and the third cutting rates, eventually leading to negative deposit rates in June 2014 and a policy rate of five basis points in September 2014. My focus here is on the first two sets of policies, as these relate to the transfer of assets and risks from banks and the markets to the Eurosystem. These two policies are therefore the ones that are most relevant with respect to bailing out the euro. They also relate to the collateral framework and therefore fit into the topic of this book.

After the introduction of the full allotment policy in October 2008, Table 3.1 shows a pattern of policies that come in three waves. Each wave starts by ratcheting up the longest maturity of the LTROs and follows this up by introducing new asset purchase programs.

The first wave commenced in June 2009 with a EUR 442 billion one-year LTRO. This was followed by a covered bond purchase program in July 2009, the Securities Markets Programme (SMP) in May 2010, and a second covered bond purchase program in November

2011. The asset purchase programs were significantly smaller than the one-year LTRO, though the SMP was a sizeable EUR 214 billion.[4]

The second wave started shortly after Draghi's appointment in November 2011. In particular, in December 2011 and February 2012 the ECB held two three-year LTROs, for a combined injection of around EUR 1 trillion. This was followed in September 2012 by an asset purchase program, the Outright Monetary Transactions (OMT) program, which promises unlimited purchases of troubled sovereigns' bonds by the Eurosystem.

The OMT has been viewed by the ECB and many commentators as the linchpin in Draghi's efforts to preserve the euro, since it promises unlimited-size bailouts – whatever it takes. But the OMT is also so controversial that it has been challenged in the courts and has never been employed.[5] The case against the OMT was heard in Germany's Constitutional Court, which handed it over to the European Court of Justice (ECJ), the highest court in the EU, in February 2014. In doing so, the German court also issued a warning that "there are important reasons to assume that [the OMT] exceeds the European Central Bank's monetary policy mandate and thus infringes the powers of the Member States and that it violates the prohibition of monetary financing of the budget."[6] The case opened in the ECJ on October 14, 2014, where, according to a *Financial Times* article, "[t]he European Central Bank on Tuesday delivered a vigorous defense of its signature bond-buying programme credited with ending the eurozone crisis, telling the EU's highest court that it was essential in preventing the break up of the common currency and

---

[4] See Eser and Schwaab (2016).

[5] I last checked the non-usage of the OMT with the ECB when touching up the final draft of this book in November 2015.

[6] See "Principal proceedings ESM/ECB: Pronouncement of the judgment and referral for a preliminary ruling to the Court of Justice of the European Union," www.bundesverfassungsgericht.de/SharedDocs/Pressemitteilungen/EN/2014/bvg 14-009.html; "German court refers ECB bond-buying programme to European justice," by Stefan Wagstyl and Claire Jones, *Financial Times*, February 7, 2014; and "ECB OMT challenge to be heard by EU top court on Oct. 14," by Aoife White and Karin Matussek, *Bloomberg*, September 23, 2014.

therefore within its legal mandate."[7] This will be discussed further in Chapter 12.

That it has not been "necessary" to use the OMT has led some observers to maintain that the mere promise of unlimited purchases is enough to preserve the euro. Given the fiscal problems in many of the euro-area countries, this always seemed premature, and even naive, a view that is supported by the third wave of policies unveiled in 2014 and finalized in January 2015.

The third wave was initially announced in June 2014. It consists of targeted LTROs (TLTROs) and asset purchase programs. The TLTROs modify the full allotment policy. In the first two TLTROs, held in September and December of 2014, banks received a cumulative initial borrowing allowance of "7% of the total amount of their loans to the euro area non-financial private sector, excluding loans to households for house purchase, outstanding on 30 April 2014."[8] All TLTRO loans were to mature in September 2018. The uptake of the first TLTRO held in September 2014 was a fairly modest EUR 82.6 billion, with the one in December reaching EUR 129.8 billion. With respect to the asset purchase programs, the June 2014 announcement provided little detail, except that ABSs would be involved.

The initial June 2014 announcement is expanded on and fleshed out in the minutes of the ECB press conference held on September 4, 2014. Two asset purchase programs were announced, one for ABSs and one for covered bonds. The ABS program is both novel and broad, with respect to both underlying assets and tranche seniority. For example, the Eurosystem can buy mezzanine tranches with government guarantees. Mezzanine tranches of ABSs are typically very risky and illiquid, but the idea is that guarantees may reduce the risk. At the same time, this policy has the potential to, and may even be intended to, extend the granting of government guarantees

[7] "ECB defends bond-buying plan at top EU court," by Peter Spiegel, *Financial Times*, October 14, 2014.

[8] ECB press release, June 5, 2014, "ECB announces monetary policy measures to enhance the functioning of the monetary policy transmission mechanism," www.ecb.europa.eu/press/pr/date/2014/html/pr140605_2.en.html.

to such relatively risky and illiquid securities. This may further strengthen the unfortunate link between sovereigns and banks and may, therefore, create its own risks.

Another significant aspect of the September 4, 2014, press conference relates to the size of the third wave of policies. During the question and answer part of the conference, Draghi indicated that the combined size of the TLTROs and the asset purchase programs would be sufficient to expand the balance sheet of the Eurosystem by close to EUR 1 trillion. The exact size was subsequently subject to some speculation, but the EUR 1 trillion (approximately) mark was reconfirmed in the Introductory Statement to the November 6, 2014, ECB press conference, when Draghi stated that "[t]ogether with the series of targeted longer-term refinancing operations to be conducted until June 2016, these asset purchases will have a sizeable impact on our balance sheet, which is expected to move towards the dimensions it had at the beginning of 2012."[9] This amounts to saying that these programs will add around EUR 1 trillion to the Eurosystem's balance sheet.

The topic of sovereign bond purchases was also raised in the September 4, 2014, ECB press conference. Being asked whether the Governing Council had considered quantitative easing, Draghi revealed that "QE was [also] discussed. Some of our Governing Council members were in favor of doing more than I have just presented, and some were in favor of doing less. . . A broad asset purchase programme was discussed, and some Governors made clear that they would like to do more."[10] Responding to a follow-up question, Draghi went on to say "Now, QE can be private sector asset-based, or also sovereign-sector, public sector asset-based, or both." These statements reveal pressure within the ECB to buy sovereign debt, perhaps even if not officially "troubled," as required by the OMT.[11]

---

[9] ECB press conference with Mario Draghi, November 6, 2014, www.ecb.europa .eu/press/pressconf/2014/html/is141106.en.html.

[10] Source: See Footnote 3.

[11] The OMT press release on September 6, 2012, states: "A necessary condition for Outright Monetary Transactions is strict and effective conditionality attached

At the time, many market participants viewed sovereign bond purchases as the next step. A Bloomberg article on September 5, 2014, quotes a former ECB economist working as a portfolio manager as believing that "[t]he ECB is ready to do more if more is needed."[12] A *Financial Times* article published online after the ECB press conference on September 4, 2014, is more explicit, quoting an economist at ING as saying "the ECB has now reached a point at which outright purchases of government bonds, is the only option left."[13]

The topic of sovereign debt purchases remained at the fore of the policy debate throughout the fall of 2014. It dominated the question and answer part of the ECB press conference on December 6, 2014. At this event, Draghi made clear that the ECB does not view buying sovereign debt as beyond its mandate and also that it does not require the unanimity of the Governing Council. This reinforces the importance attached to the buying of sovereign bonds by the ECB with respect to its fight to preserve the euro.

The third policy wave follows substantial repayments of the funds received in the three-year LTROs. Long-maturity LTROs appear to have run their course. The relatively low uptake of the first two TLTROs reflects this. To achieve the approximately EUR 1 trillion balance sheet expansion the ECB is "targeting," asset purchases will have to become more important than in the past. Thus, a significant aspect of the third wave of unconventional monetary policies is that it has moved the focus of the ECB's fight to preserve the euro from

to an appropriate European Financial Stability Facility/European Stability Mechanism (EFSF/ESM) programme. Such programmes can take the form of a full EFSF/ESM macroeconomic adjustment programme or a precautionary programme (Enhanced Conditions Credit Line), provided that they include the possibility of EFSF/ESM primary market purchases. The involvement of the IMF shall also be sought for the design of the country-specific conditionality and the monitoring of such a programme." See www.ecb.europa.eu/press/pr/date/2012/html/pr120906_1.en.html.

[12] "Draghi sees almost $1 trillion stimulus as QE fight waits," by Simon Kennedy, *Bloomberg*, September 5, 2014, www.bloomberg.com/news/2014-09-04/draghi-sees-almost-1-trillion-stimulus-with-no-qe-fight.html.

[13] "Draghi intervention on rates and bonds startles markets," by Claire Jones, Thomas Hale, and Elaine Moore, *Financial Times*, 7.14 pm, September 4, 2014.

long-maturity LTROs under full allotment on to the purchasing of assets, including sovereign bonds.

This also illustrates that the crisis in the euro area is sufficiently serious that the mere promise of unlimited asset purchases is not enough to preserve the euro. Tangible action is required. The announcement on September 4, 2014, that such action would be forthcoming is thus a highly significant event in the calendar of unconventional monetary policies in the euro area.

11.2 FULL ALLOTMENT, FRAGMENTATION, AND INEFFICIENT BAILOUTS

The full allotment policy was introduced in October 2008 and is still in force in 2015. It was introduced in response to the turmoil in the wake of the Lehman default. Interbank markets no longer functioned well, with banks reducing their lending to each other (see, e.g., Cassola, Holthausen, and Lo Duca 2010). The problems in the interbank markets that emerged in August 2007 are sketched in Chapter 1 and illustrated by the plot of the three-month Euribor–Eonia swap spread in Figure 1.1. This plot is copied over to Figure 11.1. The spread is seen to experience a sharp increase in August 2007 and shoot up to unprecedented levels after Lehman's default. This spread, the difference between Euribor and the overnight index swap rate, can be thought of as the price of liquidity, or as an interbank liquidity premium (in this case, over three months).[14] As discussed in Chapter 1, the increase in the price of liquidity was accompanied by dramatic falls in asset prices. While the discussion on this point in Chapter 1 focuses on the stock market (see Figure 1.1), it is well documented that prices of other financial and real assets fell sharply during the financial crisis.[15]

---

[14] See Chapter 1, Footnote 4. Similar increases can be seen in the USD Libor–OIS spread as well as in other currencies. See, e.g., Nyborg and Östberg (2014).

[15] Some examples: FTs Europe-wide house price database shows that house prices fell throughout Europe (see, www.ft.com/intl/cms/s/0/4fda2cc8-525a-11dd-9ba7-0000 77b07658.html#axzz3YKbFmVng). Prices of asset-backed and mortgage-backed securities also decreased strongly, as reported, for example, in the *afme/esf*

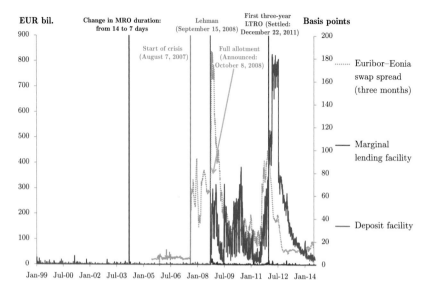

FIGURE 11.1 Euribor–Eonia swap spread (three months) and usage of standing facilities

Time period: January 1, 1999, to June 30, 2014.

Data sources: www.ecb.europa.eu/stats/monetary/res/html/index.en.html and www.euribor-ebf.eu/.

Thus, the full allotment policy has kept banks that could not access the interbank market for liquidity at reasonable prices, or at all, from having to engage in asset sales at a time when prices were plummeting. In turn, this saved these banks from financial distress and runs. It also supported asset prices. Because the full allotment policy has been in place for so many years, however, it is hard to argue that it merely has provided "liquidity" to a few banks. Rather, it can be viewed as an indirect bailout, supplying banks and the financial system with "funding." I expand on, and further substantiate, this view below.

Figure 11.2 graphs two variables, namely (i) the daily outstanding volume of the Eurosystem's open market operations

Securitisation Data Report, Q1:2010. Available on www.afme.eu/Documents/Statistics-and-Reports.aspx. Government bond yields in the euro area increased (relative to German government bond yields, see Figure 12.1).

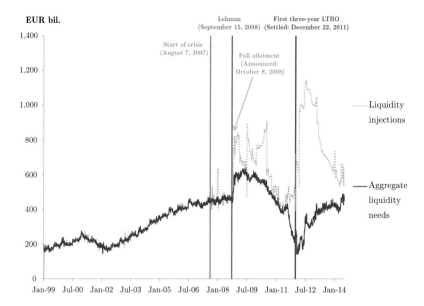

FIGURE 11.2 Eurosystem liquidity injections vs aggregate liquidity needs

Time period: January 1, 1999, to June 30, 2014.

Aggregate liquidity needs are the sum of banks' required reserves (with the Eurosystem) and the autonomous factors minus the outstanding amount from the Securities Markets Programme (SMP) purchases. Liquidity injections are the daily outstanding MRO and LTRO volumes plus the outstanding CBPP and CBPP2 amounts minus the OTs used for sterilizing the SMP. (In the publicly available data, the ECB bundles the SMP purchases with the autonomous factors. The SMP officially ended in September 2011, see Table 3.1.) *Data sources*: www.ecb.europa.eu/mopo/implement/omo/html/top_history .en.html and www.ecb.europa.eu/mopo/liq/html/index.en.html.

(labeled liquidity injections in the figure) and (ii) daily reserve requirements plus the autonomous factors and less SMP purchases (labeled liquidity needs).[16] The difference between these two variables

---

[16] The autonomous factors are "[l]iquidity factors that do not normally stem from the use of monetary policy instruments. They include, for example, banknotes in circulation, government deposits with the central bank and net foreign assets of the central bank" (www.ecb.europa.eu/home/glossary/html/act2a.en.html). The liquidity injections graph is comprised of the MROs, LTROs, and the outstanding amount from the two covered bond purchase programs (CBPP and CBPP2) as well as the OTs (other types of refinancing operations) that relate to the "sterilization" of the SMP (Securities Markets Programme, see Table 3.1). The latter absorb liquidity. With respect to the OTs, note that the ECB uses two types of liquidity-absorbing operations. One type is an overnight fixed-term deposit at the

202 BAILING OUT THE EURO

represents an excess quantity, relative to aggregate liquidity needs, of central bank money injected by the ECB into the banking sector. Figure 11.2 shows that prior to the introduction of the full allotment policy, this excess was approximately zero. In other words, the ECB pursued a liquidity-neutral policy, as described, for example, by Bindseil, Nyborg, and Strebulaev (2009), whereby aggregate liquidity injections match aggregate liquidity needs. This neutrality can be seen to have broken down after the introduction of the full allotment policy, when the liquidity injections start to exceed the neutral amount.

The flip side of the excess liquidity, seen in Figure 11.2, is the large increase in the usage of the deposit facility, seen in Figure 11.1. Since the ECB stepped in to provide funding for banks that were no longer able to meet their "liquidity needs" in the marketplace, other banks were left with excessive quantities of liquidity relative to their needs. This was placed in the deposit facility. Since the deposit rate is below the policy rate (and what banks can earn on required reserves), this is costly for the banks with excess liquidity. Perhaps to reduce the costs to these banks, the ECB moved the deposit rate to a level of 50 bp below the policy rate when it introduced the full allotment policy, as compared with 100 bp before full allotment (as shown in Table 3.1).

The full allotment-era excess of central bank money can be viewed as funding provided by the central bank, since the system as a whole did not need it for liquidity purposes and since banks in need of liquidity could, in principle, sell assets. The excess liquidity is

end of the maintenance period, in which it aims at absorbing any excess liquidity. The second liquidity-absorbing operation also takes the form of a fixed-term deposit, but with a duration of one week. The ECB started using it with the implementation of the SMP. The amount proposed to be absorbed is announced on its webpage www.ecb.europa.eu/mopo/implement/omo/html/index.en.html in its "ad-hoc communications" one day in advance. The actual amount deposited at the ECB can be found in the data it provides on its OTs. The liquidity injections series in Figure 11.2 does not include the "regular" overnight liquidity-absorbing OTs. The effect of including these would be to make the liquidity injections graph less smooth. Note also that SMP purchases, while representing a liquidity injection, are included (with a negative sign) in the liquidity needs series because this is how the data are provided by the ECB.

essentially funding banks holding on to assets instead of selling them. This was arguably necessary immediately after the Lehman default when asset markets were almost in free-fall and interbank markets experienced severe tightening. It is remarkable that it should still be necessary as late as 2015. The longevity of the full allotment policy reveals the fragility of the euro. It is highly suggestive of a policy of keeping weak banks and sovereigns from defaulting.

It is well known that it has been especially the euro-area periphery, the PIIGSC countries, that experienced problems as the crisis dragged on. This is reflected by the low sovereign ratings of these countries, as discussed in Chapter 6. There are also reports in the financial press that banks in troubled regions of the eurozone have been facing a drainage of liquidity as depositors "jog" away with their money.[17] In his comprehensive review of the euro crisis, Cline (2014) provides evidence gleaned from IMF sources that it is especially banks in Greece, Ireland, Portugal, and Spain that have been under pressure from "jogging" depositors. He also provides evidence, based on BIS statistics, that there has been a staggering outflow of capital from the euro-area periphery. In particular, from 2009 to 2012, the stock of international banks' cross-border claim on the economies of the five PIIGS countries fell by 43 percent, from EUR 4 trillion to EUR 2.3 trillion. Taking into account claims on banks only, the drop was 62 percent.[18] The imbalance in capital flows within the euro area is also demonstrated by Hans-Werner Sinn and his co-authors in a series of works focusing on the euro area's TARGET payment system.[19] Summarizing this work, Sinn (2014) shows, among other things, that the outflows from the PIIGSC countries that

---

[17] "Plug-pulling in Athens," by Joseph Cotterill, *FTAlphaville*, May 16, 2012.

[18] See Cline (2014, pp. 60–65).

[19] TARGET (Trans-European Automated Real-time Gross settlement Express Transfer system) is the central euro-area payment system. Cross-border transactions are settled via the respective NCBs and become credits or liabilities in their accounts, depending on the direction of the flow of the funds. See, e.g., Sinn (2014), Whelan (2014), or Bindseil and König (2011) for details and discussion. TARGET2 is the second-generation payment system.

started in the fall of 2008 increased rapidly over time, taking an especially large jump with the introduction of the three-year LTROs.[20] Thus, one can understand full allotment against low-quality collateral as a policy to especially sustain these troubled countries and their banks.

This view is supported by the evidence in Chapter 9 of the large three-year LTRO uptake of Spanish and Italian banks. Furthermore, Fecht, Nyborg, Rocholl, and Woschitz (2016) document that German banks' aggregate liquidity uptake from Eurosystem operations has substantially decreased over time, even as total liquidity injections have increased. Van Rixtel and Gasperini (2013) also document substantially larger reliance on Eurosystem funding among banks in the PIIGS countries as compared with banks in other euro-area member states. These disparities became especially pronounced after the August 8, 2011, re-activation of the SMP by the ECB to buy Italian and Spanish sovereign debt and after the introduction of the three-year LTROs. Overall, the story painted by the evidence is one of euro-area and money markets fragmenting along national lines, with funding holes in the periphery's banking sectors having been filled by Eurosystem credit through the full allotment procedure.

The full allotment policy is part of a package of policies that provide support to weak banks and sovereigns, and thereby help preserve the euro. The support package includes more lenient collateral eligibility rules on the extensive margin, for example, including unsecured bank bonds trading on non-regulated markets (Chapter 9) and subordinated debt instruments in the set of eligible collateral. Other elements include reduced ratings thresholds, rating-rule exemptions for some sovereigns, increased leniency with respect to collateral own use, the addition of DBRS in the set of accepted rating agencies, increased levels of outright purchases of collateral, and emergency lending assistance if all else should fail.

---

[20] See Sinn (2014, figure 6.2).

The significance of the full allotment policy is that it allows a bank to finance a large portion of its balance sheet directly from the Eurosystem and without competition from other banks or discipline from the markets. The financeable portion is made large through the eligibility of non-marketable assets. The increased usage of non-marketable and other lower-quality assets in Eurosystem operations under the full allotment era, as documented in Chapter 4, supports the view that the haircuts of these assets were set low (conversely, collateral values set high) in order to help out weaker banks. Extending the maturities in the LTROs to three years is also especially useful to weaker banks since it assures the availability of funding for this extended period of time. This is essential to the full allotment policy serving its (indirect) bailout role, since it reduces policy uncertainty with respect to the availability of funding.

However, the full allotment policy is not efficient as a bailout mechanism. It does not clean up balance sheets, inject equity, or resolve banks. Importantly, it does not solve the debt over-hang problem articulated by Myers (1977) because full allotment LTRO funding is senior, by virtue of being collateralized. Reducing debt overhang is an important objective of bailouts, to allow banks to raise external funds and lend efficiently, as discussed, for example, by Bhattacharya and Nyborg (2013), Philippon and Schnabl (2013), and others. Furthermore, as emphasized by Bhattacharya and Nyborg, constrained-optimal bailouts involve nonlinear contracts tailored to the balance sheets of individual banks, whereby the cost of bailout funding increases in the level of funding a bank asks for. Since full allotment MROs and LTROs are conducted under the fixed rate tender mechanism, this condition is violated. For all these reasons, the full allotment policy is not an efficient bailout mechanism.

A side effect of the full allotment policy is that it enhances banks' ability to arbitrage the system (Chapter 10). Using the Eurosystem's open market operations as a source of funding, Italian banks, for example, pay the same to fund Italian government bonds as they do for German government bonds, since both sets of bonds are rated at least A− (Chapter 6).[21] With respect to regulatory capital requirements, these could also be set to be the same for Italian and German government bonds, despite differences in ratings (see Korte and Steffen 2015). Italian banks thus benefit from increasing their holdings of Italian government bonds since they earn a higher yield in case of non-default and, in case of a sovereign default, Italian banks would likely end up defaulting too. Full allotment in very long-dated LTROs increases banks ability to engage in such behavior. There is evidence that this is empirically relevant. Merler and Pisani-Ferry (2012) show that the fraction of domestic government bonds held by banks in the PIIGS countries increased after full allotment was introduced, though falling again around the beginning of 2012 in Ireland and Greece. Fecht, Nyborg, Rocholl, and Woschitz (2016) document that German banks reduced their usage of PIIGSC collateral in Eurosystem operations (both in relative and absolute terms) after the introduction of the full allotment policy.[22] The growing TARGET deficits over time of the PIIGSC countries documented by Sinn (2014) may reflect, in part, these trends.

The full allotment policy also reduces the incentives for banks to create more liquid balance sheets and collateral, thus contributing further to undermining market forces and discipline (Chapter 10). The recent introduction of liquidity regulation can be understood against this backdrop. It is unclear, however, that liquidity regulation would be necessary with a more efficient collateral framework in place. It is odd to separate liquidity regulation from the collateral framework. Inconsistencies between these in the treatment of collateral may simply help grow the liquidity (or, collateral) swap market.

[21] Some Italian bonds were not rated by DBRS and thus had lower ratings and higher haircuts for a time (see Chapter 6).

[22] More generally, Fecht, Nyborg, Rocholl, and Woschitz (2016) document that systemic arbitrage has always been present, but that its intensity increased after the full allotment policy.

11.3   BUYING TIME AND SOVEREIGN FREE-RIDING

A modified perspective on the full allotment policy is that it does not represent a bailout *per se*, but rather that it is a device to buy time for banks and sovereigns to get their respective situations under control. The extensions of the maturities of the LTROs to one, three, and four years support this view. That they are ever-longer suggests that the "buying time" approach has not worked so well.

The full allotment policy also has allowed the euro area to buy time to deal with another important challenge, namely devising policies for dealing with failing banks and sovereigns. It is striking that well functioning bank resolution laws for banks did not exist in all euro-area member states seven years into the crisis and fourteen years after the start of the euro. Finally, in the spring of 2014, the European Parliament passed European Banking Union legislation. This will provide common supervisory and resolution mechanisms. This is an essential step toward cleaning up the banking sector, getting the euro-area economy going, and thereby helping preserve the euro. It came just in time too; the two three-year LTROs had maturity dates in January 2015 and February 2015, respectively. Still, there is work to be done with respect to implementing the legislation. As emphasized by the *Financial Times*: "Regulators are now faced with the challenge of putting the complex legal texts into practice."[23] The single resolution mechanism is scheduled to be operational as of January 2016.

Under the view that the full allotment policy is primarily about buying time, the shift in 2014 away from simple LTROs toward asset purchase programs can be interpreted as the endgame of the ECB's unofficial bank bailout program. A part of the impact of this shift should be to reduce the number of banks that will be resolved under the common resolution mechanism, since, for example, buying ABSs should help clean up banks' balance sheets. In this sense, the shift to asset purchases as the main unconventional monetary policy can

---

[23] "Super Tuesday for EU bank regulation," by Alex Barker and Mark Arnold, *Financial Times*, April 15, 2014.

be viewed as front-running the common bank resolution law (but the official reason for it is to fight deflation). Asset purchases may well be necessary to restore the banking sector in the euro area to "normal," but, as discussed above, an indiscriminate asset purchase program is unlikely to be efficient. It is likely to lead to larger wealth transfers than necessary.

One potential source of such wealth transfers relates to guaranteed collateral. As the Eurosystem starts buying more lower-quality collateral with government guarantees, the Eurosystem also, in effect, buys increasingly more credit insurance issued by the sovereigns. Wealth transfers arise, for example, if the central banks forgive these claims down the road, or if government guarantees are withdrawn after Eurosystem purchases. Actions such as these may turn out to be necessary to preserve the euro. Such wealth transfers may be intensified through the granting of new government guarantees to lower-quality collateral. This may also further weaken some sovereigns, which will put increased pressure on the Eurosystem to buy sovereign bonds to preserve the euro. Wealth transfers also arise if the Eurosystem buys assets at inflated prices. There are reports from the markets that covered bond and ABS prices have increased as a result of purchases by the Eurosystem. Sovereign bond spreads (relative to German bonds) also decreased for the periphery nations, except Greece, after the announcement in January 2015 that the Eurosystem would purchase such bonds.

With respect to the sovereigns, the euro area has introduced various aid schemes over the course of the crisis, such as the EFSF and the unused OMT, with especially the OMT facing severe opposition. A central concern among those that oppose the purchasing of sovereign bonds by the Eurosystem is that it will involve wealth transfers to the troubled countries whose debt will be bought. This is viewed as problematic because it appears to award irresponsible fiscal behavior and thus sets an unfortunate precedent.

This perspective can be understood in the context of the free-rider problem that is endemic in alliances of any kind (Olson and

Zeckhauser 1966). With respect to a currency alliance, such as the euro area, the free-rider problem is that some countries build up government deficits and apply lax standards with respect to supervising and regulating their banks, with the expectation that the alliance will bail them out if deficits get too large or banks get in trouble.[24]

The full allotment policy serves to keep not only banks, but troubled sovereigns alive, while politicians, central bankers, and other technocrats work to find a compromise solution to the ongoing problems in the euro area. While there has been substantial opposition to the buying of sovereign bonds, as the crisis progressed, it became increasingly hard to see the euro area staying intact without this happening. If the euro-area member states want to keep the euro as their common currency, they might find it beneficial to put more effort toward making sure free-riding in the future is reined in and that the collateral framework is cleaned up, rather than fight over the spilt milk from yesterday's free-riding. This is discussed further in Chapter 13.

While offering some benefits, there are also clear drawbacks to the "buying time" approach. Most obviously, it does not resolve uncertainty, but prolongs it. It might even be said to have heightened uncertainty, by making central bank policy so pivotal and by allowing frictions between countries to grow. That the issue as to whether the ECB can buy sovereign bonds has gone all the way to the European Court of Justice is an illustration of this.

The full allotment/buying time policy also has the potential to exacerbate the sovereign free-rider problem and strengthen the unfortunate nexus between sovereigns and banks. A case in point is the increased usage of government guarantees by Italy in time to take advantage of the second of the two three-year LTROs (Chapter 6). This benefits Italy in two different ways. First, it helps keep Italian banks afloat. Second, it indirectly supports the government itself by ensuring buyers for its debt. This is especially so under the

---

[24] See, e.g., Uhlig (2003) and the references therein.

full allotment policy, since it allows up to 99.5 percent financing of unlimited quantities of government securities. Italy auctioned off a larger than normal EUR 87.3 billion of government bonds (Treasury securities) in the primary market in the run-up to the second three-year LTRO.[25] More generally, it is well known that total Italian government debt has increased substantially over the years. From the beginning of the euro era, in January 1999, to the beginning of the financial crisis, in August 2007, the month-on-month increase in the total outstanding Italian government debt was EUR 3.5 billion. This pace was maintained until the introduction of the full allotment policy in October 2008. From then to the end of January 2015, the increase in Italian government debt has been a staggering EUR 6.7 billion per month.[26] The full allotment policy makes it easier to find a home for this debt.

The announcement on September 4, 2014, that the Eurosystem can buy mezzanine ABSs with guarantees is an extension of the policy of facilitating political influence through the back door. This may further entangle banks and sovereigns, in part because of the incentives it provides.

Linkages between governments and banks and politically motivated bailouts are not limited to the euro-area periphery. A Deutsche Bundesbank working paper finds that local politics influences the decision to bail out local savings banks in Germany (Behn, Haselmann, Kick, and Vig 2014). For a long time, German Landesbanken also had guarantees from their respective Länder. The topic of German government guarantees to eligible collateral is discussed further in Chapter 6.

---

[25] The EUR 87.3 billion is EUR 27.2 billion more than over the two preceding months and EUR 2.5 billion more than over the two following months. As an average over the two previous and two following years, the corresponding numbers are EUR 19.1 billion and 7.1 billion, respectively. So compared to the two-month period before, and the two-month period after, the "abnormal issuance" in the January to February 2012 time period can be said to be approximately EUR 8.1 and 9.6 billion, respectively. This has been calculated from numbers available on the Italian Treasury Department's webpage, www.dt.tesoro.it.

[26] Calculated from statistics available on www.dt.tesoro.it.

However, Italy is a particularly interesting case with respect to the euro crisis because it is arguably the weakest among the major euro-area countries, being its second-most indebted country after Greece. The view that the ultimate battle to save the euro will be fought on Italian ground is shared by many commentators, as illustrated, for example, by an article on the *Guardian* newspaper's economics blog from August 2014 entitled "The ECB's next problem: saving Italy," that argues that "[w]ithout a European Central Bank (ECB) rescue, in the form of large-scale quantitative easing, maybe a full-blown run on Italian debt is inevitable."[27] This highlights the importance of the sovereign bond purchases announced in January 2015, because it is questionable that the euro could withstand a run on Italian debt.

Still, it is not obvious that bailing out the euro is optimal. Many commentators believe the euro was, and is, a mistake and that it should be broken up. Finding a way to do this with a minimum of disruption was the subject of the 2012 Wolfson prize, with GBP 250,000 going to the winner, Bootle (2012). The residual uncertainty that exists with respect to the legality of the ECB buying sovereign bonds, as well as the political opposition to this in some quarters, underscores the importance of thinking not only about how to bail out the euro, but how to bail out from it.

One of the more complicated issues with respect to preserving the euro is the increased entanglement of sovereigns and banks, which has been augmented by the ECB's guarantee and haircut policies. Clearly, it should not be necessary to bail out (almost) all banks in order to preserve the euro. But the full allotment policy and the third wave of unconventional monetary policies partially announced in June 2014 and fleshed out on September 4, 2014, seem to take this tack.

---

[27] "The ECB's next problem: Saving Italy," by Phillip Inman, the *Guardian Economics Blog*, August 7, 2014, www.theguardian.com/business/economics-blog/2014/aug/07/the-ecbs-next-problem-saving-italy.

The question as to whether preserving the euro is optimal is complicated also because the answer depends on how it is done. The answer may also differ across countries. Saving the euro may involve wealth transfers from some countries (including their banks) to others. Below, I take a look at the market's assessment of this by examining the stock market's reaction to the policy announcements on September 4, 2014.

11.4   BAILING OUT THE EURO: WHO BENEFITS? GENERAL OBSERVATIONS

The question as to who benefits from the ECB's efforts to bail out the euro is clearly an important one. It is also a sensitive one, given the strained politics of the euro area. There have been calls to break up the euro and there is considerable disagreement as to what the right policies are. The purchasing of sovereign bonds is a particularly contentious policy. My investigation here is meant to be a first contribution toward addressing this sensitive question. An important sub-question is whether all countries benefit, or whether there are wealth transfers from some to others. Furthermore, if all countries benefit, do they benefit equally?

I start with some general observations distilled from the findings of the previous chapters. I then go on to the main analysis in the next section, namely an event study of the stock market's reaction to the announcement on September 4, 2014.

The first and, perhaps, most obvious observation is that the countries that have received bailout funds and ratings exemptions, Greece, Cyprus, Portugal, and Ireland, are among the main beneficiaries of crisis policies. With respect to Ireland, however, this conclusion might be contentious since it appears that Ireland was made to guarantee Irish banks by the ECB.[28] These guarantees led Ireland to needing more aid, and might have imposed more hardship on its citizens, than what might otherwise have been the case.

---

[28] See, e.g., "Poison pen," *The Economist*, November 6, 2014, www.economist.com /blogs/charlemagne/2014/11/trichet-letter.

Second, as documented in Chapter 6 (Section 6.9), some Greek banks have also benefited from abnormally small haircuts. In particular, during the time of Greece's exemption from the regular rating rules, some banks issued paper that received haircuts commensurate with ratings in the AAA to A— range, even though the banks themselves as well as Greece had ratings below BBB—. This is odd because the general policy of the ECB at the time was to set the haircuts of such paper, as well as that of Greece itself, to be commensurate with a rating in the range of BBB+ to BBB—.

Third, Greece, Portugal, Ireland, Italy, and Spain also benefited from the EUR 214 billion SMP, which involved outright purchases of the bonds of these countries.[29]

Fourth, while other countries have not received official bailout money, they (and their banks) may have benefited from indirect bailouts, as explained in the previous section, through full allotment long-maturity LTROs. As discussed above, banks in the PIIGS countries have been especially reliant on funding from the Eurosystem during the crisis. The evidence presented in Chapter 9 also shows that French banks had a large uptake in the three-year LTROs. The evidence on the usage of government guarantees in Chapter 6 and the evidence on the policies on the eligibility of marketable collateral trading on non-regulated markets in Chapter 9 also show that Italy and France, respectively, have been large beneficiaries of the ECB's unconventional monetary policies, including modifications to the collateral framework.

Fifth, Portugal, Italy, Ireland, and Spain have all benefited from a generous rating by DBRS. This is less obviously a part of the ECB's bailout policies. But the timing of the inclusion of DBRS as one of the official rating agencies under the Eurosystem's collateral framework (after the onset of the financial crisis) might be suggestive of a decision to boost ratings. The high ratings given by DBRS have helped increase the collateral values of Portuguese, Italian, Irish, and Spanish

---

[29] See, e.g., Eser and Schwaab (2016).

bonds by around EUR 200 to 300 billion (Chapter 6). Banks with paper guaranteed by these countries have also benefited.

Sixth, as documented in Chapter 6, the ECB helped Portugal emerge from its exempt status in August 2014 by lowering the minimum acceptable rating from DBRS to BBBL (from BBB). Without this, Portugal could not have become exempt. Importantly, this paved the way for Portuguese sovereign bonds to be part of the sovereign bond purchase program announced in January 2015.

Finally, it is likely that the benefits from these policies have accrued differentially across investors. The beneficiaries include creditors, as a class. For investors in general, the ECB's unconventional monetary policies have created both opportunities and risks.

11.5   EVENT STUDY: SEPTEMBER 4, 2014

Examining the stock market's reaction to the announcement on September 4, 2014, is an ideal way to address the topic of who benefits from the ECB's unconventional monetary policies to preserve the euro, because stock markets are forward looking. It also allows for an assessment of these policies that is not colored by subsequent developments. If some countries' stock markets react positively to the September 4 announcements and others negatively, this is indicative of expected wealth transfers from the negatively reacting countries to the positive ones. I also examine the behavior of bank stocks versus the rest of the market.

The September 4, 2014, announcement is particularly suitable as the subject of an event study because it represents the third wave of ECB policies, as explained above. Furthermore, the specific contents came as a surprise. A *Financial Times* article, entitled "Draghi intervention on rates and bonds startles markets," reports that:[30]

---

[30] "Draghi intervention on rates and bonds startles markets," by Claire Jones, Thomas Hale, and Elaine Moore, *Financial Times*, 7.14 pm, September 4, 2014.

Mario Draghi startled markets on Thursday cutting interest rates to a record low and pledging to buy hundreds of billions of euros of private sector bonds in a dramatic move to save the eurozone from economic stagnation... Investors had been braced for more monetary stimulus since late August when Mr Draghi signalled he was prepared to take emergency measures to combat the risk of deflation. At 0.3 per cent, eurozone inflation is at a five-year low. However, Thursday's rate cuts and the announcement of the bond purchases took analysts by surprise... Mr Draghi declined to reveal the scale of the ECB's purchases. But he said its bond buying and offer of cheap four-year loans were intended to boost its balance sheet by up to [EUR] 1tn – to levels not seen since the start of 2012... The ECB had initially signalled it would wait until the end of the year to judge the impact of its measures unveiled in June. But recent signs that the currency area's recovery has weakened and a further easing in price pressures have forced the council to act again.

That the announcements on September 4, 2014, came as a surprise is also consistent with the talk on Bloomberg TV and CNBC, where the day before the announcement most commentators predicted that the Governing Council would not do much. The scale and details of the asset purchase programs were probably what especially surprised the markets, since, in the words of the FT article, the unveiled policies "amount[] to the European Central Bank's last resort short of full-scale quantitative easing."[31] Examining the stock market's reaction to this surprising event allows us to see which sovereigns and set of banks would stand to benefit the most.

---

[31] Quantitative easing involves buying assets with "fresh" money, i.e., non-sterilized purchases. There was no indication that the asset purchase programs announced on September 4, 2014, involved sterilization. They can therefore be said to constitute quantitative easing. The FT article likely refers to quantitative easing where sovereign bonds are bought, as was eventually announced on January 22, 2015.

11.5.1   Event Study: Data and Methodology

The basic idea of the event study is to compare the difference, or spread, between two stock return indices around the event date of September 4, 2014, to the historical average difference. This allows me to comment on whether the returns associated with the event date are abnormally large or small for a particular index. I use both standard, widely available indices and ones that I have constructed using data on the common stocks of banks in the euro area. This is described in more detail below. I take account of dividends, if any, by using gross total returns. All data is downloaded from Bloomberg.

In what follows, date 0 refers to September 4, 2014. Relative to this date, I define three calendar windows: (i) $[-132, -8]$, this is a 125-day estimation window of historical average spreads and their variability, (ii) $[-7, -3]$, this is a "dead" period that does not factor into the analysis, except as discussed below within this paragraph, (iii) $[-2, +2]$, this is the longest event window. For robustness, I also use date 0 by itself, $[-1, 0]$, and $[-1, +1]$ as event windows. All indices and bank stocks are required to have return data for each day over the whole $[-132, +2]$ time period. Banks that have the same prices every day over the $[-7, +2]$ period are dropped from the sample.

While all 118 banks in the euro area with common stock found on Bloomberg are potentially part of the analysis, the filtering process described above leaves a sample of seventy-five banks, distributed across countries as shown in Table 11.1, Panels C and D. As a result of missing data, only eleven of the eighteen eurozone countries are represented in the final sample.[32] As it happens, these are the eleven original member states. For each day over the sample period, $[-132, +2]$, I use the seventy-five stocks to calculate

---

[32] Estonia and Latvia are not represented as none of the initial 118 banks were from either of these two countries. Cyprus was not included because of issues with its banks and the data on Bloomberg for these. Banks from the following countries dropped out of the final sample because of incomplete data (following the filtering procedure described in the text): Luxembourg (one bank), Malta (four banks), Slovakia (five banks), and Slovenia (one listed bank). Since these countries have no banks in the final sample, they are also excluded from Panels A and B of Table 11.1.

Table 11.1 *Event study of ECB announcements on September 4, 2014*

| | Event Window Cumulative Spreads | | | | | | | | Historical | |
| | [0] | | [-1,0] | | [-1,+1] | | [-2,+2] | | 125 obs. | |
	Spread	t-Stat.	Spread	t-Stat.	Spread	t-Stat.	Spread	t-Stat.	Mean	s.e.
Panel A: Regional Index Differences (percent)										
Euro Index – Europe Index	0.39^a	(−21.06)	0.82^a	(−22.29)	1.22^a	(−22.24)	1.67^a	(−18.35)	−0.014	0.02
Euro Bank Index – Europe Bank Index	1.09^a	(−30.18)	1.69^a	(−23.50)	2.46^a	(−22.80)	3.17^a	(−17.77)	0.013	0.04
Panel B: Country Index – Euro Index (percent)										
Austria (WBI)	-0.57^a	(11.94)	-0.71^a	(6.82)	-0.49^b	(2.35)	-1.05^a	(3.43)	−0.052	0.05
Belgium (BEL All-share)	0.38^a	(−15.18)	-0.19^a	(5.65)	-0.39^a	(7.30)	-1.31^a	(12.99)	0.036	0.03
Finland (OMX Helsinki)	-0.64^a	(18.06)	-0.93^a	(13.48)	-1.26^a	(12.23)	-0.59^a	(4.21)	0.046	0.05
France (CAC All-share)	-0.22^a	(12.39)	-0.51^a	(14.86)	-0.61^a	(11.72)	-0.77^a	(8.89)	0.002	0.02
Germany (CDAX)	-0.60^a	(25.41)	-0.55^a	(10.88)	-0.39^a	(4.55)	0.02^c	(−1.32)	−0.025	0.02
Greece (ASE)	0.40^a	(−3.48)	0.42^b	(−2.09)	1.72^a	(−4.83)	0.58^c	(−1.37)	−0.001	0.15
Ireland (ISEQ)	-0.13^c	(1.47)	-0.03	(−0.95)	0.02^c	(−1.33)	-0.98^a	(2.73)	−0.022	0.06
Italy (ITLMS)	1.11^a	(−21.13)	1.71^a	(−16.42)	1.65^a	(−10.54)	1.63^a	(−6.30)	0.016	0.05
Netherlands (AEX)	-0.48^a	(18.74)	-1.04^a	(20.44)	-1.19^a	(15.74)	-1.11^a	(9.31)	0.009	0.03
Portugal (PSI All-share)	0.13^a	(−3.81)	-0.12	(−0.85)	0.02^b	(−1.85)	-0.87	(0.93)	−0.100	0.08
Spain (MADX)	0.46^a	(−12.49)	0.58^a	(−7.36)	0.97^a	(−8.31)	0.61^b	(−2.29)	0.055	0.04

Table 11.1 (cont.)

	Event Window Cumulative Spreads								Historical 125 obs.	
	[0]		[-1,0]		[-1,+1]		[-2,+2]			
	Spread	t-Stat.	Spread	t-Stat.	Spread	t-Stat.	Spread	t-Stat.	Mean	s.e.
Panel C: Banks – Euro Index (percent)										
Austria (3 securities)	1.04^a	(-11.67)	2.70^a	(-14.67)	3.64^a	(-13.35)	2.79^a	(-6.95)	-0.155	0.10
Belgium (4 securities)	-0.25	(1.02)	-1.93^a	(4.68)	-2.11^a	(3.35)	-1.61^c	(1.40)	-0.046	0.20
Finland (2 securities)	-1.67^a	(20.16)	-2.54^a	(15.44)	-1.78^a	(7.47)	-2.83^a	(7.13)	0.039	0.08
France (17 securities)	-0.78^a	(12.61)	-1.62^a	(13.12)	-1.25^a	(6.83)	-0.86^a	(2.95)	0.013	0.06
Germany (8 securities)	-0.30^a	(3.79)	-0.85^a	(5.20)	-0.08	(0.60)	0.14^a	(-0.04)	0.024	0.09
Greece (7 securities)	4.32^a	(-22.77)	7.60^a	(-20.21)	11.22^a	(-19.92)	14.34^a	(-15.63)	-0.308	0.20
Ireland (2 securities)	3.37^a	(-15.19)	4.20^a	(-9.88)	9.95^a	(-14.97)	14.54^a	(-13.26)	-0.252	0.24
Italy (19 securities)	2.01^a	(-15.59)	2.17^a	(-8.39)	3.03^a	(-7.79)	3.22^a	(-4.94)	0.009	0.13
Netherlands (2 securities)	-0.40^a	(4.28)	-0.76^a	(4.11)	-0.74^a	(2.57)	-0.57	(1.07)	-0.019	0.09
Portugal (3 securities)	2.36^a	(-11.42)	2.97^a	(-7.45)	3.27^a	(-5.64)	3.33^a	(-3.71)	-0.148	0.22
Spain (8 securities)	0.77^a	(-9.59)	0.73^a	(-4.50)	2.20^a	(-9.15)	2.98^a	(-7.42)	0.009	0.08
Panel D: Banks – Euro Bank Index (percent)										
Austria (3 securities)	-0.76^a	(6.35)	0.04^c	(-1.36)	0.54^a	(-2.95)	-0.48	(-0.24)	-0.120	0.10
Belgium (4 securities)	-2.05^a	(10.33)	-4.59^a	(11.57)	-5.21^a	(8.75)	-4.87^a	(4.89)	-0.007	0.20
Finland (2 securities)	-3.48^a	(29.59)	-5.20^a	(22.28)	-4.89^a	(14.15)	-6.09^a	(10.73)	0.065	0.12
France (17 securities)	-2.58^a	(25.76)	-4.29^a	(21.45)	-4.35^a	(14.68)	-4.12^a	(8.57)	0.053	0.10
Germany (8 securities)	-2.11^a	(18.31)	-3.51^a	(15.34)	-3.19^a	(9.49)	-3.12^a	(5.81)	0.064	0.12

Greece (7 securities)	**2.51**^{a}	(−13.54)	**4.93**^{a}	(−13.31)	**8.11**^{a}	(−14.46)	**11.08**^{a}	(−12.09)	−0.280	0.21
Ireland (2 securities)	**1.56**^{a}	(−7.56)	**1.54**^{a}	(−4.19)	**6.85**^{a}	(−10.62)	**11.28**^{a}	(−10.51)	−0.213	0.23
Italy (19 securities)	**0.21**^{b}	(−1.68)	−0.49^a	(2.97)	−0.07	(0.69)	−0.05	(0.53)	0.043	0.10
Netherlands (2 securities)	−2.20^a	(21.70)	−3.42^a	(16.92)	−3.84^a	(12.70)	−3.83^a	(7.69)	0.020	0.10
Portugal (3 securities)	**0.55**^{a}	(−3.29)	**0.31**^{c}	(−1.32)	0.17	(−0.82)	0.07	(−0.61)	−0.108	0.20
Spain (8 securities)	−1.04^a	(22.76)	−1.93^a	(21.26)	−0.90^a	(7.33)	−0.28^b	(2.19)	0.048	0.05

This table reports on total return differences, or spreads, between various stock indices and euro-area national bank stock portfolios around September 4, 2014 (date 0). This date saw the announcement of ABS and covered bond purchase programs by the ECB. Cumulative total return spreads between two indices or portfolios are calculated over event windows [−t,s], where −t (s) represents t (s) trading days before (after) date 0. For each spread, the two rightmost columns (labeled "historical^a") report average daily spreads and the corresponding standard errors over 125 consecutive trading days for which spreads can be calculated, ending with August 25, 2014. Panel A reports on spreads between (i) a euro-area country indices versus a Europe-wide index, and (ii) a euro-area bank index versus a Europe-wide bank index. Panel B reports on spreads between euro-area country indices versus a euro-area index. Panel C (D) reports on spreads between equally weighted country bank-stock portfolios and a euro-area index (euro-area bank index), where the number in brackets indicates the number of bank stocks per country. These consist of all actively traded bank common stocks in the euro area recorded in Bloomberg (on date +3). The final sample of bank stocks includes seventy-five banks from eleven euro-area countries. Estonia and Latvia do not have any listed bank stocks in Bloomberg. Cyprus is not represented because of issues with its banks and the data on Bloomberg for these. No bank stocks from Luxembourg, Malta, Slovakia, and Slovenia fulfill filtering criteria (see the main text). These countries are also excluded from Panels A and B. Statistical significance of the cumulative spreads are tested with respect to the mean spreads and standard errors in the two rightmost columns using standard t-tests (with 124 degrees of freedom). Letters a, b, and c indicate statistical significance at the 1, 5, and 10 percent levels, respectively. Relevant t-statistics are in brackets in the first column to the right of each spread. Statistically significantly (10 percent or better) positive spreads are in boldface as are countries whose spreads overall are positive. Indices: Euro Index is EURO STOXX, Europe Index is STOXX Europe 600, Euro Bank Index is EURO STOXX Banks, and Europe Bank Index is STOXX Europe 600 Banks. Country indices are in parentheses after each country.

the equally weighted average return of the common stock for all banks within the same country.

Total returns are also collected for the following standard indices:

1. **European, euro-area indices**
   The STOXX Europe 600 Index, The EURO STOXX Index
   The STOXX Europe 600 Banks Index,[33] The EURO STOXX Banks Index
2. **Country indices**
   Austria (WBI, 75), Belgium (BEL All-share, 137), Finland (OMX Helsinki, 131), France (CAC All-share, 530), Germany (CDAX, 475), Greece (ASE , 60), Ireland (ISEQ, 47), Italy (ITLMS, 10 groups), Netherlands (AEX, 25), Portugal (PSI All-share, 50), Spain (MADX, 107).
   (The number of stocks in each index is in parentheses.)

The analysis then proceeds as follows. First, for each spread, I calculate the mean and standard error over the estimation window, $[-132, -8]$. These values are reported in the two far right columns of all four panels of Table 11.1. Second, for each spread, I calculate the (arithmetic) cumulative spread over each event window. Third, I use a standard t-test to assess whether the cumulative spread is statistically significant over the event window.[34]

11.5.2   Event Study: Results

The results are in Table 11.1. Spreads that are positive and statistically different from the relevant historical mean over the event window are indicated in bold. Thus, bold numbers highlight countries or regions that, according to the stock market, are beneficiaries of the ECB's unconventional monetary policies to preserve the euro, specifically the ones announced on September 4, 2014.

[33] This is the name of the index. It does not mean that the bank index has 600 stocks in it.

[34] The test statistic is: $t_{124} = \frac{m \times mean(spread) - ACS_{t,t}}{m \times s(spread)}$, where m is the number of days in the event window, $mean(spread)$ and $s(spread)$ are the mean and standard error of the spread over the 125 day estimation period, and ACS is the arithmetic cumulative spread over the event window. The standard error is the standard deviation divided by $\sqrt{124}$.

Panel A looks at the euro area versus Europe in general. Spreads are calculated as euro-area stock returns less Europe-wide returns. In other words, the euro area is benchmarked by Europe in general. As seen in the two far right columns, the returns on the Europe and euro-area general stock indices tend to be almost the same, the mean spread (euro area less Europe) between them being −0.014 percent. The same is true for the bank stock indices, where the spread averages to 0.013 percent. Given standard errors of 0.02 percent and 0.04 percent, respectively, this means that the average spreads are not statistically different from zero. That the spreads are zero on average is perhaps not surprising, especially because a substantial portion of the Europe-wide indices are made up of euro-area stocks.

However, things are different on September 4, 2014. On this date, the general euro-area stock market returns 0.39 percent more than the general Europe-wide returns. For banking stocks, the spread is 1.09 percent. Both spreads are highly statistically significant, when benchmarked against their typical historical mean and variation. The gains are larger for the other event windows. For the $[-2, +2]$ window the spreads are 1.67 and 3.17 percent, respectively. This illustrates that the announcement on September 4 was favorable to the euro area as a whole and especially so for its banking sector. The result is especially strong when one recognizes that a large fraction of the Europe-wide index is made up of euro-area domiciled stocks.

Panel B looks at how these gains are distributed across the countries in the euro area by looking at the spreads between country indices and the broad euro-area index. The clear winner in terms of benefiting from the ECB's policies is seen to be Italy, with a spread over the broad euro-area index of 1.11 percent on date 0 and 1.63 percent over the $[-2, +2]$ period. Greece and Spain are the other two big winners. Several countries, including Finland, Austria, and Germany have stock markets with lower returns on September 4, 2014, than Europe in general. This is suggestive of wealth transfers from these countries to the rest of the euro area. However, these underperformances disappear over longer event windows. Over the $[-1, +1]$

window, for example, Finland and the Netherlands perform about the same as Europe, with all other countries doing better. The conclusion from Panels A and B, therefore, is that the ECB's unconventional monetary policies are beneficial for the euro area as a whole, possibly with some wealth transfers from stronger to weaker member states. That the evidence with respect to wealth transfers is not stronger than it is may reflect that the failure to support the weaker nations would result in a crisis within these countries that could spill over to the rest of the euro area. However, the evidence strongly supports the view that within the euro area, the gains from the ECB's policies are not shared equally.

Panels C and D report on the results when using spreads based on the national bank indices I have calculated for the purpose of this study (described above). These national indices are benchmarked by a broad euro-area index (Panel C) and a euro-area bank index (Panel D). The spreads between the national bank indices and the broad euro-area index in Panel C reveal that the performances of Greek and Irish banks are in a class of their own, with cumulative spreads over the [−2, +2] event window of 14.34 and 14.54 percent. French banks are the worst performers, with a corresponding spread of −0.86 percent. These are all highly statistically significant.

Panel D shows a similar story, with Greek and Irish banks yielding around 11 percent more over the [−2, +2] period than other banks in the euro area. The next best performers are Austrian, Italian, and Portuguese banks, with corresponding spreads of approximately zero. The banks of all other countries are relative losers. Thus, while banks benefit especially much from the ECB's policies, the benefits are unevenly distributed across countries. This mimics the conclusion from Panels A and B.

To summarize, the conclusion from the event study is that the ECB's unconventional monetary policy benefits the euro area as a whole and especially its banking sector. No country is a spectacular loser, but the banks of Greece and Ireland are spectacular winners. The country with the largest overall gain is Italy.

That the Italian economy should be the largest winner from the ECB's fight to preserve the euro is perhaps not surprising. After Greece, Italy has the largest deficit in the euro area, and it has extended the most guarantees to its banks. This makes Italy especially fragile. The event study evidence suggests that the market expects this fragility to be reduced by the ECB's asset purchase programs.

12 The Endgame of the Euro Crisis

The endgame of the euro crisis began with the confirmation in the ECB press conference on January 22, 2015, that the Eurosystem would buy sovereign bonds. This was introduced on the back of the ABS and covered bond purchase programs announced September 4, 2014, and discussed in the previous chapter. This combined, or expanded, asset purchase program represents what central bankers refer to as quantitative easing, meaning that the purchases of the assets are financed by the creation of new (electronic) central bank money.[1]

The exact timing relates to an interim opinion by the European Court of Justice on January 14, 2015, regarding the legality of the ECB's Outright Monetary Transactions (OMT) program to buy sovereign bonds of troubled countries (ECJ 2015a). The opinion, issued by Advocate General Cruz Villalón, states that the OMT program is, in principle, within the ECB's mandate. Importantly, the Advocate General's opinion speaks not only to the legality of the OMT, but to the buying of sovereign bonds in general. His opinion is that it is within the ECB's mandate to do so, under certain basic provisos I will discuss in Section 12.2. In short, the ECB was given an amber, if not a green, light to start buying sovereign bonds. The signal was strong enough that a major buyer of euros, the Swiss National Bank, took immediate action and ended its three-year-old peg to the euro the next day.[2] The formal announcement that the Eurosystem would start buying sovereign bonds took place at the

---

[1] See, for example, information on the program from the Dutch Central Bank: www.dnb.nl/en/news/news-and-archive/dnbulletin-2015/dnb320136.jsp; or the European Parliament: www.europarl.europa.eu/RegData/etudes/BRIE/2015/548976/EPRS_BRI(2015)548976_REV1_EN.pdf.

[2] Formally, the CHF/EUR peg was a minimum exchange rate of 1.20 francs per euro. Because of the weakness of the euro, it operated as a peg in practice.

very first opportunity one week later, the scheduled press conference associated with the Governing Council meeting on January 22.

There are four elements to this chapter. It starts by providing some broader background to the fiscal sandbox of the euro area. It then goes on to discuss the ECJ's interim opinion on January 14 and the ECB's announcements on January 22, 2015. Following on from this, I discuss some scenarios as to how events may unfold as a result of the Eurosystem's expanded asset purchase program. In particular, I outline a possible strategy the ECB might pursue to deal with challenges arising from the prohibition on monetary financing. The chapter also discusses the importance of buying sovereign bonds and bank bonds. Finally, the chapter provides some thoughts as to why the announcement on January 22 does not mark the end of the fight to save the euro, but the beginning of the endgame, alternatively, the beginning of a new game.

12.1 BACKGROUND

Because of differences in economic strength and fiscal discipline across European Union countries, it was well understood by the architects of the euro that problems could arise. Thus, the Maastricht Treaty of 1992, which laid the groundwork for the euro, stipulated fiscal criteria that needed to be met prior to the adoption of the euro and maintained thereafter. These are a debt-to-GDP ratio of less than 60 percent and a deficit-to-GDP ratio of no more than 3 percent. In 1997, the Stability and Growth Pact (SGP) added guidelines and regulations relating to the enforcement of especially the 3 percent deficit ratio.[3] Even so, voters in Denmark and Sweden were sufficiently concerned that they rejected joining the euro area in 2000 and 2003, respectively. No other countries held referenda on the euro.

As seen in Table 12.1, the fiscal criteria were never honored across the board. Even in the first year of the euro, 1999, Italy and

---

[3] See European Communities (1992) for the Maastricht Treaty and European Communities (1997) and Council of the European Union (1997a, 1997b) for the Stability and Growth Pact.

Table 12.1 Euro-area member state fiscal indicators

	1999	2000	2001	2002	2003	2004	2005	2006	2007	2008	2009	2010	2011	2012	2013
Panel A: Government consolidated gross debt (percent of GDP)															
Greece	–	–	–†	–	–	–	–	*103.4*	*103.1*	*109.3*	*126.8*	*146.0*	*171.3*	*156.9*	*174.9*
Portugal	51.0†	50.3	53.4	56.2	58.7	*62.0*	*67.4*	69.2	68.4	71.7	83.6	96.2	111.1	124.8	128.0
Italy	*109.6†*	*105.1*	*104.7*	*101.9*	*100.4*	*100.0*	*101.9*	*102.5*	*99.7*	*102.3*	*112.5*	*115.3*	*116.4*	*122.2*	*127.9*
Ireland	46.7†	36.3	33.4	30.7	30.1	28.3	26.2	23.8	24.0	42.6	62.2	87.4	111.1	121.7	123.3
Belgium	*114.7†*	*109.1*	*107.8*	*104.9*	*101.3*	*96.6*	*94.8*	*90.8*	*86.9*	*92.2*	*99.3*	*99.6*	*102.1*	*104.0*	*104.5*
Cyprus	55.1	55.2	56.9	60.1	63.6	64.7	63.3	58.9	53.7	44.7†	53.5	56.5	66.0	79.5	102.2
France	60.0†	58.4	57.9	59.8	*63.9*	*65.5*	*67.0*	*64.2*	*64.2*	*67.8*	*78.8*	*81.5*	*85.0*	*89.2*	*92.2*
Spain	*60.9†*	58.0	54.2	51.3	47.6	45.3	42.3	38.9	35.5	39.4	52.7	60.1	*69.2*	*84.4*	*92.1*
Euro area (18)	–	–	–	–	–	–	–	–	–	–	–	*83.7*	*85.8*	*89.0*	*90.9*
Austria	*66.4†*	*65.9*	66.5	*66.3*	*65.5*	*64.8*	68.3	67.0	64.8	68.5	79.7	82.4	82.1	81.7	81.2
Germany	*59.9†*	58.7	57.5	59.2	*62.9*	*64.6*	*66.8*	*66.3*	*63.5*	*64.9*	*72.4*	*80.3*	*77.6*	*79.0*	*76.9*
Slovenia	23.7	25.9	26.1	27.3	26.7	26.8	26.3	26.0	22.7†	21.6	34.5	37.9	46.2	53.4	*70.4*
Malta	62.1	60.9	65.5	63.2	69.1	72.0	70.1	64.6	62.4	62.7†	67.8	67.6	69.8	67.9	69.8
Netherlands	58.5†	51.3	48.8	48.3	49.4	50.0	49.4	44.9	42.7	54.8	56.5	59.0	61.3	66.5	68.6
Finland	44.1†	42.5	41.0	40.2	42.8	42.7	40.0	38.2	34.0	32.7	41.7	47.1	48.5	53.0	56.0
Slovakia	47.1	49.6	48.3	42.8	41.5	40.6	33.8	30.7	29.8	28.2	36.0†	41.1	43.5	52.1	54.6
Lithuania	23.0	23.8	22.9	22.4	21.4	19.3	18.3	18.0	16.7	15.4	29.0	36.3	37.3	39.9	39.0
Latvia	12.2	12.2	14.0	13.2	13.9	14.2	11.7	9.9	8.4	18.6	36.4	46.8	42.7	40.9	38.2
Luxembourg	6.7†	6.1	6.6	6.5	6.4	6.5	6.3	7.0	7.2	14.4	15.5	19.6	18.5	21.4	23.6
Estonia	–	–	–	–	–	–	–	–	–	–	–	6.5	6.0†	9.7	10.1
Maximum acceptable number according to the Maastricht Treaty: 60 percent															
Number of violations	4	3	3	3	5	6	6	7	7	8	9	10	12	12	13
Percent of violations	36.4	27.3	27.3	27.3	45.5	54.5	54.5	58.3	53.8	53.3	56.3	62.5	70.6	70.6	76.5

Panel B: Government deficit (percent of GDP)

	1999	2000	2001	2002	2003	2004	2005	2006	2007	2008	2009	2010	2011	2012	2013
Greece	—	—	—†	—	—	—	—	6.1	6.7	9.9	15.2	11.1	10.1	8.6	12.2
Portugal	3.0†	3.2	4.8	3.3	4.4	6.2	6.2	4.3	3.0	3.8	9.8	11.2	7.4	5.5	4.9
Italy	1.8†	1.3	3.4	3.1	3.4	3.6	4.2	3.6	1.5	2.7	5.3	4.2	3.5	3.0	2.8
Ireland	-2.4†	-4.8	-0.9	0.3	-0.4	-1.4	-1.6	-2.8	-0.2	7.0	13.9	32.4	12.6	8.0	5.7
Belgium	0.6†	0.1	-0.2	-0.1	1.8	0.2	2.6	-0.3	0.0	1.1	5.5	4.0	3.9	4.1	2.9
Cyprus	4.0	2.2	2.1	4.1	6.0	3.8	2.2	1.1	-3.2	-0.9†	5.6	4.8	5.8	5.8	4.9
France	1.6†	1.3	1.4	3.1	3.9	3.5	3.2	2.3	2.5	3.2	7.2	6.8	5.1	4.9	4.1
Spain	1.3†	1.0	0.5	0.4	0.4	0.0	-1.2	-2.2	-2.0	4.4	11.0	9.4	9.4	10.3	6.8
Euro area (18)	—	—	—	—	—	—	—	—	—	—	—	6.1	4.1	3.6	2.9
Austria	2.6†	2.1	0.6	1.3	1.7	4.8	2.5	2.5	1.3	1.5	5.3	4.5	2.6	2.3	1.5
Germany	1.5†	-1.0	3.1	3.9	4.1	3.7	3.3	1.5	-0.3	0.0	3.0	4.1	0.9	-0.1	-0.1
Slovenia	3.0	3.6	3.9	2.4	2.6	2.2	1.5	1.3	0.1†	1.8	6.1	5.7	6.2	3.7	14.6
Malta	6.7	5.5	6.1	5.4	9.1	4.4	2.7	2.6	2.3	4.2†	3.3	3.3	2.6	3.7	2.7
Netherlands	-0.3†	-1.9	0.4	2.1	3.0	1.8	0.3	-0.2	-0.2	-0.2	5.5	5.0	4.3	4.0	2.3
Finland	-1.7†	-6.9	-5.0	-4.1	-2.4	-2.2	-2.6	-3.9	-5.1	-4.2	2.5	2.6	1.0	2.1	2.4
Slovakia	7.3	12.1	6.4	8.1	2.7	2.3	2.9	3.6	1.9	2.4	7.9†	7.5	4.1	4.2	2.6
Lithuania	—	—	—	—	—	1.5	0.5	0.4	1.0	3.3	9.3	6.9	9.0	3.2	2.6
Latvia	3.8	2.8	2.0	2.2	1.6	1.0	0.4	0.6	0.6	4.0	8.9	8.2	3.4	0.8	0.9
Luxembourg	-3.6†	-5.7	-6.0	-2.3	-0.6	1.0	-0.2	-1.4	-4.2	-3.3	0.5	0.6	-0.3	-0.1	-0.6
Estonia	—	—	—	—	—	—	—	—	—	—	—	-0.2	-1.0†	0.3	0.5
Maximum acceptable number according to the Maastricht Treaty: 3 percent															
Number of violations	0	1	3	4	4	5	4	3	1	6	13	14	11	11	7
Percent of violations	0	9.1	27.3	36.4	36.4	45.5	36.4	25	7.7	40	81.3	87.5	64.7	64.7	41.2

Panel A reports euro-area government consolidated gross debt as percent of GDP. Panel B reports euro-area government deficit as percent of GDP, where surplus is represented by negative numbers. Red italic numbers indicate violations from the Maastricht Treaty of 1992 and the subsequent Stability and Growth Pact of 1997 (maximum acceptable numbers according to the Maastricht Treaty are 60 percent debt/GDP and 3 percent deficit). Euro area (18) does not include Lithuania, which joined euro area in 2015. It does include Latvia, which joined euro area in 2014. The figures without Latvia are almost identical. A dagger, †, marks the year a country joined the euro area.

Data source: Eurostat (downloaded on February 1, 2015).

Belgium violated the 60 percent debt-to-GDP ratio threshold, having ratios of 109.6 and 114.7 percent, respectively. The Swedish and Danish electorates that rejected the euro would have seen this. Germany violated the 3 percent deficit threshold in 2001 and was joined by France in 2002. This led to a revisiting of the two rules and the penalties associated with breaking them. An updated and more forgiving version of the Stability and Growth Pact took effect in 2005.[4] Since then, the number of countries in violation of the two original thresholds has grown. In 2013, the majority of the 18 euro-area countries violated one or both of the two original fiscal ratio thresholds, with the aggregate euro-area debt and deficit-to-GDP ratios being 90.9 and 2.9 percent, respectively.[5]

Despite diverging economic performance, sovereign borrowing costs stayed in a fairly tight band until Lehman's bankruptcy in September 2008. Figure 12.1 shows ten-year yield spreads relative to German bonds for all original euro-area members plus Greece. The time period is January 1, 1999, to December 31, 2014. Figure 12.1a covers the PIIGS countries, with Figure 12.1b covering the other five. Prior to 2008, all countries except Greece had spreads below 50 basis points (bp). Greece had higher spreads until around 2002, but after this its spreads were also mostly below 50 bp until 2008. After "Lehman," borrowing costs started to diverge greatly, with those of the PIIGS countries being substantially larger than those of the others. The largest spread was reached for Greece, 35.3 percent on March 2, 2012. Portuguese spreads reached 15.6 percent on January 30, 2012, and Irish 11.4 percent on July 18, 2011.

These large yield spreads are the symptoms of dysfunction. Ireland, Portugal, Greece (and Cyprus) all ended up needing bailouts.

---

[4] Council of the European Union (2005). See, for example, also the accounts in "The ticking euro bomb: How a good idea became a tragedy," *Der Spiegel*, October 5, 2011, Buiter (2006), and Ngai (2012).

[5] At the time of writing this (January 2015), 2013 is the last year for which data is available from Eurostat. Since debt, deficit, and GDP figures from Eurostat are subject to backdated updates, the number of measured fiscal ratio violations may vary depending on when the data is downloaded. But dramatic changes to the historical figures over time should be rare and exceptional.

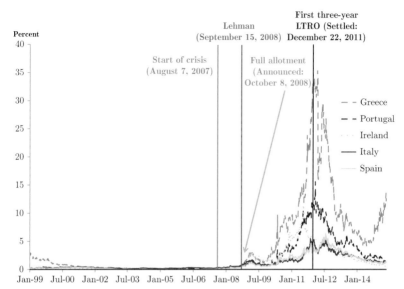

(a) PIIGS countries sovereign yield spreads over Germany

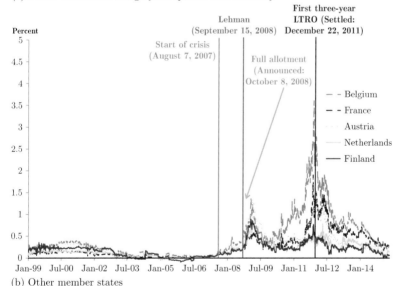

(b) Other member states

FIGURE 12.1 Euro-area sovereign yield spreads over Germany (ten years)

Time period: January 1, 1999, to April 27, 2015.

The data is based on the yield of the on-the-run ten-year sovereign bond for each country at each point in time.

Data source: Bloomberg.

The bailout negotiations with Greece proved especially difficult, with Greece essentially threatening to hold up its euro-area partners with the threat of contagion. This led to substantial turmoil in the euro area in 2011, as seen in the spreads in Figure 12.1. The oil to calm the markets from the worst of the storm were initially the two three-year LTROs in December 2011 and February 2012 and also the Treaty on Stability, Coordination, and Governance (SCG) signed by all EU member states, except the United Kingdom and the Czech Republic, March 2, 2012 (Council of the European Union 2012a).

The SCG takes us back to the Maastricht Treaty of 1992 and the Stability and Growth Pact of 1997. Article III (the Fiscal Compact) paragraph 1, reiterates the target debt and deficit-to-GDP ratios of 60 and 3 percent, respectively. Other parts of the SCG set out new monitoring and enforcement procedures. With strong echoes of the twenty-year-older Maastricht Treaty, the SCG also sets out convergence criteria for countries to comply with the 60 percent indebtedness threshold. This was needed because most eurozone member states were in violation of the 60 percent debt-to-GDP ratio, as seen in Table 12.1. As also seen, at the end of 2013, most member states were still in violation of this, as they are projected by Eurostat to be for quite some time going forward.

Getting indebtedness levels under control is critical to the survival of the euro. It is questionable whether the high current debt levels of the euro area's problem countries are sustainable.[6] Even with the Eurosystem as a backstop, many euro-area countries continue to have low ratings. The factors that can bring debt levels down are lower borrowing costs; debt repayments, writedowns, or cancellations; and growth. This is where the announcement on January 22, 2015, that the Eurosystem will start buying sovereign debt comes in.

[6] See, e.g., Eichengreen and Panizza (2014), or Broyer, Renner, Schneider, and Utermöhl (2014).

12.2 EUROSYSTEM PURCHASES OF SOVEREIGN BONDS: LEGAL ISSUES

Before examining the ECB's announcement of planned sovereign bond purchases, I first review some of the elements of the ECJ interim opinion that paved the way for them. Advocate General Cruz Villalón provides three main conditions for legitimacy of a sovereign bond purchase program:[7]

1. "the ECB must, if the programme is to retain its character of a monetary policy measure, refrain from any direct involvement in the financial assistance programme that applies to the State concerned."[8]
2. "in the event of the programme being implemented, the obligation to state reasons and the requirements deriving from the principle of proportionality are strictly complied with."
3. "the timing of its implementation is such as to permit the actual formation of a market price in respect of the government bonds."

Only the first of these points is specific to the OMT. So, in short, in the Advocate General's opinion, the Eurosystem can legitimately buy sovereign bonds provided it is done in "liquid" secondary markets and is adequately justified in terms of monetary policy. However, the ECB's mandate does not extend to engaging in economic policy or to monetary financing. The Treaty of the Functioning of the European Union (TFEU) explicitly prohibits the buying of sovereign bonds by the ECB or the national central banks *directly* from member states.[9]

[7] All the following quotes are from ECJ (2015a).
[8] Recall that the OMT is conditional on financial assistance programs. See Chapter 11, Footnote 11.
[9] See Article 123, Council of the European Union (2012b) which reads:
  1. Overdraft facilities or any other type of credit facility with the European Central Bank or with the central banks of the Member States (hereinafter referred to as "national central banks") in favour of Union institutions, bodies, offices or agencies, central governments, regional, local or other public authorities, other bodies governed by public law, or public undertakings of Member States shall be prohibited, as shall the purchase directly from them by the European Central Bank or national central banks of debt instruments.
  2. Paragraph 1 shall not apply to publicly owned credit institutions which, in the context of the supply of reserves by central banks, shall be given the same treatment by national central banks and the European Central Bank as private credit institutions.

The Advocate General interprets this prohibition as referring to purchases in the primary, but not the secondary, market. He is very clear on this, stating that:

> [I]n order to comply with the prohibition of monetary financing, the OMT programme will, in the event of its being activated, have to be implemented in such a way that a market price can form in respect of the government bonds concerned, so that there continues to be a real difference between a purchase of bonds on the primary market and a purchase on the secondary market (given that a purchase on the secondary market made seconds after the issue of the bonds on the primary market could completely blur the distinction between the two markets).

While the Advocate General refers to the OMT, it is clear that this quote applies equally to any other sovereign bond purchase program the ECB may devise.

Although there may be a legal distinction between central bank purchases in the primary versus secondary markets, the economic distinction is less clear cut. If the central bank creates new money to buy sovereign bonds, it hardly makes a difference as to whether these bonds are bought in the primary or secondary market. With respect to price impact, which is surely just one issue here, knowledge that the central bank will purchase a particular asset, or class of assets, in large quantities in the secondary market will drive its price up in both the primary and secondary markets. It is also not clear that the secondary market is more liquid. Primary markets of government bonds are typically organized as auctions, where billions of euros worth of bonds may be sold at the same time. Trades in the secondary market are typically smaller. The main distinction between primary and secondary market purchases may well be that the latter are more important with respect to controlling variations in interest

---

This is transferred more or less verbatim from Article 104 of the Maastricht Treaty (European Communities 1992). The renumbering of the article took place within the Lisbon Treaty (Council of the European Union 2007).

rates on a day-to-day basis. But if that is the purpose of central bank transactions in the secondary market, we might expect to observe sales as well as buys. Given that the ECB is targeting an increase of the consolidated Eurosystem balance sheet of around EUR 1 trillion, Eurosystem net sales of government securities are unlikely in the short to medium run.

As it turned out, the ECJ eventually ruled in this case, on June 16, 2015, along the same lines as Advocate General Cruz Villalón.[10] In the Court's opinion, the OMT is compatible with EU law. While the ECJ's ruling is binding under EU law, what this means for Germany will ultimately be decided by the German Constitutional Court, which has reserved its own ultimate judgment in the case. Meanwhile, as per the announcement on January 22, the Eurosystem started buying sovereign bonds in the secondary market, under the expanded asset purchase program, in March 2015.

12.3 THE EXPANDED ASSET PURCHASE PROGRAM

The sovereign debt purchase program announced on January 22, 2015, by the ECB complies with all of the above points from the Advocate General. It is not targeted at troubled countries or indeed any specific country, and therefore Point 1 above does not arise. It was justified as a means to fight deflation; the official inflation level in the euro area was substantially below the 2 percent target. Finally, sovereign bonds will be bought in the secondary market only.

Echoing the OMT, the program is open-ended. The stated plan is to buy EUR 60 billion per month until September 2016, but it can carry on beyond that if need be. Over twenty-one months, this amounts to EUR 1.26 trillion, which is roughly the same number as indicated by Draghi on September 4, 2014. Presumably the amount can be changed if that is deemed appropriate or necessary. The announced amount is, however, not just to cover sovereign bond purchases, but also ABSs and covered bonds. Bonds issued by agencies

---

[10] See ECJ (2015b) for details of the Court's June 16, 2015, ruling.

and European institutions are also covered by the expanded program and are to amount to 12 percent of the purchases. The mix of the other purchases was left unspecified, but Draghi made it quite clear in the press conference on January 22, 2015, that the purchasing of sovereign bonds, which was to start in March 2015, would be a significant part of the total. The emerging evidence is also consistent with this. On April 10, 2015, reported values under the expanded asset purchase program were as follows: covered bonds, EUR 67.2 billion; ABSs, EUR 5.3 billion; public sector paper, EUR 61.7 billion.[11] The takeaway is that both sovereign and bank paper will be bought in whatever quantity it takes to preserve the euro.

Sovereign and agency bonds will be bought in accordance with the ECB's capital key.[12] This structure means that sovereign bond purchases are less likely to fall foul of Point 1 from the Advocate General above. It also means that Germany is the largest beneficiary of the program, with its sovereign and agency bonds accounting for approximately 25.6 percent of the total, even though it is arguably one of the countries that needs the least aid.[13] On the other hand, Italian sovereign and agency collateral will amount to approximately 17.5 percent of the total of the sovereign and agency bond purchases. ABS and covered bond purchases do not need to comply with the capital key. Thus, these purchases can be more tilted toward weaker nations.

---

[11] See, ECB press release, April 14, 2015, "Consolidated financial statement of the Eurosystem as at 10 April 2015," www.ecb.europa.eu/press/pr/wfs/2015/html /fs150414.en.html.

[12] The capital key across EU member states' national central banks is as follows (as of January 1, 2015): Germany, 18.00; France, 14.18; United Kingdom, 13.67; Italy, 12.31; Spain, 8.84; Poland, 5.12; The Netherlands, 4.00; Romania, 2.60; Belgium, 2.48; Sweden, 2.27; Greece, 2.03; Austria, 1.96; Portugal, 1.74; Czech Republic, 1.61; Denmark, 1.49; Hungary, 1.38; Finland, 1.26; Ireland, 1.16; Bulgaria, 0.86; Slovakia, 0.77; Croatia, 0.60; Lithuania, 0.41; Slovenia, 0.35; Latvia, 0.28; Luxembourg, 0.20; Estonia, 0.19; Cyprus, 0.15; Malta, 0.06. These do not sum up to 100 percent due to rounding. See www.ecb.europa.eu/ecb/orga/capital/html/index.en.html.

[13] This percentage is calculated by taking Germany's share of the ECB's capital as a fraction of the total share of all euro-area countries, i.e., 18/70.4.

To put the size of the expanded asset purchase program in perspective, let me use Italy as an example. Recall from Chapter 11 that the month-on-month increase in Italian government debt was approximately EUR 3.5 billion prior to the financial crisis and EUR 6.7 billion after the introduction of the full allotment policy. If half of the expanded asset purchase program will be comprised of sovereign and agency bonds, the monthly purchase of such Italian bonds will be around EUR 5.2 billion. This is more than sufficient to cover "normal" monthly increases in Italian government debt and just EUR 1.5 billion short of the larger EUR 6.7 billion full allotment era monthly increase. Sovereign bond purchases of EUR 40 billion per month would be sufficient to soak up Italian government debt in full. These numbers underscore the significance of the expanded asset purchase program.

An important feature of the program is the sharing, or rather the lack of it, of potential losses on the paper that is bought. The 12 percent of the purchase that will be of European institution paper is subject to loss sharing within the Eurosystem, and the ECB will hold 8 percent of the additional assets. This means that approximately 81 percent of the purchases are going to be on the books of individual national central banks (NCBs) without being subject to loss sharing. The NCBs will buy the collateral, with the ECB coordinating the whole affair.

It is unclear which NCB will buy what paper. Still, it is difficult to see the Bundesbank, for example, buying large quantities of Italian government debt or ABSs. Thus, the program is likely to lead to further segmentation in the euro area, with each NCB buying bonds predominantly issued by its own country's banks and government. Of course, that sovereign bonds will be purchased according to the capital key is not equivalent to saying that an NCB will necessarily only buy and have on its book its own government's paper. Exactly who will end up owning what is clearly an open question and, given the disagreements on the Governing Council over the program, quite possibly subject to debate and negotiation.

12.4   ISSUES AND SCENARIOS

Regardless of who buys what, the expanded asset purchase program may represent a game-changer with respect to how the ECB conducts monetary policy. This is, perhaps, especially so given the ECJ's ruling on June 16, 2015, that the OMT is compatible with EU law (ECJ 2015b). More generally, the ruling supports the point in Advocate General Cruz Villalón's interim opinion that monetary policy can be conducted through the buying of sovereign bonds, even very large quantities of it as long as the purchases are made in liquid, secondary markets and do not violate the prohibition on monetary financing. Whereas in the past, monetary policy in the euro area has been conducted primarily through repos, in the future, open market purchases may be equally, if not more, important.

A trend toward conducting monetary policy via regular interventions in the market for government, and possibly other, bonds will have profound impact on the monetary and financial landscape of the eurozone. It is likely to result in more liquid markets for government bonds and other types of paper that the central bank decides to trade in. It will also create new opportunities for bond dealers. The composition of the Eurosystem's balance sheet will change toward outright holdings of securities. By creating permanent demand for sovereign bonds, it will enable governments to withstand higher debt levels. While the buying of sovereign bonds may help financial stability in the short run, it also caters to governments' appetites for further borrowing so that the reprieve from the euro crisis may be relatively short-lived without counter-measures being put in place.

Irrespective of whether the expanded asset purchase program marks a permanent shift in the conduct of monetary policy or is merely a temporary emergency measure, there is the fine point as to how the purchases are to be financed. In the first instance, the central bank creates new electronic money with which it purchases government debt and bank bonds and thereby sees risk transferred on to its balance sheet. The irony here is that the Eurosystem is, for the most part, owned by the sovereigns themselves. Only three of the NCBs (that I will come back to below) are not owned by their respective governments. So with respect to the buying of government bonds, the transfer is really from one branch of government to another. With respect to the buying of bank bonds, the transfer of risk is from the banks to a branch of government (the central bank). Hence, more risk ends up with government and, ultimately, tax payers. If the purchases are done along national lines, they also contribute to further fragmentation within the euro area. Since the purchases are clearly motivated by growing national debts, it is unlikely that these will magically come down just like that. So what is this likely to lead to? And how can the ECB navigate around the ban on monetary financing?

To try to answer these questions, we might take a lesson from Japan, who pioneered large-scale quantitative easing programs and is still at it. Japan's debt-to-GDP ratio ballooned to 224.6 percent as of 2013 according to the OECD and is projected to grow over the next years.[14] While we do not know for sure what will happen with Japan and its gargantuan debt, speaking at a conference in Zurich on November 17, 2014, Lord Turner, former Chairman of the United Kingdom's Financial Services Authority, declared that he was certain that Japan would never pay back all of that debt, but monetize, or effectively cancel, a large part of it.[15] After all, the Japanese government's biggest creditor is the Bank of Japan, which is owned by the government. Thus, it is a simple matter to consolidate, or cancel, that debt. As he explains in an interview in connection with the conference: "You replace the government bonds the central bank owns by a new form of debt which is perpetual and with zero interest ... If you turn government debt into a perpetual and no interest rate debt, you've turned it into money. And that is how you monetize."[16]

---

[14] See www.oecd-ilibrary.org/economics/government-debt_gov-debt-table-en.

[15] UBS Center Forum for Economic Dialogue at www.ubscenter.uzh.ch/.

[16] "There is no way Japan will ever repay its debt," by Mark Dittli and Alexander Trentin, *Finanz und Wirtschaft*, International selection, November 21, 2014.

A possible scenario is, therefore, that the government debt purchased by the Eurosystem will eventually be monetized/canceled in some way, but without falling foul of the prohibition on monetary financing. There are two main challenges to managing this. The first is that the expanded asset purchase program will increase the stock of money. Unless this is eventually reduced, it may be hard for the ECB to argue that the Eurosystem's buying of sovereign bonds does not constitute monetary financing. The second challenge is the final cancellation of government debt. It is unclear that the trick described by Lord Turner will work in the euro area given the heterogeneity across member states and the official limits on indebtedness.[17] Both of these challenges can be solved by changing legislation. For this to be politically feasible, it may well be necessary for the euro crisis to deepen further. Thus, I start by outlining an alternative scenario for how the stock of money can be reduced, even as the Eurosystem buys sovereign bonds and other assets with fresh central bank money. It bears emphasis that this scenario is hypothetical.

The strategy I have in mind involves the issuance of central bank debt certificates. These are typically considered to be liquidity absorbing monetary policy instruments. Consistent with this, under current euro-area monetary aggregate classifications, central bank paper with a maturity of less than two years does not show up in the monetary base, M1 or M2. It is only counted in M3. If the maturity is more than two years, it does not show up in M3 either.[18] Thus, if the ECB, or the Eurosystem in more generality, issues debt certificates, this will reduce the official stock of money, unless the buyers of the certificates are banks that finance their purchases by corresponding increases in their liquidity uptake in Eurosystem operations.

[17] See Chapter 13.
[18] See www.ecb.europa.eu/pub/pdf/other/manualmfibalancesheetstatistics201204en .pdf (p. 110) for definitions of euro-area monetary aggregates. When reading the definitions, note that central banks are classified with regular banks as monetary financial institutions (MFIs). See www.ecb.europa.eu/home /glossary/html/glossm.en.html#447.

The "central bank paper strategy" for reducing the official stock of money relies on the willingness and ability of various players to hold such paper. There are good reasons to believe that demand for central bank debt certificates, or bills, will be strong. Central bank bills are in some ways better than central bank money for non-bank entities that wish to hold large sums of liquid assets. The reason is that the only way non-banks can hold central bank money is by holding banknotes (paper money).[19] But a large quantity of banknotes is both costly to safeguard and cumbersome to use in transactions. Central bank bills, on the other hand, are cheap to store and easy to use, unless your want is to nip down to the pub and buy a pint. Central bank bills also have advantages over regular bank deposits. The bill gives the holder a direct claim on the central bank, thus bypassing the risk of bank default. This matters, in part, because deposit insurance does not fully protect large deposits – and operating with many bank accounts to get below the insured limit is costly in terms of time and attention. This is not to say that eliminating banks is a good thing for the economy or society. But for some entities, holding central bank bills may well be more attractive than holding banknotes or bank deposits. A drawback with central bank bills is that they may be subject to interest rate risk, depending on the terms at which they are issued.

Central bank bills may also be attractive to banks. For those with excess liquidity, holding Eurosystem bills could be a smart way to store this excess. It would pay as long as the interest rate on the bills exceeds the deposit facility rate, which is currently negative. Other banks could finance holdings of Eurosystem bills by pledging them in Eurosystem operations. Under current rules, ECB (or Eurosystem) debt certificates with maturities of less than one year have a haircut of 0.5 percent (Table 5.4). Furthermore, under the Basel regulatory framework, banks incur no capital charges against ECB debt certificates. In general, central bank paper has a risk-weighting

---

[19] By non-banks here I mean entities that do not have accounts with the central bank.

of zero as long as the central bank has at least a AA– rating.[20] All these factors would contribute to making central bank bills attractive to many banks.

Given that the Eurosystem is purchasing large quantities of government bonds, it may well be that there will be a clamor for Eurosystem debt certificates, as a substitute. End investors of today's government bonds are likely to be end investors of tomorrow's central bank paper. Central bank paper may even be viewed as preferable to government paper because default risk may be perceived to be lower. Research by Torsten Slok of Deutsche Bank shows that non-banks hold significant proportions of the outstanding stock of euro-area government bonds, though the proportion varies considerably from country to country.[21] Thus, if the ECB were to pursue the simple strategy I have outlined here to reduce the official money stock, we may see the emergence of central bank bills as an important asset class. As long as the bills are not financed by banks' pledging them in Eurosystem operations, this will reduce the monetary base.

Of course, this hypothetical strategy can be viewed as a trick. While it may help reduce the monetary base, M1, and M2, one can reasonably argue that central bank bills constitute money, just as banknotes do. Indeed, one of my arguments as to why there is likely to be a high demand for them is that they are in some ways a safer and sometimes more convenient form of money than deposits or banknotes.

Irrespective of whether we will see the emergence of central bank bills in the euro area, the expanded asset purchase program

[20] See BCBS (2006). Most euro-area NCBs are not rated (as of January 2015) because of a lack of outstanding debt. However, according to an S&P circular from 2009, when the ratings of most NCBs were discontinued, it "continues to view the creditworthiness of all national central banks within the Eurozone as being identical to that of the ECB." See "Standard & Poor's withdraws issuer credit ratings on 12 economic and monetary union national central banks," Standard & Poor's, Global Credit Portal, July 24, 2009. The ECB has a AAA rating.

[21] As reported in "Who owns the government bonds the ECB will buy?" *Wall Street Journal*, January 22, 2015 (http://blogs.wsj.com/economics/2015/01/22/who-owns-the-government-bonds-the-ecb-will-buy).

may shift the modality of the euro crisis. If the fiscal situations of troubled euro-area sovereigns are not cleaned up, and the problems within the banking sector not resolved, substantial risk will shift on to the balance sheets of central banks. This may lead markets to question the credibility of some of the national central banks and thus the euro itself. The political and economic ramifications from such a scenario are difficult to predict. It may well lead to a slide to extremism; either a fiscal/political union or the break up of the euro. A more benign outcome is that central bank asset purchases, combined with eventual debt forgiveness, will lead to a severe overshooting of the inflation target and eroding sovereign debts. This should help preserve the euro. However, at the time of writing, the low levels of long-term yields suggest that the market does not place a high probability on this high-inflation scenario.

That market fragmentation along national lines is likely to increase as a result of the expanded asset purchase program may also influence whether the euro will be preserved. Large quantities of an individual government's debt may end up being held internally, by "itself" through its central bank. Bank paper may also be held in large quantities by the respective NCBs. Such segmentation may help untie the financial strings that bind euro-area member states together and thereby alleviate the pain from a break-up of the euro. How things turn out depends, in part, on how successful the ECB will be in coordinating the asset purchases and perhaps implementing a loss sharing scheme. Financing the expanded asset purchase program by the hypothetical issuance of Eurosystem debt certificates with joint liability across the NCBs may be a vehicle for tying euro-area member states closer together.

The alternative hypothetical of issuing individual NCB debt certificates would have the opposite effect. With respect to these hypotheticals, it bears emphasis that "since the adoption of the euro and with the conduct of a single monetary policy for the euro area under the responsibility of the ECB, national central banks of the euro area no longer issue debt certificates."[22] Thus, the issuance of individual NCB debt certificates is probably quite unlikely as long as the objective is to preserve the euro.

While the doomsday scenario of central bank credibility problems may not arise, an alternative to a smooth, happy ending is that government finances do not improve and unemployment figures do not come down. While this can carry on for some time, this scenario will likely lead to a reassessment of the desirability of the euro. Under this scenario, if the euro is to be kept, an exception to the prohibition on monetary financing will probably have to be made and government debt will have to be canceled in a way that is acceptable to those that make these decisions.

The three NCBs that are not fully owned by their respective governments are those of Belgium, Greece, and Italy. Of these, the case of Italy is especially interesting, as the Banca d'Italia is largely owned by Italian banks. Thus, as the Banca d'Italia buys government bonds, the risks associated with these bonds go on the balance sheets of Italian banks, albeit in an indirect way. This further strengthens the government-bank nexus, which is already very strong in Italy. It is a rather bizarre situation that the Italian banking sector, a large part of which may be alive because of government guarantees and the full allotment policy, is who is to save the Italian government through an entity it owns, the Banca d'Italia.

12.5   THE IMPORTANCE OF BUYING SOVEREIGN AND BANK BONDS

If the euro is to survive in its current form, it is arguably necessary for the eurozone economy to improve. The economies of the periphery are especially in need of strengthening. However, over the course of the crisis, these nations have seen their indebtedness grow to levels that are too high. They do not have sufficient fiscal space to provide much by way of economic stimulus. At the same time, there is also

---

[22] Email correspondence from the ECB to the author's research team.

an unwillingness in many member states to carry out the structural reforms called on by everyone from Draghi to the Treaty on Stability, Coordination, and Governance. The problems have been made worse by weak banking sectors that have not been lending much. Monetary stimulus through the LTROs has largely gone to finance extant assets rather than new investments.

The purchasing of sovereign bonds by the Eurosystem should help the ability of the more indebted euro-area nations to carry out fiscal stimulus. This is especially so if some of the debt is eventually canceled or monetized. Fiscal stimulus is arguably necessary to invigorate the demand side of the economy. Too many people in the euro-area periphery are out of work. This is a tragedy and also an obstacle to macroeconomic improvement.

The buying of sovereign and bank bonds also works the supply side of the economy. It does this through strengthening the banks in at least three ways. First, the purchases may help get risky paper off banks' balance sheets. Second, they help create demand for banks' paper and, thereby, reduce financing costs. Third, as the prices of sovereign and bank paper improve as a result of the central banks' purchases, banks should benefit from capital gains as holders of such paper. Banks will, in effect, receive free capital injections. If periphery banks hold especially large quantities of periphery paper, they stand to benefit the most, since periphery paper has the most ground to make up. But others will benefit too. Strengthening banks' balance sheets should help stimulate bank lending and thus the economy.

The ECB's twin policies of buying sovereign and bank bonds is not efficient, because it is indiscriminate. Still, it may be sensible given the world the ECB operates in. However, if structural reforms within euro-area member states are not carried out and common, and efficient, supervision and resolution laws for banks are not implemented, Europe may go twice around the world and end up where it started, along the lines of its twenty-year trip from the Maastricht Treaty to the Treaty on Stability, Coordination, and Governance.

The dark side of the ECB's double-fronted quantitative easing is that it increases disparities before the benefits trickle down to those that need it the most. It contributes to Pikettian disparity by inflating asset prices and thus puts more money in the pockets of those that already are wealthy. To take a lesson from the United Kingdom, a Bank of England report from 2012 states that "[b]y pushing up a range of asset prices, [central bank] asset purchases have boosted the value of households' financial wealth held outside pension funds, but holdings are heavily skewed with the top 5% of households holding 40% of these assets."[23] Inflated asset prices imply that current and future savers face lower savings rates than otherwise. So it is, in part, an intergenerational wealth transfer.

Increased disparities and wealth transfers may breed tension, both within and between member states. Between those who had much and have benefited more from loose monetary policies, and those that had less and benefited less from the whole debacle. Syriza winning 36 percent of the vote in the Greek election on January 25, 2015, may be seen as a reflection of this. Protest parties gaining ground and even winning elections illustrate the pressures that exist within many euro-area countries. The swift and somewhat pugnacious foreign reactions to Syriza's election victory highlight the strained relations among euro-area countries. Already the day after the victory, the *Financial Times*, for example, reported that "Eurozone leaders reject Greek debt relief demands."[24]

Without a credible mechanism to reduce the tensions among euro-area member states, it is hard to see a healthy survival of the euro. Eurosystem purchases of sovereign bonds is not that mechanism, necessary though they might be to preserve the euro.

[23] Bank of England (2012).
[24] Alex Barker, Jeevan Vasagar, and Peter Spiegel, *Financial Times*, January 26, 2015.

13 Restoring Credibility

And indeed there will be time
. . . for a hundred indecisions,
And for a hundred visions and revisions,
Before the taking of a toast and tea.

—T.S. Eliot, *The love song of J. Alfred Prufrock*

In this chapter I argue that the pathology at the heart of the euro crisis is a lack of credibility arising from the prerogative of sovereignty. The implication is that restoring credibility necessarily must involve reining in sovereignty. A brute force approach to this is a fiscal, or full-blown political, union. Below, I propose a milder approach that targets issues that pertain more specifically to the credibility, or integrity, of the common currency. My proposal offers a different vantage point for thinking about the problems of the common currency than the standard optimal currency area approach.

On the face of it, the euro area gives the appearance of being paralyzed by indecision. The same treaty comes and goes, revisiting the same old points. Here we have the Maastricht Treaty, there the Stability and Growth Pact, and yonder comes the Treaty on Stability, Coordination, and Governance with its Fiscal Compact. The maximum debt and deficit ratios are the same, but the penalties for crossing them vary, now weakening, now getting stronger. Convergence criteria are still on the table for member states, more than a decade after the inception of the euro and two decades after the Maastricht Treaty because, as seen in Table 12.1, official thresholds are not adhered to.

At the same time, despite a no-bailout clause in the Maastricht Treaty, bailouts of member states have become an integral part of the fabric of the euro. For some countries, the bailout processes never seem to end. The reason for all this is not indecision as such, but the prerogative of sovereignty that makes it almost impossible to reach final agreements. As so vividly put by Alexis Tsipras after his Syriza party won an overwhelming victory in the Greek parliamentary elections in January 2015:[1]

> "The *sovereign* Greek people today have given a clear, strong, indisputable mandate" Tsipras told a crowd of rapturous flag-waving party supporters. "Greece has turned a page. Greece is leaving behind the destructive austerity, fear and authoritarianism. It is leaving behind five years of humiliation and pain." (italics added)

While Greece may have become the face of the crisis, other countries, including Germany, are also culpable with respect to contributing to what appears to be an endless spiral of visions and revisions (see Section 13.1).

The credibility problem in the euro area can be understood in light of Stephen Krasner's (1999) description of the interaction among sovereigns as organized hypocrisy.[2] As he summarizes it: "...the international system is an environment in which the logics of consequences dominate the logics of appropriateness."[3] In more plain language, inter-sovereign relations are dominated by game playing rather than the adherence to past agreements. There is little by way of a common understanding of what is reasonable, or expected, behavior, or, if there is, it is not kept to. The game playing may be strategic or opportunistic. It hardly matters; either way it is destructive.

---

[1] "Syriza's historic win puts Greece on collision course with Europe," by Helena Smith and Ian Traynor, *The Guardian*, January 26, 2015.

[2] The terminology has its origins in Brunsson's (1989) study of organizations.

[3] Krasner (1999), p. 6. The nomenclature logics of consequences and appropriateness is due to March and Olsen (1989, 1998) and can be described as the maximization of "utility" and the adherence to an assigned role given a set of "rules," respectively.

A feature of Krasner's perspective is also that the players in international relations are not the sovereigns as such but the leaders that represent them. These may change over time, with the ebb and flow of domestic politics. A country does not speak with one consistent voice over time. New leaders may have different agendas than the outgoing ones. Greece and Syriza represent a case in point. This makes it all the more difficult to bind countries to past agreements and helps motivate the need for supranational institutions to enforce them, as I will come back to below in the context of the euro.

Inter-sovereign euro relations, with the frequent revisiting and revisions of the same old themes, fit Krasner's description. The organized hypocrisy undermines the credibility of the very treaties that are supposed to safeguard the common currency and therefore the currency itself.

The euro's fragility was exposed at its first serious test, the financial crisis, where it started to collapse upon itself. As seen in previous chapters, it has been propped up only by ever-larger (indirect) bailouts orchestrated by the ECB. Indeed, Draghi's dramatic call to "preserve the euro, whatever it takes" speaks volumes as to the fundamental lack of credibility of the common currency. Given the absence of a check on the prerogative of sovereignty, this was perhaps no more than what could be expected.

My comments here do not speak to the optimality of the rules in the Maastricht Treaty, the SGP, or to what might be optimal European currency areas. Many commentators expressed skepticism as to the net benefits of the single currency even before the euro was introduced.[4] I am only noting that the rules have little credibility because sovereignty, as it relates to the currency, is not controlled. Before turning to my proposal for reining in sovereignty, I flesh out what I have said above with some examples that bear witness to the organized hypocrisy of the euro. These, and many other examples, are in the public domain and easily accessible.

---

[4] Feldstein (1997) is a prominent example.

13.1 ORGANIZED HYPOCRISY

Although the Stability and Growth Pact of 1997 reconfirmed the Maastricht Treaty's 3 percent deficit target and laid down, at the behest of Germany, stronger and clearer guidelines for sanctions for those countries with larger deficits, Germany itself broke through the deficit barrier in 2001. France followed suit in 2002 (Table 12.1). To avoid the sanctions due under the SGP, Germany and France pushed through a weakening of the SGP that was eventually approved in 2005. As reported in *Der Spiegel*:[5]

> [Germany and France], determined not to submit to sanctions, managed to secure a majority in the EU's council of Economic and Finance Ministers to cancel the European Commission's sanction procedure...The German-French initiative effectively did away with the Stability and Growth Pact, which the Germans had forced their partners to sign...If the two biggest economies in the euro zone weren't abiding by the rules, why should anyone else?...The process also led to a not insignificant side effect: Executive power in Europe, supposedly held by the European Commission, which is informally known as the "guardian of the treaties," was de facto transferred to the European Council, which consists of the European heads of state and government.

When a coalition of member states can overturn the "guardian of the treaties" to serve their current political purpose, the credibility of the treaties is undermined. This is a perfect example of Krasner's thesis of organized hypocrisy.[6] While many economists have

---

[5] "The ticking euro bomb: How the euro zone ignored its own rules," *Der Spiegel*, October 6, 2011.

[6] In contrast, many economists celebrated the credibility of the euro, even as the SGP was dismantled by Germany and France (see, e.g., Wyplosz 2006). But some also expressed concern. In a comment to Wyplosz' article, Martin Wolf (2006) writes, "[Wyplosz] has, to put it mildly, failed to convince me at least that [the euro] has been a 'major success,' unless one means by a success that it exists." He goes on to say: "Yet the collapse of the [SGP] leaves a big question: where is the discipline in the system?"

criticized the SGP, Martin Wolf (2006) emphasizes that "[m]aybe even bad rules, inconsistently enforced were better than none."

Later, with its house in order and the full force of the crisis upon the euro area, Germany sought to rein in its euro partners again, as it sought to do with the SGP in 1997. Craig (2012) gives the following account of the European Council meeting in December 2011 that would lead to the Treaty on Stability, Coordination, and Governance:[7]

> The core proposal in December 2011 was for reform that would further strengthen EU oversight over Member State economic policy, and the new rules were to be incorporated in the primary Lisbon Treaty through amendment requiring unanimity ... Chancellor Merkel pressed strongly for inclusion of the new measures in the Lisbon Treaty... The amendment to the Lisbon Treaty was, however, prevented by the UK veto.

The ultimate hypocrisy is perhaps that the same actors that, when it suits them, weaken a particular arrangement later turn around to strengthen it, when that suits them. The passage also illustrates the ability of individual sovereign nations to veto legislation that affects them. Not that there is anything wrong with that as such, it merely illustrates that agreements among sovereigns are difficult to achieve. It often leads to watered-down final treaties, as, for example, happened with the SCG (Craig 2012).

Another example relates to Italy's inclusion in the eurozone. Italy was allowed to join even though it was far from meeting the Maastricht Treaty's 60 percent deficit rule. In the first year of the euro, Italy's debt-to-GDP ratio was 109.6 percent. However, according

---

[7] The text by Craig (2012) refers to the Treaty of Lisbon. According to the official website of the European Union: "The Treaty of Lisbon amends the EU's two core treaties, the Treaty on European Union and the Treaty establishing the European Community. The latter is renamed the Treaty on the Functioning of the European Union. In addition, several Protocols and Declarations are attached to the Treaty." The Lisbon Treaty was signed in December 2007, entering into force December 1, 2009. Available on http://eur-lex.europa.eu/legal-content/EN/TXT/?uri=CELEX :12007L/TXT or http://europa.eu/eu-law/decision-making/treaties/index_en.htm.

to Erber (2011), "...Italy pressed the EU Commission and the other member states to focus on the three per cent deficit-to-GDP criterion as the key indicator and the *tendency* in 1997 to reduce the debt-to-GDP ratio." He goes on to claim that "The Italian government of Silvio Berlusconi also took major steps to hide its fiscal deficits from the public." This view is supported by an article in *Der Spiegel* that goes even further:[8]

> Documents from the Kohl administration, kept confidential until now, indicate that the euro's founding fathers were well aware of its deficits. And that they pushed ahead with the project regardless.
>
> In response to a request by SPIEGEL, the German government has, for the first time, released hundreds of pages of documents from 1994 to 1998 on the introduction of the euro and the inclusion of Italy in the euro zone ...
>
> The documents prove what was only assumed until now: ...The decision to invite Rome to join was based almost exclusively on political considerations at the expense of economic criteria. It also created a precedent for a much bigger mistake two years later, namely Greece's acceptance into the euro zone.

Italy also has never come close to a 60 percent debt level after joining the euro. In 2013, it stood at 129.6 percent and is not projected to get down to 60 percent anytime soon. Previous chapters have documented and discussed the central role of Italy in the euro crisis.

It is hard to believe that admitting Greece, with an economy representing 2 percent of total euro-area GDP in the year it joined (2001), could have been a worse mistake than admitting Italy, as claimed in the *Spiegel* article. Greece's impact has been felt through the fear of contagion. If countries like Italy were not part of the euro, it is unlikely that there would have been much fear of a Greek default pandemic. If Italy were to default, the end would be nigh.

---

[8] "Operation self-deceit: New documents shine light on euro birth defects," by Sven Böll, Christian Reiermann, Michael Sauga, and Klaus Wiegrefe, *Der Spiegel*, May 8, 2012.

Still, Greece offers another example of self-serving behavior undermining the basic principles on which the euro was supposedly built. Greece's creativity with its accounts is a matter of public record. Eurostat (2004) reports that:[9]

> Revisions in statistics, and in particular government deficit data, are not unusual... However, the recent revision of the Greek budgetary data is exceptional. [Deficit] [f]igures for 2003 were revised by almost 3 percentage points of GDP... Data revisions of such a scale have given rise to questions about the reliability of the Greek statistics on public finances.

The Eurostat (2004) report shows that, in contrast with what Greece had been reporting, Greek deficit figures were never below 3 percent in the 1997 to 2003 period. Thus, according to the Maastricht Treaty and the Stability and Growth Pact, Greece should not have been allowed to join the euro, as it did in 2001.[10] Greece admitted to falsifying the data, but the infringements did not lead to a revocation of Greek euro membership. As reported in the *Independent* on November 16, 2004:[11]

> Greece admitted yesterday that the budget figures it used to gain entry to the euro three years ago were fudged. The Finance Minister, George Alogoskoufis, said the true scale of Greece's budget deficit was massively understated enabling Athens to dip below the qualification bar and into the EU's single currency...

[9] "Eurostat is the statistical office of the European Union situated in Luxembourg. Its task is to provide the European Union with statistics at European level that enable comparisons between countries and regions." See http://ec.europa .eu/eurostat/about/overview.

[10] Its debt levels were also never less than 60 percent – but this was never claimed by Greece. It was not necessary either, because of the precedent set by Italy. Still, Eurostat (2004) shows that Greece under-reported debt levels too.

[11] "Greece admits deficit figures were fudged to secure euro entry," by Daniel Howden and Stephen Castle, *Independent*, November 16, 2004. Available on www.independent.co.uk/news/world/europe/greece-admits-deficit-figures -were-fudged-to-secure-euro-entry-6157967.html.

> The European Commission said there was no question of revisiting Greece's eurozone membership, but the row over budget figures has dealt another severe blow to the credibility of the single currency's battered rulebook, the Stability and Growth Pact.

The authors of this article are right. When fudging numbers to gain entry to the euro is met with not much more than a slap on the wrist, it undermines the treaties safeguarding the euro, but more than that, it undermines the euro itself.

Thus, not surprisingly, problems with Greece have persisted. It was reprimanded in 2010 by the European Commission for continued issues with the reliability of its deficit and debt figures and for a lack of co-operation to allow Eurostat to properly assess the Greek statistics.[12] The problems have perdured into 2015. When I downloaded the data for Table 12.1 in January 2015, Greek public finance data prior to 2006 were unavailable from Eurostat "due to on-going revisions related inter alia to the introduction of ESA2010. The full time series should be available in the course of 2015."[13] Checking on the status of data availability toward the end of June 2015, I found that the problem had gotten worse. Data prior to 2011 were now unavailable. Greek statistics matter a lot, because the terms of their bailout(s) depend on them. They are so important that Greek prosecutors filed felony charges against its chief statistician, Andreas Georgiou, for allegedly inflating deficit figures in 2009 – a kind of statistical treason.[14] This is not the same chief statistician that reportedly had a magic way with getting Greek deficits down below the 3 percent threshold in those heady, happy days when

---

[12] See European Commission (2010a) and European Commission and Eurostat (2010).

[13] Email from Eurostat in response to an inquiry regarding the missing Greek numbers. ESA2010 is the harmonized European System of Accounts that replaces the previous version, ESA95.

[14] See, for example, the account in "Prosecuting the messenger: Chief Greek statistician threatened with jail," by Georgios Christidis, *Der Spiegel*, February 12, 2013.

Greece joined the euro.[15] Meanwhile, Greek bailout bargaining has continued.

Greece is not the only country to join with "funny" deficit numbers. Table 12.1 shows that Malta joined in 2008 and ended its first year in the euro with a deficit of 4.2 percent, up from 2.3 percent the year before. Slovakia joined in 2009, with its deficit increasing that year to 7.9 percent from 2.3 percent the year before. It is a funny thing what being a member of the euro area can do to a country's fiscal situation.

These events of fiscal profligacy, changing the rules when it is beneficial, outright cheating, squabbling, renegotiating bailouts, and prosecuting statisticians for serving up the "wrong" statistics all serve to undermine the credibility of the common currency. They are symptoms of the (dis)organized hypocrisy at the core of the euro.

In an article entitled "Athens, Rome hold Europe to ransom," the *Wall Street Journal* discusses some of the troubles with gamesmanship in the euro area:[16]

Europe is engaged in a high-stakes game of brinkmanship that poses grave risks to the global economy. At last weekend's Villa d'Este Forum in Italy, European policy makers didn't hide their fury at Greece's back-sliding over promised structural reforms and spending cuts . . .

Greece has learned that whenever the crisis in Europe's periphery threatens to overwhelm the core, Europe will ignore previous broken promises and step up with a fresh bailout.

[15] See, for example, "How 'magic' made Greek debt disappear before it joined the euro," by Allan Little, *BBC News*, February 3, 2012, www.bbc.com/news/world-europe-16834815. A part of the magic apparently came with a little help from the magicians at Goldman Sachs (see "Goldman's Trojan currency swap," by Tracy Alloway, *FTAlphaville*, February 9, 2010, http://ftalphaville.ft.com//2010/02/09/145201/goldmans-trojan-greek-currency-swap).

[16] "Athens, Rome hold Europe to ransom," by Simon Nixon, *Wall Street Journal*, September 6, 2011, www.wsj.com/articles/SB10001424053111903648204576552833212397892.

Italy now appears to be making the same calculation
...ministers show no appreciation of the urgent need for structural reforms to address the chronic weakness of an economy that
grew on average 0.3% between 2001 and 2010 and experienced
a 25% increase in unit labor costs relative to Germany over the
same period. Instead, they talk incessantly of euro-zone bonds as a
solution to misfortunes they blame largely on external forces ...

So what can be done about Greece and Italy? Athens rejects
accusations it is dragging its feet but has promised to use a 10-day
hiatus in talks with the European Central Bank and International
Monetary Fund over progress toward its bailout targets to speed up
reforms. If it fails to deliver again, European policy makers now
talk darkly of a total loss of fiscal sovereignty. How this might
work in practice isn't clear.

In other words, Greece and Italy have the power to cause great hardship on the rest of the euro area, and indeed the global economy,
through the threat of default. We experienced this power at work
in 2010 and well into 2012, with Greek bailout negotiations caus-
ing extreme turmoil in the markets. Since then the Greek threat
has been reduced, as seen by the stock market's reaction to Syriza's
victory in the Greek election on Sunday, January 25, 2015. Greek
stocks fell approximately 9 percent over a five-trading-day window,
[−2,+3], around the election. Over the same time period, the euro-
area stock market was up almost 3 percent, just 0.2 percent below
a broader Europe index. Ten-year German government bonds were
down 9.4 bp, with Italian and Greek bonds rising 4.3 bp and 137.3 bp,
respectively.[17]

The power of Greece to wreak havoc has been waning since
late 2011 as a result of direct and indirect bailouts of the weaker
euro-area countries and banks, market fragmentation, and fiscal aus-
terity measures. But these measures and trends are not without cost.

[17] The Greek, euro area, and Europe stock indices used are, respectively, ASE, The
EURO STOXX Index, The STOXX Europe 600 Index. The returns are total gross
returns. Index and bond yield data are from Bloomberg.

While fragmented markets, for example, serve to isolate the impact of Greece (and that of the other troubled periphery countries as well), it is also inefficient and a sign of ill-health. Millions of people are without jobs and may be less than sanguine about their prospects, even as markets are holding up and the euro is not dissolving.[18] The fundamental problem of organized hypocrisy at the core of the euro has hardly been dealt with.

The *Wall Street Journal* article portrays the fragility of the euro brought about by gamesmanship. By making the threat of default credible, Greece undermined the credibility of the common currency, with obvious negative economic consequences. Greece and Italy's threat to impose losses on others could be reduced by limiting sovereignty, for example, through a fiscal or political union.

Speaking in Davos on the morning of January 22, 2015, Larry Summers, former President of Harvard and Secretary of the Treasury (United States), called the euro an act of irresponsibility, for not having set up the proper institutions in advance to use common "fiscal space."[19] But doing so might simply not have been consonant with the political realities of the time, even though there is evidence that many of the politicians that pushed through the euro saw it as a political, rather than an economic, project. Perhaps they had in mind that its fragility would eventually force political union upon the member states after a lot of trouble, toil, and suffering; a kind of modern version of Bismarck's blood and iron politics. In his treatise on the history of the European monetary union, Harold James (2012) writes, "The monetary union as conceived in the Maastricht Treaty was intended to be accompanied by a political union." He goes on to assert that a fundamental flaw resulting from this not happening

---

[18] In December 2014, the unemployment rate for the euro area as a whole was 11.3 percent, which amounts to 18.3 million people. Youth (below twenty-five years of age) was 23 percent, amounting to 3.2 million individuals. The corresponding figures for Spain, one of the hardest-hit countries, are 23.7 percent (5.9 million) and 51.4 percent (0.8 million). Data source: Eurostat, January 2015.

[19] www.bloomberg.com/news/videos/2015-01-22/lagarde-cohn-summers-botin-dalio-on-bloomberg-panel.

was that "the mechanisms for enforcing fiscal discipline were inadequate."[20] Even so, it is not obvious that creating a "United States of Europe" is "optimal." Certainly, not everyone is in favor of it.

In what follows, I discuss a less radical way to restore credibility to the common currency. A third alternative is to break the euro up into areas that are more suited to share a currency, thereby limiting the damages of what might be the inevitable organized hypocrisy of international relations.

13.2 SECURE SOVEREIGN DEBT AND MODIFY HAIRCUTS

My proposal is in the spirit of the idea in the Delors report that "[a]ll policy functions which could be carried out at a national (and regional and local) levels without adverse repercussions on the cohesion and functioning of the economic and monetary union would remain within the competence of the member countries."[21] Since more or less independent fiscal policies and gamesmanship have proved damaging to the euro and the cohesion of member states, I propose to control it in a way that is as unobtrusive to member states' sovereignty as possible.[22] Still, some sovereignty is necessarily lost.

The discussion above highlights two points, namely the lack of credibility of fiscal targets and no-bailout (now limited-bailout) clauses. We have seen over the last few years how costly this lack of credibility can be. Of course, unless you are a European federalist, dissolving the euro is not a catastrophe by itself. It is arguably more the process of dissolution that may be problematic and costly.

---

[20] For other accounts of the euro crisis and some of the political issues, see, for example, Pisani-Ferry (2014), Cline (2014), and Sinn (2014). The latter two provide further information on the macroeconomic imbalances that built up in the euro area over time.

[21] Committee for the Study of Economic and Monetary Union (1989).

[22] I initially put out my proposal in Nyborg (2011), also published in the *Neue Zürcher Zeitung* under the German title "Stabilisierung der Euro-Zone durch Besicherung von Bonds," on August 8, 2011, www.nzz.ch/aktuell/start seite/stabilisierung-der-euro-zone-durch-besicherung-von-bonds-1.11928023.

The Eurosystem's collateral framework has had a role in the crisis by allowing central bank money to be issued against sovereign debt at overly generous terms. For example, because they have an A− rating (on the S&P scale) from DBRS, Spanish and Italian bonds can be used to obtain liquidity from the Eurosystem at the same terms as German bonds, rated AAA. As late as December 2009, this was possible with Greek bonds too. The low haircuts have helped lower the funding cost for these more indebted nations.[23]

The first part of my proposal is to use haircuts to exercise a measure of fiscal control vis-à-vis euro-area member states. The idea is simple: link haircuts to indebtedness. For example, if a debt-to-GDP ratio of no more than 60 percent is desired, then increase haircuts progressively in the debt-to-GDP ratio beyond this. The same goes for the deficit; increase haircuts progressively beyond 3 percent, if that is the desired maximum level. To increase the incentives for member states to adhere to the maximum levels, haircuts could start to increase even before these levels are breached. Haircuts can also be linked to other measures and even statistics that pick up structural reforms. As this will help preserve and stabilize the euro, it should be within the ECB's mandate to do so. If it can buy sovereign bonds, it can do this.

This proposal extends the general idea I introduced in Chapter 10 (Section 10.4) to design haircut-discriminating operations. Fiscal-linked haircuts can be used as minimum bid haircuts for the relevant collateral.

My proposal works by reducing the liquidity and value of a highly indebted country's bonds. This increases its borrowing cost and, therefore, decreases its appetite for borrowing beyond the

---

[23] This relates to Nyborg, Bindseil, and Strebulaev's (2002) point that haircuts affect the opportunity costs of eligible collateral. Buiter and Sibert (2005) expand on this point, arguing that identical haircuts in Eurosystem operations for sovereign bonds serve to tighten yield spreads. What I am saying here is in line with this view. An example showing that haircuts influence sovereign bond yields is provided in Chapter 6.

threshold. The increase in haircuts when a sovereign goes beyond the threshold needs to be large to have a significant effect. Haircuts of local and regional government securities will need to be affected as well. This will have the added benefit of exerting local political pressure on reducing central government indebtedness. All this will reduce member states' appetite for borrowing beyond the threshold levels. In effect, the proposal uses the supranational status of the ECB to rein in the power of the sovereigns. The markets will do the rest.

Even with indebtedness-linked haircuts, it is not unimaginable that a country borrows too much, or even cooks its books, and ends up in a situation such as Greece in 2010. The second part of my proposal addresses this. It is more complicated than the first part and more radical, because it involves giving up more sovereignty.

The Greek debt restructuring and bailout process highlights the problems with ex-post renegotiation, whereby a defaulting debtor seeks to renegotiate her debt rather than repaying what she can. The costs associated with default are reduced if the debt is secured. Most lenders and creditors are aware of this, as illustrated, for example, by standard home mortgage contracts. Insolvency law recognizes this too, by providing mechanisms that allow creditors to take possession of the assets that secure the loans they have given as well as procedures for the orderly liquidation of a defaulting debtor's assets. Sovereign debt is a different matter because few mechanisms exist to enforce repayment. This makes it all the more important to secure sovereign debt, especially in a common currency area such as the euro area, where there is risk of contagion and where the quality of the common currency is a function of what each individual member state brings to the table to back up the currency and to secure the banking and financial system.

In the case of Greece, as for any other country, one would expect there to be assets that can be sold off to help service and repay her debt. However, we are missing a mechanism to enforce such sales and a well-considered plan as to what assets to sell. If the debt had been secured, this would already have been in place. Without this, Greece has been able to hold up the rest of the euro area with the implicit threat of a full-blown crisis, arising from contagion to other euro-area member states. If Greece were not part of the euro area, the impact on world markets would probably not be as strong. This underscores the importance of collateralizing euro-area sovereign debt, for the benefit of all of its member states and their citizens, if the euro is to be kept.

An example of a structure that does not compromise sovereignty much is offered by the oil agreements that backed up US financial assistance to Mexico in the 1990s, whereby buyers of Mexican oil paid directly into an account with the Federal Reserve rather than to Mexico. This account then served as collateral for US loans to Mexico (US GAO 1996).

More generally, collateralizing sovereign debt in a credible way requires setting up a supranational institution to hold collateral in escrow. Thus, tax receipt accounts, say, or real assets physically located in a member state could not be expropriated back by that state after a default. If physical assets are involved and there is a risk that the value of the collateral could be reduced by the actions (or inactions) of the borrowing state, debt could be structured as lease-backs, thus giving the lender a certain amount of control over the asset as long as the debt is outstanding. Under this scheme, participation in the euro requires signing away some sovereign rights under international and national law. It therefore represents a weakening of sovereignty, but this weakening can be structured to be contingent on default. Thus, in practice, its only effect is to rein in fiscal profligacy and limit the ability for brinkmanship.

The idea of my proposal is that sovereign debt must be secured, through the supranational escrow institution, for it to be eligible in Eurosystem operations.

To have a system with proper checks and balances, this institution should also be separate from the ECB. Krasner's perspective of organized hypocrisy may also be useful to understand the oddities in Eurosystem's collateral framework, which is designed by the ECB, documented in previous chapters. The substantial tinkering with it over the years is prima facie evidence of its importance. We also know there has been substantial disagreement within the ECB and among Governing Council members with respect to the use of unconventional monetary policies to (indirectly) bail out banks and sovereigns. Many of these disagreements are, roughly, on north–south lines. As emphasized by Advocate General Cruz Villalón in his interim opinion in the case against the OMT (ECJ 2015a), the ECB should be careful not to overstep its bounds.[24] Separation of the legal enforcement of financial contracts and monetary policy would be sensible.

A question under my proposal is what to do with euro-area member states that issue unsecured debt. In principle, they could do this if there is a market for it. The inability to use such paper in repos with the Eurosystem would make it unattractive. Still, investors could gamble on a bailout of the unsecured debt. Thus, measures need to be in place to deal with this contingency. For example, secured debt could become ineligible for usage in Eurosystem operations if unsecured debt is issued, or the escrow agency could be vested with powers over sovereign tax receipts and land, taking possession of assets, to be put in escrow, as unsecured debt is issued. This is necessary to reduce the possibility of game playing that so evidently has taken place and lies at the heart of the euro crisis. The euro would gain credibility if member states give up so much sovereignty as is necessary to ensure that they will not be able to hold other member states to ransom.

Making euro-area sovereign debt secured will help secure a sounder currency and financial system and reduce the incidence

---

[24] See Chapter 12.

and magnitude of future crises. In the case of default, secured debt provides for an orderly, pre-arranged settlement with minimal renegotiation or the possibility of hold-up by defaulting member states. That assets will be lost in default will incentivize nations to act more prudently in the first place, thus reducing the risk of default. Linking haircuts to the general indebtedness level of the issuing country will also help. A final advantage to making sovereign debt secured is that it would help preserve the sovereignty of member states relative to the alternative, which some have called for, of a stronger political and fiscal union.

If the ECB moves toward a policy of outright purchases of sovereign bonds, rather than conducting monetary policy mostly through repos, it may be harder to control the sovereigns. When repos are used, the terms of exchange between collateral and central bank money can be adjusted with every refinancing operation. Furthermore, such adjustments to a set of sovereign bonds would apply to the whole outstanding stock of those bonds. This flexibility and broad impact is lost under a system where the central bank mostly buys bonds on the open market.

My focus in this chapter has been on sovereign debt and indebtedness. Mass defaults of banks within a country are equally problematic. Spain offers an example of a country that used to have low government debt but a highly indebted private sector, which started to face problems with the onset of the crisis. Ireland is another example. The European Banking Union will help alleviate such problems in the future through central supervision and a common resolution mechanism of the largest banks. True to euro-area form, however, most banks are to be nationally supervised and subject to a national interpretation of the common resolution mechanism. Along the lines of my proposal for dealing with the problem of fiscal responsibility and sovereign debt, it is also possible to deal with different supervisory standards by linking haircuts on collateral issued by banks to key financial measures. These could be set according to uniform, euro-area criteria by the ECB. If banks face higher haircuts for their paper in central bank repos as their financial health declines, they may be more inclined to raise additional equity or seek resolution before the situation gets out of hand. Banks may also be discouraged from becoming "too big to fail" by raising the haircuts on their paper in central bank repos as they grow.

14 The Problem with Collateral

In the wake of the financial crisis, there have been numerous proposals for "fixing" the financial system. Many of these place increased demand on collateral. It is therefore important to realize the limitations of collateral as a problem-solving tool. In this chapter, I draw on the insights and findings from previous chapters to discuss some of the more obvious problems with systems that place large demand on collateral. In this context, I discuss two high-profile topics, namely the interbank market for liquidity and the resurrection of the 1930s-era "Chicago Plan" of full reserve banking.

14.1 THE FUNDAMENTAL PROBLEM

The fundamental problem with collateral is that there is a limited amount of it that can be considered "good." Financial systems that place large demands on collateral may face a shortage of high-quality collateral. Furthermore, as demand for collateral increases, more of it will have to be rated, or assessed in some way, and monitored. This is expensive. The ratings process is also fraught with problems, as touched on in Chapter 6. The lower down the quality scale one must go, the larger are the problems associated with the ratings process likely to be.

Collateral serves a valuable purpose because it reduces concerns about default and may therefore increase the willingness of counterparties to trade. This effect is a function of the liquidity of the underlying collateral. Securities that cannot be traded in the market, except at heavy discounts relative to fundamentals, are not suitable as collateral. The point with collateral is that losses can be covered in case of counterparty default. It is therefore important to note that there is not an active market for most securities.

As discussed in Chapter 7, conservatively estimated based on information in the Bloomberg system, only about 20 percent of the securities that are on the Eurosystem's public list of eligible collateral are sufficiently actively traded that they have fresh market prices, or quotes, on a daily basis. Furthermore, even if a security has a daily updated market price, it does not mean that arbitrarily large quantities can be traded at that price. It is well documented in the market microstructure literature that limited depth is ubiquitous in financial markets.[1] Thus, attempts to sell, or liquidate, large quantities of a specific collateral may significantly reduce its price. The more illiquid collateral is, the larger is the discount. Despite the huge amount of scientific evidence to the contrary, an enduring myth of finance and economics is that there is a well-defined market price for "everything." Based on the evidence in Chapter 7, it appears in fact that the vast majority of securities do not have market prices, never mind ones that are good for large volumes.

In financial systems that place a large demand on collateral of high quality, one would expect good-quality collateral to be produced by the system, just as illiquid collateral is being produced in the euro area for use in Eurosystem operations (Chapter 4). Thus, regulatory-induced demand for large quantities of highly liquid collateral may have unintended consequences such as bringing about an overinvestment in assets that are liquid in a real sense. On the more positive side, it may also help promote standardization of securitization products.

The large heterogeneity in securitization products in the euro area is a concern. Within the same class of products, for example, covered bonds, securities can be issued under a number of different jurisdictions and standards (see, e.g., ECBC 2015). Thus, they may behave differently in default, depending on the rules under which

---

[1] Amihud, Mendelson, and Pedersen (2013) provide an overview of the topic of market liquidity.

they are issued. This reduces substitutability and therefore liquidity. However, the incentives to standardize are impinged on by the Eurosystem's collateral framework, since haircuts are not affected by different standards across jurisdictions.

In a paper prepared for an Irish Banking Federation conference in 2008 (Nyborg 2008), I proposed that:

> [S]tandardization of securitization products and more reliable ratings of these securities would be valuable ...[This] can help promote a more resilient interbank repo market for these products and thereby: (i) provide supervisors and regulators with a market where they can fetch valuable information regarding the soundness of banks and products they have issued, (ii) help reduce bank balance sheet opaqueness, which in turn can help mitigate future extreme increases in longer term unsecured rates, (iii) help central banks such as the ECB, that rely on these products in their monetary policy implementation, to set more appropriate haircuts for eligible collateral in open market operations.

The ECB has also expressed an interest in the topic of standardization. For example, in a speech in May 2014, Mario Draghi announced that the ECB endorses a revisiting of the regulatory treatment for ABSs and "develop[ing] principles of what we call high quality securitization."[2] The motivation is the belief that this will improve liquidity. One way the ECB can help speed up this process is to reject collateral that the markets reveal to be insufficiently liquid. This could be based on standard measures of liquidity developed in the finance literature (see, e.g., Goyenko, Holden, and Trzcinka 2009, for an overview), or on something as simple as volume. For example, no volume, no Eurosystem liquidity.

---

[2] "ECB Draghi: ECB & BOE to publish line of action on ABS Friday," by Johanna Treeck, *MNI Deutsche Börse Group*, May 27, 2014, https://mninews.market news.com/content/ecb-draghi-ecb-boe-publish-line-action-abs-friday.

14.2   THE INTERBANK MARKET

The problem with collateral outlined above suggests that there is value to having unsecured interbank markets. This contrasts with the increasingly popular view that unsecured markets should be discouraged in favor of central counterparty (CCP) repos. As discussed by Rochet (2010), the argument is that CCPs reduce counterparty risk and contagion and thereby improve the interbank market and, in turn, financial stability. This is partly based on the commonly held view that many of the problems in the interbank markets during the financial crisis were related to information asymmetries between banks, leading to high borrowing costs and reduced volume. It is also based on the view that interbank markets are prone to contagion. The turmoil after Lehman Brothers' bankruptcy is often viewed in that light. The crisis made clear that a well-functioning market for liquidity is essential to the overall stability of financial markets. There are clearly many advantages to CCPs, as articulated by Rochet, but they are not a panacea.

In CCP repos, banks are likely to use the worst collateral, with the lowest opportunity cost, they can get away with, just as they do in repos with the Eurosystem. This is well understood. As an example, Eurex accepts only a subset of the ISINs on the Eurosystem's public list of eligible collateral in their GC Pooling contracts (Chapter 5). This subset consists of relatively higher-quality collateral. This reveals that Eurex is concerned about the risk it is taking when acting as a CCP. The more volume Eurex clears, the more exposed and systemically relevant it becomes. Some people close to the matter worry a great deal about CCP defaults.

A second concern with CCPs relates to how haircuts are determined. As discussed in Chapter 5, in the euro area, some CCPs are adopting the Eurosystem's haircuts for some important contracts. Thus, CCP haircuts may be as unresponsive to market conditions as those of the Eurosystem. This illustrates a general problem with centralization, namely that market forces and discipline may be lost.

Bilateral repos offer an alternative but may not provide the same protection from contagion. Furthermore, as discussed by Ewerhart and Tapking (2008), it is not only credit risk from the borrower that is an issue in bilateral repos but also the risk that the lender, or cash provider, defaults. As discussed by these authors and in Chapter 2, this gives a preference for the usage of high-quality collateral in bilateral repos. The basic logic of two-way default risk can be extended to a scenario where significant information asymmetries among banks emerge. This might stress the bilateral repo market; collateral providers (borrowers) may not be willing to post high-quality collateral to players that happen to have spare liquidity now but may default in the future; and, for similar reasons, cash providers (lenders) may not be willing to lend except at haircuts that are not acceptable to cash takers.

A potential solution to the joint problem of systemically important CCPs and bilateral repo markets that may fail under market stress is collateralized interbank loans. The advantage relative to a repo is that the collateral does not become the property of the cash provider. Instead, the collateral would be placed in escrow with a reliable custodian, for example the central bank. Large haircuts on the posted collateral that provide sufficient protection to the lender will not make the borrower concerned that the lender may not return the collateral, because it would not be hers to return. Thus, a collateralized loan contract is more resilient than a repo.[3]

What is needed to get a collateralized loan contract going is a good platform with a sound custodian. For interbank trades, it seems that this is exactly a job for a central bank, being as it is, at least in part, a coordination device for banks. Indeed, the Banca d'Italia helped set up a collateralized interbank market on the e-MID platform in 2009 with the express purpose of promoting interbank trading. It proved to be a success and may be something

---

[3] Repos are needed only if particular collateral is sought by the cash provider/lender.

to emulate elsewhere.[4] But it is not necessary to set this up as a CCP.

Despite the potential advantages of various collateralized contracts, this still requires sufficient amounts of good-quality collateral. In addition, a problem with collateralizing banks' balance sheets and then pledging this in various transactions is that depositors end up with riskier claims. Because of deposit insurance, this risk is, in turn, passed on to the deposit insurance scheme and, as shown during the crisis, ultimately tax payers. This speaks against discouraging unsecured interbank markets. A more market-oriented approach is facilitating collateralized loans by providing a trustworthy platform, for example, as on e-MID, but without biasing markets this way or that.

Unsecured trades can also be a source of information for supervisors and regulators. As emphasized by Nyborg (2008), regulators can tap into the large amount of intelligence that is produced in the unsecured, and collateralized markets alike, about the credit worthiness of banks every day by banks themselves. Unsecured rates vary across banks, reflecting, at least in part, differences in the market's assessment of their credit worthiness.[5] Thus, these rates contain valuable information to supervisors and regulators.

Using data on interbank transactions and other relevant information, appropriate algorithms can then flag problem-banks to supervisors and regulators. Quoting from Nyborg (2008), features of the data that may be useful to investigate include the following:

1. What rates do different banks pay for unsecured loans? Warning flags can be raised, for example, for banks paying unusually large rates relative to the cross-sectional mean. Unusual changes to the pattern of funding or to a bank's funding cost percentile could also give rise to warning flags.

[4] See, e.g., "There's something about the Italian interbank market," by Joseph Cotterill, *FTAlphaville*, December 7, 2010, http://ftalphaville.ft.com//2010/12/07/429286/theres-something-about-the-italian-interbank-market/. See also e-Mid's webpage, www.e-mid.it.
[5] See, for example, Furfine (2001).

2. Counterparty exposure. Large exposure to banks with high borrowing rates, for example, can give rise to a warning signal.
3. Repo rates: High rates or haircuts on particular securitization products can also be a problem for a bank that holds (on or off balance sheet) large quantities of the bad collateral. Monitoring this can therefore also be very valuable.
4. High repo rates or haircuts on particular securitization products also suggest a problem at the issuing/originating bank.

Banks that are flagged through these procedures will then have to be looked into more carefully. By doing this, it may be possible to intervene in a poorly performing bank or a particular practice before things get out of hand. In short, there are ways to deal with problems in the interbank market that do not require biasing the interbank market playing field in favor of collateralizing and encumbering banks' balance sheets. Full collateralization may well create as many problems as it may solve.

14.3   FULL RESERVE BANKING

The quest for completely eliminating the risk of crises in financial markets may be a bit like the search for the philosopher's stone. One of the more high-profile proposals involves providing a bigger role for the central bank (or the government) in the money creation process. The idea is to eliminate fractional reserve banking, i.e., require banks to hold central bank money one for one with deposits. This will eliminate traditional bank runs by depositors, assuming the absence of fraud. This idea has become known as the "Chicago Plan." As explained by Phillips (1992), the idea was originally proposed in a series of memoranda in the early 1930s by a number of economists at the University of Chicago.[6]

The idea of full reserve banking has recently received increasing interest, with a number of proposals put forth that seek to adapt the original idea to more modern financial systems (Kotlikoff 2010;

---

[6] The signatories to the original document were F. H. Knight, L. W. Mints, Henry Schultz, H. C. Simons, G. V. Cox, Aaron Director, Paul Douglas, and A. G. Hart.

Benes and Kumhof 2012; Cochrane 2014).[7] But others are more skeptical. For example, Goodhart (2013) argues that full reserve banking may possibly push problems into other arenas of the financial system and ultimately prove counterproductive. In their article on banking theory, deposit insurance, and bank regulation, Diamond and Dybvig (1986) warn that:

> Proposals to move toward 100% reserve banking would prevent banks from fulfilling their primary function of creating liquidity. Since banks are an important part of the infrastructure in the economy, this is at best a risky move and at worst could reduce stability because new firms that move in to fill the vacuum left by banks may inherit the problem of runs.

In short, full reserve banking is not as simple as it may seem.

Commenting on one of the recent proposals in his *New York Times* column, Nobel Laureate Paul Krugman asserts that it "calls for a remarkable amount of government intervention in finance; it makes liberal proposals for a transactions tax look like minor nuisances."[8] Krugman finds the debate on full reserve banking "genuinely interesting," but adds, "I'm not even sure where I stand."

It is not my intention to enter the full fray of the debate on full reserve banking here except to point out an element that is largely overlooked, namely the role of collateral. Under a full reserve system, the central bank will have to issue central bank money to cover all deposits. This raises the issue as to whether there will be a sufficient quantity of good-quality collateral to cover deposits in full.

Addressing this issue requires specifying what is meant by "deposits." The basic idea of full reserve banking is that "runnable" deposits should be covered, but the various proposals that have been put forth are not entirely clear on whether this means that the requirement of full reserves should apply to checkable, or overnight,

[7] See van Dixhoorn (2013) for an overview.

[8] "Is a banking ban the answer," by Paul Krugman, *New York Times*, April 26, 2014.

deposits only, or also include term deposits.[9] This lack of clarity may be a result of a lack of certainty as to whether term deposits are runnable. Intuitively, the effect on a bank from being served notice on all, or most, of its term deposits could be quite devastating. A run on term deposits seems at least a theoretical possibility. One way to address the question as to what deposits to count is to use the same breakdown central banks use when reporting standard monetary aggregates, such as M1 and M2.

In the euro area, M1 is comprised of currency in circulation and overnight deposits. M2 adds two types of term deposits, namely those that are redeemable at a notice of up to three months and others with a term of at most two years. The three types of deposits in M2 stood at EUR 8.7 trillion in December 2014. Of this, overnight deposits comprised EUR 5.0 trillion. These numbers represent more than a doubling of the corresponding numbers in January 2000, which were EUR 3.8 and 1.6 trillion, respectively. Most of this growth took place before the bankruptcy of Lehman. In August 2008, overnight deposits plus the two M2 deposit components totaled EUR 7.1 trillion, with overnight deposits being EUR 3.9 trillion.[10] These numbers are vastly larger than the monetary base (Table 3.2). Furthermore, from Table 7.1, we know that the aggregate par value of the Eurosystem's public list of eligible collateral is around EUR 13 trillion. Collateral with daily price updates have outstanding amounts of around EUR 9 to 10 trillion. Government bonds, exempting Greece and Cyprus, add up to around EUR 6 to 7 trillion. These numbers show that relative to current levels of deposits, there might be a shortage of good-quality collateral in the euro area with respect to implementing full reserve

---

[9] But as Phillips (1992) explains it, the original Chicago Plan proposed full reserves against demand deposits only.

[10] Definitions of M1 and M2 for the euro area can be found in www.ecb.europa.eu/pub/pdf/other/manualmfibalancesheetstatistics201204en.pdf. Monetary statistics are available at http://sdw.ecb.europa.eu/. The figures for January 2000 and August 2008 are taken from www.ecb.europa.eu/press/pr/stats/md/html/index.en.html. All figures are seasonally adjusted.

banking, especially given that there are other sources of demand for such collateral.

Of course, it is impossible to say what the levels of deposits and high-quality collateral would be in a financial system with full reserve banking. Still, the numbers suggest that markets are likely to be strained under a hypothetical move to such a system.

Much of the debate on full reserve banking is taking place in the context of the United States. Cochrane (2014) argues that the very high current level of US government debt (he cites USD 18 trillion) implies that there is plenty of good collateral to back deposits. In the United States, M1 is composed of currency in circulation, traveler's checks, and checkable deposits. M2 adds savings deposits, small-time deposits (less than USD 100,000), and money market mutual funds. In December 2014, checkable deposits were USD 1.6 trillion, with the three M2 deposit categories totaling USD 8.8 trillion, for a total deposit figure of USD 10.4 trillion.[11] The total outstanding amount of federal government debt held in the form of securities by the public in December 2014 was USD 13.0 trillion.[12] Thus, it appears that there currently is a sufficient quantity of Treasury and other government securities to back all M1 and M2 deposits in the United States. However, there is no guarantee that this "happy" state of affairs will perdure. Back in 1999, as a result of running budget surpluses, the Clinton administration started a treasury security repurchase program. At that time, the total value of these securities was around USD 3.7 trillion.[13] So under full reserve banking, it is quite possible that the United States will need to find alternatives to government debt securities to back deposits.

---

[11] See https://research.stlouisfed.org/fred2/release?rid=21. The figures are from the H.6 Money stock measures (seasonally adjusted). Of the USD 1.6 trillion of checkable deposits in 2014, USD 1.2 trillion were comprised of demand deposits.

[12] Source: *Treasury Bulletin*, March 2015, Department of the Treasury, Bureau of Fiscal Service, www.fiscal.treasury.gov/fsreports/rpt/treasBulletin/backissues.htm.

[13] Source: *Treasury Bulletin*, March 2000, Department of the Treasury, Bureau of Fiscal Service, www.fiscal.treasury.gov/fsreports/rpt/treasBulletin/backissues.htm.

In Chapter 10, I discussed various potential sources of distortions under wide collateral frameworks. The more expansive balance sheets under full reserve, as compared with fractional reserve, banking enhance the role of collateral frameworks and potentially magnify such distortions. The experience of the euro area also suggests that wide collateral frameworks enhance the role of politics in the monetary system, even though the central bank is, in principle, independent. Full reserve banking also places more power – and responsibility – in the hands of the central bank and thereby reduces the role of markets. It is unclear that this is a good thing.

15 Concluding Remarks

My main objective with this book is to raise awareness of collateral frameworks and, more generally, to advance an agenda of studying the institutional and micro-foundations of the monetary system. The aim is to draw out the wider implications for the financial system and the real economy. The book itself contributes to this agenda through unpacking the opaque foundation of the monetary system, using the complex construction of the euro as an example. In turn, this has led to the euro crisis becoming an important sub-theme in the book.

Well-functioning monetary and financial systems are important to the efficient flow of resources and private and social welfare. This point has been brought home emphatically by the global financial crisis and accompanying recession that emerged in August 2007 and that has taken years to resolve. As late as January 2015, the ECB was still heavily engaged in its fight to preserve the euro. Numerous proposals have been advanced regarding how to "fix" the monetary and financial systems and regulate banks and other types of monetary and financial enterprises. Widespread financial market interventions by central banks have made it difficult to gauge "correct" market prices and, in private, even many central bankers express this exact view. This undermines the efficient allocation of resources in the economy. Improving our understanding of the workings of the monetary and financial system is therefore of central, and also urgent, importance.

The broad perspective put forth in this book is that monetary and financial systems are fundamentally built on top of the collateral that central banks choose to accept in exchange for central bank money. To understand money and the broader financial system, it is therefore necessary to understand central bank collateral frameworks.

In this book, I have taken a first step in that direction by discussing how collateral frameworks work and interact with markets and, ultimately, the real economy. I argue that collateral frameworks can bias the private provision of *real* liquidity and thereby also the allocation of resources in the economy. They can affect market prices of financial assets and undermine the efficient working of money markets. More generally, they can impair market forces and discipline and promote politics in the monetary and financial system. Most obviously, collateral frameworks affect the balance sheets of central banks. As emphasized by Klaas Knot, President of the Dutch central bank, a weak balance sheet can undermine a central bank's credibility, with unfortunate consequences for financial stability and the real economy. These issues have been explored using the very interesting and intriguing case of the euro area as a basis of illustration and case study.

As documented in this book, the collateral framework designed by the ECB for the euro appears to suffer, to varying degrees, from all of the above predicaments. Most striking, perhaps, is how it appears to sidestep market discipline. The amount of central bank money a bank can obtain from the ECB against a given security, the security's collateral value, is set by the ECB with relatively minor input from the markets. Haircuts do not reflect market conditions and the prices to which they are applied to calculate collateral values are in the majority of cases based on theoretical models rather than direct market prices.[1] Given that there are 30,000 to 40,000 different securities on the public list of eligible collateral in the Eurosystem, the lack of market forces in setting the terms of exchange between banks and the Eurosystem is, perhaps, not surprising. Still, it should be possible to design a collateral framework that is more responsive to market forces by limiting the set of eligible collateral and, as I discuss toward

---

[1] Based on price information available on the Bloomberg system.

the end of Chapter 10, designing open market operations that are more competitive, not just with respect to repo rates, but also with respect to haircuts.

That the ECB sets collateral values with little market input points to the collateral framework being a tool of the central bank. This is especially so because the terms of exchange spill over into other markets. We know, for example, that Eurosystem haircuts are used in repos organized by central counterparties. Incentives to produce collateral are affected too. As documented in this book, there has been a growth in the production and usage of lower-quality collateral over time. This leads to the question as to why the ECB should wish to promote lower-quality collateral. More generally, what is the ECB targeting with its collateral policy and why is market discipline more or less undermined by the collateral framework? Why does its collateral framework allow for the various "oddities" documented in this book? As explained in various publications, one of the considerations the ECB has in mind with respect to its collateral policies is its own risk management.[2] What is less clear is why this should involve such a small role for market forces.

Given the role of politics in so many other spheres that relate to the euro, a plausible explanation is that market discipline is de-emphasized to accommodate the different countries that comprise the euro area. This may serve the function to ease the constraints imposed by having a single currency for disparate economies. It may reflect a wish to channel liquidity "where it is needed," although this should really be a job for the secondary market for liquidity rather than the primary market. Any such need on economic grounds must relate to a lack of integration of euro-area money markets. Whatever the case, the lack of a role for market forces in the collateral framework leaves room for politics as a source of influence over this central element of monetary policy. Politics can affect the

---

[2] See, for example, ECB (2000/7), ECB (2006/12), and the other collateral framework documents in the reference section of this book. See also Bindseil and Papadia (2006) and Bindseil (2014).

set of eligible collateral as well as collateral values. As documented in this book, government guarantees are used to gain eligibility and improve collateral values. That politics seems to have stepped into the vacuum left by the absence of market forces implies that monetary policy needs to be studied and understood in the context of political economy.

The hypothesis that the collateral framework, and monetary policy in general, is subject to politics is consistent with the commonly held view that the euro is a political, rather than an economic, creation.[3] In principle, the ECB is an independent supranational institution, but given all the evidence in the public domain, it would be naive to believe that it is insulated from political concerns. The ECB is owned by the NCBs, which, in turn, are owned by their respective governments. Its Governing Council is comprised of the Presidents of the individual NCBs and the six Executive Board members, each representing a different country. Moreover, as pointed out by former ECB board member Jürgen Stark:[4] "The EU is not a federation (and neither is the eurozone). We are a long way from reaching that level of integration in Europe."

Thus, one would expect each country to have its own agenda when it comes to the management of the monetary system, as in other matters. The existence of disagreements among Governing Council members over the crisis policies pursued by the ECB is well known. A rule of thumb is that German board members and those from other countries with relatively strong economies are less favorably inclined to accommodative policies than those from countries with more fragile or indebted economies.

Monetary politics extend to the choice of ECB President:[5]

---

[3] See, for example, Feldstein (1997).
[4] "The historical and cultural differences that divide Europe's union," by Jürgen Stark, *Financial Times*, February 11, 2015, www.ft.com/intl/cms/s/0/e08ec622-ad28-11e4-a5c1-00144feab7de.html?siteedition=intl#axzz3RiR02Zei.
[5] "German shuns top euro bank job," by Brian Blackstone, Geoffrey Smith, and Marcus Walker, *Wall Street Journal*, February 10, 2011.

> Mr. Weber's apparent withdrawal from the race [for the presidency of the ECB] is a painful blow for German Chancellor Angela Merkel, who was hoping to install Mr. Weber – a trusted if controversial ally – at the ECB's helm as part of her strategy to bolster confidence in Europe's 12-year-old single currency. Berlin is pushing for an overhaul of the euro zone's economic governance, to bring the bloc more in line with Germany's focus on fiscal prudence, inflation-fighting and business competitiveness.

Germany's Axel Weber withdrawing his candidacy opened the door to Italy's Mario Draghi and the accommodative monetary policy documented in this book, involving (indirect) bailouts of weaker sovereigns and banks. Former German ECB board member Jürgen Stark expressed the view, in the same article quoted from above, that countries in the periphery have themselves to blame for their economic woes and should bear the responsibility for their past actions. Under an ECB president with this view, monetary policy would likely have been different than what it has been under Draghi.

The Eurosystem's collateral framework and unconventional monetary policies are therefore a part of the larger political game that is played out on the euro stage among the member states. I have argued that Stephen Krasner's (1999) description of organized hypocrisy describes this game well and is at the root of the euro's fundamental problem, namely a lack of credibility. A feature of sovereign relations that makes it especially difficult to reach stable, good equilibria is that the actors change. New political leaders enter the stage, with new agendas and new mandates from their respective electorates. This is highly relevant in the euro area. As explained by a Greek official in the context of the latest round of Greek debt renegotiation that kicked off after Syriza won the elections in January 2015:[6] "You cannot ask a newly elected government that has been elected

---

[6] "Final showdown approaches for EU and Greece," by Peter Spiegel, *Financial Times*, February 13, 2015.

with a mandate for a new programme to implement the previous [bailout] as a precondition for discussion."

Unfortunately, the revisiting of monetary-relevant agreements after changes in leadership only serves to undermine the credibility of the euro, because it challenges the foundations on which the euro is built. Such revisits are disruptive and costly. The reappearance of Greek bailout talks gives a sense of waiting for Godot in reverse. Without a way to credibly commit countries to policies that safeguard the common currency, it is difficult to see a prosperous future for the euro area.

The solution to the euro's credibility problem is to rein in sovereignty with respect to decisions that affect the currency. Ever more generous and accommodative monetary policy, through, for example, buying sovereign bonds and other assets, may help alleviate the symptom but cannot reach the underlying pathology of the euro. In the longer term, such policies will only exacerbate the euro area's problems if they are not also accompanied by effective policies to control the sovereigns with respect to fiscal issues. I have suggested a mild form to control sovereignty in this book that works, in part, through the collateral framework. This involves linking haircuts to indebtedness, for example, and securing sovereign debt. A more powerful approach would be to have a fiscal or even full-blown political union. But it is not clear that this is necessarily desirable. Preserving the euro surely cannot be an aim in and of itself. If it is incompatible with economic prosperity and vitality, and perhaps well-functioning democracies, effort should instead be put toward breaking it up, rather than saving it.

While the predicament of the euro necessarily has occupied a large part of this book, its broad message is that collateral frameworks are an important part of monetary policy. Because their influence reaches to financial markets and the real economy, more knowledge and transparency about collateral frameworks would be welcome so that economists can start to gauge their impact and, hopefully, even better monetary policies can be pursued.

Transparency is also important vis-à-vis the public at large. Modern central banks are largely political creations that have come to play increasingly important roles in society. It is therefore common sense that they should be put under the light, like any other institution that affects, and matters to, people at large. The President of the Dutch Central Bank, Klaas Knot, has said as much: "central banks may need to step up their efforts on transparency and accountability."[7] Bagehot's (1873) comment that "money is economical power" also speaks to this. If money is power, it follows that whoever is bestowed with the creation of money is also bestowed with power. It is only right that such, arguably enormous, power is subject to public scrutiny, checks, and balances. This book contributes by opening up the opaque structure at the heart of central banking and the money creation process, namely the central bank's collateral framework.

---

[7] Knot (2013).

Appendix: Haircut and Rating Rules Updates

This Appendix updates the haircut and rating rules in Tables 5.4 and 6.1, respectively. It also provides an update on the extraordinary haircuts of paper issued or guaranteed by Cyprus or Greece (Table 5.5).

In the main text, the broad haircut and rating rules described in Chapters 5 and 6 are checked for validity until January 31, 2015. For the most part, however, they are valid until April 30, 2015. New rules came into force on May 1, 2015, with the adoption of a new General framework baseline document, ECB (2014/60), published in the *Official Journal* on April 2, 2015. The special case of Greece is handled separately (see Section A.5). This appendix summarizes these new rules and subsequent updates until February 29, 2016.[1] This includes a brief description of a new type of non-marketable collateral that was introduced into the collateral framework with ECB (2015/27) and eligible from November 2, 2015.

The Appendix starts by discussing two headline changes that came into force on or after May 1, 2015. It then moves on to providing updated haircut and rating rules tables. This includes a review of the Eurosystem's harmonized rating scale, which plays a more significant role after May 1, 2015, than previously. A discussion of the extraordinary haircuts of paper issued or guaranteed by Cyprus and Greece closes out the Appendix.

A.1 HEADLINE CHANGES

By way of background, I start by providing two notable changes to the Eurosystem's collateral framework that came into force on or after May 1, 2015. These relate to eligibility, haircuts, and rating rules.

---

[1] The February 29, 2016, cutoff date reflects when this Appendix was written.

1. As of May 1, 2015 (ECB 2014/60): The rating categories used in the haircut table are modified. In particular, the main classification variable is not long-term ratings anymore, but the credit quality steps in the harmonized rating scale. This means that short-term ratings can substitute for long-term ratings (with some exceptions).

   Recall from the "haircut tables" (Tables 5.1 to 5.4) and the "rating rules table" (Table 6.1) that there are two rating categories with respect to haircuts. Rating category 1 is comprised of Credit Quality Steps 1 and 2 of the harmonized rating scale, while rating category 2 consists of Step 3 only. However, the rating categories are not defined by the steps, but in terms of them. Whereas the steps are officially defined in terms of both long- and short-term ratings from the accepted rating agencies, for the most part, it is only the highest long-term rating that matters with respect to haircuts and eligibility (details are in Chapter 6 and Table 6.1). In other words, the rating categories in the haircut tables in Chapter 5 are primarily defined by long-term ratings, rather than the full credit quality steps. As of May 1, 2015, however, the rating categories for haircut setting purposes are primarily defined by the full credit quality steps (ECB 2014/60). Both long- and short-term ratings are now relevant, though with some exceptions (see Table A.3).

2. As of November 2, 2015 (ECB 2015/27): The set of eligible non-marketable assets is expanded to include a new category, namely Debt Instruments Backed by Eligible Credit Claims (DECCs).

   ECB (2015/27) lists the following three general properties of eligible DECCs: (i) As their name says, DECCs are backed by credit claims that would be eligible on a stand-alone basis. (ii) DECCs offer dual recourse to the underlying cover pool and the originators of the credit claims. (iii) Unlike ABSs, for example, eligible DECCs cannot tranche risk.

   Initially, DECCs were only eligible as collateral if used by an entity in the same member state as where the DECC was issued. From January 25, 2016, DECCs can also be used on a cross-border basis, but must be issued in a euro-area member state to be eligible collateral (ECB 2015/34).

A.2 THE HARMONIZED RATING SCALE

As discussed in Section A.1, the harmonized rating scale took on new significance as of May 1, 2015, when Guideline ECB (2014/60) came

Table A.1 *Harmonized rating scale*

Panel A: Before April 1, 2014			
Long-term	**Step 1**	**Step 2**	**Step 3**
S&P	AAA to AA–	A+ to A–	BBB+ to BBB–
Fitch	AAA to AA–	A+ to A–	BBB+ to BBB–
Moody's	Aaa to Aa3	A1 to A3	Baa1 to Baa3
DBRS	AAA to AAL	AH to AL	BBBH, BBB
Short-term			
S&P	A-1+	A–1	A–2
Fitch	F1+	F1	F2
Moody's	–	P–1	P–2
DBRS	R–1H	R–1M, R–1L	R–2H, R–2M

Panel B: From April 1, 2014			
Long-term	**Step 1**	**Step 2**	**Step 3**
S&P	AAA to AA–	A+ to A–	BBB+ to BBB–
Fitch	AAA to AA–	A+ to A–	BBB+ to BBB–
Moody's	Aaa to Aa3	A1 to A3	Baa1 to Baa3
DBRS	AAA to AAL	AH to AL	BBBH *to BBBL**
Short-term			
S&P	–	*A–1+**, A–1	A–2
Fitch	–	*F1+**, F1	F2
Moody's	–	P–1	P–2
DBRS	–	*R–1H**, R–1M	*R–1L**, R–2H, R–2M, *R2–L**

The terminology "harmonised rating scale" is introduced in Annex II of ECB (2010/13), which applies from January 1, 2011. Panel A (from January 1, 2011): Long-term and Step 1 short-term ratings are from ECB (2010/13). Steps 2 and 3 short-term ratings are from archived ECB webpages (valid from at least May 28, 2011) and are verified through correspondence with the ECB. Panel B (from April 1, 2014): Long-term ratings are from ECB (2014/10). Short-term ratings are from archived ECB webpages and verified through correspondence with the ECB. Panel B is valid at least until February 29, 2016. Changes from Panel A to B are in (red) italic type and starred, *.

into force. This scale classifies marketable collateral into three steps, with each step being defined in terms of both long- and short-term ratings by the official rating agencies.

The mapping from ratings to credit quality steps was changed as of April 1, 2014 (ECB 2014/10). Details are given in Table A.1, which provides the full harmonized rating scales before and after that date. The most significant change here is that the ECB lowered the threshold of acceptable ratings from DBRS by including a long-term rating of BBBL and a short-term rating of R2–L into Step 3.

Note that Credit Quality Step 2 is meant to correspond to a maximum probability of default over a one-year horizon of 0.10 percent (ECB 2006/12, p. 42 and 2014/60, p. 38). The corresponding number for Step 3 is 0.40 percent (ECB 2010/13, p. 51 and 2014/60, p. 38).

A.3 HAIRCUTS

Table A.2 provides an updated haircut table. The two main changes are already discussed in Section A.1. First, from May 1, 2015, the rating categories are defined by the full credit quality steps (exceptions are detailed in Table A.3). Second, there is a new type of eligible nonmarketable collateral, namely DECCs. For these instruments, each individual credit claim that makes up the cover pool receives its own individual haircut. Apart from the possible reclassification of some collateral arising, for example, from the expansion of relevant ratings to include short-term ones, the haircuts in Table A.2 are the same as in Table 5.4.

In the fall of 2015, the ECB decided to separate out the documentation regarding haircuts from the rest of the collateral framework (ECB 2015/34 and 2015/35). This came into force on January 25, 2016. The rationale is that "[t]his [separation] would enable risk control parameters to be provided in a compact and self-contained form and enable the streamlining of the implementation of amendments to the relevant framework promptly once the corresponding decisions are adopted by the Governing Council" (ECB 2015/35). This suggests that haircuts may be updated more frequently in the future than they have been in the past. However, the haircuts in Table A.2 are still valid as of February 29, 2016.

Table A.2 Haircuts and liquidity categories from May 1, 2015 (The information in this table was still in force as of February 16, 2016)

Panel A: Levels of valuation haircuts applied to eligible marketable assets

			Haircut categories for marketable assets						
		Category I Debt instruments issued by central governments, ECB debt certificates, Debt certificates issued by NCBs prior to the date of adoption of the euro in their respective Member State		**Category II** Debt instruments issued by local and regional governments, Debt instruments issued by entities classified as agencies by the Eurosystem, Debt instruments issued by multilateral development banks and international organisations, Jumbo covered bonds		**Category III** Traditional covered bonds and other covered bonds, Debt instruments issued by non-financial corporations		**Category IV** Unsecured debt instruments issued by credit institutions, Unsecured debt instruments issued by financial corporations other than credit institutions		**Category V** Asset-backed securities[a]
Credit quality	Residual maturity (years)	Fixed coupon	Zero coupon	Fixed coupon	Zero coupon	Fixed coupon	Zero coupon	Fixed coupon	Zero coupon	
*Steps 1 and 2**	[0–1]	0.5	0.5	1.0	1.0	1.0	1.0	6.5	6.5	10.0
	[1–3]	1.0	2.0	1.5	2.5	2.0	3.0	8.5	9.0	
	[3–5]	1.5	2.5	2.5	3.5	3.0	4.5	11.0	11.5	
	[5–7]	2.0	3.0	3.5	4.5	4.5	6.0	12.5	13.5	
	[7–10]	3.0	4.0	4.5	6.5	6.0	8.0	14.0	15.5	
	[10,∞)	5.0	7.0	8.0	10.5	9.0	13.0	17.0	22.5	

Table A.2 *(cont.)*

Credit quality	Residual maturity (years)	Category I		Category II		Category III		Category IV		Category V
		Fixed coupon	Zero coupon	Fixed coupon	Zero coupon	Fixed coupon	Zero coupon	Fixed coupon	Zero coupon	
Panel A – continued										
Step 3*	[0–1]	6.0	6.0	7.0	7.0	8.0	8.0	13.0	13.0	
	[1–3]	7.0	8.0	10.0	14.5	15.0	16.5	24.5	26.5	
	[3–5]	9.0	10.0	15.5	20.5	22.5	25.0	32.5	36.5	22.0‡
	[5–7]	10.0	11.5	16.0	22.0	26.0	30.0	36.0	40.0	
	[7–10]	11.5	13.0	18.5	27.5	27.0	32.5	37.0	42.5	
	[10,∞)	13.0	16.0	22.5	33.0	27.5	35.0	37.5	44.0	

Floating rate debt instruments:
Haircut applied to marketable debt instruments included in categories I to IV is that applied to zero-to-one-year maturity buckets of fixed-coupon instruments in liquidity and credit quality *step** to which the instrument is assigned.

ABSs, covered bonds and unsecured debt instruments issued by credit institutions that are theoretically valued: [see Note 6 to Table 5.4]
Subject to an additional valuation haircut in the form of a valuation markdown of 5 percent.

Own-use covered bonds: [see Note 6 to Table 5.4]
Subject to an additional valuation haircut (markdown) of (a) 8 percent for own-use covered bonds in Credit Quality Steps 1 and 2, and (b) 12 percent for own-use covered bonds in Credit Quality Step 3.

Note 1: " '[O]wn-use covered bonds' means covered bonds issued by either a counterparty or entities closely linked to it, and used in a percentage greater than 75 percent of the outstanding notional amount by that counterparty and/or its closely linked entities" (ECB 2014/60).
Note 2: The 75 percent limit in Note 1 was removed in ECB (2015/35), effective from January 25, 2016.

Debt instruments issued by credit institutions and traded on non-regulated markets: Same haircuts as for other marketable assets.

Panel B: Haircuts applied to eligible non-marketable assets

Credit claims with fixed interest payments:

Haircuts applied to fixed interest credit claims differ according to the residual maturity, the credit quality *step** and the valuation methodology applied by the NCB. Haircuts as a function of residual maturity (residual maturity, haircut), if the valuation is based on

(1) a theoretical price assigned by the NCB:

*Steps 1 and 2**: [0–1), 10.0; [1–3), 12.0; [3–5), 14.0; [5–7), 17.0; [7–10), 22.0; [10,∞), 30.0 *Step 3**: [0–1), 17.0; [1–3), 29.0; [3–5), 37.0; [5–7), 39.0; [7–10), 40.0; [10,∞), 42.0

(2) the outstanding amount assigned by the NCB:

*Steps 1 and 2**: [0–1), 12.0; [1–3), 16.0; [3–5), 21.0; [5–7), 27.0; [7–10), 35.0; [10,∞), 45.0 *Step 3**: [0–1), 19.0; [1–3), 34.0; [3–5), 46.0; [5–7), 52.0; [7–10), 58.0; [10,∞), 65.0

Credit claims with variable interest payments:

The haircut is that applied to fixed interest credit claims in the zero-to-one-year maturity bucket corresponding to the same credit quality *step** and the same valuation methodology.

Retail mortgage-backed debt instruments:

Non-marketable retail mortgage-backed debt instruments are subject to a valuation haircut of 39.5 percent. The rating must be *Step 2** at least [ECB 2014/60].

Non-marketable debt instrument backed by eligible credit claims (DECCs):* [Eligible as of November 2, 2015 [ECB 2015/27]]

*Each underlying credit claim included in the cover pool of a non-marketable debt instrument backed by eligible credit claims (DECC) shall be subject to a valuation haircut applied at an individual level following the rules set out above. The aggregate value of the underlying credit claims included in the cover pool after the application of valuation haircuts shall, at all times, remain equal to or above the value of the principal amount of the DECC that is outstanding. If the aggregate value falls below the threshold referred to in the previous sentence, the DECC shall be valued at zero.**

Fixed-term deposits (with Eurosystem): No haircut.

Updates to the General framework, published in ECB (2014/60, from December 19, 2014) are in (red) italic type and starred, * (except changes to the wordings in the liquidity (or, haircut) categories). Updates that relate to the introduction of DECCs (ECB 2015/27) are indicated the same way. From May 1, 2015, haircuts are based on a collateral's credit quality step as defined in Table A.1, but with some exceptions relating to the admissibility of short-term ratings as detailed in Table A.3. Features in the table that are from the Temporary framework are indicated in (light blue) slanted type with a double dagger, ‡. *¹ Except ABSs backed by residential mortgages or loans to SMEs issued before June 20, 2012 that do not fulfill certain standard eligibility criteria, but have a credit quality of at least BBB–. These have a haircut of 22 percent (see ECB 2013/36, and ECB 2014/31).‡*

A.4   RATING RULES

As discussed above, the main change to the rating rules involves the full use of the harmonized rating scale. Apart from this, the rules are largely the same. For example, the first-best rating rule still applies for all marketable assets except ABSs, for which the second-best rule applies (see Table A.3 for details).

Finally, observe that what I have called "privately eligible collateral" is still a feature of the Eurosystem's collateral framework. If ratings from an accepted rating agency (S&P, Fitch, Moody's, and DBRS) do not exist and the issuer or guarantor is a non-financial corporation from the euro area, high credit standards can be established by in-house, NCB, or third-party rating models. Such collateral will not appear in the public list of eligible collateral (ECB 2014/60, p. 48).

A.5   GREECE AND CYPRUS

As discussed in Chapters 5 and 6, Greece and Cyprus have been exempted from normal Eurosystem haircut and rating rules for substantial periods of time. The extraordinary haircuts for Cyprus listed in Table 5.5 are still in force as of February 29, 2016. However, the special haircuts for Greece listed in the same table lost force on February 11, 2015, when Greece lost its exempt status. As explained by the ECB on February 10, 2015:

> On the basis of the information available, the Governing Council has made an assessment, according to which it is not currently possible to assume a successful conclusion of the review of the European Union/International Monetary Fund programme for the Hellenic Republic. Consequently, the Hellenic Republic is no longer deemed to be in compliance with the conditionality of the programme and, as a result, the conditions for the temporary suspension of the Eurosystem's credit quality thresholds... are no longer fulfilled. As a consequence, the Governing Council has decided that the Eurosystem's credit quality thresholds shall apply

Table A.3 *Credit quality and ratings rules*

Credit Quality Rules	*Applies to:*
Baseline Rule (ECB 2014/60, pp. 38, 46–49, G)	

High credit standards are now defined in terms of the full credit quality steps of the harmonized rating scale: "All eligible assets for Eurosystem credit operations shall comply, as a minimum, with a credit quality requirement corresponding to credit quality step 3" [ECB 2014/60, Article 59 3.(b), p. 38, G). With respect to the priority of different ratings, the order is still issue, programme/issuance series, and issuer or guarantor ratings. Further details are provided below. Accepted rating agencies: S&P, Fitch, Moody's, DBRS.

I. Ratings by accepted rating agencies exist for either the issue, issuer, or guarantor

1. Definitions and background:

(a) In what follows, issue rating "…refers to [a] …credit assessment [from an accepted rating agency] assigned to either an issue or, in the absence of an issue rating from the same [rating agency], the programme or issuance series under which an asset is issued. …Any …rating [[short- or long-term]] assigned to the issue or programme or issuance series shall be acceptable" (ECB 2014/60, Article 83[a], p. 46, G).

(b) Acceptable issuer ratings:

   (i) "For short-term assets [[those assets with an original maturity of up to and including 390 days]], …short-term and long-term issuer ratings [from an accepted rating agency] shall be acceptable. For long-term assets [[those assets with an original maturity of more than 390 days]], only …long-term issuer ratings [from an accepted rating agency] shall be acceptable" (ECB 2014/60, Article 83[b], p. 46, G).

   (ii) "For the purpose of …issuer ratings [from an accepted rating agency], a foreign currency rating shall be acceptable. If the asset is denominated in the domestic currency of the issuer, the local currency rating shall also be acceptable" (ECB 2014/60, Article 86, p. 48, G).

(c) "For marketable assets with more than one issuer (multi-issuer securities), the applicable …issuer rating …[is] determined …as follows" (ECB 2014/60, Article 85, p. 47, G):

   (i) "If each issuer is jointly and severally liable for the obligations of all other issuers under the issue or, if applicable, for the programme, or issuance series, the …issuer rating [from an accepted rating agency] to be considered shall be the highest rating among the first-best …issuer ratings of all the relevant issuers" (ECB 2014/60, Article 85, p. 47, G).

   (ii) "If any issuer is not jointly and severally liable for the obligations of all other issuers under the issue or, if applicable, for the programme, or issuance series, the …issuer rating [from an accepted rating agency] to be considered shall be the lowest rating among the first-best …issuer ratings of all the relevant issuers" (ECB 2014/60, Article 85, p. 47, G).

(d) Acceptable guarantor ratings: "Only …long-term guarantor ratings [from an accepted rating agency] shall be acceptable" (ECB 2014/60, Article 83[c], p. 47, G).

Table A.3 *(cont.)*

Credit Quality Rules	Applies to:
2. Determination of Eurosystem collateral framework rating:	For marketable assets[1] other than asset-backed securities and those listed in item 3 below.
(a) "The Eurosystem shall consider . . . issue ratings in priority to . . . issuer or . . . guarantor ratings" (ECB 2014/60, Article 84[a][i], p. 47, G].	
(b) " . . . [A]t least one . . . [rating from an accepted rating agency] must comply with the Eurosystem's applicable credit quality requirements [of a rating in Step 3 or better]" (ECB 2014/60, Article 84[a][i], p. 47. See also Article 82 1.[a], G].	
(c) If issue ratings from an accepted rating agency exist:	
"If multiple . . . issue ratings are available . . . the first-best [rule is applied] . . . If the first-best . . . issue rating [is not in Step 3 or better] . . . , the asset shall not be eligible, even if a[n otherwise acceptable] guarantee . . . exists" (ECB 2014/60, Article 84[a][ii], p. 47. See also Article 82 1.[a], G].	
(d) If no issue ratings from an accepted rating agency exist:	
"In the absence of any . . . issue rating, an . . . issuer or . . . guarantor rating may be considered . . . If multiple . . . issuer and/or . . . guarantor ratings are available [from accepted rating agencies] for the same issue, then the first-best [rule is applied] . . . " [ECB 2014/60, Article 84[a][iii], p. 47, G].	
3. Determination of Eurosystem collateral framework rating:	For marketable assets issued by central governments, regional governments, local governments, agencies (except covered bonds), multilateral development banks or international organizations.
(a) "The Eurosystem shall only consider . . . issuer or . . . guarantor ratings" (ECB 2014/60, Article 84[b][i], p. 47, G].	
(b) " . . . [A]t least one . . . [rating from an accepted rating agency] must comply with the Eurosystem's applicable credit quality requirements [of a rating in Step 3 or better]" (ECB 2014/60, Article 84[b][i], p. 47. See also Article 82 1.[a], G].	
(c) "If multiple . . . issuer and . . . guarantor ratings are available, the first-best [rule is applied] . . . " (ECB 2014/60, Article 84[b][ii], p. 47, G].	

4. Determination of Eurosystem collateral framework rating:

(a) "The Eurosystem shall only consider … issue ratings [from accepted rating agencies]" (ECB 2014/60, Article 84(c)(i), p. 47, G).	Asset-backed securities.
(b) At least two issue ratings (from two different rating agencies) must be in Step 2 or higher (ECB 2014/60, Article 84(c)(ii), p. 47. See also Article 82 1.(b), G).	
(c) Temporary framework exception: ABSs can also be accepted as eligible collateral with a second highest long-term rating in Step 3 but, in this case, are subject to stricter criteria with respect to the underlying assets and non-performing loans among other things (see ECB 2014/31, Article 3 1., pp. 31–32, T).	
II. If neither the issue, issuer, or the guarantor is rated	
(a) If the issuer or guarantor is a local authority, regional government, or a qualified public sector entity, established in a Member State whose currency is the euro, the applied credit quality step depends on how relevant competent authorities treat the issuer or guarantor for capital requirement purposes. In particular,	All marketable assets[1] except for asset-backed securities.
(i) If the issuer or guarantor is treated equally to the central government in the jurisdiction where they are established, the assigned credit quality step is that of the central government (as determined by the rules in item 3 above).	
(ii) If the issuer or guarantor is treated equally to a credit institution, the assigned credit quality step is one below that of the central government (logic suggests that the word "below" here should be interpreted with reference to the following order: Step 1 > Step 2 > Step 3). See ECB (2014/60, Article 87, p. 48, G) for further details.	
(b) If the issuer or guarantor is a non-financial corporation established in a Member State whose currency is the euro, the credit quality step that applies is determined by in-house, NCB, or third-party rating models. See ECB (2014/60, Articles 87, 108–110, and 119, pp. 48–58, G) for further details.	
Note: Asset-backed securities require issue ratings from acceptable rating agencies and are not covered by II (a) and (b). See ECB (2014/60, Article 88, p. 49) for further details.	Asset-backed securities.

This table provides eligibility criteria with respect to credit quality standards from May 1, 2015, until February 29, 2016, for marketable assets. General framework documents are denoted by a "G," Temporary framework documents by a "T."

Notes: [1] "All marketable assets" excludes debt certificates issued by (i) the ECB (or the Eurosystem), or (ii) the national central banks prior to the adoption of the euro in their respective Member State. Securities in (i) and (ii) are eligible without rating considerations.

in respect of marketable debt instruments issued or fully guaranteed by the Hellenic Republic.

ECB (2015/6)

At the time of this decision, Greece's highest rating was B by DBRS and Fitch, five notches below the BBB− minimum requirement for eligibility.[2] Its ratings went even lower as the year progressed. By the end of 2015, Greece's highest ratings were CCC+ from S&P and CCCH from DBRS (both −10 on the scoring system used in Chapter 6). The Governing Council's decision on February 10, 2015, thus meant that paper issued or guaranteed by Greece was no longer eligible as collateral in Eurosystem operations.

Since Greece lost its exempt status and its ability to make collateral eligible through guarantees, it has been on emergency liquidity assistance (ELA). Greece has also been involved in various debt renegotiation processes and received a third bailout package (stability and support program) from the European Stability Mechanism (ESM) in the summer of 2015. This amounts to up to EUR 86 billion over three years (European Commission 2015), which, by way of comparison, is approximately 48 percent of Greece's GDP in 2014.[3]

---

[2] By a simple notch count, a rating of B from DBRS corresponds to a rating of B as well on the S&P scale. Source of ratings information: Bloomberg.

[3] Using the Eurostat GDP figure for Greece of EUR 177.5 billion, as reported on February 17, 2016.

References

GENERAL

Abbassi, Puriya, Falk Bräuning, Falko Fecht, and José-Luis Peydró, 2014, Cross-border liquidity, relationships and monetary policy: Evidence from the euro area interbank crisis, Discussion paper 45, Deutsche Bundesbank.

Afonso, Gara, Anna Kovner, and Antoinette Schoar, 2011, Stressed, not frozen: The federal funds market in the financial crisis, *Journal of Finance*, 66, 1109–1139.

Allen, Franklin, Elena Carletti, and Douglas Gale, 2014, Money, financial stability and efficiency, *Journal of Economic Theory*, 149, 100–127.

Allen, Franklin and Douglas Gale, 1994, Limited market participation and volatility of asset prices, *American Economic Review*, 84, 933–955.

Allen, Franklin and Douglas Gale, 1998, Optimal financial crises, *Journal of Finance*, 53, 1245–1284.

Allen, Franklin and Douglas Gale, 2007, *Understanding financial crises*, Clarendon Lectures in Finance, Oxford University Press, New York.

Amihud, Yakov and Haim Mendelson, 1986, Asset pricing and the bid-ask spread, *Journal of Financial Economics*, 17, 223–249.

Amihud, Yakov, Haim Mendelson, and Lasse H. Pedersen, 2013, *Market liquidity: Asset pricing, risk, and crises*, Cambridge University Press, Cambridge.

Angelini, Paolo, 2008, Liquidity and announcement effects in the euro area, *Giornale degli Economisti e Annali di Economia*, 67, 1–20.

Ashcraft, Adam, Nicolae Gârleanu, and Lasse H. Pedersen, 2010, Two monetary tools: Interest rates and haircuts, *NBER Macroeconomics Annual 2010*, 25, 143–180.

Ayuso, Juan and Rafael Repullo, 2001, Why did the banks overbid? An empirical model of the fixed rate tenders of the European Central Bank, *Journal of International Money and Finance*, 20, 857–870.

Bagehot, Walter, 1873, *Lombard street: A description of the money market*, Richard D. Irwin, Inc., Homewood, Illinois, 1962, reprinted from the Scribner, Armstrong & Co., edition, New York, 1873.

Bank of England, 2012, The distributional effects of asset purchases, July 12, www.bankofengland.co.uk/publications/Documents/news/2012/nr073.pdf.

Bartolini, Leonardo, Spence Hilton, Suresh Sundaresan, and Christopher Tonetti, 2011, Collateral values by asset class: Evidence from primary securities dealers, *Review of Financial Studies*, 24, 248–278.

BCBS (Basel Committee on Banking Supervision), 2006, International convergence of capital measurement and capital standards, Bank for International Settlements, June, ISBN 92-9197-720-9 (online).

BCBS, 2011, Basel III: A global regulatory framework for more resilient banks and banking systems, Bank for International Settlements, June, ISBN 92-9197-859-0 (online).

BCBS, 2013, Basel III: The liquidity coverage ratio and liquidity risk monitoring tools, Bank for International Settlements, January, ISBN 92-9197-912-0 (online).

Behn, Markus, Rainer Haselmann, Thomas Kick, and Vikrant Vig, 2014, The political economy of bank bailouts, Working paper, Deutsche Bundesbank.

Beirne, John, 2012, The EONIA spread before and during the crisis of 2007–2009: The role of liquidity and credit risk, *Journal of International Money and Finance*, 31, 534–551.

Benes, Jaromir and Michael Kumhof, 2012, The Chicago Plan revisited, Working paper 202, International Monetary Fund.

Bernanke, Ben S. and Mark Gertler, 1989, Agency costs, net worth, and business fluctuations, *American Economic Review*, 79, 14–31.

Bernanke, Ben S. and Mark Gertler, 1990, Financial fragility and economic performance, *Quarterly Journal of Economics*, 105, 87–114.

Bernanke, Ben S. and Kenneth N. Kuttner, 2005, What explains the stock market's reaction to Federal Reserve policy, *Journal of Finance*, 60, 1221–1257.

Bhattacharya, Sudipto and Douglas Gale, 1987, Preference shocks, liquidity and central bank policy, *New approaches to monetary economics*, Chapter 4, 69–88, W. Barnett and K. Singleton, eds., Cambridge University Press, Cambridge.

Bhattacharya, Sudipto and Kjell G. Nyborg, 2013, Bank bailout menus, *Review of Corporate Finance Studies*, 2, 29–61.

Bindseil, Ulrich, 2014, *Monetary policy operations and the financial system*, Oxford University Press, Oxford.

Bindseil, Ulrich, and Philipp J. König, 2011, The economics of TARGET2 balances, SFB 649 Discussion paper 35.

Bindseil, Ulrich, Andrés Manzanares, and Benedict Weller, 2004, The role of central bank capital revisited, Working paper 392, European Central Bank.

Bindseil, Ulrich and Kjell G. Nyborg, 2008, Monetary policy implementation: A European perspective, *Handbook of European financial markets and institutions*, Chapter 28, 742–778, X. Freixas, P. Hartmann, and C. Mayer, eds., Oxford University Press, Oxford.

Bindseil, Ulrich, Kjell G. Nyborg, and Ilya A. Strebulaev, 2009, Repo auctions and the market for liquidity, *Journal of Money, Credit and Banking*, 41, 1391–1421.

Bindseil, Ulrich and Francesco Papadia, 2006, Credit risk mitigation in central bank operations and its effects on financial markets: The case of the Eurosystem, Occasional paper 49, European Central Bank.

Blanchard, Olivier J. and Stanley Fischer, 1989, *Lectures on macroeconomics*, MIT Press, Cambridge, MA.

Bofinger, Peter, 2001, *Monetary policy: Goals, institutions, strategies, and instruments*, Oxford University Press, New York.

Bootle, Roger, 2012, Leaving the euro: A practical guide, A submission for the Wolfson Economics Prize MMXII by Capital Economics.

Breitung, Jörg and Dieter Nautz, 2001, The empirical performance of the ECB's repo auctions: Evidence from aggregated and individual bidding data, *Journal of International Money and Finance*, 20, 839–856.

Broyer, Claudia, Nicoletta Renner, Rolf Schneider, and Katharina Utermöhl, 2014, Scenarios for government debt in the eurozone, Working paper 179, Allianz Economic Research.

Brunnermeier, Markus K. and Lasse H. Pedersen, 2009, Market liquidity and funding liquidity, *Review of Financial Studies*, 22, 2201–2238.

Brunsson, Nils, 1989, *The organization of hypocrisy: Talk, decisions and actions in organizations*, Wiley, Chichester.

Buiter, Willem H., 2006, The "sense and nonsense of Maastricht" revisited: What have we learnt about stabilization in EMU? *Journal of Common Market Studies*, 44, 687–710.

Buiter, Willem H., 2008, Can central banks go broke? CEPR Discussion paper 6827.

Buiter, Willem H. and Anne C. Sibert, 2005, How the Eurosystem's treatment of collateral in its open market operations weakens fiscal discipline in the eurozone (and what to do about it), CEPR Discussion paper 5387.

Buraschi, Andrea and Davide Menini, 2002, Liquidity risk and specialness, *Journal of Financial Economics*, 64, 243–284.

Calomiris, Charles W., 2009a, The subprime turmoil: What's old, what's new and what's next, *Journal of Structured Finance*, 15, 6–52.

Calomiris, Charles W., 2009b, A recipe for ratings reform, *The Economists' Voice*, 6, 1–4.

Calomiris, Charles W. and R. Glenn Hubbard, 1990, Firm heterogeneity, internal finance, and "credit rationing," *Economic Journal*, 100, 90–104.

Carpenter, Seth and Selva Demiralp, 2006, The liquidity effect in the federal funds market: Evidence from daily open market operations, *Journal of Money, Credit and Banking*, 38, 901–920.

Caruana, Jaime, 2011, Why central bank balance sheets matter, Keynote address at the Bank of Thailand, BIS conference.

Cassola, Nuno, Cornelia Holthausen, and Marco Lo Duca, 2010, The 2007/2009 turmoil: A challenge for the integration of the euro area money market? Working paper, European Central Bank.

Cassola, Nuno, Ali Hortaçsu, and Jakub Kastl, 2013, The 2007 subprime market crisis through the lens of European Central Bank auctions for short-term funds, *Econometrica*, 81, 1309–1345.

CGFS (Committee on the Global Financial System), 2013, Asset encumbrance, financial reform and the demand for collateral assets, CGFS Paper 49, Bank for International Settlements, May, ISBN 92-9197-935-X (online).

Chailloux, Alexandre, Simon Gray, and Rebecca McCaughrin, 2008, Central bank collateral frameworks: Principles and policies, Working paper 222, International Monetary Fund.

Champ, Bruce, Bruce D. Smith, and Stephen D. Williamson, 1996, Current elasticity and banking panics: Theory and evidence, *Canadian Journal of Economics*, 29, 828–864.

Chapman, James T.E., Jonathan Chiu, and Miguel Molico, 2011, Central bank haircut policy, *Annals of Finance*, 7, 319–348.

Chesterton, Gilbert K., 1911, The invisible man, in *The innocence of Father Brown*, Cassell & Company, London.

Cheun, Samuel, Isabel von Köppen-Mertes, and Benedict Weller, 2009, The collateral frameworks of the Eurosystem, the Federal Reserve System and the Bank of England and the financial market turmoil, Occasional Paper 107, European Central Bank.

Chordia, Tarun, Asani Sarkar, and Avanidhar Subrahmanyam, 2005, An empirical analysis of stocks and bond market liquidity, *Review of Financial Studies*, 18, 85–129.

Cline, William R., 2014, *Managing the euro area debt crisis*, Peterson Institute for International Economics, Washington, DC.

Cochrane, John H., 2014, Toward a run-free financial system, *Across the great divide: New perspectives on the financial crisis*, Chapter 10, 197–249, M.N. Baily and J.B. Taylor, eds., Hoover Institution, Stanford University.

Cœuré, Benoît, 2013, The single resolution mechanism: Why it is needed, Speech at the ICMA Annual General Meeting and Conference, organized by the International Capital Market Association, Copenhagen, May 23.

Committee for the Study of Economic and Monetary Union, 1989, Report on economic and monetary union in the European Community [The Delors report], presented April 17, http://ec.europa.eu/economy_finance/publications/publication6161_en.pdf.

Council of the European Union, 1997a, Council Regulation (EC) No 1466/97 of 7 July 1997 on the strengthening of the surveillance of budgetary positions and the surveillance and coordination of economic policies, *Official Journal of the European Communities* L 209, http://eur-lex.europa.eu/legal-content/EN/ALL/?uri=CELEX:31997R1466 (January 24, 2015).

Council of the European Union, 1997b, Council Regulation (EC) No 1467/97 of 7 July 1997 on speeding up and clarifying the implementation of the excessive deficit procedure, *Official Journal of the European Communities* L 209, http://eur-lex.europa.eu/legal-content/EN/ALL/?uri=CELEX:31997R1467 (January 24, 2015).

Council of the European Union, 2005, Council Regulation (EC) No 1055/2005 of 27 June 2005 amending Regulation (EC) No 1466/97 on the strengthening of the surveillance of budgetary positions and the surveillance and coordination of economic policies, *Official Journal of the European Union* L 174, http://eur-lex.europa.eu/legal-content/EN/ALL/?uri=CELEX:32005R1055 (January 24, 2015).

Council of the European Union, 2007, Treaty of Lisbon amending the Treaty on European Union and the Treaty Establishing the European Community (2007/C 306/01), *Official Journal of the European Union* C 306, http://eur-lex.europa.eu/legal-content/EN/TXT/?uri=OJ:C:2007:306:TOC (April 21, 2015).

Council of the European Union, 2012a, The Treaty on Stability, Coordination and Governance [SCG], http://ec.europa.eu/economy_finance/economic_governance/sgp/legal_texts/index_en.htm (January 26, 2015).

Council of the European Union, 2012b, Consolidated versions of the Treaty on European Union and the Treaty on the Functioning of the European Union (2012/C 326/01) [TFEU], *Official Journal of the European Union* C 326, http://eur-lex.europa.eu/legal-content/EN/TXT/?uri=OJ:C:2012:326:TOC (April 21, 2015).

Craig, Paul P., 2012, The Stability, Coordination and Governance Treaty: Principle, politics and pragmatism, *European Law Review*, 37, 231–248.

Diamond, Douglas W. and Philip H. Dybvig, 1986, Banking theory, deposit insurance, and bank regulation, *Journal of Business*, 59, 55–68.

Diamond, Douglas W. and Raghuram G. Rajan, 2006, Money in a theory of banking, *American Economic Review*, 96, 30–53.

van Dixhoorn, Charlotte, 2013, Full reserve banking: An analysis of four monetary reform plans, A study for the Sustainable Finance Lab, Utrecht, The Netherlands.

Duffie, Darrell, 1996, Special repo rates, *Journal of Finance*, 51, 493–526.

Eberl, Jakob and Christopher Weber, 2014, ECB collateral criteria: A narrative database 2001–2013, Ifo Working Paper 174.

ECB (European Central Bank), 1999, *Monthly Bulletin*, November, ISSN 1561-0136 (online).

ECB, 2004, *Monthly Bulletin*, April, ISSN 1725-2822 (online).

ECB, 2007, Decisions taken by the Governing Council of the ECB (in addition to decisions setting interest rates), October, www.ecb.europa.eu/press/govcdec/otherdec/2007/html/gc071026.en.html.

ECB, 2011, The monetary policy of the ECB, ISBN 978-92-899-0778-1 (online).

ECB, 2012, Indicators of market segmentation: Media request following the ECB press conference on 2 August 2012, www.ecb.europa.eu/pub/pdf/other/is120802_media_request.en.pdf.

ECB, 2013, Collateral eligibility requirements: A comparative study across specific frameworks, July, ISBN 978-92-899-1014-9 (online).

ECBC (European Covered Bond Council), 2015, European covered bond fact book, August.

ECJ (Court of Justice of the European Union), 2015a, Press release No 2/15, Luxembourg, January 14, http://curia.europa.eu/jcms/upload/docs/application/pdf/2015-01/cp150002en.pdf.

ECJ, 2015b, Press release No 70/15, Luxembourg, June 16, http://curia.europa.eu/jcms/upload/docs/application/pdf/2015-06/cp150070en.pdf.

Eichengreen, Barry and Ugo Panizza, 2014, A surplus of ambition: Can Europe rely on large primary surpluses to solve its debt problem? CEPR Discussion paper 10069.

Erber, Georg, 2011, Italy's fiscal crisis, *Intereconomics*, 6, 332–339.

Ernhagen, Tomas, Magnus Vesterlund, and Staffan Viotti, 2002, How much equity does a central bank need, *Sveriges Riksbank Economic Review*, 2, 5–18.

Eser, Fabian and Bernd Schwaab, 2016, Evaluating the impact of unconventional monetary policy measures: Empirical evidence from the ECB's Securities Markets Programme, *Journal of Financial Economics*, 119, 147–167.

European Commission, 2010a, Report on Greek government deficit and debt statistics, January 8, http://eur-lex.europa.eu/legal-content/EN/TXT/PDF/?uri=CELEX:52010DC0001&from=EN (February 1, 2015).

European Commission, 2010b, Annotated presentation of regulated markets and national provisions implementing relevant requirements of MIFID (Directive 2004/39/EC of the European Parliament and of the Council), *Official Journal of the European Union* C 348/9, `http://eur-lex.europa.eu/legal-content/EN/ALL/?uri=CELEX:52010XC1221%2802%29` (February 10, 2015).

European Commission, 2015, Commission signs three-year ESM stability support programme for Greece, Press release, Brussels, August 20, `http://europa.eu/rapid/press-release_IP-15-5512_en.htm`.

European Commission and Eurostat, 2010, Information note on Greece, February 24, `http://ec.europa.eu/eurostat/de/web/products-eurostat-news/-/INFO-GREECE` (February 1, 2015).

European Communities, 1992, Treaty on European Union (92/C 191 /01) [The Maastricht Treaty], *Official Journal of the European Communities* C 191, `http://eur-lex.europa.eu/legal-content/EN/ALL/?uri=OJ:C:1992:191:TOC` (January 24, 2015).

European Communities, 1997, Resolution of the European Council on the Stability and Growth Pact, Amsterdam, June 17, 1997 (97/C 236/01) [SGP], *Official Journal of the European Communities* C 236, `http://eur-lex.europa.eu/legal-content/EN/ALL/?uri=OJ:C:1997:236:TOC` (January 24, 2015).

Eurostat, 2004, Report by Eurostat on the revision of the Greek government deficit and debt figures, *Eurostat News*, December 1, 2004.

Ewerhart, Christian and Jens Tapking, 2008, Repo markets, counterparty risk and the 2007/2008 liquidity crisis, Working paper 909, European Central Bank.

Fair, Ray C., 2002, Events that shook the market, *Journal of Business*, 75, 713–731.

Fecht, Falko, Kjell G. Nyborg, and Jörg Rocholl, 2008, Liquidity management and overnight rate calendar effects: Evidence from German banks, *North American Journal of Economics and Finance*, 19, 7–21.

Fecht, Falko, Kjell G. Nyborg, Jörg Rocholl, and Jiri Woschitz, 2016, Collateral, central bank repos, and systemic arbitrage, Working paper, University of Zurich and Swiss Finance Institute.

Feldstein, Martin, 1997, The political economy of the European economic and monetary union: Political sources of an economic liability, *Journal of Economic Perspectives*, 11, 23–42.

Fitch, 2014, Fitch Ratings Global Corporate Finance 2013 Transition and Default Study, Special report.

Flannery, Mark J. and Aris A. Protopapadakis, 2002, Macroeconomic factors do influence aggregate stock returns, *Review of Financial Studies*, 15, 751–782.

Fleming, Michael J. and Eli M. Remolona, 1997, What moves the bond market? *Federal Reserve Bank of New York Economic Policy Review*, 3, 31–50.

Friedman, Milton, 1970, A theoretical framework for monetary analysis, *Journal of Political Economy*, 78, 193–238.

Furfine, Craig H., 2001, Banks as monitors of other banks: Evidence from the overnight federal funds market, *Journal of Business*, 74, 33–57.

Gabrieli, Silvia and Co-Pierre Georg, 2014, A network view on interbank market freezes, Discussion paper 44, Deutsche Bundesbank.

Goodhart, Charles A.E., 2013, The optimal financial structure, Special paper 220, LSE Financial Markets Group.

Gorton, Gary and Andrew Metrick, 2010, Haircuts, *Federal Reserve Bank of St. Louis Review*, 92, 507–519.

Gorton, Gary and Andrew Metrick, 2012, Securitized banking and the run on repo, *Journal of Financial Economics*, 104, 425–451.

Goyenko, Ruslan Y., Craig W. Holden, and Charles A. Trzcinka, 2009, Do liquidity measures measure liquidity? *Journal of Financial Economics*, 92, 153–181.

Griffin, John M., Jordan Nickerson, and Dragon Y. Tang, 2013, Rating shopping or catering? An examination of the response to competitive pressure for CDO credit ratings, *Review of Financial Studies*, 26, 2270–2310.

Gurley, John G. and Edward S. Shaw, 1960, *Money in a theory of finance*, Brookings Institution, Washington, DC.

Hamilton, James D., 1996, The daily market for federal funds, *Journal of Political Economy*, 104, 26–56.

Hamilton, James D., 1997, Measuring the liquidity effect, *American Economic Review*, 87, 80–97.

Hau, Harald, Sam Langfield, and David Marques-Ibanez, 2013, Bank ratings: What determines their quality? *Economic Policy*, 28, 289–333.

Hawkins, John, 2003, Central bank balance sheets and fiscal operations, BIS Paper 20, 71–83.

Heider, Florian and Marie Hoerova, 2009, Interbank lending, credit-risk premia and collateral, *International Journal of Central Banking*, 5, 5–43.

Heider, Florian, Marie Hoerova, and Cornelia Holthausen, 2009, Liquidity hoarding and interbank market spreads: The role of counterparty risk, Working paper 1126, European Central Bank.

Holmström, Bengt and Jean Tirole, 2011, *Inside and outside liquidity*, MIT Press, Cambridge, MA.

James, Harold, 2012, *Making the European monetary union*, The Belknap Press of Harvard University Press, Cambridge.

Jeanne, Olivier and Lars E.O. Svensson, 2007, Credible commitment to optimal escape from a liquidity trap: The role of the balance sheet of an independent central bank, *American Economic Review*, 97, 474–490.

Jordan, Thomas J., 2012, Some lessons for monetary policy from the recent financial crisis, *International Journal of Central Banking*, 8, 289–292.

Jordan, Bradford D. and Susan D. Jordan, 1997, Special repo rates: An empirical analysis, *Journal of Finance*, 52, 2051–2072.

Kashyap, Anil K. and Jeremy C. Stein, 2000, What do a million observations on banks say about the transmission of monetary policy? *American Economic Review*, 90, 407–428.

Keloharju, Matti, Kjell G. Nyborg, and Kristian Rydqvist, 2005, Strategic behavior and underpricing in uniform price auctions: Evidence from Finnish Treasury auctions, *Journal of Finance*, 60, 1865–1902.

Kindleberger, Charles P., 1978, *Manias, panics and crashes: A history of financial crises*, Basic Books, New York.

Kisgen, Darren J. and Philip E. Strahan, 2010, Do regulations based on credit ratings affect a firm's cost of capital? *Review of Financial Studies*, 23, 4324–4347.

Kiyotaki, Nobuhiro and John Moore, 1997, Credit cycles, *Journal of Political Economy*, 105, 211–248.

Kiyotaki, Nobuhiro and John Moore, 2003, Inside money and liquidity, Working paper, London School of Economics.

Knot, Klaas, 2013, Central bank independence and unconventional monetary policy: Challenges for the ECB, Speech at the Bank of Mexico international conference.

Korte, Josef and Sascha Steffen, 2015, Zero risk contagion – banks' sovereign exposure and sovereign risk spillovers, Working paper, Goethe University Frankfurt and ESMT.

Kotlikoff, Laurence J., 2010, *Jimmy Stewart is dead: Ending the world's ongoing financial plague with limited purpose banking*, Wiley, NJ.

Krasner, Stephen D., 1999, *Sovereignty: Organized hypocrisy*, Princeton University Press, Princeton, NJ.

Krishnamurthy, Arvind, Stefan Nagel, and Dmitry Orlov, 2014, Sizing up repo, *Journal of Finance*, 69, 2381–2417.

Lagos, Ricardo, 2006, Inside and outside money, Staff Report 374, Federal Reserve Bank of Minneapolis.

Mancini, Loriano, Angelo Ranaldo, and Jan Wrampelmeyer, 2014, The euro interbank repo market, Working paper 1316, University of St. Gallen, School of Finance.

March, James G. and Johan P. Olsen, 1989, *Rediscovering institutions: The organizational basis of politics*, The Free Press, New York.

March, James G. and Johan P. Olsen, 1998, The institutional dynamics of international political orders, *International Organization*, 52, 943–969.

Markets Committee, 2013, Central bank collateral frameworks and practices, Bank for International Settlements, March, ISBN 92-9197-926-0 (online).

Merler, Silvia and Jean Pisani-Ferry, 2012, Who's afraid of sovereign bonds? *Bruegel Policy Contribution*, 2, 1–8.

Miles, David and Jochen Schanz, 2014, The relevance or otherwise of the central bank's balance sheet, *Journal of International Economics*, 92, 103–116.

Myers, Stewart C., 1977, Determinants of corporate borrowing, *Journal of Financial Economics*, 5, 147–175.

Nautz, Dieter and Christian J. Offermanns, 2007, The dynamic relationship between the euro overnight rate, the ECB's policy rate and the term spread, *International Journal of Finance and Economics*, 12, 287–300.

Ngai, Victor, 2012, Stability and Growth Pact and fiscal discipline in the eurozone, Thesis supervised by Franklin Allen, Wharton School, University of Pennsylvania.

Nyborg, Kjell G., 2008, Bank supervision after the financial crisis: Signals from the market for liquidity, Working paper, Norwegian School of Economics.

Nyborg, Kjell G., 2011, Stabilisierung der Euro-Zone durch Besicherung von Bonds, *Neue Zürcher Zeitung*, www.nzz.ch/aktuell/startseite/stabilis ierung-der-euro-zone-durch-besicherung-von-bonds-1.11928023, August 8. English version: The euro area sovereign debt crisis: Secure the debt and modify haircuts, Occasional paper 2011-01, Swiss Finance Institute.

Nyborg, Kjell G., Ulrich Bindseil, and Ilya A. Strebulaev, 2002, Bidding and performance in repo auctions: Evidence from ECB open market operations, Working paper 157, European Central Bank.

Nyborg, Kjell G. and Per Östberg, 2014, Money and liquidity in financial markets, *Journal of Financial Economics*, 112, 30–52.

Nyborg, Kjell G. and Ilya A. Strebulaev, 2001, Collateral and short squeezing of liquidity in fixed rate tenders, *Journal of International Money and Finance*, 20, 769–792.

Nyborg, Kjell G. and Ilya A. Strebulaev, 2004, Multiple unit auctions and short squeezing, *Review of Financial Studies*, 17, 545–580.

Nyborg, Kjell G. and Suresh Sundaresan, 1996, Discriminatory versus uniform Treasury auctions: Evidence from when-issued transactions, *Journal of Financial Economics*, 42, 63–104.

Olson Jr., Mancur and Richard Zeckhauser, 1966, An economic theory of alliances, *The Review of Economics and Statistics*, 48, 266–279.

Paul, Ron, 2009, *End the Fed*, Grand Central Publishing, New York.

Philippon, Thomas and Philipp Schnabl, 2013, Efficient recapitalization, *Journal of Finance*, 68, 1–42.

Phillips, Ronnie J., 1992, The "Chicago Plan" and New Deal banking reform, Working paper 76, Jerome Levy Economics Institute of Bard College.

Pisani-Ferry, Jean, 2014, *The euro crisis and its aftermath*, Oxford University Press, New York.

van Rixtel, Adrian and Gabriele Gasperini, 2013, Financial crises and bank funding: Recent experience in the euro area, BIS Working paper 406.

Rochet, Jean-Charles, 2010, Systemic risk: Changing the regulatory perspective, *International Journal of Central Banking*, 6, 259–276.

Rösler, Cornelia, 2015, Frictions in the interbank market: Evidence from volumes, Working paper, University of Zurich and Swiss Finance Institute.

Sims, Christopher A., 2004, Fiscal aspects of central bank independence, *European Monetary Integration*, Chapter 4, 103–116, H.W. Sinn, M. Widgrén, and M. Köthenbürger, eds., MIT Press, Cambridge, MA.

Singh, Manmohan, 2013, The changing collateral space, Working paper 25, International Monetary Fund.

Singh, Manmohan and Peter Stella, 2012, Money and collateral, Working paper 25, International Monetary Fund.

Sinn, Hans-Werner, 2014, *The euro trap: On bursting bubbes, budgets, and beliefs*, Oxford University Press, Oxford.

Skeie, David R., 2008, Banking with nominal deposits and inside money, *Journal of Financial Intermediation*, 17, 562–584.

Stella, Peter, 1997, Do central banks need capital? Working paper 83, International Monetary Fund.

Stella, Peter, 2005, Central bank financial strength, transparency, and policy credibility, Staff paper 52, International Monetary Fund.

Tobin, James, 1980, Redefining the aggregates: Comments on the exercise, in *Measuring the Money Aggregates: Compendium of Views Prepared by the Subcommittee on Domestic Monetary Policy of the House Committee on Banking, Finance, and Urban Affairs*, 96th Congress, 2nd Session, Washington, DC.

Uhlig, Harald, 2003, One money, but many fiscal policies in Europe: What are the consequences? *Monetary and fiscal policies in EMU: Interactions and coordination*, Chapter 2, 29–64, M. Buti, eds., Cambridge University Press, Cambridge.

US GAO (United States General Accounting Office), 1996, Mexico's financial crisis: Origins, awareness, assistance, and initial efforts to recover, www.gao.gov/products/GGD-96-56 (January 23, 2015).

Whelan, Karl, 2014, TARGET2 and central bank balance sheets, *Economic Policy*, 29, 79–137.

White, Lawrence J., 2010, The credit rating agencies, *Journal of Economic Perspectives*, 24, 211–226.

Wolf, Martin, 2006, Comment on Wyplosz (2006), *Economic Policy*, 21, 253–256.

World Bank, 2012, Global financial development report 2013: Rethinking the role of the state in finance, Washington, DC: World Bank, doi:10.1596/978-0-8213-9503-5, License: Creative commons attribution CC BY 3.0.

Wyplosz, Charles, 2006, European monetary union: The dark sides of a major success, *Economic Policy*, 21, 207–261.

EUROSYSTEM COLLATERAL FRAMEWORK

ECB (2000/7), Guideline of the European Central Bank of 31 August 2000 on monetary policy instruments and procedures of the Eurosystem, *Official Journal of the European Communities* L 310, General framework, December 11, 2000, 1–2 and 31–44.

ECB (2002/2), Guideline of the European Central Bank of 7 March 2002 amending Guideline ECB/2000/7 on monetary policy instruments and procedures of the Eurosystem, *Official Journal of the European Communities* L 185, General framework, July 15, 2002, 1–2 and 31–45.

ECB (2003/16), Guideline of the European Central Bank of 1 December 2003 amending Guideline ECB/2000/7 on monetary policy instruments and procedures of the Eurosystem, *Official Journal of the European Union* L 69, General framework, March 8, 2004, 1–2 and 31–47.

ECB (2005/2), Guideline of the European Central Bank of 3 February 2005 amending Guideline ECB/2000/7 on monetary policy instruments and procedures of the Eurosystem, *Official Journal of the European Union* L 111, General framework, May 2, 2005, 1–2 and 32–46.

ECB (2006/12), Guideline of the European Central Bank of 31 August 2006 amending Guideline ECB/2000/7 on monetary policy instruments and procedures of the Eurosystem, *Official Journal of the European Union* L 352, General framework, December 13, 2006, 1–2 and 35–56.

ECB (2007/10), Guideline of the European Central Bank of 20 September 2007 amending Annexes I and II to Guideline ECB/2000/7 on monetary policy instruments and procedures of the Eurosystem, *Official Journal of the European Union* L 284, General framework, October 30, 2007, 34–43.

ECB (2008/11), Regulation (EC) No 1053/2008 of the European Central Bank of 23 October 2008 on temporary changes to the rules relating to eligibility of collateral, *Official Journal of the European Union* L 282, Temporary framework, October 25, 2008, 17–18.

ECB (2008/13), Guideline of the European Central Bank of 23 October 2008 amending Guideline ECB/2000/7 on monetary policy instruments and procedures of the Eurosystem, *Official Journal of the European Union* L 36, General framework, February 5, 2009, 31–45.

ECB (2008/18), Guideline of the European Central Bank of 21 November 2008 on temporary changes to the rules relating to eligibility of collateral, *Official Journal of the European Union* L 314, Temporary framework, Novermber 25, 2008, 14–15.

ECB (2009/1), Guideline of the European Central Bank of 20 January 2009 amending Guideline ECB/2000/7 on monetary policy instruments and procedures of the Eurosystem, *Official Journal of the European Union* L 36, General framework, February 5, 2009, 59–61.

ECB (2009/16), Decision of the European Central Bank of 2 July 2009 on the implementation of the covered bond purchase programme, *Official Journal of the European Union* L 175, Temporary framework, July 4, 2009, 18–19.

ECB (2009/24), Guideline of the European Central Bank of 10 December 2009 amending Guideline ECB/2008/18 on temporary changes to the rules relating to eligibility of collateral, *Official Journal of the European Union* L 330, Temporary framework, December 16, 2009, 95.

ECB (2010/1), Guideline of the European Central Bank of 4 March 2010 amending Guideline ECB/2000/7 on monetary policy instruments and procedures of the Eurosystem, *Official Journal of the European Union* L 63, General framework, March 12, 2010, 22–23.

ECB (2010/3), Decision of the European Central Bank of 6 May 2010 on temporary measures relating to the eligibility of marketable debt instruments issued or guaranteed by the Greek Government, *Official Journal of the European Union* L 117, Temporary framework, May 11, 2010, 102–103.

ECB (2010/13), Guideline of the European Central Bank of 16 September 2010 amending Guideline ECB/2000/7 on monetary policy instruments and procedures of the Eurosystem, *Official Journal of the European Union* L 267, General framework, October 9, 2010, 21–55.

ECB (2010/30), Guideline of the European Central Bank of 13 December 2010 amending Guideline ECB/2000/7 on monetary policy instruments and procedures of the Eurosystem, *Official Journal of the European Union* L 336, General framework, December 21, 2010, 63–67.

ECB (2011/4), Decision of the European Central Bank of 31 March 2011 on temporary measures relating to the eligibility of marketable debt instruments issued or guaranteed by the Irish Government, *Official Journal of the European Union* L 94, Temporary framework, April 8, 2011, 33–34.

ECB (2011/10), Decision of the European Central Bank of 7 July 2011 on temporary measures relating to the eligibility of marketable debt instruments issued or guaranteed by the Portuguese Government, *Official Journal of the European Union* L 182, Temporary framework, July 12, 2011, 31–32.

ECB (2011/14), Guideline of the European Central Bank of 20 September 2011 on monetary policy instruments and procedures of the Eurosystem (recast), *Official Journal of the European Union* L 331, General framework, December 14, 2011, 1–2 and 29–53.

ECB (2011/17), Decision of the European Central Bank of 3 November 2011 on the implementation of the second covered bond purchase programme, *Official Journal of the European Union* L 297, Temporary framework, November 16, 2011, 70–71.

ECB (2011/25), Decision of the European Central Bank of 14 December 2011 on additional temporary measures relating to Eurosystem refinancing operations and eligibility of collateral, *Official Journal of the European Union* L 341, Temporary framework, December 22, 2011, 65–66.

ECB (2012/2), Decision of the European Central Bank of 27 February 2012 repealing Decision ECB/2010/3 on temporary measures relating to the eligibility of marketable debt instruments issued or guaranteed by the Greek Government, *Official Journal of the European Union* L 59, Temporary framework, March 1, 2012, 36.

ECB (2012/3), Decision of the European Central Bank of 5 March 2012 on the eligibility of marketable debt instruments issued or fully guaranteed by the Hellenic Republic in the context of the Hellenic Republic's debt exchange offer, *Official Journal of the European Union* L 77, Temporary framework, March 16, 2012, 19.

ECB (2012/4), Decision of the European Central Bank of 21 March 2012 amending Decision ECB/2011/25 on additional temporary measures relating to Eurosystem refinancing operations and eligibility of collateral, *Official Journal of the European Union* L 91, Temporary framework, March 29, 2012, 27.

ECB (2012/11), Decision of the European Central Bank of 28 June 2012 amending Decision ECB/2011/25 on additional temporary measures relating to

Eurosystem refinancing operations and eligibility of collateral, *Official Journal of the European Union* L 175, Temporary framework, July 5, 2012, 17–18.

ECB (2012/12), Decision of the European Central Bank of 3 July 2012 amending Decision ECB/2011/25 on additional temporary measures relating to Eurosystem refinancing operations and eligibility of collateral, *Official Journal of the European Union* L 186, Temporary framework, July 14, 2012, 38.

ECB (2012/14), Decision of the European Central Bank of 18 July 2012 repealing Decision ECB/2012/3 on the eligibility of marketable debt instruments issued or fully guaranteed by the Hellenic Republic in the context of the Hellenic Republic's debt exchange offer, *Official Journal of the European Union* L 199, Temporary framework, July 26, 2012, 26.

ECB (2012/18), Guideline of the European Central Bank of 2 August 2012 on additional temporary measures relating to Eurosystem refinancing operations and eligibility of collateral and amending Guideline ECB/2007/9, *Official Journal of the European Union* L 218, Temporary framework, August 15, 2012, 20–23.

ECB (2012/23), Guideline of the European Central Bank of 10 October 2012 amending Guideline ECB/2012/18 on additional temporary measures relating to Eurosystem refinancing operations and eligibility of collateral, *Official Journal of the European Union* L 284, Temporary framework, October 17, 2012, 14–15.

ECB (2012/25), Guideline of the European Central Bank of 26 November 2012 amending Guideline ECB/2011/14 on monetary policy instruments and procedures of the Eurosystem, *Official Journal of the European Union* L 348, General framework, December 18, 2012, 30–41.

ECB (2012/32), Decision of the European Central Bank of 19 December 2012 on temporary measures relating to the eligibility of marketable debt instruments issued or fully guaranteed by the Hellenic Republic, *Official Journal of the European Union* L 359, Temporary framework, December 29, 2012, 74–76.

ECB (2012/34), Decision of the European Central Bank of 19 December 2012 on temporary changes to the rules relating to the eligibility of foreign currency denominated collateral, *Official Journal of the European Union* L 14, Temporary framework, January 18, 2013, 22–23.

ECB (2013/4), Guideline of the European Central Bank of 20 March 2013 on additional temporary measures relating to Eurosystem refinancing operations and eligibility of collateral and amending Guideline ECB/2007/9 (recast), *Official Journal of the European Union* L 95, Temporary framework, April 5, 2013, 23–30.

ECB (2013/5), Decision of the European Central Bank of 20 March 2013 repealing Decisions ECB/2011/4 on temporary measures relating to the eligibility of marketable debt instruments issued or guaranteed by the Irish Government, ECB/2011/10 on temporary measures relating to the eligibility of marketable debt instruments issued or guaranteed by the Portuguese Government, ECB/2012/32 on temporary measures relating to the eligibility of marketable debt instruments issued or fully guaranteed by the Hellenic Republic and ECB/2012/34 on temporary changes to the rules relating to the eligibility of foreign currency denominated collateral, *Official Journal of the European Union* L 95, Temporary framework, April 5, 2013, 21.

ECB (2013/6), Decision of the European Central Bank of 20 March 2013 on the rules concerning the use as collateral for Eurosystem monetary policy operations of own-use uncovered government-guaranteed bank bonds, *Official Journal of the European Union* L 95, General framework, April 5, 2013, 22.

ECB (2013/13), Decision of the European Central Bank of 2 May 2013 on temporary measures relating to the eligibility of marketable debt instruments issued or fully guaranteed by the Republic of Cyprus, *Official Journal of the European Union* L 133, Temporary framework, May 17, 2013, 26–28.

ECB (2013/21), Decision of the European Central Bank of 28 June 2013 repealing Decision ECB/2013/13 on temporary measures relating to the eligibility of marketable debt instruments issued or fully guaranteed by the Republic of Cyprus, *Official Journal of the European Union* L 192, Temporary framework, July 13, 2013, 75.

ECB (2013/22), Decision of the European Central Bank of 5 July 2013 on temporary measures relating to the eligibility of marketable debt instruments issued or fully guaranteed by the Republic of Cyprus, *Official Journal of the European Union* L 195, Temporary framework, July 18, 2013, 27–29.

ECB (2013/35), Decision of the European Central Bank of 26 September 2013 on additional measures relating to Eurosystem refinancing operations and eligibility of collateral, *Official Journal of the European Union* L 301, General framework, November 12, 2013, 6–12.

ECB (2013/36), Decision of the European Central Bank of 26 September 2013 on additional temporary measures relating to Eurosystem refinancing operations and eligibility of collateral, *Official Journal of the European Union* L 301, Temporary framework, November 12, 2013, 13–14.

ECB (2014/10), Guideline of the European Central Bank of 12 March 2014 amending Guideline ECB/2011/14 on monetary policy instruments and procedures of the Eurosystem, *Official Journal of the European Union* L 166, General framework, June 5, 2014, 33–41.

ECB (2014/12), Guideline of the European Central Bank of 12 March 2014 amending Guideline ECB/2013/4 on additional temporary measures relating

to Eurosystem refinancing operations and eligibility of collateral and amending Guideline ECB/2007/9, *Official Journal of the European Union* L 166,
Temporary framework, June 5, 2014, 42–43.

ECB (2014/31), Guideline of the European Central Bank of 9 July 2014 on additional temporary measures relating to Eurosystem refinancing operations and
eligibility of collateral and amending Guideline ECB/2007/9 (recast), *Official
Journal of the European Union* L 240, Temporary framework, August 13, 2014,
28–38.

ECB (2014/32), Decision of the European Central Bank of 9 July 2014 repealing
Decision ECB/2013/22 on temporary measures relating to the eligibility of
marketable debt instruments issued or fully guaranteed by the Republic of
Cyprus and Decision ECB/2013/36 on additional temporary measures relating
to Eurosystem refinancing operations and eligibility of collateral, *Official
Journal of the European Union* L 240, Temporary framework, August 13, 2014,
26–27.

ECB (2014/38), Decision of the European Central Bank of 1 September 2014
amending Decision ECB/2013/35 on additional measures relating to Eurosystem refinancing operations and eligibility of collateral, *Official Journal of the
European Union* L 278, Temporary framework, September 20, 2014, 21–23.

ECB (2014/40), Decision of the European Central Bank of 15 October 2014 on
the implementation of the third covered bond purchase programme, *Official
Journal of the European Union* L 335, Temporary framework, November 22,
2014, 22–24.

ECB (2014/45), Decision (EU) 2015/5 of the European Central Bank of 19
November 2014 on the implementation of the asset-backed securities purchase programme, *Official Journal of the European Union* L 1, Temporary
framework, January 6, 2015, 4–7.

ECB (2014/46), Guideline of the European Central Bank of 19 November 2014
amending Guideline ECB/2014/31 on additional temporary measures relating
to Eurosystem refinancing operations and eligibility of collateral and amending Guideline ECB/2007/9, *Official Journal of the European Union* L 348,
Temporary framework, December 4, 2014, 27–29.

ECB (2014/60), Guideline of the European Central Bank of 19 December 2014
on the implementation of the Eurosystem monetary policy framework
(ECB/2014/60) (recast), *Official Journal of the European Union* L 91, General
framework, December 4, 2014, 3–135.

ECB (2015/6), Decision (EU) 2015/300 of the European Central Bank of 10
February 2015 on the eligibility of marketable debt instruments issued or fully

guaranteed by the Hellenic Republic (ECB/2015/6), *Official Journal of the European Union* L 53, Temporary framework, February 25, 2015, 29–30.

ECB (2015/27), Guideline (EU) 2015/1938 of the European Central Bank of 27 August 2015 amending Guideline (EU) 2015/510 of the European Central Bank on the implementation of the Eurosystem monetary policy framework (ECB/2015/27), *Official Journal of the European Union* L 282, General framework, October 28, 2015, 41–51.

ECB (2015/34), Guideline (EU) 2016/64 of the European Central Bank of 18 November 2015 amending Guideline (EU) 2015/510 on the implementation of the Eurosystem monetary policy framework (General Documentation Guideline) (ECB/2015/34), *Official Journal of the European Union* L 14, General framework, January 21, 2016, 25–29.

ECB (2015/35), Guideline (EU) 2016/65 of the European Central Bank of 18 November 2015 on the valuation haircuts applied in the implementation of the Eurosystem monetary policy framework (ECB/2015/35), *Official Journal of the European Union* L 14, General framework, January 21, 2016, 30–35.

COLLATERAL FRAMEWORK RELATED

Directive (85/611/EEC), Council Directive 85/611/EEC of 20 December 1985 on the coordination of laws, regulations and administrative provisions relating to undertakings for collective investment in transferable securities (UCITS), *Official Journal of the European Communities* L 375, December 31, 1985, 3–18.

Directive (88/220/EEC), Council Directive 88/220/EEC of 22 March 1988 amending, as regards the investment policies of certain UCITS, Directive 85/611/EEC on the coordination of laws, regulations and administrative provisions relating to undertakings for collective investments in transferable securities (UCITS), *Official Journal of the European Communities* L 100, April 19, 1988, 31–32.

Directive (2000/12/EC), Directive 2000/12/EC of the European Parliament and of the Council of 20 March 2000 relating to the taking up and pursuit of the business of credit institutions, *Official Journal of the European Communities* L 126, May 26, 2000, 1–59.

Directive (2001/107/EC), Directive 2001/107/EC of the European Parliament and of the Council of 21 January 2002 amending Council Directive 85/611/EEC on the coordination of laws, regulations and administrative provisions relating to undertakings for collective investment in transferable securities (UCITS) with a view to regulating management companies and simplified prospectuses, *Official Journal of the European Communities* L 41, February 13, 2002, 20–34.

Directive (2001/108/EC), Directive 2001/108/EC of the European Parliament and of the Council of 21 January 2002 amending Council Directive 85/611/EEC on the coordination of laws, regulations and administrative provisions relating to undertakings for collective investment in transferable securities (UCITS) with regard to investments of UCITS, *Official Journal of the European Communities* L 41, February 13, 2002, 35–42.

Directive (2004/39/EC), Directive 2004/39/EC of the European Parliament and of the Council of 21 April 2004 on markets in financial instruments amending Council Directives 85/611/ECC and 93/6/EEC and Directive 2000/12/EC of the European Parliament and of the Council and repealing Council Directive 93/22/EEC, *Official Journal of the European Union* L 145, March 30, 2004, 1–43.

Directive (2005/1/EC), Directive 2005/1/EC of the European Parliament and of the Council of 9 March 2005 amending Council Directives 73/239/EEC, 85/611/EEC, 91/675/EEC, 92/49/EEC and 93/6/EEC and Directives 94/19/EC, 98/78/EC, 2000/12/EC, 2001/34/EC, 2002/83/EC and 2002/87/EC in order to establish a new organisational structure for financial services committees, *Official Journal of the European Union* L 79, March 24, 2005, 9–17.

Directive (2009/65/EC), Directive 2009/65/EC of the European Parliament and of the Council of 13 July 2009 on the coordination of laws, regulations and administrative provisions relating to undertakings for collective investment in transferable securities (UCITS), *Official Journal of the European Union* L 302, November 17, 2009, 32–96.

European Commission (May 2010), European Economy – The Economic Adjustment Programme for Greece, *Occasional Papers* 61, `http://ec.europa.eu/economy_finance/assistance_eu_ms/greek_loan_facility/index_en.htm` (September 10, 2014).

European Commission (February 2011), European Economy – The Economic Adjustment Programme for Ireland, *Occasional Papers* 76, `http://ec.europa.eu/economy_finance/assistance_eu_ms/ireland/index_en.htm` (September 10, 2014).

European Commission (June 2011), European Economy – The Economic Adjustment Programme for Portugal, *Occasional Papers* 79, `http://ec.europa.eu/economy_finance/assistance_eu_ms/portugal/index_en.htm` (September 10, 2014).

European Commission (March 2012), European Economy – The Second Economic Adjustment Programme for Greece, *Occasional Papers* 94, `http://ec.europa.eu/economy_finance/assistance_eu_ms/greek_loan_facility/index_en.htm` (September 10, 2014).

European Commission (May 2013), European Economy – The Economic Adjustment Programme for Cyprus, *Occasional Papers* 149, http://ec.europa.eu/economy_finance/assistance_eu_ms/cyprus/index_en.htm (September 30, 2014).

European Commission (June 2013), Memo – Statement by the European Commission and the IMF on Cyprus, MEMO/13/624, http://europa.eu/rapid/press-release_MEMO-13-624_en.htm (September 30, 2014).

European Commission (April 2014), European Economy – The Economic Adjustment Programme for Portugal – Eleventh Review, *Occasional Papers* 191, http://ec.europa.eu/economy_finance/assistance_eu_ms/portugal/index_en.htm (September 29, 2014).

European Commission (June 2014), European Economy – Post-Programme Surveillance for Ireland – Spring 2014 Report, *Occasional Papers* 195, http://ec.europa.eu/economy_finance/assistance_eu_ms/ireland/index_en.htm (September 10, 2014).

Index

ad-hoc and privately eligible collateral, 24, 94–96
agency debt, 56–58, 233–235
aggregate liquidity needs
full allotment policy and, 199–206
full reserve banking and, 269–273
arbitrage
collateral framework and, 183–185
full allotment policy and, 205–206
Ashcraft, Adam, 14–17, 20
asset-backed securities (ABS), 10, 23, 44–45
credit standards for, 107–109
euro area bailout and, 196–197
expanded purchase of, 233–235
full allotment policy and purchase of, 207–212
haircut effects on, 60–79, 82–84
price volatility for, 199, 200
ratings for, 80–82
second-highest rule for, 109–110
assets
bias toward illiquid collateral as, 185–189
in central bank balance sheets, 11–14, 49–51
collateralized borrowing and, 14–17, 52–56, 60–62, 256–262
default probabilities of, 65
financial crisis of 2008 and price of, 7–11
financing for purchase of, 236–242
illiquid *vs.* liquid, 19–23
liquidity pull-back and, 5–6
price volatility for, 29–32, 199–206
purchase programs for, 192–197, 199, 207–212, 214, 223, 233–235
targeted purchase of, 198–199

auctions
discriminatory auctions, 189–191
refinancing operations and, 42–45
Austria, bank stock performance in, 216–223
automobile corporations, banking subsidiaries of, 146–147

Bagehot, Walter, 18, 277–278
bailouts
buying time and free-riding problems with, 207–212
collateral framework facilitation of, 19–23
costs and benefits of, 212–214, 253–255
euro area integration of, 245–247
full allotment policy and, 205–206
Italian government guarantors and, 136–141
negotiations history for, 225–230
overview of, 192–194
political motivations for, 209–212
ratings exemptions and, 112–114
balance sheets
asset purchase programs and TLTROs, impact on, 196–197
central banks, 11–14, 49–51
collateral framework and, 14–17
full allotment policy and, 203–205
illiquid collateral and asymmetry among, 185–189
sovereign bond purchases and, 236–242
Banca d'Italia, 241–242, 267
bank bonds
collateralization using, 54–56
economic stimulus through purchase of, 242–244

in Greece, 143–146
haircut policy and, 60–62
banking institutions
CCP repos and, 266–269
corporate guarantees and, 146–147
defaults by, 261–262
full allotment policy and, 183–185, 199–206
German guarantees and, 142–143
government guarantors and, 132–136, 209–212
illiquid collateral bias and, 185–189
indirect bailouts of, 212–214
Italian government guarantors for, 136–141
monetary policy and, 1–3, 42–45
own-use collateral and, 178–182
ratings for, 87–93
stock spread analysis of, 216–223
Bank of Canada, balance sheets, 11–14
Bank of England, balance sheets, 11–14
Bank of Japan, balance sheets, 11–14
Basel II and III bank regulation frameworks, 178
Belgium
fiscal indicators for, 225–230
national central bank in, 241–242
benchmark allotment, 42
BGN pricing source, 161–162
Bhattacharya, Sudipto, 20, 205–206
bias in market discipline, 183–185
bid price, marketable collateral, 149–162
bilateral repos, 266–269
Bindseil, Ulrich, 6–7, 25, 189–191, 257
Blanchard, Olivier J., 19
Bloomberg data
asset classes and, 29–32
bond yield and price data from, 117
eligible marketable collateral pricing and, 149–162
event study of bank stocks using, 216–223
Italian government guarantees data, 136–141
pivotal ratings data from, 128–131
pricing data, 29–32, 166–167
on securities, 263–265
Bootle, Roger, 209–212
borrowing

collateralization of, 14–17
haircut-linked cost increases for, 256–262
bubbles, collateral frameworks and risk of, 19–23
Buiter, Willem H., 14–17
Bundesbank, ECB Pooling Baskets and, 87–93
buying time approach, full allotment policy and, 207–212
"by count" numbers
pledged collateral, 162–166
theoretical prices, liquidity category, 159, 160
"by value" numbers, theoretical prices, liquidity category, 159, 160

Calomiris, Charles W., 65, 92–93
capital key (ECB), asset purchase program expansion and, 233–235
central banks
asset purchase financing and, 236–242
balance sheets, 11–14, 49–51
bills, monetary policy and, 238–240
collateral frameworks and, 274–280
debt certificates issued by, 238–240
fixed rate tender offers, 189–191
full allotment policy and, 199–206
haircut policies and, 62
illiquid collateral bias and, 183–189
liquidity pull-back and, 4–6
monetary policies of, 1–3, 194–199
MRO/LTROs and money injection in, 45–49
central counterparty (CCP) repos
eligibility of collateral and, 87–93
interbank market and, 266–269
low-quality collateral bias and, 183–185
Chapman, James T. E., 14–17, 20
Chesterton, G. K., xiii–xiv
Chicago Plan, 269–273
Chiu, Jonathan, 14–17, 20
Cline, William R., 203–205
Cochrane, John H., 272–273
Coeuré, Benoît, 188–189
collateral
asset classes of, 52–54

eligibility and usage patterns for, 23–26
Eurosystem holdings of, 49–51
financial markets and, 14–17
fundamental problems with, 263–265
government guarantees and ratings for, 94–96
guarantees and distribution of, 94–96, 132–136
illiquidity of, 19–23
liquidity effects on, 19–23
marketable collateral, pricing rules, 149–162
pledged collateral, 162–166
usage trends for, 54–56, 162–166
value determination for, 26–28, 32–34, 94–96, 149–162
collateral central counterparty (CCP) repo contracts, 14–17, 87–93, 183–185
collateral framework
bias toward illiquid collateral and, 185–189
ECB rules for, 59–63
euro-area securities, 49–51
financial markets and, 14–17
full reserve banking and, 269–273
future challenges and issues for, 274–280
general and temporary frameworks, 60–62
interbank market and, 14–17, 266–269
liquidity pull-back and, 6–7
market discipline and, 19–23, 178–191
market forces in, 32–34, 189–191
monetary policy and, 1–3, 49–51, 194–199
opacity of, xiii–xiv
overview, 18–19
potential impact of, 19–23
ratings role in, 94–96, 105–107
sovereign debt and, 256–262
value determination in, 26–28
collateralized loans, liquidity injection through, 35–45
constrained-optimal bailouts, 205–206
corporations

guarantees, cheap funding accessibility and, 146–147
ratings for, 87–93
counterparty risk
bias toward illiquid collateral and, 185–189
haircut policy and, 78–79, 84–85
interbank market and, 266–269
coupon effects
haircut policy and, 65
liquidity categories and, 78
sovereign ratings and, 119–132
covered bonds, 10
euro area bailout and, 196–197
expanded asset purchase program and, 233–235
haircuts for, 82–84
purchase program for, 194–199
Craig, Paul, 248, 249
credibility issues
collateral framework and, 274–280
limits on sovereignty and, 245–247
sovereign debt and, 241–242
credit claims, haircut variations over time for, 79–85
credit institutions and standards
Eurosystem Credit Assessment Framework, 105–107
expansion of ratings agencies and relaxation of, 107–109
German guarantees and, 142–143
haircut policies and, 60–62, 281–282
harmonized rating scale, 109–110, 282–284
Italian government guarantors and, 136–141
ratings rules and, 96–112, 281–282
Cruz Villalón, Pedro (Advocate General), 224, 225, 231–233, 236–242
Cyprus
bailout funds for, 212–214
haircut rules for, 85–87, 143–146, 288–292
ratings exemption for, 94–96, 112–114, 212–214, 288–292
sovereign debt crisis in, 188–189, 225–230
standard minimum ratings requirements for, 31–32

daily outstanding amounts, monetary base and, 45–49
daily reserve requirements, full allotment policy and, 199–206
debt certificates, central bank issuance of, 238–240
Debt Instruments Backed by Eligible Credit Claims (DECCs), 281–282
debt-to-GDP ratio
  euro area inclusion and, 248–256
  euro crisis and, 225–230
  in Japan, 237–238
default probabilities, asset classes and, 65
deficit threshold violations
  credibility of euro area and, 248–256
  euro crisis and, 225–230
  haircuts linked to, 256–262
deficit-to-GDP ratio, euro crisis and, 225–230
Denmark, 225–230
deposit insurance, 268–269
deposit rates
  euro crisis and, 194–199
  full allotment policy and, 199–206
  full reserve banking and, 269–273
Diamond, Douglas W., 269–273
discriminatory auctions, 42–45, 189–191
Dominion Bond Rating Services (DBRS), 30–31, 94–96, 107–109
  extra collateral value in pivotal ratings of, 128–131
  harmonized rating scale and, 109–110
  long-term scales and scoring system, 146–147
  sovereign ratings by, 119–132
  Spanish bond rating by, 115–118
  yearly average score comparisons with other agencies, 126–128
Draghi, Mario, xiii–xiv, 9–11, 192–199, 214–223, 233–235, 242–244, 265, 277–278
Duffie, Darrell, 14–17
Dybvig, Philip H., 269–273

Economic Adjustment Programmes (EAP)
  haircut policy and, 85–87

ratings exemptions and, 112–114
EFSF program, 207–212
eligibility criteria for collateral frameworks, 23–26
  asset classes, 52–54
  changes to, 80–82, 281–282
  ECB guidelines for, 60–62
  guarantees and, 132–136
  non-regulated market inclusion in, 171–182
  own-use collateral, 168–170
  in primary/secondary repo markets, 87–93
  rating agency ratings and, 31–32, 94–96
  rating categories and, 79–85
  weakening of, 32
Eliot, T. S., 245
emergency liquidity assistance (ELA), 146, 292
Eurex Clearing Margining process, 87–93
  CCP repos and, 266–269
Eurex GC Pooling ECB Baskets, 25, 29–32, 87–93, 266–269
Euribor-Eonia swap spread
  full allotment policy and, 199–206
  liquidity effects and, 8–9
  swap rates, 118
euro area
  asset purchase and euro preservation in, 241–242
  background on crisis in, 225–230
  bailout benefits and drawbacks in, 212–214
  bond purchases in, 242–244
  calendar effects on, 6–7
  collateral framework in, xiii–xiv, 256–262, 274–280
  credibility issues for, 245–247
  eligibility guidelines for collateral in, 60–62
  endgame of crisis in, 224–244
  event study of bank stocks in, 216–223, 274–280
  fiscal indicators for member states in, 225–230
  free-rider problem in, 207–212
  full allotment policy and fragility of, 199–206

gamesmanship in, 253–255
heterogeneity in securitization
    products of, 263–265
inequality in stock returns in, 32
Italy's inclusion in, 248–256
monetary policy event study of,
    214–223
negotiations over bailouts in,
    225–230
Outright Monetary Transactions
    mechanism and, 9–11
overview of bailouts in, 192–194
possible breakup of, 22–23, 211
ratings comparisons in, 94–96
securities of, 49–51
segmentation within, 188–189
sovereign ratings for countries in,
    119–132
European Banking Union, 207–212,
    261–262
European Central Bank (ECB), xiii–xiv
asset classes of, 52–54
asset purchase program expansion
    by, 233–235
bailout measures of, 192–194
collateral framework in, 14–17,
    274–280
collective structure of, 1–3
Credit Quality Steps of, 78, 109–110
debt certificates issued by, 238–240
Economic Adjustment Programmes
    and, 85–87
fixed rate tender offers and, 43–44,
    189–191
foreign currency reverse operations,
    42
haircut policy and, 59–63, 92–93,
    178–182, 256–262, 281–282,
    284–287
liquidity policies in, 9–11, 199–206
monetary policies of, 194–199,
    214–223, 236–242
non-regulated markets accepted by,
    171–177
own-use collateral and, 168–170
ratings agencies expansion and,
    107–109
ratings rules and, 94–96, 112–114,
    281–282

reverse operations for liquidity
    injection, 35–45
sovereign debt and, 197–198,
    242–244, 256–262
standardization of collateral and, 265
target rate, 42
theoretical pricing by, 183–185
European Commission (EC)
Economic Adjustment Programmes
    and, 85–87
German guarantees and, 142–143
Greece reprimanded by, 250–253
ratings exemptions and, 112–114
European Court of Justice (ECJ),
    195–196, 224, 225, 231–233,
    236–242
European Economic Area (EEA), 60–62
European Financial Stability
    Facility/European Stability
    Mechanism, 9–11, 43–44
ratings exemptions and, 112–114
European Stability Mechanism (ESM),
    292
European Union
bailout support from, 112–114
euro area stock performance
    compared with stocks of,
    216–223
possible breakup of, 22–23
"STEP market" in, 171–177
Eurostat, 248–256
Eurosystem
asset and risk transfer to, 194–199
asset purchase financing and,
    236–242
balance sheets, 11–14, 49–51
bond purchases by, 10
collateral framework in, 14–17,
    32–34, 274–282
collateral usage in, 54–56
collective structure of, 1–3
corporate guaranteed securities in,
    146–147
debt certificates for, 238–240
ECB Pooling Baskets and, 87–93
eligibility criteria for collateral in,
    96–112
fixed-term deposit in, haircut for,
    80–82

guidelines for collateral framework
of, 60–62
haircuts in, 29–32, 178–182
legality of sovereign bond purchases
by, 231–233
liquidity injections *vs.* aggregate
liquidity in, 199–206
low-quality collateral in, 25
market and theoretical prices in,
149–167
mezzanine tranches purchased by,
196–197
monetary policy instruments over
time, 35–45
non-regulated market securities in,
171–177
open market operations of, 199–206
ratings process in, 30–31, 107–109
repo collateral eligibility and, 56–58
theoretical pricing in, 149–162
Eurosystem Credit Assessment
Framework (ECAF), 105–107
Ewerhart, Christian, 25–26, 266–269
excess liquidity, full allotment policy
and, 199–206
exemptions from ratings, 31–32,
112–114
external ratings
collateral eligibility and, 23–26
eligibility criteria for collateral and,
94–96
haircut policy and, 178–182
longer-dated bonds, 115–118
non-marketable assets and, 178–182
of issuers and guarantors, 105–107
role of, 29–32
extra collateral value
in DBRS pivotal ratings, 128–131
Italian government guarantors
impact on, 136–141

Fecht, Falko, 203–206
federal funds rate, calendar effects on,
6–7
Federal Reserve System
balance sheets, 11–14
eligibility criteria for collateral, 24
financial crisis of 2008
collateral framework and, 274–280
EU fiscal indicators prior to, 225–230

euro crisis and, 192–194
monetary policy and, 7–11, 43–44
MROs/LTROs and effect of, 45–49
financially sound guarantors,
guarantee rules and, 104–105
financial markets
collateral framework and, 1–3, 14–17
eligibility of collateral criteria and,
82–84, 263–265
future challenges for, 274–280
illiquid collateral bias and, 185–189
monetary policy in, 3–6
Finland, bank stock performance in,
216–223
Fischer, Stanley, 19
Fitch rating agency, 30–31, 88, 94–96,
115–118
long-term scales and scoring system,
146–147
yearly average score comparisons
with other agencies, 126–128
fixed rate tender mechanism
central bank money injection and,
45–49
full allotment policy and, 205–206
implementation of, 43–44
market forces and, 189–191
fixed-term deposits, collateral
eligibility of, 80–84
FMS Wertmanagement, 142–143
foreign currency
marketable securities, 80–82
reverse operations for, 42
fragmentation of markets
asset purchase expansion and,
241–242
bias toward illiquid collateral and,
188–189
economic impact of, 253–255
full allotment policy and, 203–205
France
collateral eligibility criteria in, 32
deficit sanctions and, 248–256
non-regulated markets and, 171–177
free-rider problem
full allotment policy and, 207–212
private liquidity and, 19–23, 185–189
"French Medium-Term Notes (BMTN)
market", 171–177

fresh market pricing, marketable
    collateral and, 149–162
Friedman, Milton, 4–6, 192–194
full allotment policy
    as bailout mechanism, 183–185,
        199–206, 212–214
    buying time and free-riding
        problems with, 207–212
    central bank money injection and,
        45–49
    corporate guaranteed securities and,
        146–147
    ECB liquidity and, 9–11, 80–82
    EU stability and, 19–23
    illiquid collateral and, 183–185
    implementation of, 43–44
    own-use collateral and, 168–170
    refinancing operations and, 194–199
    targeted longer-term refinancing
        operations (TLTROs) and,
        196–197
    weaknesses of, 205–206
full reserve banking, 269–273
fundamental liquidity, 118
funding, corporate guarantees and
    access to, 146–147

Gale, Douglas, 21
gamemanship, in euro area, 253–255
Gârleanu, Nicolae, 14–17, 20
Gasperini, Gabriele, 203–205
General framework document (ECB
    2008/13), 80–82, 109–110
    non-regulated market inclusion in,
        171–177
Georgiou, Andreas, 250–253
Germany, 225–230
    asset purchase program expansion
        and, 233–235
    bailouts in, 209–212
    bank stock performance in, 216–223
    collateral framework politics and,
        277–278
    Constitutional Court of, 195–196
    deficit sanctions and, 248–256
    government guarantees in, 31–32,
        142–143, 205–206
    non-regulated markets in, 171–177
    SGP treaty and, 248–256
    sovereign debt crisis and, 188–189

gold prices, bias toward illiquid
    collateral and, 185–189
Goodhart, Charles A., 269–273
government bonds/government debt
    collateralization using, 54–56
    DBRS sovereign ratings for, 119–132
    debt certificates and, 238–240
    extra collateral value of, 128–131
    full allotment policy and, 209–212
    haircut policy and, 60–62, 256–262
    monetary policy and market for,
        236–242
    monetization of, 237–238
    primary and secondary market
        purchases of, 231–233
    ratings rules for, 87–93, 115–118
government guarantees
    distribution of collateral and,
        132–136
    free-rider problem and, 207–212
    in Germany, 142–143
    in Greece, 143–146
    issue ratings and, 105–107
    in Italy, 136–141
    market fragmentation and, 188–189
    mezzanine tranches and, 196–197
    own-use collateral and, 168–170
    programme/issuance ratings,
        111–112
Greece
    bailout funds for, 212–214
    bank stock performance in, 216–223
    credibility of eurozone membership,
        250–253
    electoral politics in, 242–247
    government guarantees in, 143–146
    haircut policies in, 85–87, 143–146,
        212–214, 288–292
    "jogging depositors" problem in,
        203–205
    national central bank in, 241–242
    pivotal ratings for, 125–126
    ratings exemption for, 94–96,
        112–114, 143–146, 212–214,
        288–292
    sovereign debt crisis in, 188–189,
        225–230, 256–262
    standard minimum ratings
        requirements for, 31–32

gross domestic product (GDP), balance
sheets as percentage of, 11–14
guarantee rules
changes over time, 96–112
collateral value and, 26–28, 31–32,
207–212
corporate guarantees, funding
accessibility and, 146–147
distribution of collateral and,
132–136
in Germany, 142–143
in Greece, 143–146
haircuts and theoretical price
increases and, 183–185
issuer ratings and, 105–107
in Italy, 136–141
market segmentation, 19–23
programme/issuance ratings,
111–112
ratings boost and, 178–182
sovereign ratings and, 94–96
*Guideline of the European Central
Bank of 31 August 2000 on
monetary policy instruments and
procedures of the Eurosystem
(ECB 2000/7)*, 60–62

haircut policy
asset classes and, 52–54
biases and systemic arbitrage and,
183–185
CCP repos and, 266–269
collateral frameworks and, 14–17
collateral value and, 26–28, 32–34
credit standards and, 96–112
discriminatory auctions and,
189–191
documentation and overview, 59–63
evolution of, 29–32
extraordinary rules, 85–87, 281–292
fundamental liquidity and, 118
in Greece, 143–146, 212–214
high-quality collateral and, 25–26
liquidity categories and, 63–79,
84–85, 166
market conditions and, 115–118,
189–191, 274–280
marketable assets and, 84–85
own-use collateral and, 168–170
pledged collateral, 162–166

potential impact of, 19–23
for primary/secondary repo markets,
87–93
proposed modifications for, 256–262
ratings exemptions and, 288–292
ratings rules and, 79–85, 115–118,
178–182
rules for setting, 63–79, 281–292
updated table for, 284–287
Hamilton, James D., 6–7
harmonized rating scale, 109–110,
282–284
Hau, Harald, 90–93
high-quality collateral, bilateral repos
and, 25–26
Holmström, Bengt, 19
housing
as illiquid asset, 19–23
mortgage contracts for, 256–262
price volatility for, 199, 200

illiquid assets
bias toward, 183–185
collateral framework and, 19–23,
263–265
costs of, 185–189
as eligible collateral, 178–182
market forces and, 189–191
incentives, in collateral frameworks,
19–23
income disparity, wealth transfer and,
242–244
inflation, sovereign debt erosion and,
241–242
inside/outside money distinction, 19
insolvency regulations, sovereign debt
and, 256–262
inter-sovereign relations, credibility
challenges and, 245–247
interbank market
collateral framework and, 14–17,
266–269
financial crisis of 2008 and, 7–11
liquidity pull-back and, 4–6
weakness of, 199–206
interest rates, monetary policies and,
214–223
International Monetary Fund (IMF)
bailout support from, 112–114

Economic Adjustment Programmes and, 85–87
International Securities Identification Number (ISIN)
collateral eligibility and, 23–26, 87–93
marketable collateral pricing and, 149–162
pledged collateral, 162–166
Ireland
bailout funds for, 212–214
extra collateral value of bonds in, 128–131
"jogging depositors" problem in, 203–205
ratings exemption for, 112–114, 212–214
sovereign debt crisis in, 188–189, 225–230
sovereign ratings for, 125–126
standard minimum ratings requirements for, 31–32
issuer ratings
for German guarantees, 142–143
government bonds, 105–107
government guarantors and, 132–136
Italian government guarantors and, 136–141
programme/issuance ratings, 111–112
Italy
asset purchase program expansion and, 233–235
bank stock performance in, 216–223
bond ratings for, 115–118
collateral eligibility criteria in, 32
credibility of eurozone membership, 248–256
extra collateral value of bonds in, 128–131
government guarantees in, 31–32, 94–96, 136–141, 209–212
haircuts for government bonds in, 91–93
national central bank in, 241–242
non-regulated markets in, 171–177
open market operations of banks in, 205–206
pre-crisis fiscal indicators in, 225–230

sovereign debt in, 203–205
sovereign rating for, 94–96

James, Harold, 255–256
Japan debt-to-GDP ratio, 237–238
"jogging depositors" problem, 203–205
Jordan, Thomas, 13–14, 185–189

Kiyotaki, Nobuhiro, 19, 185–189
Knot, Klaas, 13–17, 185–189, 274–278, 280
Krasner, Stephen, 245–249, 260, 277–278
Kreditanstalt fürWiederaufbau, 142–143
Krugman, Paul, 269–273

Landesbanken/Girozentral, 142–143, 209–212
Langfield, Sam, 90–93
Latvia, sovereign ratings for, 125–126
Lehman bankruptcy, 8–9, 32–34
full allotment policy as response to, 183–185, 199–206
liquidity markets and, 266–269
non-regulated markets in wake of, 171–177
sovereign debt following, 225–230
liquidity categories
changes to, 80–82
collateral framework and, 263–265
Eurosystem liquidity injections vs. aggregate liquidity, 199–206
fundamental liquidity, 118
guarantee rules and, 132–136
as haircut categories, 84–85
haircut rules and, 60–79
non-regulated markets and, 171–177
pledged collateral, 162–166
ratings over time, 79–85
theoretical pricing and, 149–162
updated haircuts for, 284–287
Liquidity Coverage Ratio, 14–17
liquidity pull-back, 4–6
market inefficiencies and, 6–7
Lisbon Treaty, 249
longer-dated bonds
ratings for, 115–118
repayment of, 198–199

longer-term refinancing operations
(LTROs), *see also* targeted
longer-tem refinancing operations
(TLTROs)
corporate guaranteed securities and,
146–147
economic effects of, 242–244
EU stability and, 19–23
euro area bailouts and, 225–230
evolution of, 43–44
full allotment policy shift from,
207–212
as funding supply, 48–49
government guarantees and, 31–32
haircuts and, 82–84
Italian government guarantors and,
136–141, 209–212
monetary base and, 45–49
non-regulated markets and, 171–177
own-use collateral and, 168–170
PIIGS sovereign debt and, 203–205
refinancing using, 194–199
repayment of, 198–199
unsecured bank debt and, 171–177
weaknesses of, 205–206
long-term ratings
credit standards and, 105–107
harmonized rating scale and,
109–110
loss sharing
asset purchase program and lack of,
233–235
collateral and, 263–265
low-quality collateral
bias toward, 183–185
full allotment policy and eligibility
of, 203–205, 207–212
increased production of, 23–26
potential costs of, 185–189
usage fraction of, 56–58

Maastricht Treaty of 1992, 225, 230,
242–256
main refinancing operations (MROs),
9–11
evolution of, 42–45
monetary base and, 45–49
marketable assets, 60–62
haircuts for, 84–85

marketable collateral, pricing rules,
149–162
market discipline
biases and systemic arbitrage and,
183–185
CCP repos and, 266–269
collateral frameworks and, 19–23,
178–191, 274–280
costs of undermining, 185–189
discriminatory auctions and,
189–191
impairment of, 178–182
low-quality collateral and, 29–32
own-use collateral and, 168–170
theoretical prices and, 166–167
unsecured markets and, 32–34
market forces
CCP repos and, 266–269
in collateral framework, 32–34,
189–191
collateral frameworks and, 274–280
fundamental liquidity and, 118
haircuts and, 115–118
liquidity and, 6–7
sovereign debt and, 241–242
theoretical prices and, 149–167
Marques-Ibanez, David, 90–93
Merler, Silvia, 205–206
Mexico, US oil agreement with,
256–262
mezzanine tranches, 196–197
minimum rating requirements,
collateral eligibility and, 80–82
Molico, Miguel, 14–17, 20
monetary bases (M1/M2)
debt certificates and, 238–240
full reserve banking and, 269–273
refinancing operations and, 45–49
monetary policies
bailouts and, 236–242, 260
central banks and, 1–3
euro crisis and, 192–194
event study in, 214–223
financial crisis of 2008 and, 7–11,
32–34
financial markets, 3–6
future challenges for, 274–280
implementation instruments for,
35–45
patterns and key issues in, 194–199

unequal gains in EU policies,
216–223
monetary shocks, liquidity pull-back
and, 4–6
money markets, financial market and,
6–7
money stock, central banks' reduction
of, 238–240
Moody's rating agency, 30–31, 94–96,
115–118
long-term scales and scoring system,
146–147
sovereign ratings and, 119–132
yearly average score comparisons
with other agencies, 126–128
Moore, John, 19, 185–189
moral hazard, inside/outside money
distinction and, 19
mortgage-backed securities, price
volatility for, 199, 200
Myers, Stewart C., 205–206

national central banks (NCBs)
asset classes for, 62
asset purchase program and,
233–235, 241–242
collateral eligibility and credit
standards of, 96–112
collateral framework and, 188–189,
274–280
defaults by, 261–262
German guarantees and, 142–143
market fragmentation and, 188–189
monetary policy implementation
through, 35–45
own-use collateral and, 168–170
ratings and role of, 105–107
sovereign bond purchasing and risk
transfer to, 236–242
stock indices for, 216–223
Netherlands
bank stock performance in, 216–223
non-regulated markets in, 171–177
nominal balances, central bank control
of, 19–23
non-marketable assets, 60–62
as eligible collateral, 178–182
full allotment policy and eligibility
of, 203–205

haircut variations over time for,
79–85
ratings for, 80–82
theoretical prices, 162–166, 183–185
non-regulated markets, collateral
framework and, 171–177
non-subordination requirement,
haircut policy and, 60–62
Norges Bank, balance sheets, 11–14
Nyborg, Kjell G., 8–9, 14–17, 19–23,
25, 42, 185–191, 203–206, 257,
268–269

*Official Journal of the European
Union*, 59–63, 80–82
harmonized rating scale and,
109–110, 281–292
open market operations
arbitrage and, 205–206
collateral framework and, 189–191
sovereign bond purchases and,
236–242
volume of, 199–206
opportunity costs, for eligible
collateral, 178–182, 257
organized hypocrisy theory
collateralization of sovereign debt
and, 260
credibility of euro area and, 248–256
Östberg, Per, 4–6, 8–9, 19–23
Outright Monetary Transactions
(OMT) program, 9–11, 43–44,
194–199, 207–212, 224, 225,
231–242
overnight index swap rate
full allotment policy and, 199–206
reserve supply and, 6–7
own-use collateral
corporate guaranteed securities and,
146–147
defined, 168–170
haircut policy and, 78–79, 84–85
low-quality collateral as, 183–185
"own-use" collateral, 32–34, 64

Pedersen, Lasse H., 14–17, 20
People's Bank of China, balance sheets,
11–14
Philippon, Thomas, 205–206
Phillips, Ronnie J., 269–273

PIIGS countries
  bailouts and, 212–214
  sovereign debt crisis in, 203–205
Piraeus Bank, 143–146
Pisani-Ferry, Jean, 205–206
pivotal ratings
  extra collateral value of, 128–131
  rules for determining, 119–132
pledged collateral, 162–166
  ratio of aggregate liquidity to,
    178–182
politics
  bailouts and role of, 209–212
  collateral framework and, 274–280
  of eurozone establishment, 255–256
  monetary policies and, 242–244
  of sovereign debt, 241–242
  sovereignty issues in, 245–247
pooling systems, collateralization
  through, 35–45, 266–269
Portugal
  bailout funds for, 212–214
  extra collateral value of bonds in,
    128–131
  government securities ratings for,
    109–110
  haircut rules for, 143–146
  "jogging depositors" problem in,
    203–205
  ratings exemption for, 94–96,
    112–114, 126–128, 212–214
  sovereign debt crisis in, 188–189,
    225–230
  sovereign ratings for, 125–126
  standard minimum ratings
    requirements for, 31–32
pricing rules
  collateral value and, 29–34
  liquidity and asset price changes
    and, 199–206
  market and theoretical prices,
    149–167
  marketable collateral, 149–162
  non-marketable assets, 178–182
  pledged collateral, 162–166
  for securities, 263–265
primary markets
  collateral eligibility and ratings for,
    87–93
  haircuts in, 29–32

  sovereign debt purchases in, 231–233
private collateral, 31–32, 94–96,
  274–280
  free-rider problem and, 19–23,
    185–189
  non-marketable assets and, 31–32,
    112–114, 178–182
  ratings for, 288–291
programme/issuance series, rating for,
  111–112

quantitative easing, 197–198, 214–223
  economic effects of, 242–244
quantity-rate pairing, 189–191

rate-cutting policies, euro crisis and,
  194–199
ratings agencies
  credit standards and long-term
    ratings of, 105–107
  expansion of, 178–182
  government bond ratings, 115–132
  long-term scales and scoring system,
    146–147
  rules of, 94–96
  yearly average score comparisons,
    126–128
ratings rules
  collateral framework and, 1–3
  collateral value determination by,
    26–28, 30–34
  DBRS impact on sovereign ratings,
    119–132
  evolution of, 63–85, 96–112,
    115–118, 281–292
  exemptions from, 31–32, 112–114,
    178–182, 288–292
  for Greek government-guaranteed
    bonds, 143–146
  for primary/secondary repo markets,
    87–93
  harmonized rating scale, 109–110,
    282–284
  inflation of, 90–93
  Italian government guarantors
    impact on, 136–141
  liquidity category changes, 80–82
  long-term scales and scoring system,
    146–147
  monetary policies and, 214–223

procedure for determination of, 107–109
programme/issuance series, 111–112
role in collateral framework, 94–96
shopping for low-quality collateral and, 183–185
updates for, 288–291
refinancing operations
monetary base and, 45–49
monetary policies and, 35–45, 194–199
repo markets
collateral eligibility in, 14–17, 87–93
discriminatory auctions in, 189–191
ECB shift from, 256–262
haircuts in, 29–32, 87–93
high-quality collateral and, 25–26
interbank market and, 266–269
liquidity injection through, 35–45
low-quality collateral bias and, 56–58, 183–189
ratings for, 14–17, 87–93
representative price selection, marketable collateral, 149–162
reserve requirements, monetary policy and, 44–45
residual maturity effects
haircut policy and, 65
liquidity categories and, 78
sovereign ratings and, 119–132
retail mortgage-backed debt (RMBD), own-use collateral and, 168–170
retained collateral, see own-use collateral
revers operations, monetary policy implementation, 35–45
risk transfer
asset purchasing and, 236–242
collateral safety and, 14–17
van Rixtel, Adrian, 203–205
Rochet, Jean-Charles, 266–269
Rocholl, Jörg, 203–206

Schnabl, Thomas, 205–206
secondary markets
collateral and liquidity in, 14–17
haircuts and, 29–32
repo market collateral eligibility and ratings, 87–93

sovereign debt purchases in, 231–233, 236–242
securities
corporate guarantees for, 146–147
guarantees for, 132–136
haircut variations over time for, 79–85
Italian government guarantors for, 136–141
lack of market for, 263–265
Securities Markets Programme (SMP), 42–44, 194–206, 212–214
securities purchases, monetary policy and, 43–44
shocks to liquidity, illiquid collateral bias and, 185–189
Sibert, Anne C., 14–17
Sinn, Hans-Werner, 203–205
Slok, Torsten, 240
Slovenia, sovereign ratings for, 125–126
SoFFin (Special Financial Market Stabilization Funds), 142–143
sovereign bonds/sovereign debt
bailouts and purchase of, 197–198, 224, 225
bias toward illiquid collateral and, 188–189
collateralization of, 256–262
credibility issues and, 274–280
DBRS impact on ratings for, 119–132
economic stimulus through purchase of, 242–244
expanded asset purchase program and, 233–235
financial crisis and evolution of, 192–194, 203–205, 225–230
full allotment policy and, 207–212
haircut policies and, 115–118
legality of purchases of, 231–233, 236–242
pros and cons of purchasing, 212–214
rating exemptions, 94–96
sovereign guarantees
collateral framework and, 1–3
full allotment policy and, 183–185
Spain
bank stock performance in, 216–223
extra collateral value of bonds in, 128–131

government bond ratings in, 94–96, 115–118

haircuts for government bonds in, 91–93

"jogging depositors" problem in, 203–205

sovereign debt in, 94–96, 261–262

Stability and Growth Pact (SGP), 245–256

euro crisis and, 225–230

stale prices

Eurosystem collateral framework and, 178–182

illiquid collateral and, 183–185

marketable collateral, 149–162

pledged collateral, 162–166

summary of, 166–167

Standard & Poor's rating agency, 30–31, 94–96, 115–118

long-term scales and scoring system, 146–147

yearly average score comparisons with other agencies, 126–128

Stark, Jürgen, 277–278

state development banks (Förderbanken), German guarantees and, 142–143

Stella, Peter, 185–189

sterilized purchases, 44–45

stock market

liquidity effects in, 9, 199–206

monetary policies and, 214–223

spread analysis in, 216–223

stock returns, inequality in euro area of, 32

Strebulaev, Ilya A., 6–7, 14–17, 25, 42, 189–191, 257

subordinated bonds, 60–62

collateral eligibility for, 80–82

Summers, Larry, 255–256

supranational debt institutions, 56–58, 256–262

swap rates

full allotment policy and, 199–206

government bond ratings and, 118

Sweden, 225–230

Swiss National Bank, 224, 225

Syriza party, 242–244, 253–255

systemic arbitrage, market discipline and, 183–185

Tapking, Jens, 25–26, 266–269

targeted longer-tem refinancing operations (TLTROs), 196–197

repayment of, 198–199

TARGET payment system, 203–206

Temporary framework document (ECB 2008/11), 80–82, 107–109

ratings exemptions in, 112–114

term deposits, full reserve banking and, 269–273

theoretical prices

bias toward low-quality collateral and, 183–185

for eligible collateral, 178–182

illiquid collateral and, 183–185

marketable collateral, 149–162

markets and, 149–167

pledged collateral, 162–166

summary of, 166–167

Tier 1/Tier 2 assets

credit standards and ratings for, 96–112

haircut policies and, 60–85

Tirole, Jean, 19

Tobin, James, 4–6

transparency, collateral framework and, 277–278

treasury security repurchase program, 272–273

Treaty of the Functioning of the European Union (TFEU), 231–233

Treaty on Stability, Coordination, and Governance (SCG), 230, 242–247

Troika (IMF, EC, and ECB)

haircut rules and, 85–87

ratings exemptions and, 112–114

Tsipras, Alexis, 245–247

Turner (Lord), 237–238

UCITS-compliant covered bonds, 104–105

non-regulated markets and, 171

ratings exemption for, 105–107

unemployment

bond purchases as remedy for, 242–244

in euro area, 255

uniform haircut rules, discriminatory auctions and, 189–191

United Kingdom

non-regulated markets in, 171–177
wealth transfer in, 242–244
United States
  full reserve banking in, 272–273
  oil agreement with Mexico and,
    256–262
  ratings inflation in, 90–93
unsecured bank debt
  collateral eligibility and, 32–34,
    80–84
  interbank markets and, 268–269
  LTRO uptake, 171–177
unsecured debt instruments
  collateral eligibility of, 80–82
  guarantees and bias toward, 183–185

in Greece, 143–146
off-again/on-again clause for, 82–84

variable rate tender, 42–45

wealth transfer
  bank stock performance and,
    216–223
  bond purchases and, 242–244
  full allotment policy and, 207–212
Weber, Axel, 277–278
Wolf, Martin, 248, 249
Wolfson Prize, 209–212
Woschitz, Jiri, 203–206

Printed in the United States
By Bookmasters